The Magic Circle: Principles of

MODELING AND SIMULATIONS FOR LEARNING AND INSTRUCTION
Volume 1

Series Editors
J. Michael Spector
Learning Systems Institute, Florida State University, Tallahassee, USA
Norbert M. Seel
University of Freiburg, Germany and Florida State University, Tallahassee, USA
Konrad Morgan
Human Computer Interaction, University of Bergen, Norway

Scope
Models and simulations have become part and parcel of advanced learning environments, performance technologies and knowledge management systems. This book series will address the nature and types of models and simulations from multiple perspectives and in a variety of contexts in order to provide a foundation for their effective integration into teaching and learning. While much has been written about models and simulations, little has been written about the underlying instructional design principles and the varieties of ways for effective use of models and simulations in learning and instruction. This book series will provide a practical guide for designing and using models and simulations to support learning and to enhance performance and it will provide a comprehensive framework for conducting research on educational uses of models and simulations.

A unifying thread of this series is a view of models and simulations as learning and instructional objects. Conceptual and mathematical models and their uses will be described. Examples of different types of simulations, including discrete event and continuous process simulations, will be elaborated in various contexts. A rationale and methodology for the design of interactive models and simulations will be presented, along with a variety of uses ranging from assessment tools to simulation games. The key role of models and simulations in knowledge construction and representation will be described, and a rationale and strategy for their integration into knowledge management and performance support systems will provided.

Audience
The primary audience for this book series will be educators, developers and researchers involved in the design, implementation, use and evaluation of models and simulations to support learning and instruction. Instructors and students in educational technology, instructional research and technology-based learning will benefit from this series.

THE MAGIC CIRCLE:
PRINCIPLES OF GAMING & SIMULATION

Second Edition, 2008

By

Jan H. G. Klabbers
KMPC, The Netherlands

SENSE PUBLISHERS
ROTTERDAM / TAIPEI

A C.I.P. record for this book is available from the Library of Congress.

ISBN 90-8790-006-6 (paperback)
ISBN 90-8790-007-4 (hardback)

Published by: Sense Publishers,
P.O. Box 21858, 3001 AW Rotterdam, The Netherlands
http://www.sensepublishers.com

Second Edition, 2008

Printed on acid-free paper

For my parents, my wife Catharine, and daughters Catja and Lara

Dr. Jan H.G. Klabbers (1938) has been founder of the Social Systems Research Group (SSRG) at Radboud University, Nijmegen, the Netherlands; Harkness Fellow, while at MIT-Sloan School of Management (1968-1970); and Research Fellow at Case Western Reserve University (USA) (1973-1974). He is former Professor at Leiden University, Utrecht University, University of Amsterdam, and Erasmus University in the Netherlands, and University of Bergen, Norway. From 1976-2004 Dr. Klabbers has been General Secretary of the International Simulation And Gaming Association (ISAGA), its President in 1988-1989, and since 2004 Honorary Member. His publications cover social systems theory, design science and analytical science methodology, and the design and application of gaming and simulation in a wide variety of areas of application such as, health care systems, educational systems, human resources, general management, and global climate change policy development. Dr. Klabbers is currently involved in management & policy development, entrepreneurship & innovation, action-based learning and coaching. He is Founder & Managing Director of KMPC, an international management and policy consultancy.

TABLE OF CONTENTS

TABLE OF CONTENTS

PART IV: EPILOGUE

PREFACE

The field of gaming and simulation resembles a flowering orchard. It is very diversified in two respects. Firstly, scholars and practitioners in gaming and simulation represent a great variety of expertise, knowledge, and disciplinary background. Moreover, they apply games and simulations in numerous contexts of use. Secondly, games and simulations come in many different varieties, covering the whole spectrum from role-play to digital games. Grasping the big picture is not simple. Key terms are "play", "game", and "simulation". "Play" refers to a certain kind of human activity, and "game" to a certain setting, or form of play, which allows for, or triggers playful behavior. The term "simulation" refers both to a dynamic model, an image that represents a reference system, and the running of that model. A simulation is a functional model that imitates the behavior of a reference system. That reference system can relate to an existing system − in real life − or to a purely abstract system with no direct connotation to empirical reality. In other words, with respect to such an abstract system − expressed in a formal mathematical language − the rules of correspondence with some reference system may not be defined, or they may not yet be relevant.

To grasp the meaning and potential of gaming is an important goal for a variety of disciplines, each of which use different theoretical backgrounds and methodologies. This diversity of approaches results in a many-sided image of gaming and it makes building bridges between particular perspectives both necessary and difficult. One possible solution is to explore specific domains, where different fields of study converge. Such an approach can provide a more detailed characterization of the common problems, as well as highlight the interpretative limitations of the specialized areas of research and practice. That is, defining and investigating the existing points of convergence promotes establishment of foundations for a more coherent understanding of the field. In this book, I will present such a common and converging perspective. It goes beyond the specific knowledge domains of (mono-)disciplines and enlightens gaming from the viewpoint of social systems, more particularly social systems as complex adaptive systems. It offers a meta-disciplinary view, connecting various levels of organization, and understanding.

The terms "play" and "game" have been used interchangeably as if the two are the same. In this book, I will focus attention on games − forms of play − and gaming, which is a basic form of both human activity, and human expression. While entering a game, and assuming the role of player, people temporarily enact a world, which is a class of its own. Interactively they shape a narrative and write local history. The enacted worlds can be purely virtual, imaginary, even disobeying laws of nature. Games can be designed as images of existing social systems with certain rules of correspondence in mind. As Huizinga pointed out in his book *Homo Ludens*:

All play moves and has its being within a play-ground marked off beforehand, either materially, or ideally, deliberately or as a matter of course. Just as there is no formal difference between play and ritual, so the "consecrated spot" cannot be formally distinguished from the playground. The arena, the card-table, **the magic circle** [emphasis added-author], the temple, the stage, the screen, the tribunal (court of justice), etc., are all in form and function playgrounds: forbidden spots, isolated, hedged around, hallowed, within which special rules obtain. All are temporary worlds within the ordinary world, dedicated to the performance of an act apart (Huizinga, 1985, p. 10).

Learning to understand and to read what happens in the magic circles of games is not straightforward. Playing games is a total experience. Are we able to produce a coherent image, a leitmotiv, to capture it in scientifically sound terminology? The structure of scientific research forces knowledge to be extracted from a fully integrated world into disciplinary knowledge domains and inference schemes. The gamed experience becomes des-integrated by disciplinary units that is, faculties and departments. Thus, the way scientific research is organized aggravates the lack of coherence in game studies. Proper approaches to gaming require at the least an interdisciplinary, or transdisciplinary frame of reference.

Playing a game is a total event of being involved in a temporary, provisional, and integrated world. In current scientific research, play- and game-studies are scattered over various disciplines. Providing a comprehensive frame-of-reference for addressing the great variety of approaches to gaming and simulation is not a simple task. Such a synthetic perspective on inquiry and practice should allow the gaming and simulation communities to accumulate a common understanding of principles. Making coherent distinctions between the different types of games and simulations - to learn to see the wood for the trees - requires a commonly accepted conceptual framework. That does not yet exist. Gaming is a science, an art, as well as a craft. Especially as a specific craft within various professional communities, it is stubborn to change and adjust to outside incentives. This hampers cross-fertilization.

Games and simulations as a particular field of scientific enquiry and professional practice have been developed since the beginning of the twentieth century. Simulation and game design and their use, on the basis of varying tools, such as paper, pencil, boards, computers, simulation software, multi-media hard- and software, and the Internet, have been addressed widely in the literature. Simulation and gaming methods are being used in the natural sciences such as physics, chemistry, biology, computer science, in engineering, especially by those who are active in advancing cybernetics, control theory, and (general) systems theory, as well as by behavioral and social sciences such as psychology, sociology, anthropology. More recently, the humanities have become increasingly engaged in the study of video- or computer games as expressions of new media cultures. They approach those games - mainly used in the entertainment business - as interactive narratives. Mathematical game theory, and the more recent offspring "multi-agent-based modeling" have gained a solid position in economics. Business simulations and general management games are embedded in the curricula of many business administration schools.

The purpose of the book is to present principles underlying the design and use of gaming and simulation. That frame-of-reference will enlighten the characteristics of particular games and simulations from a common perspective. I will pay less attention to instrumental reasoning than on methodological questions. The main reason for choosing this road is the lack of a robust methodology that underpins gaming and simulation methods. Gaming and simulation are more than methods and tools. They are firstly a way of thinking, and secondly, a method and a technique. In addition, the framework presented will help to grasp the interplay between forms of knowledge and knowledge content in connection with gaming, which evolves through the action of the players. These notions I consider preconditions for raising epistemological questions in relation to the educational value of games and simulations. They will provide a proper context for addressing design science and analytical science approaches to artifact assessment and theory development and testing.

Due to the high diversity of approaches, the field has to accommodate the great variety of views on gaming, games, simulations, models, and modeling. Therefore, as mentioned above, I will choose an interdisciplinary and where appropriate a meta-disciplinary approach.

Itinerary for reading the book

Those readers who are mainly interested in getting familiar with gaming are invited in reading Chapters 1, and 2 of Part I, and Part III: Cases. Teachers and trainers in addition, should read Chapters 3, and 7. Those who are mainly involved in game design should focus on Part II, particularly to Chapters 4, 5, and 7. Finally, those readers who are involved in research on gaming should pay attention to Part II. All readers are invited to select relevant cases from Part III, to see how gaming and simulation work in practice. In every chapter, due to the focus on methodology, some parts are abstract and theoretical, other parts are practical.

Jan H.G. Klabbers
August 2006

KALEIDOSCOPIC PERSPECTIVE ON GAME, PLAY, AND SIMULATION

HISTORIC TRACES

Suppose you would have the opportunity to visit the Museum Het Valkhof ("Falcon House") at Nijmegen, the Netherlands. It houses among others, a large and important collection of Roman antiques. The museum is situated at the edge of the historic Valkhof Park with a nice panorama of the river Rhine, with at its other side, up North, the open and flat area where two thousands years ago the Batavians used to live. Het Valkhof was also two thousands years ago the site of a Roman encampment on which about 800 A.D. the Emperor Charlemagne built a castle. Today it is an exciting modern location for art and culture.

The large and varied archeological collections of the museum reveal the prehistoric, Roman and medieval past of the city of Nijmegen, with a wealth of information on various themes – the Roman army, Roman religion and burial traditions, trade and crafts, and games to pass the time – all of which conjure a picture of everyday life in Noviomagus (Nijmegen), once the most important Roman city in the Netherlands.

At the exhibition floor with its light, airy space, you will find a stone bench with three game boards printed on it. For each game, pieces are provided and the rules are printed on the bench. The games are LUDUS LATRUNCULORUM (the SOLDIERS GAME); the MILL GAME, and the CIRCULAR MILL. Youngsters play those games while their parents visit the museum. The MILL GAME is also part of the decorations put on the floor of the Antonio Fortress in Jerusalem by Roman soldiers (Grunfeld et al., 1994). The game board of the MILL GAME looks as follows; see Figure 1.1.

In 1283 the book "Libro de Jeugos" (Book of Games) was published. It was the first book in European literature devoted to games (Grunfeld et al. 1994). It was part of a series of books, covering the most important issues of that time: history, law, religion, astronomy, and magic. The compendium was established through the personal leadership of Alfonso X, king of Castile and León, who brought together a group of experts. The king – known as Alfonso the Sage – was an eminent scholar himself. The fact that games – in all their known appearances – received considerable attention, gives evidence of their importance in medieval Spain. In his introduction the king points out that it is God's disposition that human beings unwind and relax through a variety of games, and that this pleasure will offer solace, and drives away boredom. Alfonso's editors limited themselves to the Spanish and Moorish medieval culture. Libro de Juegos describes for example 'NINE MEN'S MORRIS' ('MILL GAME'), which was played by the ancient Egyptians.

'nine men's morris' ('mill game')

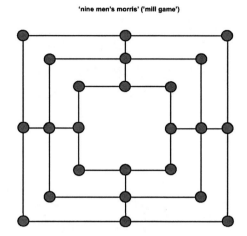

Figure 1.1. Game board of the MILL GAME

It is probably one of the oldest board games in the world. The English name 'Morris' could be linked to the earliest Medieval French version with the name 'merrils' or 'morell' (Grundfeld et al., 1994). It could however also refer to old English folk-dance for men, with in this case the nine pieces of the game representing nine dancing men. Another ancient game called "WARI" or "AWARI" is a variation of the so-called Mancala games, played in ancient Egypt. Game boards, carved in stone, have been found in the pyramid of Cheops and in the temples of Luxor and Karnak. Games are spread too over Asia and Africa. In Surinam playing games is part of funeral rituals to entertain the soul of the deceased person (Grunfeld et al., 1994). It is interesting to note that Backgammon, one of the great pleasures of 13th century nobility, originated from the Roman game 'Tabula', by Arabs called 'Nard.' A global perspective on games shows that they are embedded in human culture. For example, African tribes, Eskimos, Japanese intellectuals, and Mexican Indians play games. Games have crossed borders and cultures without asking for permission from rulers.

PLAY ELEMENT OF CULTURE

The shifting meanings on the terms *play*, and *game*, presented above, lack a more fundamental view on the play element of culture. Without a basic understanding of the play concept, it will be difficult, if not impossible to address related scientific questions and puzzles. It will moreover hamper grasping its significance in human society.

Play in the blood. The many manifestations of play and their widespread use show that it is connected through an indissoluble tie to human culture. Huizinga (1985) was explicit about the nature and meaning of play. He argued that play precedes culture, because the idea of culture, however vaguely described, always presupposes human society, while animals have not waited for the human being to teach them to play. One can safely assert that human society has not added significantly to the general notion of play. Animals play just like humans. All the essential features of human play are present in playing animals. Watching young dogs playing with each other, one can notice these features. They invite one another by posture and gestures to join in. They obey the rules not to eat through each other's ears. They pretend to be angry. Particularly, they apparently seem to enjoy it. Such playing of young dogs is only a simple form of animal play. There are examples of more highly developed forms of play: real contests and fine performances before an audience. Play is more than a physiological phenomenon. It goes beyond boundaries of purely biological or physical activity. In play, there is something at stake that goes beyond the immediate desire of survival. Each play is a meaningful activity, and foremost a free act. Because of its quality of freedom, it exceeds the confines of nature. Play is not ordinary or 'real' life. It is departing from ordinary life in a temporary atmosphere of activity with its own purpose. Based on these notions, Huizinga defined play as follows:

> Play is a voluntary activity or occupation, executed within fixed limits of time and place, according to rules freely accepted but absolutely binding, having its aim in itself and accompanied by a feeling of tension, joy, and the awareness that it is different from ordinary life (Huizinga, 1985, p. 28).

Through this limits of time and space, players (actors) enter a magic circle and enact a world, which is both real and imagined. The scope of this definition is both very broad, and very limiting. It is broad as it covers animal, child, and adult play, as well as the whole variety of games, exhibitions and performances. It is limiting because it requires a "stop rule", and a well-specified location, while it seems to exclude the linkages of play with law, war, knowing and wisdom, and art, topics that Huizinga addressed in the chapters of the book. The purpose of law, knowing and wisdom, and, art is to keep the game going which implies that there is no stop rule. If one considers war as form of diplomacy and international relations with particular means, than underlying play and war is a game without stop rule. The connotation of play and law, war, knowing, and art presumes an ongoing game without clearly defined stop rules. Huizinga called the category *play* one of the most fundamental in life. While reflecting on the expressions of the play concept, he observed that languages have varied in getting the numerous aspects of play into one word. There are highly developed languages, which have retained totally different words for the various play forms. This multiplicity of terms has hampered the aggregation of all play forms under one term. Huizinga illustrated this by discussing expressions for play activity in languages such as, Greek, Chinese, Sanskrit, English, Japanese, the Germanic group of languages, etc. From this review of play related terms, he gathered that cultures generally refer to play as contest, as battle: "Play is battle, and battle is play" (Huizinga, 1985, p. 40).

Compared to the English-American language, which has two words "play" and "game", the Dutch and German language for example have only available one generic term: "spel" and "Spiel", for expressing playful kinds of activities. The more subtle differentiations that the terms "play" and "game" offer are more difficult to express in Dutch. This becomes clear when comparing the original Dutch text of Huizinga's Homo Ludens with the English translation.

Huizinga (1985) − in his foreword of "Homo Ludens" − mentioned that he was convinced that civilization arises and unfolds in and as play. The Dutch subtitle of his book is: "The play element *of* culture". When giving lectures in Zürich, Vienna, and London, his hosts wanted to correct it to "The play element *in* culture". Each time Huizinga protested and clung to the genitive "of". It was not his object to define the place of play among all the other manifestations of culture, "but rather to ascertain how far culture itself bears the character of play". He approached play historically, not scientifically. In the English translation (Huizinga, 1955), the translator, who prepared the English version from the German edition, noted that as English prepositions are not governed by logic, it was decided to retain the more euphonious ablative "in" in the sub-title. I think that it is not the whole story for the following reason. In the Dutch version, at p. 74, Huizinga stated: "Culture does not begin *as* play, and it does not begin *from* play. It begins *in* play". That particular sentence is missing in the English translation. Nonetheless, the English text (p. 75) continues, similar to the Dutch text with: "In play, therefore, the antithetical and agonistic basis of civilization is given from the start, for play is older and more original than civilization". Comparing the original Dutch and the English text, I notice some important differences. The English translation is less consistent with Huizinga's basic thesis: underpinning the play element *of* culture. Huizinga pointed out that as "culture artifacts" grow more composed and elaborate, their production becomes more high-wrought. The basis of civilization becomes increasingly overgrown with ideas, systems, concepts, norms, skills, and traditions (customs), which seem to have lost their connections with play. Culture grows increasingly serious, and while it evolves, it seems to give only incidental prominence to play. So it seems. In the following chapters on play and law, play and war, playing and knowing, etc, he argued that such a view is not correct. In the chapter "Play and War" Huizinga (1955) reflected on the "Law of Nations", and observed that

Its principle of reciprocal rights, its diplomatic forms, its mutual obligations in the matter of honoring treaties, ... all bear a formal resemblance to play-rules inasmuch as they are only binding while the game itself is recognized (p. 100).

Then he drew the interesting conclusion: "We might, in a purely formal sense, call all society a game, if we bear in mind that this game is the living principle of all civilization" (pp. 100-101). This observation upsets the idea of play executed within fixed limits of time and place. Viewing all society a game implies that games can and should go on without a stop rule. It forms a marked and interesting contrast with the definition of play, mentioned above, which states that "play is a voluntary activity or occupation, executed within fixed limits of time and place." Moreover, the notion that society is a game is consistent with the subtitle of the book: the play element *of* culture.

Huizinga checked the conceptual value of the word "play" by the word, which expresses the opposite. For this he chose the word "earnest", used in the sense of "work". The opposite of work can either be play, jesting, or joking. He chose the complementary pair *play-earnest* as the most interesting one. Leaving aside here linguistic questions, Huizinga argued that the two terms are not of equal value. The significance of the term "earnest" is defined by and exhausted in the negation of "play", earnest is equivalent to "not-playing", and nothing more. The significance of "play", on the other hand, is not defined or exhausted by calling it "non-earnest". Players can be both playful and serious, while playing. Therefore, the play concept is much broader and of higher order than is seriousness. Seriousness seeks to exclude play, whereas play can very well include seriousness.

It is out of the scope of this chapter to discuss in detail Huizinga's views on play. In line with the kaleidoscopic perspective of this introduction, a few critical comments should however be made. Huizinga emphasized that the great variety of cultural manifestations, whether they are rituals, contests, or ceremonies, are all forms of play. His definition of play sheds light on the human activity as embedded in institutional settings, he left however in the dark the qualities of games, their peculiar forms, that enhance or trigger typical playful behavior. That is a serious omission, for it hampers the more precise descriptions of human actions during a game. The examples provided remain anecdotic. In the next chapter I will address explicitly the diversity of forms of play, their classifications and typologies.

Games of chance

More recent advances in complexity science are shedding light on the fundamental role of the play element of nature. Eigen and Winkler (1975) stated that play is a natural phenomenon that has determined the course of nature right from its beginning. It has shaped matter, the organization of matter to become living organisms, and social behavior of man. While referring to the origin of play, they expressed its fundamental characteristic as follows.

> The history of play goes back to the beginning of time. The energy of the Big Bang set everything in motion and caused a whirl in matter that never will end. Organizing forces tried to catch everything that dissipated, and they tried to tame chance. What resulted is not the rigid order of a crystal. It is the order of life. Chance is from the beginning the undeniable opponent of the organizing forces. Chances and rules are the elements of the game. Similar to its beginning with elementary particles, atoms and molecules, it finds its continuation in our brains. It was not the human being that invented play. It is play and nothing but play that makes up the human being (p. 17-18).

Eigen and Winkler (1975) paid attention to elementary forces, laws of nature and chance, and demonstrated the wide variety of structure, patterns, and forms that emerge from applying simple rules of chance. They connected self-organizing forces of nature with the idea of an evolutionary game of life on earth, to organizations in transition. The related organizational complexity is explored as it emerges through far-from-equilibrium dissipative, autopoietic, or self-organizing systems in evolutionary space. Such games increase or decrease in complexity via their co-evolving component systems. They refer to a-priori indeterminable number of microstates, and processes. Specific organization, structure and process produce order within such huge sequence spaces. The evolutionary game concerns the narrowing down of these sequence spaces to a few biologically or socially viable ones.

Caillois (2001) elaborated games of chance as an important category of as well as attitude to play. He referred to state lotteries, casinos, hippodromes, pari-mutuels of all kinds as forms of pure play following laws of chance: mathematical laws of probability. For those playing such games of chance, "it is not an abstract expression of a statistical coefficient, but a sacred sign of the favor of the gods" (Caillois, 1958, p.126). That connotation of the term chance brings us back again to the play element of culture. It is not contradictory to Eigen and Winkler's approach. It expresses a notion of play and chance complementary to and following from laws of nature. It shows the equivocality (ambiguity) of the idea of play. I will discuss Caillois' ideas in more detail in Chapter 2.

QUESTIONS OF TERMINOLOGY

From the play element of culture, and the use of games, sketched above, one can gather the high diversity and broad scope of this field. In the following sections, I will address both gaming and simulation, referring to activities and processes related to games as products of the human minds: artifacts. I would like to stress that the perspectives offered, usually do not address the same readers. Each view offers a different scope and pays attention to distinct goals and questions. Together, they illustrate the richness and reach of this subject of study. The nouns 'play', 'game', and 'simulation' refer to both products of human invention – artifacts – and activities such as expressed through the verbs 'to play', 'to game', and 'to simulate'. The artifacts, expressed through their nouns, only obtain meaning in the activities they trigger. A game is a form of play, and it is only a game if being played. A simulation is only a simulation if set in motion. To advance the study of these artifacts, and the related playful activities, it is therefore needed to bring order in the terminology. A common understanding of the key terms paves the road for having constructive conversations and for addressing corresponding methodological questions.

Monitoring the ongoing discussions and debates on the meaning of those terms since the 1960s, I have learned that there is still little agreement among scholars and practitioners about terminology. From a scientific viewpoint that is understandable, as those who are involved in gaming and simulation represent the whole spectrum of academic disciplines. However, the confusion about terms is broader than strictly academic. It precedes academic reflection and is more fundamental than basic research. It refers to man as a playful animal, and the play element of culture – see above – (Huizinga, 1985). The kaleidoscopic view on activities such as, playing, gaming, and simulating – presented here – indicates that for developing an integrative perspective, it is worthwhile to choose an appropriate level of aggregation. Moreover, to be able to understand their diversity of appearances and practices, we should take on board their *contextuality, problem orientations*, and *method diversity*. Fruitfully dealing with method diversity is only possible from a proper methodological perspective. It will provide a deeper understanding of gaming methods and techniques in Part II.

The idea of games in philosophy

In *Philosophical investigations*, Ludwig Wittgenstein (1968) argued that there is no fixed set of features that define a game. As a game is a form of play, with emphasis on rules, Wittgenstein's main focus seems to be on games as human constructs, or artifacts. This applies to language as well. According to Wittgenstein, games encompass a loose set of features. A simple criterion for demarcating games from non-games is difficult to offer. It is not clear whether Wittgenstein had in mind the same ambiguity that Huizinga referred to when addressing the question of play and non-play in relation to being playful and/or earnest. Wittgenstein held that language was itself a game, consisting of tokens governed by mutually agreed upon rules that influenced the usage of words. Wittgenstein proposed performing a thought experiment. First he asked the readers to propose a definition of the word "game", and he then went on to lead them through the problems with each of the possible definitions of the word "game". Any definition which focuses on amusement leaves us unsatisfied since the feelings experienced by a world class chess player are very different than those of a circle of children playing FOLLOW THE LEADER. Any definition, which focuses on competition, fails to explain the game of catch, the game of solitaire, or any cooperative game. And a definition of the word "game", which focuses solely on rules, will fall on similar difficulties, as there are games that are not rule-driven (see next chapters). Wittgenstein's main point was not that it is impossible to define "game", but that we don't have a clear cut definition, and we don't need one. The meaning of the term "game" shows itself in its use. A "game" does not exist in a cultural or social vacuum. Therefore, shifting contexts of playing games offer a variety of meanings to the word. Everybody in a certain cultural setting understands what we mean when we talk about playing a game.

We are able to identify and correct inaccurate uses of the word "game". Wittgenstein argued that "definitions" are emergent forms from what he termed "forms of life", which are the culture and society from which they emerged. Wittgenstein stressed very strongly the social aspects of cognition. To see how language works, we have to see how it functions in a specific social situation. It is this emphasis that may explain Wittgenstein's comment that "if a lion could speak, we would not understand him." When speaking of the variety of games, we refer to *family resemblances*. Family resemblances and classifications, how exactly do they work? Why is it that we are sure a particular activity such as, Olympic target shooting, is a game while a similar activity such as, military sharp shooting is not? Wittgenstein's explanation is tied up with an important analogy. How do we classify objects and ideas? If we see enough matches between their attributes, we say we have noticed a family resemblance, which helps us to classify them. This usually is not a purely conscious and rational process. We intuitively see the resemblances. Wittgenstein suggested that the same might be true with games. Perhaps we are all familiar (i.e. socially tuned) with enough things, which are called games, and enough things, which are not games, that we can instantly categorize related artifacts and activities intuitively. According to Wittgenstein, this also applies to language games.

He paid special attention to indirect communication, and thought experiments, and argued that many philosophers are confused, because they are not able to *see* family resemblances, and have difficulties in understanding the vague intuitive rules of the language game, thereby tying themselves up in philosophical knots. He suggested that untangling these knots requires more than simple deductive arguments. He tried to divert his colleagues from their philosophical problems to indirectly retrain their intuitive ability to notice family resemblances. It applies to language games as well as to the broader class of artifacts called "games."

Family resemblances on "play", "game", "playful gaming"

As demonstrated above, the terms "play" and "game" have been used interchangeably as if the two are the same. Makedon (1984) reflected on the playfulness of games, and argued that playing and gaming are each a necessary but not sufficient condition for covering all aspects of gaming. "The characteristics that are commonly held to play include voluntariness, spontaneity, and desirability for its own sake" (Makedon, 1984, p. 30). Games, as special forms of play, are linked to rules. "Its essential quality is not subjective or attitudinal, as is the quality of play, but objective or formal. Unless the game is played according to its rules, it is not the same game or even a game at all" (Makedon, 1984, p. 31). The system of play rules fixes the range of ideas and symbols to be used in a game. They both enable and constrain the players' activities and their inter-actions. Makedon did not make a distinction between the designer of a game and as such the key person who defines the rules, and the players who play by those rules. Therefore, I guess that he implicitly focused on rule-driven games only, with the rules set by the game designer, and subsequently executed by the game facilitator. This limited scope excludes games that are driven by the rules being shaped and negotiated among the players themselves during the game session (Klabbers, 1996). His frame-of-reference seems to exclude *free-form* or *open games* in which the players have the freedom to self-organize the rules.

Play is an activity that is desired and enjoyed for its own sake. Makedon summarized the differences between play and game by pointing out that play is subjectively grounded in the player, while game is objectively grounded in the game rules (Makedon, 1984, p. 32). A game is only a game if being played. Therefore, in practice both terms are intertwined. Although pinpointing key qualities of play and game, Makedon misses a third key quality, which emerges when considering gaming from the perspective of the anthropology of knowledge. Barth (2002) distinguished *three interrelated faces of knowledge*:
- A substantive corpus of assertions;
- A range of media of representation; and
- A social organization.

Assertions convey how people connect objects, and actions to explain events, and processes. These explanations may have a mythical or a rational connotation. The related "causal" inferences usually are expressed in games in terms of behavioral (descriptive) or normative (prescriptive) rules. In cultures, the *media of representation* range from signs, symbols that are being used during consecrations, holy dances, sacral contests – all part of a festival or mythical ritual – to mathematical knowledge used for computations, to images in gross anatomy atlases, technical laboratory equipment for microbiological experiments, chemical models, geography atlases and scale models, and so on. These representations shape both thought and action and thus the practices of the people involved. The players of a game enact the real, imaginary, or virtual world, and shape a *social organization*, through these assertions and interventions in the media of representation. These three faces of knowledge interrelate in particular ways in different knowledge traditions (cultures), and they generate tradition-specific criteria for validity of knowledge-about-the-world. The substantive corpus of assertions is based upon various types of rules about how to interpret and act on the world. It refers to insights, information, verbal taxonomies, concepts and their interrelationships, and prescriptive and descriptive action repertoires. The play element of a game is embedded in its social organization. The rules encompass the corpus of assertions about the gamed reality. They represent as such a *necessary* but *insufficient condition* for playing games such as CHESS, GO, MONOPOLY, etc. Makedon does not refer to media of representation as a key element of a game. I consider this a serious omission for two reasons. Firstly, with rules but without media of representation such as for example a game board, a game is an abstract entity that cannot be played. CHESS for example, cannot be played without its game board and the pieces with their peculiar qualities.

Secondly, media of representation refer to resources available to players to move within the game space. They symbolize both the real and imaginary, or virtual world that is acted upon by the players. Both MONOPOLY and GRAND THEFT AUTO symbolize a city, however from very distinct viewpoints in terms of the resources – and media of representation – available to the player(s).

Makedon, and with him, many authors on gaming and play, restrict themselves to the rules as the key characteristic – the back bone – of play and game, while omitting their linkages to the resources as conveyed through the media of representation. As a consequence, they are not able to deal properly with the concept "game space", and the way the players – through their actions – move through this space. A game is both objectively grounded in the rules and in their linkages to the resources. For example CHESS: changing the board, the pieces, or the rules, will change both the game and its play. The media of representation typify reference systems in real or imaginary worlds. They constitute basic ingredients of games.

Participating in a game is performing symbolic acts, which constitute our ways of understanding major aspects of the world, ways to think and feel about the world, and ways to act on it. Tracing the history of play and game is not straightforward, as the play element refers to narratives of game experiences, while the game element emphasizes their form as embedded in the rules, and media of representation. "Game archaeologists" will find traces of games in the written rules, by oral tradition, and in media of representation such as a variety of game boards engraved in stone in ancient Egypt, Rome and many other places. It will be more difficult to find narratives about what happened in a particular game, because only on rare occasions will those stories have been collected.

AREAS OF APPLICATION

Outdoor gaming exercises

Outdoor gaming is a form of experiential learning under natural conditions. Natural circumstances provide a great variety of options for learning to cope with physical, mental, and social challenges. Typical outdoor programs are: rappelling, ropes or challenge courses, assembling large wooden structures such as watch towers, kayaking, canyoning, hiking, bicycling, horse riding, rock climbing, and wilderness adventure programs. Eberle (2004) observed that one of the major goals of this type of gaming exercises is the development of new and reinforcement of desirable and existing competencies of groups and individuals. These forms of experience-based training and development aim at improving teamwork (teambuilding). Priest (1986) mentioned the following goals of outdoor (outward bound) programs: enhancing cultural change, changing motivational climate in companies, influencing risk taking propensity, leadership, improving self-confidence and trustworthiness (acceptance, believability, confidentiality, dependability, and encouragement). The peculiar settings of these programs make them also suitable for therapeutic use, and for helping deviant juveniles or adolescents at risk (Eberle, 2004).

The social setting of outdoor training programs is primarily being used for experience-based training. It can however also be used to develop and test theories. David Berreby (2005-a) described some interesting outdoor programs to underpin his ideas about the emerging science of "tribal" psychology. He recalled an intriguing exercise by Muzafer Sherif, a social psychologist, in 1954 (see also: Berreby, 2005-b). Under the auspices of the University of Oklahoma, Sherif designed the following experiment. Twenty two fifth-graders from Oklahoma City were invited in the summer of 1954 to spend three weeks in the Sans Bois mountains at a 200-acre campground – the Robbers Cave State Park – with swimming holes, streams, canoes, baseball, campfires, caves, and snakes. They were invited to explore the woods where Jesse James's gang hid out, to have cookouts, and play tug of war. Sherif's goal was to advance social psychology. That was his hidden agenda. All the boys were strangers. Sherif and his counselors observed the birth, life, and death of tribal feelings. Sherif aimed at showing that circumstances could create tribes, and tribal feeling, and subsequently that a change in circumstances could change those perceptions, and the related behavior and handling repertoire.

The boys arrived in two separate groups of 11 each, and each band had time to explore and claim some territory – a bunkhouse, a swimming hole, a ball field. Each group soon decided it needed a name and a symbol. On the sixth day of camp, one group called themselves the "Rattlers". The Rattlers learned that they were not alone. They could hear other boys in the distance, playing on the ball field. That group also had invented a name. They called themselves the "Eagles". The Rattlers and Eagles elaborated their differences. Different incidents that happened in both groups, and the way they were handled by individuals – nude swimming, clean language the Eagles way, toughing it out when hurt the Rattlers ethos, formed the identity and behavioral rules of both "tribes".

Sherif implemented some meta-rules to induce competition between both tribes. He set up a tournament of ball games, bean tosses, tug-of-war and other contests, with prizes for the team that won the most games. Within two days, feelings of mutual antagonism became manifest. The counselors had to keep a close eye on both cabins at night. Both tribes went in for raids and counter-raids. The game facilitators had to step in to prevent real bloodshed.

At the beginning of the third week Sherif had to show that changing circumstances of the boys' lives would get them to drop the Rattler-Eagle divide. He gave the two warring cultures a shared goal, which demanded that they all perceived themselves as "in the same boat." He blocked the faucet leading from the camp's one water tank. Both sides had to figure out how to unblock the spigot. During the following days he wanted them to work out several common bottlenecks. For example, he staged the mechanical breakdown of one truck, so that only one truck was available to return to the base camp. That was a moment of truth. If they stayed true to their Rattler and Eagle loyalties, they had to make two separate 60-mile round trips, or they could decide to go as one. After a long debate, they chose to go as one group. On the way back, the boys traded stories about raids and fights. Slights and attacks that made them furious before made them now laugh and brag (Berreby, 2005-a, p. 12).

In this social psychological experiment, the experimenter takes first the role of game designer, subsequently of game operator, and finally of outside game evaluator, explaining what happened. By setting and changing the conditions for the participants to act, he shaped conditions for the game (social system) to shape itself. The boys were not aware that they were involved in a game. Within the physical settings, which he created, the "players" enacted (accidentally) a system of rules, and symbols that conveyed their identity as group ("tribe"). The outdoor game became a real and temporary social system for them. Through their insider stories they gave the social system *meaning*. For Sherif it was a model of a social system. Through his outside observer's position, he provided an explanation at a level of abstraction, which was distinct from the "players" level of understanding. He provided a social psychological, and Berreby gave it tribal psychological explanation. Other inference schemes may offer still other explanations. Conclusion: One dynamic system of interactions produces many stories of insiders, and many explanations by qualified outsiders.

This story is one example of an outdoor game to test a theory about social psychology, and tribalism. Berreby argued that "tribal" perceptions and feelings about race, religion, and nation, arise from a built-in mental faculty. I would argue that the interplay between that mental faculty and the enacted social and physical environment are triggers for constructing and continuously reconstructing a particular social system. "Tribal" psychology, so framed, connects anthropology, social and cognitive psychology.

Game theory

Operational gaming has a long history. Sun Tsu, the great Chinese general of the 5th century B.C. used concepts of operational gaming and some elements of the theory of games, in its two-person zero-sum form (Shubik, M. 1983). 23 centuries later the Prussian war staff used war games to experiment with strategies and tactics, and another two centuries later, Von Neumann and Morgenstern elaborated on mathematical game theory.

Modern game theory became prominent with the classic work *The Theory of Games and Economic Behavior* by John von Neumann and Oskar Morgenstern (1944). It contained a mathematical theory of economic and social organization. They elaborated the method for finding optimal solutions for two-person zero-sum games. Initially work on game theory was primarily focused on *cooperative games*. Such games refer to social systems that have the capacity to enforce coordinated behavior on agents (social or institutional actors), which become members of coalitions. The related game theoretical mechanisms − from law to legal contracts − are abundant in societies. Cooperative game theory analyses optimal strategies for institutional actors, presuming that they can enforce formal agreements between them about proper strategies for handling their varying interests. For example, two players are involved, one positioned over the rows and the other over the columns of the payoff matrix in Table 1.1. In game theory, the players are actors that represent institutions or agencies with opposite interests. Therefore, I will use the term *actor* to indicate the distinction with individual persons and their assumed positions in the game. For example, BRIDGE is a two-actor game, because it deals with two opposite interest groups or stakeholders' positions. Even in case of changing partners, the game still deals with two opposite interest groups. In the case of Table 1.1, each actor has two options, each option leading to a specific payoff. In game theory, the term *strategy* refers to a rational and exhaustive plan that cannot be disturbed by the actions of the opposite actors, or by "nature". When a game is presented in this form it is presumed that both actors act simultaneously or, are not informed in advance about the actions of the other. The state of the world is represented via the payoffs in the matrix. The classic form of a two-person game is depicted in Table 1.1.

Table 1.1 State space of two-person game

Payoff matrix	*Actor 2 chooses* **Option1**	*Actor 2 chooses* **Option2**	*Row* *Maximum*
Actor 1 chooses **Option1**	Payoff 6	Payoff 5	5*
Actor 1 chooses **Option2**	Payoff 5	Payoff 4	4
Column minimum	6	5*	

A simple example will illustrate the style of reasoning of game theory. The numbers in the matrix refer to the payoffs, pending the options the actors choose. In case of Table 1.1, by definition, the numbers represent the payoffs that actor 2 will have to pay actor 1. Both actors try to maximize their profits or minimize their losses. Whatever strategy actor 1 will choose, actor 2 will always make the most profitable counteroffer. Taking into account the options of actor 2, for actor 1, strategy 1 is most profitable choice. Similarly, taking into account the options of actor 1, for actor 2, strategy 2 is most profitable. After a number of iterations, both actors will find out that this strategy is most beneficial for both of them. It is the optimum strategy. Changing the state space of payoffs and extending the matrix to n players, very elaborate strategies may evolve that −expressed in formal, mathematical, language − predict optimal solutions. John Nash (1950-a; 1950-b; 1951; 1953) developed an optimum strategy for non-cooperative multi-player games: the Nash equilibrium, for which he received the Nobel Prize in 1994. Thomas C. Schelling and Robert J. Aumann shared the 2005 Nobel Prize in Economic Science. The two scientists have been awarded the prize for their fundamental works on game theory. Aumann (1959) dealt with cooperative N-Person games, while Schelling (1960) elaborated the strategy of conflict.

Paul Walker (1995) traced game theory back to the Talmud. He noted that the Babylonian Talmud is the compilation of ancient law and tradition set down during the first five centuries A.D. which serves as the basis of Jewish religious, criminal and civil law. One problem discussed in the Talmud is the marriage contract. A man has three wives whose marriage contracts specify that in the case of this death they receive 100, 200 and 300 respectively. The Talmud gives apparently contradictory recommendations. When the man dies leaving an estate of only 100, the Talmud recommends equal division. However, if the estate is worth 300 it recommends proportional division (50,100,150), while for an estate of 200, its recommendation is (50,75,75). This peculiar ruling has baffled Talmudic scholars for two millennia. From the perspective of modern game theory with its state space represented through the payoff matrix such as depicted in Table 1.1, it was recognized that the Talmud anticipated with these alternative solutions the theory of cooperative games.

Game theory distinguishes two approaches: the theoretical, which is formal and mathematical, and the experimental approach. Game theory progresses by the continual interplay of theory and experiment. Game theorists hypothesize ideas and principles, which are subsequently explored by stating them in precise mathematical language. This allows predictions to be made, which experimentalists can test. With the theoretical approach, a mathematical model, based upon axioms of rational decision-making, predicts optimal solutions to N-persons games. It is a normative theory that prescribes which strategy is most optimal for rational decision makers. The experimental approach puts subjects in a setting such as for example depicted in Table 1.1 (see above), and studies how the strategies of both players evolve over time. By developing and testing hypotheses, experiments falsify theories of human sequential decision-making, which are framed according to the layout of payoff matrices. When there are surprising new experimental findings, theorists attempt to model them in order to test the adequacy of current theories. If a gap emerges between theory and experiment, which lasts for a long time, then the theorists will have to reexamine the assumptions behind such unsuccessful theories. Although being focused on the mathematical analysis of economic behavior, game theory provided strong conditions in the 1950s for a favorable reception by sociologists and psychologists, especially from the viewpoint of interactive decision theory. However, as Luce and Raiffa stated:

> Initially there was a naïve bandwagon-feeling that game theory solved innumerable problems of sociology and economics, or at least, that it made their solution a practical matter of a few years' work. That has not turned out to be the case (Luce and Raiffa, 1957, p. 10).

It is still problematic in 2006. One of the major obstacles for embedding game theory in mainstream sociological and psychological research was the question about the correctness and fruitfulness of the economist's paradigm of rational action. The concept of *rationality* is defined in a way that it suits the formal theory and its underlying axioms. Through its axiomatic approach, game theory offered a context free, universal approach to interactive decision making. However, as Jessie Bernard (1954) had pointed out, sociological phenomena are context dependent. Institutions affect the way a game is played, and culture affects what is happening in a society, which impacts on the rules of the game (Bernard, 1954). Moreover, human behavior does not fit into the strict definition of rationality of game theory. Bernard mentioned another difficulty with game theory. It refers to determining exactly what the rules and payoffs are. Both need elaborate empirical research before the game exercise can start. She mentioned that in many cases it might be impossible to determine what the payoff for a specific strategy is or to compare the payoff of one strategy to that one of another. The comparison of *utilities* in the payoff matrix is another obstacle. If a millionaire and a beggar would jointly play a zero-sum game, the winning or losing of for example 25 Euro would have a significant higher utility for the beggar than for the millionaire. "Utility" in rational economic terms is not similar to its meaning in psychological terms. In addition, I argue that human decision-making is a self-referential process, meaning that the interpretation of the rules and the payoffs fluctuate over time, and vary over contexts. These obstacles have turned out to be major impediments to mathematical game theory in the social and behavioral sciences. Empirical verification of game-theoretical analysis was and still is a major problem.

William Gamson carried game theory a step further by investigating what it had to say about building coalitions (Gamson, 1961). Some years later Gamson published the game SIMSOC – simulated society (Gamson, W. 1968). SIMSOC resembles conceptually an extended prisoner's dilemma game. Many business simulations can be described as extended prisoner's dilemma games. They do not apply the rigor of the axiomatic game theory, and give the players more freedom to interpret the rules and appreciate the multiple meanings of the payoffs. Current developments in game theory relate to multi-agent modeling (agent-based simulation), which are used for designing so-called artificial societies. Game theory is primarily academic of nature.

Functionally integrated business games and simulations

War games and game theory stimulated the development of a new class of games and simulations. A short history of the field of business games and simulations reflects the predominant management paradigms of 20th century. The first of these types of games is THE MONEY GAME, developed in 1912 in the UK. In the Leningrad Textile Factory (USSR) M. Bierstein developed the ORGANISATION OF PRODUCTION GAME in 1932. After World War II, large companies increasingly were seeking the same optimal market position, each one responding to actions taken by competitors. As many former army officers entered business, they brought with them knowledge about and experience with war games. Business was and still is viewed as war among competitors. It is obvious that in such an atmosphere corporate managers became interested in adopting war games as prototypes for running a business.

In 1957 the American Management Association introduced the first functionally integrated business game. It was the start of a whole series of general management games, developed in the 1950s and 1960s in the USA, such as the UCLA Game, the Harvard Business School Game, the Carnegie Tech. Management Game, The New York University Game, INTOP (International Operations Simulation), and The Executive Game. In Japan the Top-Management-Decision-Game, model 625-B, was developed. These first generation games ran on main-frame computers. Nowadays they run on PC's. Usually, decisions of the participating management teams deal with selling price; production volume; R&D budget; marketing budget; materials purchase budget; plant and equipment investment budget; and dividend. These decisions are made quarterly or annually, and the results from the simulation model are fed back to the teams for assessment and adjustment for the next time increment. Profitability is the major goal of these games.

Thorelli (2001) expressed the spirit of 1950s well by telling the story about the development of the business simulation International Operations Simulation (INTOP) in an ignorant and hostile academic environment. He was a GE executive when he first became excited about management games. This was the Sales Management game developed by G.R. Andlinger, published in the Harvard Business Review in 1958 (Andlinger, 1958). It was a hand-scored board game. Andlinger's game was certainly a pioneer effort. Joining the University of Chicago in the following year, Thorelli brought the game into his marketing and business policy classes, pending the development of a new, computer-based game. He continued:

> An underlying educational premise was a strong belief that different people learn in different ways – calling for a varied set of pedagogical instruments. A related idea was that business schools – like other professional schools –

should have the mission to strike bridges between classical (as well as applied) disciplines on one hand and practical applications on the other. Aside from class discussions of cases, relatively little was really being done in this area at the time. Perhaps the single most important objective was to develop an exercise to demonstrate the interaction between *structure* (of the organization as well as the task environment), *strategy*, and *performance* (SSP) in the business world. By making the game international, participants would naturally expect different business environments and presumably they would begin to see the interactions of SSP variables. It was easy to foresee the imminent rapid growth of international business and its importance to management. Both to reach a broader audience and to focus on cross-functional interaction, the aim was to create a general management game useful in both functional (production, marketing, finance, and so on) and integrative capstone courses. The notion of a 'business management laboratory' was prominent in our minds. With colleague Robert L. Graves and then graduate assistant L.T. Howells we spent the next three years developing the first IB strategy simulation on the UNIVAC 1 (Thorelli, 2001, pp. 492-493).

The structure of INTOP and its more recent version INTOPIA reflect the generic structure of well-known business simulations. Several companies operate in the same national and/or international market. They manufacture goods with the available facilities. The core mechanism for representing the dynamics of such games is micro-economic theory. That theory is formalized in the computer program, which calculates the consequences of the decisions of each of the companies, in terms of turn over, costs, market share, profits, etc. Emphasis is on business strategy vis-à-vis the market. The internal organization of the companies is modeled via functional subsystems such as production, finance, marketing, personnel, etc.

Behavioral simulations

Closely linked to business simulations of the type sketched above, and emerging in the US in the 1960s, are behavioral simulations. Contrary to business simulations with their focus on economic theory, this type of games pays special attention to learning about organizational behavior, organizational design, change, development, and management. They simulate the many aspects of organizational life such as, the development of work teams, informal groups, organizational differentiation and integration, leadership, organizational conflict, information processing systems, politics, etc. Emphasis is mainly on the wheeling and dealing of the internal organization of a manufacturing or service company. A classic example is THE ORGANIZATION GAME (Miles & Randolph, 1985).

Video games

Traditional board and card games still enjoy high interest, and annually many new games of such type are being designed for commercial reasons. Since the advent of the PC in the 1980s a new variety of games has rapidly proliferated: video- or computer games that run on PCs or on specifically designed consoles such as

Xbox, PlayStation, or the Gamecube. Publishers such as, Electronic Arts, Atari, Activision, etc. distribute the games, and pay for using, and for the privilege of producing games for their consoles. The publishers cooperate with numerous design studios from all over the world, which envision and develop the digital games. On average, it takes three years to design and market a game. At November 30, 2005, Sony announced that it had supplied one hundred million game computers – Playstation 2 – to retailers. Playstation 2 entered the market in March 2000. Similar figures apply for Xbox. They offer an indication of the global market of digital games. The games PRINCE OF PERSIA, GRAND THEFT AUTO, F.E.A.R, CIVILIZATION, CALL OF DUTY, AGE OF EMPIRES, WORLD OF WARCRAFT, the SIMS etc. represent a multi-billion market for the game industry. Especially the younger generation – thirty years of age and younger – is very much involved in playing such games. They enter a virtual space through their *avatars*, which have to *conquer a whole variety of odds*, defending themselves from being attacked by odd characters popping up in endless repetition, even after they have been destroyed. The odds in physical space may take shape in the form of walls, barred doors or corridors, ditches, canals, sweeping obstacles, etc. By conquering the odds, the avatars – as the extension of the players in virtual space – find their trails though the maze, and by doing so, they frame interactively their narratives.

These highly competitive games require a high level of cognitive and psychomotor skills. The Cyberathlete Professional League (CPL) organizes annually a World Tour Grand Finals, awarding $500,000 in cash prizes in 2005 to the top 16 competitors over the course of the three days. The 2005 winner received $150,000, the largest cash prize ever for a computer game tournament (see: http://www.thecpl.com/league/). Although purely developed for commercial reasons, these video games impact on youth culture, the way youngsters spend their time at home and at school, communicate with their friends, and the way they learn. Gradually universities are becoming aware of the social and cultural impact of video games, of their reach, which is extending beyond the traditional boundaries of play and entertainment in family homes and arcades, into the classroom. That emerging youth culture is influencing social and group dynamics at playgrounds and other local youth facilities.

Many traditional board and card games such as, CHESS, GO, etc. have been digitalized and included in standard software for PCs. That adaptation implies both a shift in media of representation of those games – the interaction between the game board and the pieces on it – and the roles of the player(s). With CHESS, the computer assumes the role of the opponent. It becomes a rule-driven agent, who makes choices and moves pieces, based on a built in algorithm. Through the Human Computer Interface (HCI) the player interacts both with that agent (the artificial competitor) and the digital game board.

The commercial sector is still the major source of video game development. The initial costs of developing and marketing video games are very high. Also the financial risks are high. Property rights of game console manufacturers place high financial constraints on the development and use of digital games. They form bottlenecks in the flow of new and innovative game design.

Through so-called game engines – software packages that generate a variety of images – commercial, digital game design tends to a repetitive process in terms of form and content. Commercial success with one genre of play tends to repeat its prior success. Successful games tend to become pioneers of a certain genre, leading to a series of games of similar form and content. Informatics, Computer science and Information Science departments at universities are becoming a major source of innovations for game design. Humanities, and the social and behavioral sciences are gradually showing a keen interest in game studies, from various perspectives such as, multi-media studies, game cultures, social interaction, and cognition. Computer science and language faculties are increasingly joining efforts in video game design, the computer science taking care of software development, and linguistics and humanities of the narrative aspects. Video games – viewed as interactive narratives – offer a rapidly developing new area of research. Contrary to the other varieties of gaming – sketched in this chapter, which are driven by scientific curiosity, video games are mainly commercial products, and only recently – through their technological and social impact, and vast financial resources – they are becoming object of scientific study.

THE ADVENT OF GAMING ASSOCIATIONS

Via games and simulations, developed since the 1950s, we are witnessing their rapid proliferation to areas such as, social studies, urban and land use management, ecology, education (classroom instruction), international relations, health care, natural resources, etc. In addition, the field offered a broadening scope of forms: role-playing games, board games, computer-assisted and computer-supported games, frame games, exercises, simulation games, behavior simulations, and a variety of computer simulations.

In the early 1960s, James Coleman, William Gamson, Garry Shirts, Clark Abt, and a few others were pioneering the development of simulation games for use in classroom instruction (Stadsklev, 1974). Richard Duke and Allan Feldt were pioneers of urban and land use gaming. Duke designed METROPOLIS (1964), METRO-APEX (1964), METRO (1965) and Allan Feldt the COMMUNITY LAND USE GAME (CLUG) (1966). Harold Guetzkow developed INTER-NATION SIMULATION (1966), and Gary Shirts STARPOWER (1969), opening gaming to International Relations studies. Many others followed their footsteps in the 1970s and 1980s, diversifying the field of simulation gaming to many new areas.

In line with the spirit of the 1960s, associations such as ISAGA (International Simulation and Gaming Association), NASAGA (North-American Simulation and Gaming Association), SAGSET (Society for the Advancement of Games and Simulations in Education and Training), and ABSEL (Association for Business Simulation and Experiential Learning) have been established in the early 1970s. They have carried out pioneering work to establish gaming and simulation in academia and professional practice. More recently, associations such as, JASAG (Japan Association of Simulation And Gaming), SAGSAGA (Swiss Austrian German Simulation And Gaming Association), a Dutch special interest group called SAGANET, and DiGRA (Digital Game Research Association), have been established. All these fellow associations propagate gaming and simulation, both as a way of thinking, a methodology (study of methods), and a technique.

TENSIONS

The kaleidoscopic perspective, presented above, shows the richness and reach of human activities vis-à-vis the play character of human society. I have touched on several approaches to play, game, and simulation. Their core idea refers to activities, embodied experiences, drama, and to the playground of the mind, bound by ties of logic, causality, imagination, myths, poetry, and to social play as a form of social reproduction. Game sessions may very well develop beyond the reach of reason. Although also animals play, it should be noted that they do not develop and posses games. Games have additional quality to play. Forms of play can be traced as artifacts over thousands of years of history, and at very different locations such as in China, India, Arabic world, Africa, Europe, and America, by people very far apart in time and space. Games result from the artificial, artful (craftsmanship), and since the 1940s, from scientific conceptions (phrases, formal languages, and utterances) about the world. They are artifacts that derive their meaning from the activity called "play". Human activities become play in situations of strife, challenge, contest, ritual, and competition for whatever cause or goal. In due process, they become social games.

Games are forms of play. The linkages between the rules and the resources define the variety of play forms. It is worthwhile to note the important distinction between *rule-based*, *principle-based*, and *free-form* games. In rule-based games, the rules are not questioned. They are just followed. The actors play by the rules. Those, who do not obey the rules, are out. In principle-based games, the actors have freedom to interpret the rules, based on the underlying norms, before acting. The actors have some freedom to play with the meaning of those rules. This distinction applies as well to the North-American society, which is more rule-based then European societies, which tend to be more principle-based. In free-form games, only a few ground rules or "rules of nature" exist, such as the time of the beginning, the stop rule, the role of the facilitator, and the location in which the game takes place. All other rules that seem to be suitable evolve during the game session, and are being negotiated and shaped by the actors themselves. Therefore, free-form games are self-organizing, or self-reproductive systems (autopoietic systems).[1] These distinctions have so far received only minor attention in the literature.

Playing games implies that the players engage in an evolving process. Playing a game is a total event of being involved in a temporary, provisional, and integrated world. A key question is: How can knowledge about a reference system be gained, assimilated among the actors, re-integrated and disseminated to enhance the social system's performance? Answers to this question may be considered simple and straightforward. However, providing the way academia is structured, I argue that we are dealing with a self-made problem. The structure of scientific research forces knowledge to be extracted from a fully integrated world into disciplinary knowledge domains and inference schemes. Such knowledge becomes des-integrated by disciplinary units called departments in universities. As a consequence, the integrated experience of playing games becomes des-integrated in scientific research. An integrative theory of knowledge – to deal coherently with the many faces of a gaming experience – is lacking.

To illustrate the scattered world of gaming and game studies in academia, I present a random list of disciplines and departments of fellow scholars globally

---

[1] *Poïesis* means in ancient Greek: "to make", "to produce". This word, the root of our modern poetry, was first a verb, an action that (re-) produces and transforms the world. Autopoiesis means self-reproduction. See also Maturana & Varela (1980) *Autopoiesis and Cognition*.

involved in gaming: *architecture (& building); biology; business administration; cognitive economics; cognitive engineering; communication; computer science; computing arts and design sciences; design & environment; economics; education; environmental information; information science; information systems; integration of technology in education; interactive arts; international relations; language; linguistics; management; marketing; mathematical economics; media studies; natural resource management; policy studies; organizational behavior; political science; project management; psychology (leadership/work & organization); public administration; research methodology and methods; social psychology; social sciences; sociology; systems agronomics; systems management; teacher studies; technology education; telecommunication; urban planning; etc.*

To underpin my argument about the diversity of disciplines involved, and to indicate which key concepts they use, I wrap up results of a study by colleagues from JASAG (Japan Association of Simulation And Gaming) (Klabbers, 2004). At the 34th ISAGA annual, international conference, held at Kazusa Akademia Park in Chiba, Japan from August 24–29, 2003, the first day was dedicated to ISAGA/JASAG Symposia with as special topics, "The past, present, and future of JASAG," and "The contribution of JASAG to S&G."

Yusuke Arai (2003) and Fumitoshi Kato (2003) reported on a study about concept mining in JASAG related publications since 1991. The purpose of the study was:

- To (re-) identify the domains of research;
- To understand the characteristics of interdisciplinary approaches.

The research projects carried out covered a wide variety of domains of research such as, management, System Dynamics, artificial society, systems science, information and decision-making, multi-agent approaches, education, play therapy, agricultural policy, environmental issues, conflict resolution, international relations, intercultural communication, consensus formation, policy studies, game theory, group dynamics, business gaming, organizational behavior, and others.

Major contributors were:

- Information engineering, information science, knowledge science (22%);
- Social engineering (19%);
- Management, organization theory, decision-making (19%);
- Business game practitioners, business consulting (10%);
- Social psychology;
- Economics;
- Political science;
- Others.

The list of 33 key concepts from 129 publications in the journal *Simulation and Gaming* run from "simulation" (50 references), "game" (47 references), to "earth" (6 references) and "Internet" (3 references).

Concept mining in the proceedings of the JASAG annual conferences produced a list of 80 key concepts. They run from simulation (132 references), game (98 references), through society (40), decision-making (13), theory (8), multimedia (8), to cognition (5), and eco (4). It is an impressive list of contributors and concepts, illustrating the great diversity of the Japanese gaming and simulation community.

Considering these listings, I notice that many of my dedicated colleagues work in distinct university departments. On the instrumental level, noticed during numerous international meetings over many years, I have seen a growing understanding about gaming and simulation methods and techniques. Nevertheless, as gaming and simulation is also, and more importantly, a way of thinking, on a theoretical and methodological level, professionals have difficulty in speaking with the same tongue. The high diversity of the field is both strength, and a weakness. A proper rhetoric for cross-fertilization about theoretical questions is still missing. Professionals and scholars, by lack of a common theoretical framework, fall back on the inference schemes of their particular disciplines.

In the following chapters I will address this problematical issue in more detail, and pay attention to the scope of activities covered by the terms *play, game, and simulation*. For that matter, I will use "gaming" as the common term, encompassing the terms "play", "game", "simulation", and the interesting connection "playful gaming". I do not intend to discuss in detail the various disciplinary approaches to gaming with their emphasis on methods and techniques per se. Such an approach would be lacking coherence due to the many distinct and often disjoint conceptions underlying gaming methods and tools. Moreover, it would not due justice to key questions about this trans-discipline. More particularly, I will focus on methodological issues on an appropriate level of aggregation, to offer an integrated view on this currently diverse and scattered field of study and professional practice. My purpose is to enlighten common principles underlying the field. Such commonly held views will eventually improve professional practice.

It is a commonly held opinion among professionals that games and simulations offer a shared "language" to enhance stakeholders' competency in handling multifaceted issues. I have indicated above that the field itself needs such a common language as well, if it will evolve as a trans-discipline in its own right. To summarize: gaming contains many methods. Moreover, it is a way of thinking. In the following chapters, I will address practical, theoretical and methodological questions to improve the way we conceptualize these artifacts. Therefore, in Part II, I will emphasize first the position of the designer, and design science as the frame-of-reference for addressing key questions. Subsequently, I will pay attention to the analytical science domain of gaming and simulation.

Working definitions

A **game** is a *form of play*. It is an activity involving one or more players who assume roles while trying to achieve a goal. Rules determine what the players are permitted to do, or define constraints on allowable actions, which impact on the available resources, and therefore influence the state of the game space. Games deal with well-defined subject matter (content and context).

Play is a voluntary activity or occupation, executed according to rules freely accepted but absolutely binding, having its aim in itself and accompanied by a feeling of tension, joy, and the awareness that it is different from ordinary life.

In these working definitions, I have not yet addressed questions about forms of knowledge and knowledge content; competition and cooperation; extrinsic and intrinsic rules; entertainment, education, and training.

THE GAMING LANDSCAPE IN THE 20TH CENTURY

INTRODUCTION

In Chapter 1, I have sketched general ideas about and approaches to play and game. In this chapter I will pay major attention to classifications, typologies, and taxonomies. Therefore, focus will be on games as products – *artifacts* – of human creativity, ingenuity and craftsmanship. Purpose is to bring order to the variety of appearances of those artifacts. While discussing classifications and typologies, I am mostly interested in the viewpoints of the authors that underlie those schemes, asking myself whether the perspectives offered may bear fruit in developing a common perspective, an integrated framework to the gaming and simulation landscape. In addition, I am interested in the question: What makes a game unique? The idea of singularity, of being distinctive and unique applies particularly to the field of gaming with its wide variety of appearances of those artifacts. Studying the classifications – referring to the question what these artifacts have in common – as well as reflecting on what makes games unique, points to the need for a deeper understanding of their architecture. To be able to unravel it, I will present a generic framework.

THE GAME ELEMENT OF WESTERN CIVILIZATION SINCE THE 20TH CENTURY

When Huizinga (1985) wrote the book "Homo Ludens" in the 1930s, he paid major attention to the play element of archaic societies, and early civilizations with special emphasis on the linkages between play and law, war, knowing and wisdom, philosophy, and art. Subsequently, he sketched the ludic qualities of western civilization since the Roman Empire. To illustrate his viewpoint, he discussed more in depth the rituals, festivities, contests, and play qualities of the ancient Greek culture. In the last chapter of the book, he addressed the play-element of contemporary civilization that is, the late 19th century until the 1930s. He observed the increasing influence of sports, and especially ball games in the late 19th century in England to the extent that the term *sport* gradually replaced the term *game*. This was the current history of the early 20th century. Sport in current society that is, in the early 21the century, has become big and serious business. Its commercial racket has great impact on the true play spirit: spontaneity and carelessness that were so characteristic of the play qualities of ancient civilization. Huizinga claimed that the professional [*of the 1930s: note author*] lacks spontaneity and carelessness.

In modern social life sport occupies a place alongside and apart from the cultural process. The great competitions in archaic cultures had always formed part of the sacred festivals and were indispensable as health and happiness bringing activities. "This ritual tie has now been completely severed: sport has become profane, "unholy" in every way and has no organic connection whatever with the structure of society, least of all when prescribed by the government" (Huizinga, 1955, pp. 197-198). Considering the position of sport in contemporary cultures, and the linkages of the Olympic games, soccer world championships, and other national and regional tournaments with government policies, one could question their play element of culture in Huizinga's sense. Observing the rituals of soccer fans in Latin-America and Europe in behavior and outfit, I would argue that the strong agonistic habit that is so peculiar of modern sports, both at the playing fields and at the stadiums, are very closely connected to modern high-tech cultures vis-à-vis networks of hooligans. Commercial sports competition may not belong to sacred play-forms of an ancient past, I still view it a basic play element of culture, however dismantled its magic may be. Business has become a game, and gaming has become business.

In the same vain, Huizinga dismissed already in the 1930s "modern" science as play. "The logical development of civilization which we call science is more inextricably bound up with dialectics than is the aesthetic ... By way of tentative conclusion we might say that modern science, so long as it adheres to strict demands of accuracy and veracity, is far less liable to fall into play as we have defined it, than was the case in earlier times and right up to the Renaissance, when scientific thought and method showed unmistakable play-characteristics" (Huizinga, 1955, p. 204). Since science increasingly is feeling the political pressure to produce knowledge usable to society, a pressure that materializes through budget allocations, latitude for play is becoming tight.

Regarding the play-element in contemporary social and political life, I note that Huizinga's observations of the 1930s still apply in even more naked form. Certain play forms may be used consciously to cover up a social or political agenda. Spin-doctors in government make it their trade, using mass media to disguise questionable political designs. This is a form of false play. Watching TV in many countries, and especially the high proportion of games and 'run-arounds", one notices that post-modern life is being dominated to an ever increasing extent by a quality that has something in common with play and yields the illusion of a strongly developed play-factor. Huizinga (1955) called this quality of play *puerile (childish, foolish)*. It is the most appropriate appellation for that blend of adolescence and barbarity, which is increasingly rampant over the Western world. That world, mediated through the mass-communication infrastructure demonstrates an insatiable thirst for trivial recreation and crude sensationalism, the delight of mass-meetings, mass-demonstrations, parades, etc. Whole nations turn into clubs, flattering self-love and narrow group-consciousness, with politicians dancing on the waves of such popular entertainment. These forms of play, demonstrating the infantile play elements in culture, should not distract us from the more sincere characteristics of (fair) play that I am addressing here. I do not suggest that children's play as such is puerile, as it usually is sincere with much magic involved.

Since the first Industrial Revolution there is decreasingly little room for the play element of culture. Utilitarianism, rationalism, and efficiency propagated through technological progress, and scientific management with its machine bureaucracy of work and production, have forced an over-estimation of the economic factor in life. Huizinga noted (1955) that they have killed the mysteries and acquitted man of guilt and sin. Weber (1947) speaks of a disenchanted world.

Contemporary civilization cannot exist in the absence of a certain play-element. It presupposes limitation and mastery of the self, the ability not to confuse its own tendencies – expressed in the private space of life – with the ultimate and highest goals of a community, conveyed in the public domain. Mastery of the self implies the understanding that it is enclosed within certain bounds freely accepted. Huizinga (1955) stated that civilization will, in a sense, always be played according to certain rules, and true civilization will always demand fair play: good faith expressed in play terms. He recollected the endless rotation of the tension between play and earnest. Looking for a pivot to resolve that question, we will not find it in logic, and we have to look for it in the sphere of ethics, and esthetics. Play in itself is neither good nor bad. It lies beyond morals. However, if we have to decide whether an action to which our will impels us is a serious duty, or is permitted through play, then our moral conscience will at once provide the touchstone. The play-seriousness duality loses all meaning as soon as truth and justice, compassion and forgiveness become embedded in the way we act. "One drop of pity is enough to lift our actions beyond intellectual distinctions and classifications" (Huizinga, 1985, p. 209). Therefore play surpasses rational and logic analysis.

Since the beginning of the 20th century a more profane interpretation of play and game has gained prominence, especially through scientific endeavors linked to the growing awareness of social questions raised during the First Industrial Revolution: business has become a form of play, and play has become business. The related issues became more manifest during the Second Industrial Revolution. Characteristic of the First Industrial Revolution was the transformation of energy from one form to another. Through artificially constructed engines such as, the heat engine, a whole new complex technology emerged, replacing natural (physiological) engines (animals and human beings) as sources of mechanical work. Heat engines became the slaves of the industrial societies. Human beings were responsible for their maintenance, for tending them and steering their work through routine control operations. The increasing complexity of the industrial enterprises through mass production, and the resulting auxiliary social and political organizations, required a new way of thinking about the efficient organization and management of work. The counterpart of the complex technology became scientific management, advocated by Henri Fayol, F.W. Mooney, Lyndall Urwick and Frederick Taylor. They saw management as a process of planning, organization, command, coordination, and control, while drawing on a combination of military and engineering principles. The classical management theory with its emphasis on designing bureaucratic organizations, combined the way the machine routed production with the way the bureaucracy routed the process of administration. (For more details about scientific management, see for example, Morgan, 1986.)

In such a setting the idea of play as an activity valued for itself (autotelic) lost much of its appeal. The term *game,* with its connotation of rule-driven contest and competition, moved to the foreground. It fitted better with utilitarianism, rationalism, and efficiency of industrial practice. The autotelic character of play shifted to the allotelic quality of game. It became functional to a goal outside the immediate sphere of play. The functionally integrated business games and simulations, discussed in Chapter 1, illustrate my point. Their main purpose was and is to train general management skills, and business administration. The expertise gained through these business games proliferated during the 1960s to areas such as, social studies, urban and land use management, ecology, education (classroom instruction), international relations, health care, natural resources, etc. In addition, the field offered a broadening scope of play forms: role-playing games, board games, computer-assisted and computer-supported games, frame games, exercises, simulation games, behavior simulations, and more recently, digital, or video games. So, how is current practice shaping the gaming landscape?

THE CURRENT LANDSCAPE

Since the beginning in 1970, the International Simulation And Gaming Association (ISAGA) has mapped its activities in a common scheme, taking into account *foci of interest* and *areas of application*. Areas of application represent the reference systems that are being used for gaming and simulation. ISAGA has distinguished the following foci of interest:
- Theory and methodology
- Design
- Assessment & evaluation

More particularly, under those general headings, attention is focused on the following themes:
- Learning & education
- Individual & collective competence
- (Intra- and cross-cultural) communication
- Management development
- Organizational (institutional) change
- Policy-development

These themes are not mutually exclusive. They refer to relevant contexts of use, and intended audiences.

The following areas of application – reference systems – are distinguished:
- Business administration
- Public administration
- Environment (eco-systems)
- Entertainment
- Health care
- Human/cultural resources
- Human settlements/geography
- International relations
- Military
- Natural resources
- Religion
- Services
- Technology

Since the late 1990s increasingly the area of research of digital games is for a variety of reasons gaining prominence. The main goal of these games is entertainment. Scientific interests focus on multi-media, language (interactive narratives), and computer science applications. Gradually, the competency developed extends to more regular foci of interest, and areas of application such as, military training, leadership training, training firefighters, etc. Areas of application represent virtual reality, and imaginary worlds.

Game design has received wide attention. However, it has been limited so far to instrumental design, the design of the artifact as such. More recently, due to the growing awareness of the broader potentials of gaming, attention is shifting towards the use of games/simulations to enhance change, to improve the capacities of participants to support change, and to their impact on (youth) culture. That understanding requires a distinction between two levels of design: the instrumental design of the game/simulation as such, and organizational design on the basis of the game, designed for such special purposes. I have coined the terms "design-in-the-small" (DIS), and "design-in-the-large" (DIL) to take both levels of design on board (Klabbers, 2003, 2006). Design-in-the-large is linked to social system's development. In all cases, what matters is the interplay between both design levels. I will not elaborate here the underlying ideas. For more details, see Chapter 6.

When digital gaming gradually becomes embedded in the broader area of gaming, as developed, and practiced by ISAGA, NASAGA, SAGSET, ABSEL, JASAG, SAGSAGA, etc. (see Chapter 1) then it will immerse into the more general framework, presented in Table 2.1. As the field is advancing rapidly, Table 2.1 should be considered work-in-progress. Its form and especially, its content will change over time.

In each cell of the matrix of Table 2.1, a variety of games, forms of play, may be used. They range from role-play, frame games, board games, behavioral simulation, management & business simulation, computer-assisted and computer-supported games, to digital games. Many classifications on play and games have been developed to capture the variety of *forms, functions, activities, and processes*. Each of them highlights certain characteristics, while ignoring others. Before discussing several classifications in more detail, I first will present terms that are related to gaming and simulation, and that are being used in common as well as in scientific language. That list will help sorting out some key features of gaming/simulation. I will start with further elaborating the term *play*, which, as learned from Huizinga's exposé, incites so much confusion.

AMBIGUITY OF THE TERM PLAY

It is difficult – and I would say fruitless – to provide a purely functional explanation of play. Above, I have indicated a diversity of forms of play in the gaming landscape, expressed by Table 2.1. I have not yet addressed the wide variety of experiences of playing games. Brian Sutton-Smith (2001), in his book "The ambiguity of play", in search for definitional clarity, aimed to develop a coherent theory of play. He found himself in the position of having to deal simultaneously with seven types of ambiguity, presented by William Empson (1955). Referring to play, he denoted the following ambiguities:

1. The ambiguity of reference (is that a pretend gun sound, or are you choking?);
2. The ambiguity of the referent (is that an object or a toy?);
3. The ambiguity of intent (do you mean it, or is it pretend?);
4. The ambiguity of sense (is this serious, or is it nonsense?);
5. The ambiguity of transition (you said you were only playing);
6. The ambiguity of contradiction (a man playing at being a woman);
7. The ambiguity of meaning (is it play or play fighting?) (Sutton-Smith, 2001, p. 2).

Table 2.1. Realm of Gaming & Simulation

Areas of application:	Foci of Interest						
	I. Theory & Methodology						
	II. Artifact design (DIS)						
	III. Assessment & Evaluation						
	IV. Systems development (DIL)						
	V. Education & Training: topics						
	Skills & abilities	Communication	OD	Policy Formation	MD & Decision-making		Multi-media & Computer science
1. Business administration							
2. Public administration							
3. Environment							
4. Human services							
5. Health care							
6. Intern. Relations							
7. Military							
8. Religion							
9. Technology							
10. Human settlements							
11. Virtual worlds & entertainment							

Sutton-Smith presented a list of activities that relate to play form and play experiences. It is arranged from the more private to the more public forms of play:

- *Mind and subjective play*: dreams, daydreams, fantasy, etc.;
- *Solitary play*: hobbies, collections, writing to pen pals, etc.;
- *Playful behavior*: playing tricks, playing around, playing for time, etc.;
- *Informal social play*: joking, parties, cruising, etc.;
- *Vicarious audience play*: television, films, cartoons, etc;
- *Performance play*: playing the piano, playing music, being a play actor, etc.;
- *Celebrations and festivals*: birthdays, Christmas, Easter, etc.;
- *Contests (games and sports)*: athletics, gambling, casinos, etc;
- *Risky or deep play*: caving, hang gliding, kayaking, etc. (Sutton-Smith, 2001, pp. 4-5).

To bring more coherence to the idea and experience of play, he has chosen *rhetoric* as his main approach. Rhetoric in his view is "a persuasive discourse, or an implicit narrative, wittingly or unwittingly adopted by members of a particular affiliation to persuade others of the veracity and worthwhileness of their beliefs" (Sutton-Smith, 2001, p. 8). He did not have in mind a discussion of the substance of play, or its science, or its theories, rather the way, in which the underlying values – attributed to play – are conveyed. He noted that play rhetorics are part of multiple broad symbolic systems – political, religious, social, and educational – through which we construct the meaning of the cultures in which we live.

Sutton-Smith (2001) discussed the following seven rhetorics of play as:

- *Progress*: usually applied to children's play;
- *Fate*: usually applied to gambling;
- *Power*: usually applied to sports, contests;
- *Identity*: usually applied to traditional and community celebrations;
- *Imaginary*: usually applied to playful improvisation of all kinds (imagination);
- *Self*: usually applied to solitary activities (hobbies, bungee jumping);
- *Frivolity*: usually applied to the activities of the idle or the foolish.

Sutton-Smith hoped that via the seven rhetorics he presented, he would be able to build a bridge based on some *unifying discourse*, a more genuinely *interdisciplinary organization of play*. To catch the multiplicity of concepts he has applied to play, he finally offered "play as a model of adaptive variability" as an integrative eighth rhetoric with the following basic features:

- *Evolution of the brain*: play to increase the brain's variability;
- *Redundancy*: reproduction of useful structures to enhance adaptation;
- *Flexibility*: play to improve adaptability – the capacity to adapt.

In attempting to present a coherent discourse on play, Sutton-Smith put himself in the observer's position. Considering the seven ambiguities of play – presented above – through that outsider's position, he was not able to cope adequately with the intentions and perspective of the players themselves. Nevertheless, he was aware of the duality of play both from the perspective of the outside observer, and the inside participant of a game. Sutton-Smith's puzzle was:

... it is clear that verbalizations about a ludic experience are not the same as that experience. When the adult says play is a developmental experience, for

27

the child it may be nothing but hide-and-seek. What the Puritan says is character destroying gambling may be, for the player, the one satisfying experience in the week. Because forms of play, like all other cultural forms, cannot be neutrally interpreted, it is impossible to keep ambiguity from creeping into the relationship between how they are perceived and how they are experienced. ... Scholars also seem to have in common, wittingly or not, the way they manipulate these rhetorics to justify their own preoccupations with the different play forms (Sutton-Smith, 2001, p. 216).

I would rephrase it as follows:

It is clear that theorizing about a ludic experience is not the same as that experience. When the scholar says play is a developmental experience, for the player it may be a satisfying and joyful experience. Because forms of play, like all other cultural forms, cannot be neutrally interpreted, it is impossible to keep ambiguity and discrepancy from creeping into the relationship between how they are observed by scholars, and experienced by the players.

The notion of rhetorics (*theory or discourse*) is a notion that pertains to the domain of descriptions, and as such it is relevant only in the meta-domain in which the observer makes his commentaries (theories, rhetorics), which cannot be deemed to be operative in the experiential domain of the players of a game, the object of the description. As long as such rhetorics (theories) are not connected to the experiential domain, they are fictions. In the ludic experiential domain of playful gaming, the conceptual is intertwined with the embodied experience, which links explicit with tacit knowing. The seven ambiguities of play, referred to above, result from the choice to theorize about play from the position of the meta-domain. From the position of the player − the experiential domain − those ambiguities will evaporate easily, being replaced by ambiguities related to making sense of the situation that is, produce meaning while playing. Sutton-Smith was aware of it, yet he did not switch perspective, to take on board the rhetorics of the players as well. He chose to stay an outside observer, while ignoring the knowledge domain of the players, and as a consequence he was not able to deal adequately with the ambiguity of play. He was only able to tell one part of the story.

SYNONYMS

Providing the lessons learned from Huizinga's and Sutton-Smith's exposés, it will be tricky to offer a list of terms that relate to the terms *play*, and *game*, in the hope that they shed better light on this ambiguous phenomenon. Presenting a list of synonyms implicitly offers an analogical line of reasoning: objects are different even though they look similar. Nevertheless, I will take that risk, as in common use these terms are often linked with play and game. I will start with a comprehensive work definition of a game. It is an adjustment of Abt's (1968), and Ellington's *et al.* (1982) definitions.

Working definition of a game

A game is any contest or effort (play) among adversaries or teammates (players) operating under constraints (rules and resources) for an objective (winning, victory, prestige, status, or pay-off). The exercise, or activity, should involve overt competition, or cooperation between the individuals or teams, who are competing

against each other, or together (while jointly conquering circumstances) fighting the odds.
Next, I will list terms that are related to the terms *play* and *game*, referring to their common use.

Play

- Spending time, doing enjoyable things;
- Taking part in games;
- Including a person as a member of a team;
- Performing an activity guided by the rules of a game.

Game

- An activity or sport involving skill, knowledge, or chance, in which you follow fixed rules and try to win against an opponent or to solve a puzzle;
- A particular occasion, usually, arranged in advance, on which a game is played;
- A part of a match, for example in tennis or bridge, consisting of a fixed number of points;
- The degree of skill or the style that someone uses when playing a particular game;
- The equipment that you need to play a particular indoor game, for example a board, dice, cards;
- An activity that children do, for example pretending to be someone or using toys;
- A situation that you do not treat seriously;
- A way of behaving in which a person uses a particular plan, especially to gain an advantage;
- Games: an organized event in which competition in several sports takes place.

Model

- A physical representation that shows what an object looks like or how it works;
- A theoretical description of a system or process that can help you understand how the system or process works, or how it might work;
- An example that has been especially built and organized to demonstrate how it can function;
- An example of a person's behavior you copy, because you admire it, and want to be like that person.

Simulation

- The process of simulating something that is, reproducing a set of conditions, or the result of simulating it;

- An attempt to solve a problem or to work out the consequences of doing something by representing the problem or possible course of events mathematically, often using a computer.

Simulator

- A device designed to reproduce actual conditions to train people.

Gamble

- A risky action or decision in the hope of gaining money, success, or an advantage.

Exercise

- A series of energetic movements which you do in order to get fit or remain healthy;
- A short piece of work that you do, which is designed to help you learn a particular mental skill;
- An activity planned to achieve a particular purpose.

Sports

- Amusement, fun, not seriously;
- Activity for amusement and exercise;
- Meeting for athletic contests;
- Sports are games such as football, soccer, and cricket, and other activities which need physical effort and skill;
- Any kind of enjoyable activity for which you need physical or mental skill.

These terms have in common the following attributes: players, activities, concepts, forms, contests, places, and purposes. Subsequently, let us see in which form these attributes are embedded in several classifications and typologies of games.

CLASSIFICATIONS OF GAMES

Games are forms of play. Referring to Sutton-Smith (2001), I already have presented various views on play. The following classifications are based on those broad ideas, and focus more on special forms of play. They take their broad scope of play for granted. I will not discuss these classifications in great detail. They serve to illustrate the variety of views on, and approaches to gaming.

Caillois

Caillois (2001) has presented a classification that is close to Huizinga and Sutton-Smith's notions of play (Table 2.2). The classification makes an important distinction between two kinds of rules, and four forms of activities in culture. The *paida* element concerns the free play of a game, based on its intrinsic values for the players. The *ludus* element pays more attention to institutionalized rules and conventions imposed on the players. The paida-ludus dimension refers to ways of playing. Caillois considered both game qualities to be the extremes of a continuum. Many games are a mixture of the paida and ludus elements. The four cultural activities – categories of play: *agôn, alea, mimicry,* and *ilinx* vary with respect to locus of control of the players. With agôn and mimicry, the players can control events. With alea and ilinx, when entering the game, they leave control to the circumstances. Caillois speaks of four categories of play – *competition, chance, simulation,* and *vertigo* – and in addition calls them basic attitudes governing play. He mentioned that they are not always encountered in isolation. In many games the various attitudes of play become associated. He presented six possible pairs:

- Competition & chance (agôn – alea)
- Competition & simulation (agôn – mimicry)
- Competition & vertigo (agôn – ilinx)
- Chance & simulation (alea – mimicry)
- Chance & vertigo (alea – ilinx)
- Simulation & vertigo (mimicry – ilinx).

Table 2.2. Classification of games adapted from Caillois (2001)

	AGON *Competition* Equal probability of success	MIMICRY *Imitation* Players pretending to be someone else	ALEA *Chance* Players cannot exert control over outcomes	ILINX *Vertigo* Attempts to disrupt regular perception patterns
PAIDA (Free-form, improvisation) ⇓	Racing, athletics Playing jazz	Children's imitations, masking & pretending to be someone else	Counting out rhymes, heads and tails	Acrobatics, horseback riding, merry go round
⇑ LUDUS (Rule-driven, conventions)	Soccer, chess, sports tournament	Theater	Lottery, roulette	Mountain climbing, tightrope walking

Based on this scheme, Caillois (op cit.) distinguished forbidden, contingent, and fundamental relationships between these four attitudes of play. Vertigo and agôn are incompatible. The conditions for ilinx destroy the conditions for agôn: respect for rules, self-control, efforts to win, testing oneself under conditions of equality. In a similar vain, simulation and chance are mutually exclusive. Regarding contingent relationships, chance and vertigo, as well as, competition and imitation can be associated without harm. A fundamental relationship exists between *agôn* and *alea*.

They are symmetrical to each other, and complement one another. A multitude of games exist that combine the two attitudes in varying degrees. Card games, golf, poker, soccer, etc., are not purely games of chance. They also require skills, self-control, testing oneself under conditions of equality, and prior submission to the decision of a referee. Many board games are a combination of skill and chance. *Agôn* and *alea* are regulated through the rules of the game. Without rules there would be no competition. *Mimicry* and *ilinx* form another kind of fundamental relationship. Both presume a world without rules and regulations. Caillois said:

> The combination of *alea* and *agôn* is a free act of will, stemming from the satisfaction felt in overcoming an arbitrarily conceived and voluntarily accepted obstacle. The alliance of *mimicry* and *ilinx* leads to an inexorable, total frenzy, which in its most obvious forms appears to be the opposite of play, an indescribable metamorphosis in the conditions of existence. The fit so provoked, being uninhibited, seems to remove the player as far from the authority, values, and influence of the real world, as the real world seems to influence the formal, protected, regulated, and protected activities that characterize the wholly inhibited games subsumed under the rules of *agôn* and *alea*. The association of simulation and vertigo is so powerful and so inseparable that it is naturally part of the sphere of the sacred, perhaps providing one of the principal bases for the terror and fascination of the sacred (pp. 75-76).

Although tripartite combinations occur, Caillois considered them rare juxtapositions that do not influence the character of the games involved. For example, a horse race is typical *agôn* for the jockeys, at the same time a spectacle that stimulates *mimicry* among the spectators, and a pretext for betting on the winner -- a game of chance: *alea*. Caillois' interpretation of term simulation (mimicry), although related, is not equal to the meaning of simulation presented in Chapter 4.

Ellington, Addinall, & Percival

Ellington, Addinall, & Percival (1982) developed a classification, using different game formats (Table 2.3).

Table 2.3. Classification of games according to format (adapted from Ellington et al., 1982)

Non-electronic games		Electronic games
Psychomotor skill games	Intellectual skill games	Games of chance
Field games (outdoor athletics) Table games (snooker, pool)	Simple manual games Card games Board games Device-based games	Video games Computer games

They distinguished pure games, pure simulations, pure case studies, and their overlaps: simulation games, games used as case studies, simulated case studies, and simulation games used as case studies. Pure games, according to their point of view, contain all exercises that include competition and rules. Pure simulations contain all exercises that represent a dynamic representation of real situations. Pure case studies are non-interactive, in-depth studies and illustrations of special or general features, concerning the history of cases that happened in health care, legal procedures, companies, etc. Their definition of pure games emphasizes the agôn/ludus combination from Caillois' classification.

Shubik

Shubik (1983) focused on the use of games, contrasting rigid-rule and free-form games. He distinguished for practical reasons five kinds of use (Table 2.4).

Table 2.4. Taxonomy of games (adapted from Shubik, 1983)

	From → Rigid-rule games:		To Free-form games
Use	Manual games	Computer- based games	
Training			
Teaching			
Operational: • Policy formation • Dress rehearsals • Sensitivity analysis			
Research • Theory generation • Theory validation			
Futures Studies • Structured brain storming • Policy exercises			

Shubik made a distinction between *gaming, simulation,* and *game theory.* He referred to gaming as being people oriented, and having close connections with the behavioral sciences. For him simulation was more linked to computers, and becoming increasingly intertwined with econometric modeling. He connected game theory to mathematical methods in the study of decision systems – sequential, and iterative decision-making – related to a study of conflict and cooperation. Apparently, for him the paida/ludus continuum was important in connection with the various kinds of use. In his review, he paid no attention to the broader cultural context of play, and considering the context of his publication, emphasized the academic and professional use of games. Interestingly, he recognized the research potential of games, *research gaming* as he called it, as a growing and important field of use. He referred to managerial issues, and experimenting in social, experimental psychology, and experimental economics. Nowadays, experimental economics is strongly related to agent-based modeling. It combines both theory generation and validation.

Since the 1960s games and simulations have been used as future studies to develop and experiment with future scenarios on large-scale social issues such as global and regional economic development, global climate change, regional, national, and local environmental pollution, health care, etc. During several of these studies, the gaming approach, embedding behavioral aspects, became integrated with simulation, including technological-economic-ecosystems aspects, in one integrated framework. I will discuss such studies in more detail in Part III.

These three examples, in combination with Huizinga and Sutton-Smith's classes of play, illustrate a common academic understanding of play and game during the 20th century. Since the rapid advent of digital games for entertainment since the 1980s, that picture needs some adjustments for at least two reasons. The development of digital games for entertainment until recently was not driven by scientific curiosity, but by conquering a highly profitable market. Moreover, those who developed a keen academic interest in those games came from disciplines that previously had not shown much interest in gaming. These newcomers from the humanities, linguistics, media studies, and computer science, were, and to a large extent still are, not aware of the gaming tradition that had emerged since the 1950s. They not only have started to re-invent the wheel, increasingly they have started to develop their own branch of academic gaming, introducing new concepts and terminology. I will pay attention to this new gaming culture by discussing the following two characteristic approaches to classifying computer games.

Rollings & Adams

Rollings & Adams (2003) have distinguished genres in interactive entertainment (Table 2.5).

Table 2.5. Genres in Interactive entertainment (adapted from Rollings & Adams, 2003)

Genres in Interactive entertainment	
Action games	Physical challenges, puzzles, races;
Strategy games	Strategic, tactical, & logistical challenges;
Role playing games	Tactical, logistical and exploration challenges;
Real world simulations	Physical and tactical challenges (sports games & vehicle simulations)
Constrctn&Mngmnt games	Economic and conceptual challenges;
Adventure games	Exploration, puzzle solving, conceptual challenges;
Puzzle games	Logical challenges;

A *genre* is a figure of speech, in this case, about a play form, which people consider to have the same style or subject. It refers to key elements that games have in common: rules, roles, challenges, etc. The types of games, and the related challenges are not mutually exclusive. They overlap. As common elements, and styles of play make the distinctions, a genre is more related to the practice of play, and to a certain play culture, and less to a conceptual class such as applied in Table 2.2, 2.3, and 2.4. They allow games to cross genres, by combining elements of play. Their approach to classifying digital games is more fluid than the classifications mentioned above.

Aarseth

Aarseth (1997) has taken a more rigorous approach to classifying computer games. Relating games to text, his focus is on textuality, on story telling, or interactive narrative. Games are viewed as communication devices, generating text. His style of reasoning is related to concepts from ergodic theory.

Ornstein (1989) pointed out that ergodic theory resulted from an attempt to understand the long-term statistical behavior of dynamical systems such as the motions of a billiard ball, or the motions of the earth's atmosphere. The theory aims at abstracting out the statistical properties of dynamical systems. Two systems are considered the same (isomorphic) when viewed as an abstract system or object, if, after ignoring sets or event with probability zero, there is a one-to-one correspondence between the points in their phase spaces. Corresponding sets have the same probability and evolve in the same way. Abstract dynamical systems arise in many different contexts. Brown & Nilsson (1962) stated that in an ergodic random process, time wise sampling leads to the same statistical results as ensemble sampling. Ensembles are time series data collected from experiments. Suppose, we would sample any one member of the ensemble at a large number of points in time, then the data obtained should have the same statistical distribution as would be obtained if each member of the ensemble were sampled once at any particular time, for example t=1. Aarseth (1997) applied these notions to games, viewing them as abstract objects that generate text: strings of signs. He pointed out that text is an object with as a primary function to send out verbal information. Therefore, a text does not operate independently from a material medium, and is not equal to information – a string of signs transmitted to an observer. Aarseth viewed information as a string of signs, which may make sense to an observer. To make that distinction clear, he introduced the following terms: *scriptons, textons*, and the *traversal function*. Scriptons are strings of signs as they appear to the reader. Textons are strings of signs, as they exist in the text. The traversal function is the mechanism by which scriptons are revealed or generated from textons and presented to the user of the text. Based on this terminology, he introduced a typology enabling the description of any text (read: game) according to their model of traversal. Seven variables constitute that typology (Aarseth, 1997, pp. 62-64):

- *Dynamics*: changing contents of scriptons, or the number (and content) of textons.
  - o Scripton: strings of signs as they appear to the reader;
  - o Texton: strings of signs as they exist in the text;
  - o Traversal function: the mechanism by which scriptons are revealed or generated from textons and presented to the user of the text.
  If scriptons are constant, then the text is static.

- *Determinability*: A text is determinate if the adjacent scriptons of every scripton are always the same. If not, then the text is indeterminate.
- *Transiency*: Text is transient if it passes (scrolls over the screen) and the user does not need to do anything to the passing of scriptons. If the user scrolls text – self-pacing – then the text is intransient.
- *Perspective*: If the text requires the user to play a strategic role, as a character in the world described by the text, then the perspective of the text is personal (see interactive narratives in MUDs); if not, then it is impersonal.
- *Access*: If all scriptons of the text are readily available to the user at all times, then the text is random accessible. If not, then access is controlled.
- *Linking*: A text may be organized by explicit links for the user to follow. Links may be conditional, or no links may exist.
- *User functions*: The user may perform the following functions:
  - ○ Explorative function – choice of path to take;
  - ○ Configurative function – scriptons are chosen or created by the user;
  - ○ Interpretive function;
  - ○ Textonic function; the user can add textons and traversal.

These seven variables with their various possible values create a multidimensional space of 576 unique media positions. For example, the game MULTI-USER DUNGEONS (MUD1) will produce the following profile: static, indeterminable, transient, permanent, controlled, conditional, and explorative (Aarseth, 1997). Based on this typology, digital games – as text objects – can be classified with unique profiles.

A precondition for this approach is that all text, and its *scriptons*, *textons*, and the *traversal function* are predefined otherwise the game-artifact cannot be identified. Therefore, this typology will only be of use for digital games. I consider it too limited to characterize for example MMORPGs (massively multi-player online role-playing games)

Aarseth's approach demonstrates the elegance and strength of a theoretically underpinning of a classification. It focuses on computer games as narratives, and deals with computer semiotics. The resulting demarcation line excludes many games from the classification.

Next, I will present a classification that includes key characteristics of games from the perspective of the setting that players step into: competition or cooperation.

Klabbers

Game theory has provided the following key concepts on gaming: competitive and cooperative games, and zero-sum and non-zero-sum games. Systems theory, and computer science have introduced concepts such as, goal-, and non-goal-seeking, common- and distributed access. Combining these terms in a coherent scheme brings forward the following functional classification (Table 2.6). The classification does not make distinctions along the paida/ludus dimension (Table 2.2). The contest may be between teams of players, competing against each other, or among teams of players, engaging in common activity, while fighting the odds. They may or may not have common access to rules and resources, the loss of one player may be the gain of the other one. They may seek to achieve a common goal, or they just like to meet each other in cyberspace, just for the fun of it. Although one may question whether with respect to MMORPGs (massively multi-player online role-playing games) a stop rule applies, finite games obey the "rule of nature": there is a beginning and an end. Goal seeking, cooperative games require an attitude of play, which is distinct from zero-sum competitive games. These differences impact on the way the players will communicate and interact with one another.

Table 2.6. Functional Classification of Games

Finite Games – stop rule			
Competitive Games		Cooperative Games	
Common access Games	Distributed access Games	Common access Games	Distributed access Games
Zero-sum games; *Chess Tennis, Monopoly*	**Zero-sum games**; *Bridge Simsoc**	**Goal seeking**; *Rock-climbing charades*	**Goal seeking**; *Bafa-bafa* Beer game* Dentist* Hexagon* Funo* Perform**
Non-zero-sum games; *Poker Hide-and-seek*	**Non-zero-sum games**; *Business simulations Clug* Funo**	**Non-goal seeking**; *frame narratives*	**Non-goal seeking**; *Mmorpg***

** Mmorpg (massively multi-player online role-playing games)

Note *: BAFA-BAFA (1973); BEER GAME (1966); CLUG (1966); DENTIST (Chapter 8); FUNO (Chapter 11); HEXAGON (1976); PERFORM (Chapter 9); SIMSOC (1978).

ARCHITECTURE OF GAMES AND SIMULATIONS

All classifications presented above convey a perspective on games and simulations, which denotes their internal structure, their *architecture* so to say, without describing it in detail. An additional and more serious objection against these classifications is the concept of game as external to the actors, the players. This is strange, as they are *artifacts*: human constructions, developed with clear intentions in mind that only receive their meaning while being played. Their architecture preconditions the dynamics of play, and include forms of knowledge that can make knowledge content meaningful while playing. Therefore, classifications of the kinds discussed above, are flawed. They miss the core idea that brings forward such a variety of appearances and functions: their *morphology* with *actors included*. Aarseth (1997) referred implicitly to the internal structure of games-as-text. I consider this too limited a view on games for the following reason.

Huizinga (1985) has discussed the play element of culture, arguing that play is a culture shaping human activity. Acknowledging that basic role implies that the morphology of games should receive more attention. The study of form and structure of these artifacts should be at the basis of their classifications, generating classes and specimen with distinct qualities. The morphology of games and simulations should provide the foundations for developing a coherent taxonomy. Studying the architecture of games covers three aspects:

- Art and science of design of the artifacts;
- Style and layout of particular artifacts;
- Structure, design, and assessment of an artifact.

In this chapter, I will focus on the second aspect: style and layout of particular artifacts. In Part II, I will address the other two aspects in more detail.

Strongly related to the play element of culture is the notion that games – as forms of play – are expressions of human and social systems that generate culture. If play is valued for itself, it can only intrinsically be valued, if it creates a human and social system that temporarily is a world of its own. What will happen within the magic circle is both real and imagined. To be able to interconnect both worlds, we need a suitable core concept. My thesis for the study of the architecture of games is the following: *games are social systems, as well as models of social systems*. This notion implies that for the study of games and simulations, we need to be aware of, and accept a *dual position*. We should study games both from the position of the insiders, who play the game, and of the outsiders, who observe the game being played. As a consequence, we will have to acknowledge two linked but separate knowledge domains. In Chapter 3, and Part II, I will elaborate further the implications of this thesis.

GAMES ARE SOCIAL SYSTEMS

For a proper approach to gaming, as a particular kind of human activity, it is worthwhile to understand it from the perspective of human organization & social system. Therefore, I will start with wrapping up key notions of social systems. Subsequently, I will use that frame-of-reference for elaborating the architecture of games.

Social systems

While playing games, adults and children give shape to human organizations. When considering the variety of games, an equal variety of organizational forms can be observed. For that reason organization theory offers a fruitful frame-of-reference for reflecting on gaming. The way people organize themselves in various social settings tells much about their culture, and their codes of conduct. Because of the variety of forms of organization, the generic term *social system* captures their common features. Nations, companies, institutions, collective networks, and groups are examples of social systems. All show particular structural characteristics. In organization theory, structure is viewed as the arrangement of parts, components or subsystems of the entire organization. Weick (1979) has pointed out that the structure that determines how an organization acts and how it appears, is the same structure established by regular patterns of interlocked behavior. Reproduction of such a structure is the outcome of collective behavior: systems of interaction.

Giddens (1993) speaks of duality of structure.

> Interaction is constituted by and in the conduct of subjects; structuration, as the reproduction of practices, refers abstractly to the dynamic process whereby structures come into being. Social structure is both constituted *by* human agency and is at the same time the *medium* of this constitution (Giddens, 1993, p. 128).

The study of social systems deals with the various kinds of human organization, from the societal level down to small groups, and individuals in social settings. Organization science, organizational psychology and sociology, management science, political science, and systems science contribute to this vast area of research. I will highlight two features of social systems, drawn from the above-mentioned disciplines that are of relevance for linking social systems with games. Social systems:

- Are boundary maintaining entities;
- Consist of three interlocked strata (levels of description) (Figure 2.1):
    o *Culture* that is, norms, values, beliefs, attitudes, etc. of the actors involved;
    o *Structure* that is, vertical and horizontal communication and coordination;
    o *Technology* that is, the whole complex of routine and non-routine procedures to handle material processes (Klabbers, 1986).

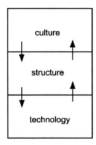

Figure 2.1. Representation of strata of social systems

Members of a social system draw hypothetical lines to enable them to distinguish between 'us' and 'them'. That hypothetical line frames the interface with its environment. Every social system – through converting and harnessing matter and energy – has a material basis. The resulting physical infrastructure – the arrangement of material objects in the space that the social system occupies – generates products, artifacts, and services. All the related processes are part of the technology stratum in the broad meaning of the word. Steering, or governing that stratum requires appropriate communication and coordination procedures. The resulting structure drives the flow of data and information between the actors. In current industrial societies, Information technology (the Internet, mobile phones, etc.) enables that flow in time and space. Structural conditions enhance or limit the interactions between actors. The system of interactions between the actors produces a social organization with its values, norms, beliefs, symbols and rituals: its particular culture. Motivational conditions – being part of a culture – stimulate or inhibit the actor's interests in communication, and in exercising or accepting control over their actions. That control structure, which is embedded in the communication rules, also impacts on the control over the processes of the technology stratum: the material resources. The communication and coordination structure interlock with the material processes. Through the structure of a social system, special activities and tasks are integrated and coordinated. The dialogic forces of *differentiation* and *integration* of tasks produce a hierarchy of regulation and control in the social system. Contrary to the general notion in organization science, the concept of structure in social systems should not be seen as fixed or external to social action. Giddens (1993) made an interesting point, which implicitly links the morphology of social systems with games. He introduced the notion of *duality of structure*: structure being a constraint upon action, as well as enabling action. He pointed out that actors routinely draw upon rules and resources, and thereby reproduce them in the course of their daily activities. He quoted Mouzelis for saying:

> Actors often distance themselves from rules and resources, in order to question them, or in order to build theories about them, or – even more importantly – in order to devise strategies, for either their maintenance or their transformation (Mouzelis, 1991, pp. 27-28).

By speaking of actors, rules, and resources, and linking them with the duality of structure, Giddens presented not only a particular meaning to the culture, structure, and technology strata, introduced above, in addition, he offered a framework for isomorphic mapping human organization on gaming. By doing so, he opened the realm of social theory to gaming theory. I will illustrate the meaning of these abstract concepts by the following example.

A family is a social system. The parents and kids shape a certain familiy culture with its particular beliefs, attitudes, norms and values. Those norms, values, etc. do not need to be exactly the same for both parents and the children. Usually, family members disagree about norms and attitudes, especially when the children are teenagers. So, the family exercises a mixed set of individual and collective qualities. The parents and kids communicate: they co-construct and sustain a system of interactions, based on the way they relate to one another, the specific context in which they interact, and the content of their conversations. That system of interactions and the related communication rules define the structure of the family: the vertical and horizontal communication. Parents tune tasks among each other, coordinate the tasks of the children and follow through whether they are carried out as agreed. These tasks may relate to homework from school, cleaning the rooms, cleaning the dishes, doing groceries, etc. A family earns income for living in a house, uses water, electricity, and gas, and appliancies such as the refrigerator, the TV, etc. These are the basic resources for maintaining the family's household. Teenagers usually start distancing themselves from the parental authority, and the rules of conduct, in order to question them, or in order to build "theories" about them, or – even more importantly – in order to devise strategies, for either their maintenance or their transformation. Parents usually disagree with their teenagers, and together they engage in an ongoing conversation about norms and values, and ways of communicating/interacting with each other. They continuously produce and reproduce their family, living in this city, in this country or state, and in this part of the globe: an extending horizon of social and physical environments.

Steering social systems & games

Connected to the concept of control is the notion of steering, and the position from which it happens. Steering is *allopoietic* if it happens by an outside actor, or agency. It is *autopoietic* if the internal actors are in control. As regards allopoietic steering, the behavior of the system is controlled by the function it fulfills in the larger social system and by the input it receives from its environment. The system involved is viewed as an instrument, produced and used by another external system to reach its goals (Maturana & Varela, 1980). This distinction also applies to games. They may be used as instruments to achieve a goal defined on a game and its actors. In such case, the game is functional to an outside purpose. Its use is allopoietic. If games are used solely for training skills, and the outcomes are graded accordingly, then they are allopoietic. In general, those games are rule-driven. If playing a game is valued for itself, and the actors are free to shape their own rules of play (a free-form game), then these actors also shape the goals of play. Such games are autopoietic. They are not structured by external information they receive, but by their internal system of interactions. Therefore, the (meta-) cognitive structures used by the system (game) are constructed (produced) by the system (game) itself. Maturana and Varela (op. cit.) rejected the concept of knowledge as a representation or image of some external reality. Cognitive interaction between the system and its environment is restricted to triggering internal processes by external perturbations (Heylighen, 1990). Thus, a social system is not reactive to its environment. It first enacts (constructs) that environment, and subsequently acts on that image. Evidently in social systems – as in games – the actors enact these internal processes, while producing a system of interactions: their social organization. They form the autopoietic (self-reproducing, self-organizing) forces within the system.

These core ideas about social systems apply to all kinds of human organization, and by definition, they also apply to games. It is out of the scope of this chapter to discuss social systems theory in more detail. In Chapter 4 I will discuss this gaming theory.

BUILDING BLOCKS OF GAMES

Social systems approach

Social systems as well as games consist of three interconnected building blocks: actors, rules, and resources (Figure 2.2), which are similar to the strata described in Figure 2.1. Actors constitute systems of interactions: a social organization. They draw upon rules and resources while functioning in organizations. In a soccer game for example, the players, the coaches and the referees are the main actors. They interact according to the rules. Their resources are the ball, the soccer field, the stadium, etc. While confirming their roles, and making use of the rules and resources, they produce and reproduce the social system concerned (that is, a particular match, and the annual competition in the league). By changing the rules and/or the resources, they either transform the system or produce a completely new one. They may switch from soccer to rugby. Because of the duality of structure, they can also change position, from inside participant (actor) to outside observer. In that case, they can question the motives and effectiveness of the actors; the rules as applied by the referee, and the quality of the resources: the right of wrong ball, proper lighting in the stadium, etc. That could help to develop strategies for the maintenance or transformation of the social system that is, the soccer game, and the competition.

From a morphological viewpoint, Figure 2.2 represents the basic architecture of games and simulations. It is the starting point of any game, running from one actor to multiple actor configurations. In each game, the players (actors) interact with one another, while applying rules, and utilizing resources. In a one actor setting, such as in many digital games, the player – through the avatar – enters a virtual world, which represents a particular social system with its rules and resources. The rules and resources may be the same for every actor, they may overlap, or they may be even distinct from one another. Actors may also violate those rules.

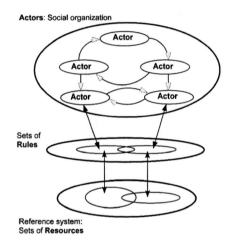

Figure 2.2. A generic model of games and simulations

Classification of games & simulations

The generic model of Figure 2.2 enables us to make a clear distinction between games and simulations with respect to the form of the artifact. So far I have used the terms *games*, *simulations*, *gaming simulations*, and *simulation games* interchangeably, not taking the precaution to be accurate about their meaning. In the areas of gaming, addressed in Table 2.1 this mixture of terms is used for pragmatic reasons, blurring the distinction between form and function. Games, as artifacts of a certain form, can be used to simulate certain social systems. This way of phrasing implies that the function of simulating refers to rules of correspondence between the artifact and a real life reference system. However, as pointed out earlier, simulation can also refer to a model of some particular form. In this case, form and function overlap. In this book, when using the terms *game* and *simulation*, it will mean artifacts of a certain form. Connected to this, when I describe games to simulate a certain social system, I will be explicit about that role, and about the function of the game that is, to simulate a system and a process. When I further use the term *game*, I will refer to its form. Therefore, I will not use terms such as *simulation game*, and *gaming simulation* as they mix up the terminology.

Figure 2.2 represents a fully-fledged representation of a game, with all the ingredients of a game: actors, rules, and resources. Many forms of play exist that do not define explicitly the resources. They represent a subset of the building blocks of Figure 2.2. Examples are role-playing games, frame games, and certain types of scenario games. Such forms of play are depicted in Figure 2.3.

If the actors are excluded from the game model, leaving two interconnected ingredients for modeling the social system: rules and resources, then the artifact will represent a dynamic feedback model, see Figure 2.4. Decision rules, embedded in feedback loops, such as applied in System Dynamics, define the processing of resources. These decision rules can also be defined as formal algorithms, which then become conceptualized as *agents*: rule-driven sequences of events. The generic scheme of Figure 2.4 represents the field of *computer simulation, agent-based simulation* included. (For more details, see Chapter 5.)

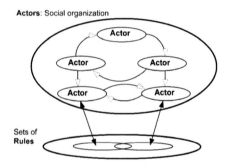

Figure 2.3. Representation of role-playing games

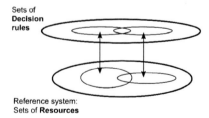

Figure 2.4. Representation of feedback systems, and agent-based models

A third option for modeling social systems, is to only address the resources of social systems that is the input-throughput, and output of matter, energy, and information as for example in supply-chains: energy supply and demand, and information systems. Such input-output models may be driven by a transfer function, which links time series of inputs to time series of outputs, ignoring the internal structure or throughput of the system, see Figure 2.5.

Dynamic models, depicted by Figures 2.4 and 2.5, represent the domain of simulations, both in form and function. Therefore, I consider simulation models to be a subset of the more encompassing game model of Figure 2.2. It is out of the scope of this chapter to discuss simulation modeling. For more details, see Chapter 5.

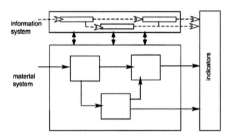

Figure 2.5. Representation of resources modeling

ABOUT RULES

Rules are associated with regularity, the common order of things, instructions, prescriptions, orders, directions, measures (of length), customs, influences, procedures, codes of conduct, government, and law.

The following distinctions between rules are relevant for gaming.

- *Regulative rules* – instructions often written down.
- *Functional* and *substantive* (fundamental) rules. Functional rules serve a pragmatic purpose, while substantive rules have an existence, independent of circumstances such as, a Constitution.

Rules are:
- Official instructions, which tell people what they are allowed to do and what they are not allowed to do in game, or in a particular place or situation, or during pomp & circumstances.
- Courses of action to do something properly or to achieve a particular goal;
- Statements, or assertions that describe the way things happen in a system. Such rules are often considered behavior rules, or laws of nature in terms of correlations, if-then, or deterministic, stochastic, or fuzzy causal inference schemes;
- Ways of behaving or taking part in something that is right and acceptable (rules of conduct);

To rule is equivalent with:
- To have the power to control affairs, and to use that power (autocratic, democratic rule);
- To govern a country; to regulate conditions of a state by rule of law;

- To have the power of control or the system of control over a group of people, even if they are not required by any rules or laws;
- The most powerful and influential feature of a particular situation;
- To have an idea or feeling that controls or strongly influences thinking or doing;
- To make official decisions;
- To control an activity or process, usually by means of rules of law.

Rules are synonym to *codes* that is,
- A set of ideas by a group of people about the proper way to behave;
- A set of written rules which state how people should behave in a particular country, society, or business;
- Any system of signs or symbols that has a meaning for example, language, gestures, or social behavior.

Rules are linked to, or embedded in steering and control.

Wrapping up these interpretations, it is important to distinguish between rules as *prescriptions* – normative rules – and rules as *descriptions* of processes, which result from the execution of normative rules. The idea is that normative rules bring forward regularities, or order. The rule "No Trespassing" could mean: trespassing not allowed, or trespassing does not occur. So, to understand the meaning of a rule, it should be put into context. Rules may differ in their measure of detail, and in their reach (Klabbers & van der Waals, 1989). The more detailed they are, the more they exclude. As regards the domain of a rule, it is important to know which activities are allowed or prohibited by a particular rule. The smaller the domain and the more detailed a rule, the more rigidity it causes in the social system. This combination of detail and domain may cause a dilemma. It may be that detailed rules may be only applicable to a very limited domain. In such a situation, detailed rules call for many rules to control the system. The game designer will have to decide how important it is to write down detailed rules. Compare for example the following instructions:

"Bake an apple pie for George"; and
"Cook a dinner for fifteen people."

The first instruction is more detailed than the second one. It leaves at best some freedom for choosing among various recipes for apple pie. There are far more alternatives open for cooking a dinner. One should be aware that the sheer existence of a rule-base does not necessarily imply that the anticipated activities and processes actually will take place. A rule taking effect, presupposes both acceptance by the people involved, and the capacity to execute and uphold it. Acceptance can have various grounds such as, coercion, morals, self-interest, etc. The capacity to apply a rule depends on its phrasing. If it is equivocal, then people tend to partly play *by*, and partly *with* the rules. This ambivalence becomes even trickier when multiple rules apply that are inconsistent or in conflict with each other that is, they are mutually exclusive. Those considerations are important for the game designer and facilitator to be aware of. It influences the transparency and playfulness of a game. Inconsistent and conflicting rules may be designed into a game in order to question for example ethical issues among actors.

This diversity of terms associated with the rules of the game, provides a continuum running from *rigid-rule* to *free-form games*. In rigid-rule games, the rules are detailed, and refer to a well-defined domain of application. Free-form games include a few basic rules, such as the start and stop rules, the use of space and equipment, the authority of the game facilitator to intervene for example to insert time-outs, intermediate debriefings, etc. Rigid-rule games are usually operational games. They are triggered at the beginning with the instruction (Christopher & Smith, 1987): This is the problem. How will you solve it? Free-form games start with: This is the situation, how will you deal with it? The dynamics of a rigid-rule game aim at convergence of ideas and actions. A free-form game may lead to convergence, or divergence, of ideas, and accepting a multiple reality about the issue at stake. Facilitating and debriefing a rigid-rule game is easier that facilitating and debriefing a free-form game. The last one requires the higher competency to deal with a more fuzzy and volatile process that tends to duck out of the facilitator's control. The players are in control of the process, and they self-organize their social system to meet their needs and interests. The choice between using rigid-rule or free-form games depends on purpose, context of use, and the intended audience.

It is important to know that a certain class of rules will directly impact on the system's resources. They are the rules that is, statements, or assertions that describe the way things happen in a system. Such rules are often considered behavior rules, or laws of nature in terms of correlations, if-then, or deterministic, stochastic, or fuzzy causal inference schemes. They express our understanding of the world: the reference system, and the way we have arranged the order of things. Descriptive rules either result from the execution of normative rules, or are expressed in terms of cause-effects between variables, or events, or in terms of if-then relations in terms of activities. As a rule of thumb, normative (prescriptive) rules are included in the rule-base of the game, and descriptive rules are embedded in the processes that model the resources, see Figure 2.2. Understood in this way, normative rules belong to the manipulation set of the game designer and facilitator.

MORPHOLOGY OF GAMES

The social systems approach to gaming offers a complete and coherent model by combining institutional and behavioral aspects about the game situation in relation to reference system. The institutional aspects include the physical, environmental, and the socio-economic infrastructure that structurally condition the activities of individuals and groups of individuals. The behavioral aspects concern the capabilities and related actions and efforts of the players. In Part II, I will discuss these qualities in more detail.

From the designer and facilitator's viewpoint, it is worthwhile to note that games convey a message that is to be learned and understood while playing. In Chapter 3 I will elaborate how to conduct gaming sessions to make that message clear to the participants, and to guarantee that the lessons learned make a lasting impression. When entering the magic circle, the players enter a symbolic world, with its peculiar signs, references, conventions, rituals, and practices. Each game represents a local language to convey the embedded message. For that reason, I will combine the frames-of-reference of social systems and a semiotic theory of gaming.

Social systems & linguistic approach

Marshev and Popov's semiotic theory of gaming (Marshev & Popov, 1983) is fruitful for two reasons. It offers a general outline for understanding the basic elements of gaming, and it presents games as languages that is, vehicles for communication.

Table 2.7. Syntax of a game

Syntax	
The syntax defines the grammatical arrangement of a game: the formal system.	
Actors Number of actors: individual and aggregate actors (teams). The number of game places of actors. In case of digital games, the *avatars* that connect the actors to the virtual world.	Participants of the social system. The number of persons participating in the game. Actors are capable of carrying out activities. They can be individuals or groups (teams): aggregate actors The dynamic coupling of actors and avatars in digital games.
Rules Game manipulation set	This subset of rules defines the manipulations allowed, communication rules, and the possible moves with the pieces, as transitions of the positions over time, and possibly − in case of digital games − an algorithm for the right moves.
Evaluation function	Rules describe the initial game positions. Dependent on the type of game, they may also define the intermediate and final positions, including the rules for finishing the game.
Resources *Game space* Set of game positions Set of pieces to play with	The set of places for resource allocation. The arrangement of the set of pieces (positions in the frame) at a certain moment in time defines their position in the scheme or *state space* of the game. The set of all theoretically available state spaces define the game space. The game space symbolizes a real or imaginary world (reference system): the physical environment & the infrastructure. *The way the pieces interrelate is defined by the rules. The pieces are arranged in the game space via the initial setting, and change during the process of playing.* The set of places defines the game space: the evolving states with the state space.

Each game is a language with its particular *syntax, semantics,* and *pragmatics.* Combined with the generic structure of games: actors, rules, and resources, the linguistic approach provides the following gaming framework (Table 2.7; 2.8; 2.9; and 2.10). As a language it conveys and produces meaning and context dependent situated knowledge. As mentioned earlier, the purpose of a game can be autotelic or allotelic. It is autotelic if the players have the freedom to act according to own

47

goals and sources of motivation. They are free from dependence on authority and be allowed to reason for themselves (Moore & Anderson, 1975).

Table 2.8. Semantics of a game

Semantics	
The way a game corresponds with our understanding, with our conceptual frames that is, their general interpretation is called the semantics.	
Actors Roles of participants; The symbolic representation of the system of interactions: the social organization.	The *role* is a key term in the semantics of a game. It provides a context for interpreting a game place. It offers a lens and a perspective for interpreting and acting. The role structure gives shape to the theoretical (formal) structure of the system of interactions. Actors assume those roles and express them according to formal and informal rules. Actors may take multiple roles. They have available pieces (resources) in the game space. They can make a sequence of moves with these pieces while trying to achieve their goals. They have access to various sorts of information during the game.
Rules Valuation set	Relationships between roles. The relationships between the roles shows the communication and coordination structure. Conventions, regulations, procedures, and codes of conduct, rituals: evaluation of social situations. Who is allowed to interact with whom, and when? Assertions about cause-effect relationships.
Resources	The placement of pieces at one moment in time is understood as a particular state of the social system, expressing the socio-economic and cultural situation. The symbolic meaning of the pieces in the game space, referring to their real life meaning. Places for resource allocation. During the game pieces are allocated in the game space. This allocation, from its initial position onwards, defined by the rules, is for the actors to decide. Initial and intermediate positions are evaluated to make subsequent moves. Meaning of the initial, intermediate and final positions for each actor.

A game is allotelic if the players act according to pre-determined goals and sources of motivation, often embedded in the rules. The game itself and the efforts of the players represent means to some end.

Table 2.9. Pragmatics of a game

Pragmatics	
Designing, preparing, conducting and assessing a game session comprise the pragmatics of a game. It includes the macro-, and micro-cycle of a game (see Chapter 3). During the preparations, the game facilitators allocate the actors to their roles. The materials for the game, the facilities and equipment are prepared. Conducting a game starts with the instructions to the players (briefing) and proceeds by facilitating, debriefing and assessing the game.	
Actors Learning context	Allopoietic vs. autopoietic steering: If the goals of the game are external, as usually happens in professional training, its steering is allopoietic, emphasizing the training of skills. If the game is valued for itself (autotelic), then steering is autopoietic.
Learning goals	Knowledge as acquisition, as interaction. If transfer of explicit knowledge is the primary goal, in terms of concepts, cognitive maps etc., players' minds are viewed as mental containers. That knowledge is acquired. If knowledge is the result of meaning processing between the players, knowledge is the consequence of the system of interactions (for further details, see Chapter 3).
Rules	The team of facilitators applies the rules. Format & instructions: The format defines the procedures for conducting the game, and methods for presenting information. Games can be rule-driven of free-form, requiring a different format and phrasing of the instructions. Assessment functions: Assessing a game, after its final position has been reached, starts with the debriefing, including a thorough evaluation of the subsequent positions of actors and resources in the game space, the moves the actors have made and the motives for making those moves. Also intermediate assessments (time-outs) are possible.
Resources	Materials of the game: equipment, paraphernalia, and facilities. The participants may use equipment such as computers, paper and pencil, scissors, etc. For conducting games appropriate facilities are needed: rooms, tables, chairs, projectors, etc.

The players are recipients of information that they will handle according to the rules of play. They depend on the authority of the game facilitator and are forced to reason according to the knowledge provided by the game. Most operational games that are used for skill training are allopoietic. They are training tools.

Combining the social systems and linguistic approaches to gaming brings forward a generic framework for defining the morphology of games and simulations in great detail. It includes the actors, and allows for making fingerprints of any game.

Table 2.10. Basic ingredients of game architecture

Architecture of games			
Social System	**Syntax** *Form*	**Semantics** *Content*	**Pragmatics** *Usage*
Actors	Number of players Number of game places of actors	Roles Composition of roles in social organization	Learning context: types of steering; Learning goals: kinds of knowing;
Rules	Game manipulation set: Preparatory rules; Start & stop rules; Rigid-rules; Principle-based rules; Free-form. Initial game positions; Allowable moves; Final game positions	Relationships between roles, communication rules, procedures Evaluation of places for resource allocation, and relative position within team of players	Team of game facilitators Format & instructions for rigid-rule vs. free-form Assessment functions
Resources	Game space; Set of game positions; Set of pieces	Positioning of pieces: meaning of cultural, socio-economic situation Set of occupied & available positions	Materials: Equipment Paraphernalia Facilities

To give an idea of the meaning of the game space, consider for example to board game AWARI. It consists of two rows of six boxes, and at the opposite ends two boxes for collecting the chips won. Providing the initial condition: four beans in each box, these beans are divided over the boxes, following the rules. The AWARI game space is in the order of magnitude of 900 billion positions (NRC, 2002). For games such as CHESS and GO the game space is still incalculable. These positions are discrete. If a dynamic, non-linear mathematical model is used to represent the resources, such as in a System Dynamics model, then the state space of that model defines the game space.

Marshev & Popov (1983) said that the interpretation of a game is *correct* if each correct position in the game corresponds with a similar time dependent description of the social system. The interpretation is *adequate* if every position in the game corresponds with a true position in the social system and can be reached from the initial position. Both conditions ensure that the game and the social system match, that they do not contradict each other. The game – as formal system – is complete. Table 2.10 summarizes the key characteristics of the morphology of games, embedding the social systems with the linguistic approach in one framework.

Basically, referring to the pragmatics of gaming, playing games implies learning, unlearning or even breaking habits.

DECONSTRUCTION OF GAMES

Marshev & Popov (op. cit.) distinguished three areas of application: education, research, and operational/practical. Taking their views on board, I have adjusted and updated these three areas. Educational functions of games are:
- Demonstration function – enlightenment of concepts, principles, methods, processes, and procedures of the socials system involved;
- Training function – developing skills, problem solving, decision making etc.;
- Motivation function – involving learners in the educational process, and to stimulate intrinsic motivation;
- Arousal function – increasing the level of activation of learners.

The research function of games includes:
- Formalization function – artifact design;
- Heuristic and creative function – developing search strategies and envisioning new opportunities;
- Verification function – artifact assessment & theory testing (see Chapter 7);
- Organizational function – project management & organization (see Chapter 5).

The operational function of games includes:
- Games as interventions (change agent) – culture reshape, improving the internal organization of the social system, competency of staff, decision making procedures etc.;
- Planning function – organization design, scenario design;
- Experimental function – using games to experiment with various strategies to explore viable options. (See also Chapter 7.)

The operational function broadens the scope of gaming to organization design, and social systems development. From that perspective, I have linked gaming in its capacity of change agent to *design-in-the-large*, while for the design of the artifact as such I have denoted the term *design-in-the-small* (Klabbers, 2003, 2006). (For more details, see Chapter 5.)

Whenever gaming is used for these areas of application, it is recommended to apply the framework of Table 2.10 when selecting an existing game to see whether it suits the requirements. In my teaching, I have extensively used Table 2.10, and the underlying concepts. Through its application the students learned to read and understand the architecture of a whole variety of games, from traditional board games to currently available computer games. For them often it came as a surprise to see that the scope of computer games is less complex on the conceptual level, and more complicated on the purely instrumental level than many conventional games. The architecture of many existing games, developed since the 1950s, turned out to be more complex in terms of their conceptualization – their theoretical framework. A reason may be that they address different audiences.

A few years ago, I applied the scheme of Table 2.10 in a legal case. A Dutch consultancy had charged a Scottish consultancy to have copied their game without paying a proper fee for buying or licensing it. The Scottish consultancy approached me to support their case on short notice. They were very explicit in stating that their game was not only distinct from the Dutch game in form and content, moreover, it had been designed on the basis of a unique design specification provided by a major client. The Scottish consultancy claimed that they had not committed piracy. However they had to prove it for the Netherlands Institute of Arbitration. I accepted their request under the clear precondition that, if on the basis of my deconstruction of both games, I should come to the conclusion that the games were basically similar, I would be explicit about it in my report to the board of arbitrage. That precondition was accepted.

On the basis of the frame-of-reference of Table 2.10, I deconstructed the architecture of both games in great detail. The results, written down in a lengthy report, underpinned the conclusion that the Scottish game was distinct from the Dutch game in terms of its design specifications, in particular with respect to its rule-base, the resources and their form of presentation. What looked similar on the surface was very distinct in its architecture. The complaining party, the Dutch consultancy, was not able to substantiate their charge on the same level of detail, and lost the arbitration. In my teaching and in the legal case, deconstructing games according to the schemes of Table 2.7, 2.8, 2.9, and 2.10, presented above, has turned out to be productive and worthwhile.

Using the generic framework presented above for deconstructing games, the next challenge is to use the classifications discussed in this chapter for arranging interesting existing games. Once they have been classified (grouped), each class should be deconstructed applying Table 2.10 to figure out key qualities of those classes, and to look for a more fundamental taxonomy on games.

INTERACTIVE LEARNING THROUGH GAMING

GAMING AS AN EMBODIED EXPERIENCE

The use of games depends on four general indicators (Duke, 1974):
- Purpose – primary purpose to be achieved through the game.
- The subject matter – what is the game about?
- Context of use;
- Intended audience(s).

Games are specific as regards their purpose, subject matter, form, and content. Via concrete gaming experiences it is expected that the participants will become more knowledgeable about the subject matter through learning by doing. Through their generic forms, and playful experiences, games shape interactive learning environments (Klabbers, 2003). Lessons can be learned from playing games that transcend the unique setting of any particular game. Playing a game is performing symbolic acts that fit into the very idea of Huizinga's (1985) notion of the play element of culture.

All learning aims at developing expertise, broadening our scope, and improving our capacities and response repertoire. Motivation is the driving force of developing capabilities. Therefore, a game should be motivating for the participants, stimulating them to perform to the best of their abilities. They should feel competent to achieve the goals set by the game, and the facilitator should provide them with a safe learning environment to experiment in a playful manner with the options available. To enter the magic circle with sufficiently confidence, the participants should be made aware of their achievement and competence motivation. Achievement motivation refers to people attracted to tasks that are neither very easy nor very hard. People high on *achievement motivation* strive to constantly better themselves and their accomplishments. *Competence motivation* refers to people's beliefs in their own ability to solve the problems at hand (Sternberg, 1998; McClelland, 1985; Bandura, 1996). Engaging in the playful act of gaming, presupposes that the players (actors) consider themselves sufficient competent to achieve their goals. It is the primary task of the game designer, and subsequently the game facilitator, to provide the participants with an interactive learning environment that matches their abilities.

Interactive learning through gaming and simulation includes the following five interacting key elements of learning: *meta-cognitive skills, learning skills, thinking skills, knowledge and motivation* (Sternberg, 1998). Meta-cognitive skills refer to people's cognition of their cognition, which is their understanding and handling of their own cognition. Meta-cognition is a second-order concept. It refers to itself. Sternberg mentioned seven modifiable meta-cognitive skills: problem recognition, problem definition, problem representation, strategy formulation, resource allocation, monitoring of problem solving, and evaluation of problem solving. As such skills go beyond the unique setting of a game, they result from playing games in general. Therefore, playing games helps to improve meta-cognitive skills.

Examples of learning skills are selective encoding, distinguishing relevant from irrelevant information, selective combination, putting together the right information, selective comparison, relating new information to information, stored in memory (Sternberg, 1985). It also here applies that playing games enhances learning skills, for in the dynamics of game play, the actors are continuously engaged in making sense of what is happening in their dynamic game space.

Thinking refers to:
- Critical (analytical) thinking, i.e., analyzing, critiquing, judging, evaluating, comparing and contrasting;
- Creative thinking skills, i.e., creating, discovering, inventing, imagining, supposing, and hypothesizing;
- Practical thinking skills, i.e., applying, using, utilizing, and practicing (Sternberg, 1998).

Again, games and simulations offer interactive learning environments that challenge the players to practice such skills.

All these skills are related to gaining knowledge. Two kinds of knowledge play an important part in learning through gaming: *declarative* and *procedural knowledge*. Declarative knowledge refers to facts, concepts, principles, and laws. It is "knowing that". In games, declarative knowledge is mainly embedded in the rules and resources. It refers to assertions, prescriptions, and descriptions about the gamed world. Procedural knowledge concerns procedures and strategies. It is "knowing how". Sternberg et al. (1995) mentioned that procedural tacit knowledge enhances knowing how the system functions in which one is operating. While declarative knowledge is mainly built into the game, procedural knowledge is more a capacity of the players.

Once players enter the magic circle, and assume their roles, in the rituals of play, they apply these skills, and become more knowledgeable. As their action repertoire increases they become more adaptable to shifting conditions and circumstances. They engage in a playful act, motivated to apply their meta-cognitive skills, learning skills, thinking skills, knowledge and experience, being aware of their attitudes, beliefs, and feelings. Playing games is an embodied experience, interconnecting the knower and the known. How can their capacities and competency be improved in game sessions? In the next section, I will elaborate a typical game session.

SETTING OF A TYPICAL GAME SESSION

When preparing a game session, the facilitator has to design a specific interactive learning environment for the intended audience of players. The following questions need to be addressed up-front. Is the subject matter tuned to context of use, and to the initial capabilities of the players? Does the goal of the game fit the purposes of group of players, and the client? While selecting a suitable game, the facilitator needs to check whether the framework of the game − its form and content − is tuned to the behavior styles of the participants. If for example the participants are not familiar with computers, or the Internet, then it will discourage them from engaging themselves in a computer-supported game. Similar impediments, however for different reasons, may concern board games and role-play.

The macro-cycle

A typical game session for professionals includes two interconnected levels of use: the macro-cycle and the micro-cycle (Figure 3.1 and 3.2).

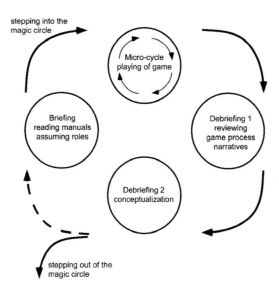

Figure 3.1. Macro-cycle of game session

The preparations of a game session start with the *briefing*. A short time before the participants meet – usually a few weeks before the session – they receive an invitation with a short description of the game, and further relevant reading material. This is the beginning of the briefing. The day they arrive to actually play the game, the meeting starts with an introduction by the facilitator, player manuals are handed out, and teams are arranged. As part of the briefing, the participants read the manuals, assume their roles, and arrange a first team meeting. Sometimes, when participants do not know each other in advance, a simple role-play may help as an icebreaker. The purpose of the briefing is to ensure that everyone is mentally ready to step into the magic circle.

As games either evolve in cycles or in an iterative sequence of steps, the facilitator monitors the dynamic process of play, and intervenes only when needed to guide its proper continuation. In a rigid-rule game, the facilitator makes sure that everyone plays by the rules. In a free-form game the players have in principle the freedom to shape their own rules within the constraints of a few "rules of nature". These rules concern, the start and stop rules, use of the physical game space and its facilities, and break out times for meals. Facilitating a free-form game presupposes that the facilitator does not impose rules while the games goes on, and only intervenes when participants may get hurt, physically or mentally. Within those boundaries, all that happens is part of the learning process, and should be taken on board for the debriefing. I will discuss the micro-cycle in more detail below.

Once the facilitator applies the stop rule, the debriefing starts. During the first stage of the debriefing, focus is on reviewing the gamed process, to allow the players to "blow off steam", unwind, and metaphorically "play again and comment on the video of the game". They engage in reviewing their experiences, being part of a common process, and through conversations interactively construct the game narrative. They shape the individual histories and common history of the game reality. Based on that shared perspective, they enter the second stage of the debriefing, paying attention to key concepts and their interrelationships. Debriefing 2 aims at sense making and meaning construction, and agreeing on the vital *schemas* triggered by the game. I will discuss the meaning and role of schemas below. After the second debriefing, the participants usually step out of the magic circle. Pending the context of use, for example the game being a part of an ongoing educational program, the participants may repeat the macro-cycle, switching roles and playing a leveled up game that requires a higher level of skill and competence.

The micro-cycle

Providing this general scheme of the macro-cycle, next it is worthwhile to look into the performances during the game in more detail (Figure 3.2). Once the participants have agreed to enter the magic circle, while having assumed their roles, they enter an imaginary world − valued for itself. They accept to play by the rules. Providing the composition of roles, conveying various positions and perspectives on the game reality, the players will deal with a multiple reality. During the game they are involved in four interrelated sets of activities:
- Actions and interactions: through bodily activities increasing arousal and awareness;
- Sense making and meaning construction: figuring out what is happening;
- Formation and adjustment of schemas: understanding the behavior patterns that emerge;
- Adjusting the action repertoire: improving the capacity to adapt to shifting circumstances.

Although, on an aggregate level, these four activities follow the sequence as depicted in Figure 3.2, in practice the players perform these activities simultaneously. They are part of a total engagement of the persons involved. Only when they take distance from the ongoing process − by mentally taking a "time out" − they become aware of the four kinds of activities and the way they interrelate. When they enter the magic circle, some of the players may start with taking action, some may start figuring out what is happening in the physical space, trying to make sense of the new situation, and others may try to refer to schemas they are familiar with to decide which action repertoire may be most worthwhile for a start. To illustrate the dynamics of a game, I will present the metaphor of gas in a drum. The four activities represent gas molecules that move with a certain speed through the space, continuously bumping into each other. At any moment in time, it will be difficult (impossible) to define the location and speed of the individual gas molecules.

However on an aggregate level – looking at the totality of all molecules – a general pattern emerges that informs us about the interrelationship between volume, temperature, and pressure within that drum.

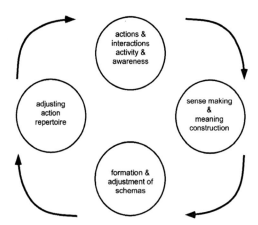

Figure 3.2. Illustration of the micro-cycle

The interplay between the players' activities may also look like the performance of jugglers trying to keep their four saucers simultaneously spinning on rods. During the debriefings, as part of the macro-cycle – it is the main task of the facilitator to – raise the level of players' awareness about the four activities – depicted in Figure 3.2 – allowing them through story telling and reflection to share their views on the set of four activities, and to bring order to their composition within the context of the game session, to render meaning to the joint effort and performance. The micro-cycle as depicted in Figure 3.2 resembles Kolb's theory of experiential learning (Kolb & Fry, 1975). The frame and underlying ideas look similar, the concepts and the related theory of knowledge are different, as I will explain below.

SITUATED LEARNING

Gaming sessions are examples of situated learning: learning being contextualized. In addition to offering interactive learning environments, games also shape *multi-modal learning* conditions. This means that a mixture of sensory-motor capacities is required to perform in a game. Above, I have linked interactive learning through gaming and simulation to five interacting key elements of learning: meta-cognitive skills, learning skills, thinking skills, knowledge and motivation. Combining views on learning, a tension may occur between claims about situated learning and about the transfer of skills and knowledge beyond the situation in which the tasks are performed. A claim on situated learning could imply that the more general skills and knowledge from a gaming experience cannot be transferred to real-world situations. To make my point clear, I do not support the assertion that all knowledge and skills gained during a gaming session are situation specific. For example, various skills such as, reading, calculating, communicating – verbally and in writing – transfer from one context to another. Games may have different surface structure, and nevertheless show common abstract structures, which require similar skills and knowledge to handle them. However, as I will describe later, some kinds of knowledge are specific to the situation in which the players perform their tasks.

Action and interaction are basic ingredients of playing games. It is important to note that action is grounded in the concrete situation in which it occurs (Anderson, Reder, & Simon, 1996). Actions during the game, and the related embodied experiences, are the basis for the debriefing, which is a process of abstraction from the individual bodily experience to the shared conceptual understanding. If well designed, and suited to the occasion, games are capable to bridging education-by-abstraction with on-the-job training. They can also be used as suitable forms of apprenticeship training (Part II). Although games provide complex social environments, enhancing the five key elements of learning, some skills do not necessarily need to be practiced in such social settings. Providing that related *schemas* are in preliminary form available, it is not necessary to learn to use a calculator, to skate, and to ride a bike, while interacting with others. Even for team sports it may be more effective to learn some special skills in private. Declarative knowledge lends itself more for individual learning than procedural knowledge, which presupposes a common understanding about how to act. That common understanding may need continuous negotiation among the players, and acceptance by the facilitator in accordance to the rules of the game. Such skills cannot be practiced in a social vacuum. Practicing skills in complex social settings is effective for special skills that are unique to the complex situation, and that require skills of fellow players that complement each other. In such circumstances, social learning is a prerequisite for improving capabilities. It is worthwhile however to stress that related skills refer to social settings, and that the related schemas link the knower and the known in such contexts. Their meaning derives from their context of use.

Wenger (2002) distinguished four components of social learning: *meaning, practice (mutual engagement), community*, and *identity*. He considered learning a transformation of knowing, a change in the alignment between experience and competence. From the viewpoint of Figure 3.2, I prefer the expression: a change in the alignment between schemas and action repertoires. Underlying the idea and practice of situated learning is the ongoing scientific debate about the connotation of the terms *knowledge*, and *knowing*. Roughly speaking in terms of folk theory, learning increases knowledge. Sfard (1998) proposed two ways of thinking about the act of gaining knowledge through learning. She referred to the acquisition and participation metaphor. The mind – in the view of the acquisition metaphor – is a mental container of knowledge, and learning is a process of concept development, of filling up that container. Such knowledge is a capacity of the individual mind. It is a process of gaining possession over some commodity. Learning, in this view, is a matter of acquisition, construction, and application of new knowledge in new situations. The teacher's role is to help the learner to construct and internalize the material, to become owner of it. Knowledge acquisition through the mind as mental container is predominant in professional education. Such knowledge is general, theoretical, and propositional. It enjoys a privileged position in academia. While teaching professional knowledge, many methods of didactic education assume a separation between knowing and doing. Knowledge is treated as an integral, self-sufficient substance, theoretically independent of the situations in which it is learned and used (Brown, Collins & Duguid, 1989). In terms of Sfard, these substances are the concepts that are to be understood as basic units of knowledge. Accordingly, professional activity consists of instrumental problem solving made rigorous by the application of scientific theory and technique (Schön, 1983).

From a practical point of view there is a growing crisis of confidence in this type of professional knowledge and consequently in this type of knowledge transfer by our educational institutions. Schön (1983, 1987) has argued that professionally designed solutions to public problems have had unanticipated consequences, sometimes worse than the problems they were designed to solve. He observed that newly invented technologies, professionally conceived and evaluated, have turned out to produce unintended side effects unacceptable to large segments of our society. In order to be able to cope with complex, uncertain and unique social situations, Schön has proposed the term *problem framing*: a process in which we interactively name the elements and attributes to which we will pay attention, and frame the contexts in which we will pay regard to them (Schön, 1983). Such kind of problem framing is precisely what is happening in a self-organizing learning environment such as in free-form gaming (Klabbers, 1996). Brown et al. (1989) pointed out that knowledge is situated. It is in part a product of the activity, context, and culture in which it is developed and used. Gaming is appropriate for supporting situated learning. Free-form gaming especially is a fruitful cognitive apprenticeship method. It enhances enculturation among learners via authentic practices that is, activities and social interactions in a way similar to the successes of craft apprenticeship. This understanding is more in tune with Sfard's second metaphor: the participation metaphor. In the context of gaming, and more in line with the gaming terminology I have introduced, I prefer to use the term *interaction metaphor*.

The acquisition metaphor is strongly entrenched in the rationalist tradition in science. In this tradition, knowledge is composed of abstract, context-independent, formally interconnected domain-specific concepts. It focuses mainly on declarative knowledge. How do learners build for themselves concepts that seem fully congruent with those of others? This simple question is difficult to answer. Take for example into account the philosophical debate about the meaning of words. Fodor (1998) pointed out that we should get rid of the idea of the internally structured meaning of words. Considering the prototype theory, that human beings associate words with prototypes (i.e., the prototype of an apple, a table, a car, etc.), implies that words can function in compositional connections such as in sentences. The meaning of words is not fixed and the same for every individual. Marconi (1998) noted that in linguistic usage we are guided by norms. Often we have to find the right word. It is our lexical competence to judge whether a word fits. Everyone using a language assumes that he or she speaks like everyone else. Testing the meaning of words is actually an interactive process that converges to a common understanding, even a common understanding of distinct meanings.

Rogoff (1990) – in the context of the interaction metaphor – spoke of learning as an apprenticeship in thinking. Sfard (1998) signaled an extensive change in thinking by the fact that, although referring to learning, recent literature in educational sciences does not mention the terms *concept* or *knowledge*. They have been replaced with the noun *knowing*, which indicates action. She stated that the talk about states has been replaced with attention to activities. The image of learning that emerges from this linguistic turn, the permanence of possessing (*knowledge*) gives way to the constant flux of doing. The new set of key words is *practice*, *discourse*, and *communication*. They suggest that the learner is a person interested in participation in certain kinds of activities rather than in accumulating private possessions. From the viewpoint of the interaction metaphor, learners contribute to the existence and functioning of a community of practitioners (Sfard, op. cit.). Greeno (1997) defined learning as the improved participation in interactive systems. Although Greeno did not make explicit reference to gaming, it is reasonable to link such interactive systems with games.

Underlying the acquisition metaphor are many dualist notions, centering on the antagonistic distinction between subject and object, process and content, knower and known. Prawat (1998), while referring to Dewey, pointed out that attention has been focused on the mental representation aspects of knowledge (see the mind as mental container) at the expense of the all important environment-person interaction. Dewey (1989) argued that the ontology that gives rise to dualism has emphasized the origins of knowledge and not its consequences. The origins' argument is central in the thinking of traditional rationalist and empiricist philosophers (Prawat op. cit.). Dewey argued that emphasizing origins that is, raising the question where the idea came from, is like looking through a rear-view mirror. The acquisition metaphor focuses on retrospective factors. Highlighting the consequences of knowledge looks at the prospective factors of knowledge. Dewey rejected the origins' argument. He developed further the *idea*, as a key knowledge construct. For an inquirer the true test of an idea is thought to lie in its ability to open up new aspects of the world, in a cognitive-perceptual sense (Prawat op. cit.). Dewey's pragmatism implies abandoning the mental container metaphor for knowledge in favor of the non-dualist perceptual metaphor, referring to an ongoing process of sense making of the world. Dewey abolished the epistemological gap between thought and reality (Diggins, 1994). Pragmatists locate meaning in the present and future (Prawat op. cit.). Prawat argued that both in simple and complex situations, the need to test ideas leads to operations being performed on objects and events, either in fact or in imagination. Ideas lead to changes in prior conditions. Performing operations on objects in imagination, for example during a game session, can help in testing ideas in Dewey's sense. Dewey further argued that while individuals test ideas, they do not necessarily author them (cited in Diggins, 1994). Ideas typically are tested and negotiated in a social context. To understand is to anticipate together (Dewey, 1981). Prawat mentioned that Dewey viewed idea generation as a process best carried out in a *learning community*, a community devoted to disciplined inquiry. Dewey's pragmatism connects the interaction metaphor with the perceptual metaphor. It underpins the notion of interactive learning environments as an environment for testing ideas (i.e., testing the consequences of knowledge) in a learning community.

Schemas

McVee, Dunsmore, and Gavalek (2005) have concisely reviewed in their article "Schema theory revisited" the distinct views on learning and knowledge, expressed above, since the 1970s. The recent history of the term *schema* illustrates the ongoing debate on cognition, mind, learning and knowledge.

During the early use, schema theorists have provided the theory prominence in various areas of research such as cognition, participative model building, and artificial intelligence. Key question is: What is the role of schemas in knowing about the world? For Piaget (1952) schema was a central construct in his theory of the origins and development of children's cognition. He used two terms to convey the meaning of cognitive development: *assimilation* of new experience in line with existing schemas, and *accommodation* (adjustment) of schemas to fit the individual's experience. Accommodation is more profound. Similar to Dewey, Piaget emphasized the importance of the person-environment and related sensory-motor qualities of schema formation. In the 1970s the focus of attention was the role of individual meaning-making processes: knowledge and knowledge construction. Schemas were in the head of the person, and meaning was stored in mental structures as representations of something in the world, separating the knower and the known. McVee, Dunsmore, and Gavalek (op. cit.) explained that such a view on cognition expresses a rationalist worldview that is inherently dualistic. The individual knower stands separate and apart from the world-as-known: a separation between subject and object. The basic idea was that cognition exists as an isolated process within the individual. McVee, Dunsmore, and Gavalek traced the origin of the concept of schema to Plato, Aristotle, and Kant. They mentioned that Kant (1929) is considered to be the first to talk about schema as organizing structures that mediate how we see and interpret the world (Johnson, 1987, cited in McVee et al.). For Kant schemas were go betweens, linking the external world with internal mental structures: knowledge structures stored in the brains, or minds, of the individual. Rumelhart (1984, p. 169, cited in McVee et al.) characterized schemas as follows. Schemas:

- Have variables;
- Can be embedded in one another;
- Represent knowledge at all levels of abstraction;
- Represent knowledge rather than definitions;
- Are active processes;
- Are recognition devices for evaluating the goodness of fit between data and knowledge structures.

Anderson and Pearson (1984, p. 259, cited in McVee et al.) define schema theory to be a model for representing how knowledge is stored in human memory. In the practice of (participative) model building and evaluation studies of gaming and simulation sessions, cognitive mapping techniques are used that are based on the idea of schemas as cognitive structures stored in individuals. These views on schema theory are closely connected to the acquisition metaphor, and the notion of cognition as mental container. From such a cognitive perspective of knowledge, in a variety of ways the mind creates inner representations that correspond to reality. This kind of knowledge:

- represents a pre-given world.
- is explicit.
- is universal and objective.
- is context independent.
- results from information processing.
- is cumulative.
- is transferable.
- enables instrumental problem solving.

This type of knowledge is explicit, articulated and can be packaged and transferred easily between agencies with the use of information and communication technology (see also von Krogh & Roos, 1996).

That interpretation of schema theory has increasingly drawn criticism since the 1990s, among others due to the understanding that it is not able to take on board the origins and development of schemas. Moreover, and in line with this criticism, that typical interpretation of schema theory uses the model of the mind as machine, information processor, or computer. The mind is a reactor, and a mirror. Another interpretation of schema is gaining prominence, offering a socio-cultural perspective, which is more suitable to learning through gaming.

Recent social and cultural perspectives consider schemas as *transactional* and *embodied* constructs. That interpretation of schemas as transactional and embodied is tuned to processes between ideas – in Dewey's terminology – and artifacts. Based among others on the role of human activity (Vygotsky, 1978, 1986), socio-cultural theories enlighten the role of meaning making processes, and social interactions in learning, and the situatedness of language and social interactions within cultural and historical systems (McVee et al., 2005). Basically, this perspective on schemas addresses properties of adaptation and adaptability between persons and their physical and social environments. Hacking (1999) noted that ideas and classifications – schemas – do not exist in a vacuum. They inhabit a social setting, which Hacking calls the *matrix*. Interactions and transactions happen within matrices, such as institutions and practices. Therefore, individual knowledge is embedded in matrices, which condition that knowledge in social and cultural practice. Through this understanding of schemas as inter- and transactional, the notion that they are fixed and rigid structures has to be abandoned. Activating schemas in ambiguous social settings requires that in an ongoing dialectic between the person and his enacted environment, they either frame experience to be coherent with existing schemas – a process of assimilation – or adapt schemas to fit a person's experience – a process of accommodation. The related practices are situated, and happen within particular contexts through specific activities. They are forms of (future) history writing. McVee, Dunsmore, and Gavalek (op. cit.) denoted that schemas are cultural historical constructions that emerge within the individual through inter- and transactions with others. They argued that material and ideational tools and embodiment mediate the origins and development of schemas. This view on schemas is in line with understanding of the *Self*, based on current brain research. Dennett (2003) observed that at some evolutionary point the brain started creating floating inner models or *schemas* of the organism in space and time, in reference to certain *goal states* and the prediction of results of *action*. New environmental complexities arose, and social interaction increasingly has become a modality for survival and reproduction. Dennett argued that in order to be capable of considering different courses of action in advance of committing to any one of them, that predictive function necessarily focuses on a person's "I" insofar as it had to relate to others and their relation, in turn, to that "I." He said that this added recursivity, building stable, predictive models hierarchically, underlies communication. It is what I consider a precondition for shaping and sustaining double interacts (Weick, 1979, see Chapter 4). Dennett (2003) wrapped up his ideas by expressing that once – in our evolution – we began to develop the activity of communication, and in particular communications of our actions and plans, we had to have some capacity for monitoring not just the results of our actions, in addition we needed that capacity for monitoring prior evaluations and formations of intentions as well. The resulting schemas convey the "self" of communication that has the job of maintaining a relationship to the past and to the future. This self-monitoring function of schema, Dennett calls it the "center of narrative gravity", underlies our sense of being in control of actions and of participating as free individuals in an ongoing and stable social and moral community (see also Moss, 2003).

This brings into the fore the question about the nature of schemas and their use. Holland and Cole (1995) (cited by McVee et al.) distinguished *schemas*, representing ideas, and *discourse* (conversation), representing material aspects. They viewed schemas and discourses as artifacts. In gaming terms it is more appropriate to view ideas as meta-artifacts, and the material aspects – the artifacts – both collective tools with histories and functions contingent with social practice (see also Chapter 6). Cole (1996) asserted that no word exists apart from its material instantiation. Vygotsky (1986) has pointed out that the sense of a word is aroused via the sum of all psychological events connected to it. Wittgenstein (1961) argued that meanings arise only within the rules of the language game. McVee, Dunsmore, and Gavalek (op. cit.) stated that by attending to the materiality of artifacts, we are able to explore the interrelationship between cognitive processes and social and physical practices that both enable and constrain their meaning potential. In gaming terms: cognitive processes by the players are strongly related to the characteristics of the game-artifact: the rules and resources, and the social and physical practices they trigger. It is an embodied experience. Bereiter (1997) argued that humans can overcome the limitations of situatedness, which is biologically based, by transforming physical environments and social practices, and creating knowledge objects whose abstract and symbolic representations free them from situation dependency. With games we have the capacity to learn to go beyond the situatedness, the "hic et nunc". McVee, Dunsmore, and Gavalek (op. cit.), while referring to Vygotsky (1978), stated that cognition is a culturally situated process. It involves problem solving in a particular context. In the setting of a game, not only that type of cognition is relevant. In addition, games are artifacts that mediate culturally situated processes and enhance meta-cognition as a culturally shared process. The inter- and transactions involved represent recursive processes between ideas and artifacts. As material and ideational tools, and embodiment mediate the origins and development of schemas, it is worthwhile to grasp their relevance for gaming, and to look into related knowing in more detail. These ideas about schemas are embedded in the micro-cycle of a game (Figure 3.2).

Explicit & tacit knowing

Participants engage in many simultaneous activities while playing a game. They learn while playing. Not only their minds, also their whole bodies are very present in a game. While participating in a game, they deal with embodied experiences. To be able to connect the minds and bodies during an experiential situation in one coherent framework implies that we have to take on board modern and post-modern Western thought about objective knowledge, realism, nominalism, and deconstructionism. Basing himself on Polanyi's treatment of the structure of human experience (Polanyi, 1964, 1966), Gill (2000) elaborated the dynamics of cognitive experience. By emphasizing the crucial role of the body in all human experiences, he distinguished three dimensions: the *awareness, activity, and cognitivity dimension* (Figure 3.3). For reasons I will explain below, I have adjusted the term cognitivity to *articulation*.

Explicit knowing is conceptual, in the focus of our attention, and well articulated. In science it is a form of abstract knowledge, expressed in formal language, laws of nature, equations, molecular structures, mathematical proofs, algorithms, etc. *Tacit knowing* is in the background, it is bodily experienced, and private, in the sense of not pronounced. We should however be aware that while playing a computer game such as, AMERICA'S ARMY, PRINCE OF PERSIA, GRAND THEFT AUTO, WORLD OF WARCRAFT, the SIMS, our focus of attention is the virtual world that unfolds while we play. We know explicitly what is going on. Actions that take place obey laws of nature. That abstract knowledge is tacitly available to the players. It has been embedded in the game as explicit, abstract, knowledge. Next, I discuss Figure 3.3 in more detail.

The awareness dimension. In his book *Personal Knowledge,* Polanyi (1964) stated that when we are relying on our awareness of something (A) for attending to something else (B), we are but subsidiarily aware of A. In terms of Gestalt psychology: object B is the figure at the foreground, while A is in the background. The object B, which is the focus of our attention, is then the meaning of A. The focal object B is always identifiable, while background objects such as, A, may be unidentifiable. The two kinds of awareness are mutually exclusive. Would we switch our attention from B to A, of which we have hitherto been subsidiarily aware, than object B will lose its previous meaning (Gill, 2000, pp. 31-32; Polanyi, 1964, p. xiii).

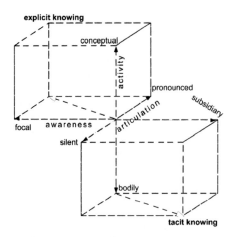

Figure 3.3. Representation of explicit & tacit knowing

During a game session, the players are continuously shifting their focus of attention, while simultaneously being aware of the game situation, which provides the background, or context for our ideas, inter-, and transactions. Taking into account the different roles they play, the participants are continuously positioning themselves on different locations of the awareness dimension, switching between the focal and subsidiary poles (see Figure 3.3).

The activity dimension. The activity dimension connects the *bodily* and the *conceptual poles.* Gill pointed out that through our embodiment, we interiorize, indwell things and ideas, people and institutions that shape the natural and social worlds that surround us. Once we are participants in conceptual reality − indwelling in our schemas − we find that our ideas, as well as those of others, may cycle back to have an effect on our bodily activity in the form of instruction – directions of movements – and motivation (Gill, 2000, pp. 39-40).

The articulation dimension. Even if objects, people, or institutions are the focus of our attention, and we have conceptually clear ideas about them, it is still open to us whether to articulate them, or keep them for ourselves, either to go public, or to keep them private. Gill, while referring to the *cognitivity* dimension, is not explicit about its meaning. Moreover, it seems to me that he described with that concept, the movement from tacit to explicit knowing. In that case, cognitivity is the vector that connects both kinds of knowing. It is not a third dimension. I consider the articulation dimension a necessary precondition for making schemas explicit that are in the focus of our attention. If it is not articulated in precise and accurate terms, it cannot be shared with others.

The interplay between these three dimensions can be seen in complex situations such as in games, and athletic contests, when the participants have to judge continuously, and quickly, how to best respond to the evolving situation. Such settings demonstrate the structure and dynamics of experience, the origins and development of schemas, and the interplay between ideas and material artifacts (in gaming terms: the linkages between actors, rules, and resources).

Through understanding the intricate interplay between explicit and tacit knowing, we are also able to take into consideration the role of the visceral (autonomous) nervous system in tacit and explicit knowing. We are not able to fully articulate our tacit knowing, and we are aware that it is beyond immediate conceptual control. Tacit knowing refers to feelings, beliefs, and emotions that are instinctive rather than rational and carefully thought out. Tacit knowing is richer than can be expressed through language.

The views about schemas and knowing, expressed above, should be understood in the context of a theory of mind. Following Premack and Woodruff (1978), *theory of mind* refers to the everyday ability to attribute independent mental states to self and others in order to predict and explain behavior. Lewis (2003) has distinguished four interconnected levels in the development of a theory of mind:

- Level 1 – *I know.* It is the basic level, common to other animals as well. It is built into the perceptual-motor system of many organisms. It is based on implicit consciousness, and involves little or no language. It does not involve a mental state of explicit consciousness, the idea of me.
- Level 2 – *I know I know.* This level includes the capacity to reflect on one's self and to reflect on what one knows. This mental state is a meta-representation, involving explicit consciousness and self-referential behavior. It refers to the mental state of me.
- Level 3 – *I know you know.* This form of knowing not only includes levels 1 and 2, the mental state that I know something and am aware of it, in addition I believe and expect others know it as well. Level 3 offers the ability of shared meaning. The representation of what I, and you know does not need to be accurate. Adults know more than a child. Once a child has reached this level of development, it has the ability to deceive. It knows that it knows (level 2), and it knows that you know (level 3). Thus deception is possible. A two and a half-year-old child has developed that capacity.
- Level 4 – *I know you know I know.* This level presumes at least two actors, similar to level 3, with each actor having a perspective. These perspectives

may be different. Both actors can check their knowledge of what they know about each other, against what each individually knows. At the level of "they know I know", your knowledge about what they know can be adjusted. Lewis said that once a child knows that it can be the subject and also the object of the knowledge of another, it is capable of recognizing the difference in perspectives between individuals. Level 4 of perspective taking allows for mature meta-knowledge to emerge.

Once these levels of knowing are reached and mastered, they enhance general cognitive competence, in particular language use. Figure 3.3 includes these four levels of knowing. I presume that every activity starts with level 1, to a large extent operating autonomously, and beyond control of the others levels.

While designing, facilitating, and debriefing games, we need to be aware of the three interconnected dimensions of Figure 3.3, their unpredictable impact on the cognitive processes, and the embedded social and physical practices that both enable and constrain their meaning potential.

USABLE KNOWLEDGE & MEANING PRODUCTION

In the previous section I have paid attention to gaming and situated learning, arguing that, although grounded in the concrete situation in which it occurs, it is not confined to local circumstances. The five interacting key elements of learning: meta-cognitive skills, learning skills, thinking skills, knowledge and motivation, exceed local conditions, mainly due to the schemas that emerge during play. The debate about schema theory, and the distinct theories of knowledge underlying the meaning of schemas, is not restricted to situated learning as such. It touches upon a wider debate that is ongoing in the philosophy of science.

All the aspects of learning, discussed above, somehow obscure the underlying philosophical views on knowledge and knowing. According to Hacking (1999), it makes for example a difference, if one hopes that the world, of its own nature, is structured in the ways in which we describe it, or that all the structure of which we can conceive lies within our representations. Hacking referred to the first position as the *realist*, or inherent-structurist, and to the second one as the *nominalist* position, constructionism. The realists are convinced that the world has an inherent structure, and that the task of science is to discover it. The nominalists argue that we only can know the world through our representations. It is out of the scope of this chapter to discuss at length the pros and cons of both positions. That is the turf of philosophers of science. Providing the purpose of this chapter: interactive learning through gaming, I will further deal with this controversy pragmatically.

I will make one remark about the ongoing debate about realist and nominalist positions in science that I view relevant for the further line of reasoning. It is related to the roles of perception, observation, explicit knowing, schemas, and paradigms in scientific research. To illustrate my point, I will address the question of dark matter and dark energy in cosmology. The term *dark* means not-yet-visible via currently available measuring instruments. Dark matter is a hypothetical substance – particles – of unknown composition. They do not emit or reflect enough electromagnetic radiation to be detected directly. Its effect can only be inferred indirectly from gravitational effects on visible matter such as stars and galaxies. That hypothetical matter would resolve a number of inconsistencies in the Big Bang theory, and would explain among others the abundance of gamma radiation in the galaxy. If dark matter exists it would explain several anomalous astronomical observations. The total amount of matter of the universe is yet unknown. Inferred from gravitational effects, only 4% of the total mass can be observed directly that is, through appropriate measuring instruments. About 22% is assumed to be composed of dark matter. The remaining 74% is considered dark energy. Determining the nature of this missing mass is one of the most important problems in modern cosmology and particle physics. The reason, I bring this question forward is that the demarcation line between realism and nominalism in dealing with these inconsistencies in the theory is not clear-cut. Dark matter, which is a hypothetical construct, emerging from inconsistencies in the Big Bang theory, is currently the prevailing paradigm in physical cosmology. It can only be inferred from the application of other constructs such as electromagnetic radiation, invisible to the human eye. The Big Bang theory itself is a social construct, social in the sense that it is the paradigm for proper scientific research by most cosmologists.

The human eye cannot directly observe most of the visible matter (*white matter* in physical terms). We need special instruments for their detection. Such instruments enlarge our capacities to observe matter from a far distance in time and space. Other instruments such as the microscope and special microphones make things visible that are too tiny to see, and audible for ultrasound that is beyond our hearing capacity. Therefore, science builds artifacts – instruments – that enlarge our sensory capacities. The history of such scientific artifacts is a recollection of human ingenuity to build and develop schemas: both ideational and material artifacts in a community of researchers. They are social constructions in a historic context that enlarge our capacities for advancing explicit knowing. However, there is more to say to this. Because dark matter, and the Big Bang theory are expressions of a paradigm, the related scientific community applies procedural tacit knowing to be able to communicate effectively with peers. It involves knowing how the scientific community, as an organization in which one is operating, works. So, for the sake of the argument, the question whether reality is "out there", or a construction, a schema, embedded in social and physical practices, does not seem to be of less relevance pragmatically. Physics, whether it be cosmology or quantum physics, is first and foremost a formal mathematical construct, and secondly, it is instrumentation to test those constructs while pursuing the scientific method. Those constructs convey a common formal language, linked to natural language to enable communication with other research communities, and the public at large. Learning the proper rethorics of such scientific community takes time for two reasons. It is highly abstract and therefore difficult to grasp. Moreover, it is embedded in social (read: scientific) practice with its many ambiguities. To underpin this argument, I refer to Booth's (1987) Ryerson Lecture "The idea of a university as seen by a rhetorician." Booth mentioned that he had been asking colleagues in various disciplines about how much they understand of other people's work. He asked them whether they – on short notice – could read an article or book in a given field and then enter into a serious dialogue with the author, at a level of understanding that the author would take as roughly comparable to his or her own? The answers in general were that no one claimed to be able to understand more than a fraction of what their colleagues publish. One colleague, Roger Hildebrand, provided Booth with the climax to his survey. Hildebrand mentioned his switch from particle physics to astrophysics. To outsiders of both communities of research, that might look like a small leap, a small shift within the same general field, as compared with the distance, between for example art history and chemistry. Hildebrand said that he had to spend the equivalent of about three full years "becoming a graduate student again" before he could feel some confidence in a dialogue with front-liners in his new field, and before he could judge the importance of a new article in that field. Booth elaborated the meanings of understanding, and presented four rhetorics. (For more details, see Chapter 6.) What he had to say about rhetorics, and what is relevant for this line of reasoning is the following. Booth noted that there are many and diverse rhetorics peculiar to each various front-lines of research. Each group of experts relies on what Aristotle called *special topics of persuasion*, the often *tacit convictions* that are shared by all within a discipline and that are therefore available in constructing arguments within the field. Examples are the assumption that photographs of bubble chambers and their interpretations can somehow be relied on with respect to electrically charged particles, or the conventional agreements about how to deal with normal curves and chi squares, and with the proper use of graphs etc. These assumptions shift over time and while peers construct their arguments, they can only during a given period of time be relied on without argument in their support. Booth (op. cit.) asserted that few specialists would want to claim that they or their successors will find themselves fifty years later relying on the same tacit assumptions, leading to the same conclusions, that they share today. Booth's argument illustrates that as regards front-line research, tacit understanding of the meaning of assumptions, play a serious role to persuade their fellow researchers. With respect to Hildebrand, it seems reasonable to assume that the difficulty of switching from particle physics to astrophysics was less a matter of intellectual capacity, than to learn to understand and deal with the tacit convictions that are shared by his new colleagues: to learn to handle well that embedded language. Wrapping up: for knowledge to become usable, professionals need to be competent in handling the intricate linkages between explicit and tacit knowing. Two other kinds of knowing need to be addressed to complete that picture on usable knowledge and meaning production: local and enculturated knowledge.

Local knowing

Suppose we chose the cooperative game of mountain climbing as an example. To accomplish that goal with a team, it is important to know about the local circumstances. Climbing Mount Everest will require knowledge of the local conditions, which are different from climbing Mont Blanc, or the Zugspitze. So, physical, geographic, and ecological conditions matter in such circumstances. In the case of choosing a competitive game, and providing the actors distributed access to available information, they can only act on the basis of local knowledge that is, knowledge that pertains to their position in the broader play arena. For example, in a business simulation with six companies operating in the same market, each company has a limited view on that market – the other companies included – and can only manage the company through its local knowledge of the market. As markets have emerging properties, a sector of the economy – represented in the framework of a business simulation – acts like a complex adaptive system (see Chapter 4). Each company, co-evolving with the other competing companies, will act on the basis of local knowledge. The development of all companies is a composition of the actions of all players in that market. Therefore, local knowledge provides a context for understanding the potential impact of all actors involved. It sets conditions for meaningful action.

Enculturated knowing

In chapter 1 I have referred to the play element of culture, and the creation of culture through play (Huizinga, 1985). Culture includes values, beliefs, attitudes, esthetic standards, linguistic expression, thinking styles, behavior codes, and communication styles to survive and prosper in particular social and ecological environments. Culture is produced and reproduced through individual and collective actions of the members of a culture. It emerges through systems of interactions between people, institutions, agencies, and societies. It is a way of living in a particular physical and social environment. It is an expression of a group of people, addressing valid needs of its members. A subculture in a culture represents the way of living of a group of people within the larger socio-political community. Members of a sub-culture share certain cultural characteristics such as linguistic or dialectical features that distinguish them from the broader culture in which they are embedded. Members of a culture communicate through a variety of codes: language, gestures, images, signs, and written symbols, to which they attach meaning. Multicultural education is a structured process designed to foster understanding, acceptance, and constructive relations among people of different cultures (Hoopes & Pusch, 1979). Intercultural communication often includes bilingual education, cross-cultural awareness of all aspects of culture, mentioned above. I will not discuss games for multicultural communication and education. That topic is more relevant for details on game design (Chapter 5). In the context of this chapter, I will address culture as the mental equipment players will bring with them when they enter the magic circle of a game, any game. Referring to Le Goff (1977), the term *mental equipment* ('outillage mental') is less on the content of communication, assertions, or special topics of persuasion, and more on the underlying thinking styles (schemas). Within a cultural setting it is not straightforward to trace that orchestration of thinking and acting, because it is part of the realm of thought and ideas shared by all members of that cultural community. For that reason they in general do not feel the need to make it explicit, risking that it will stay unnoticed. It frames a form of non-verbal communication – a silent language – shared by members of a (sub-)culture. It is always present in a game setting both implicitly and explicitly: implicitly, as part of the mental equipment of the participants, explicitly in the rules of the game, including communication rules, and in the resources (material artifacts).

Enculturation happens through interacting with people in the form of speech, words, and gestures. It encompasses learning the following cultural characteristics: ideological, political, technological, and economic qualities of a society. Enculturation helps mold a person into an acceptable member of society. Gaming, being fruitful for supporting situated learning, is a suitable apprenticeship method to enculturate learners into authentic practices through activity and social interaction in a way similar to that evidently successful craft apprenticeship. Therefore, and in line with play element of culture, games influence and are influenced by enculturated knowing.

Local knowledge refers more to the physical, ecological, and geographical environment of the actors in a game, while enculturated knowledge pays more attention to their mental, symbolical equipment. Cultural knowing is related to tacit knowing, which emphasizes the individual meaning creation. Cultural knowing taps more the shared and hidden codes of a group or community.

Generally, knowledge will be usable when the situation in which the four forms of knowing: explicit, tacit, local, and cultural knowing, are interconnected in an action-based setting such as in a game. Only such preconditions will enhance the actors to make sense of the situation – the interactive learning environment – they enact. Figure 3.4 depicts the conditions for meaning production in a game, more in general, in social systems.

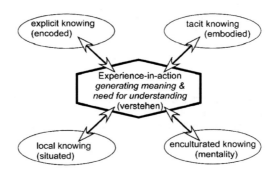

Figure 3.4. Illustration of meaning production in an interactive learning environment

Performance and affective appraisal of the participants need to take the four forms of knowledge into account, acknowledging that experience-in-action is an emergent process. Combined with the five interacting key elements of learning, mentioned above, situated learning is not confined to the local setting of a game. Playing games enhances the transfer of learning capabilities from current or previous tasks to novel tasks. This is in line with Sutton-Smith (2001) eighth rhetoric: "play as a model of adaptive variability" with the following basic features:
- *Evolution of the brain*: play to increase the brain's variability;
- *Redundancy*: reproduction of useful structures to enhance adaptation;
- *Flexibility*: play to improve adaptability – the capacity to adapt.

Anthropology of knowledge & gaming

The question arises how Figure 3.4 fits into the general scheme of a game. In Chapter 2, I have presented games to be constituted by three interrelated building blocks: actors, rules, and resources. From the viewpoint of game design, and facilitation, the four kinds of knowledge – depicted in Figure 3.4 – should be mapped into the gaming framework. Barth's views on the anthropology of knowledge offer are interesting and fruitful. Barth (2002) distinguished three faces of knowledge: *a social organization, a substantive corpus of assertions, and a range of media of representation*. These faces interrelate in particular ways in different traditions of knowledge, and they generate tradition-specific criteria for the validity of knowledge-about-the-world. He illustrated his approach with studies of the

Baktaman community of New Guinea, people living in North Bali, and a modern academic work environment in the UK.

Barth (op. cit.) noted that knowledge is what a person employs to interpret and act on the world. He included feelings (attitudes), information, embodied skills as well as verbal taxonomies and concepts. This includes all means of understanding that we use to make up our experienced, grasped reality: explicit, tacit, local, and enculturated knowing. Knowledge, according to Barth, is a way to understand major aspects of the world, ways to think and feel about the world, and ways to act on it.

I will paraphrase Barth's views on knowledge to connect them to gaming. Any game represents a tradition of knowledge. It is distributed, communicated, employed and transmitted within a series of instituted social relations. It contains assertions and ideas about aspects of the world. This tradition must be instantiated and communicated in one or several media of representation in the form of words, concrete symbols, pointing gestures, languages, images, etc. These three aspects of knowledge determine each other. They constrain and enable one another. They are embedded in the play element of culture. To paraphrase Chi-Yue Chiu's comments on Barth's paper, during a game session, meaning is constructed, transmitted and applied in social transactions. These symbolic actions take place among socially situated persons with particular communicative intentions (Chi-Yue Chiu's, 2002). Within such a setting, the interplay between explicit, tacit, local, and enculturated knowing, will bring forward meaning. Learning has only taken place, if as a result of playing a game, increased awareness enhances our understanding of (parts of) the world, our thinking and feeling about the world, and our ways of acting on it.

Media of representation and communication run in the field of gaming and simulation from game boards, paper and pencils, snow cards, and computer interfaces with underlying mathematical models, to web-based multi-media configurations. Different branches of academic knowledge use different media of representation. Mathematical knowledge uses computations, gross anatomy uses atlases, microbiology, its technical laboratory equipment and chemical models, geography uses atlases and scale models, and so on. Barth (2002) pointed out that these representations shape both thought and action and thus the practices of scholars in different disciplines, and the practices of human beings in society. They shape the style of game design through the media or representation in the game. By selecting certain media of representation, game designers construct imagery that affects the learning in a game that is, the construction of new knowledge. In addition to and distinguished from the modes of representation, the organizational face of knowledge determines criteria of validity, trajectories of evolving knowledge, and forms of coherence that govern knowledge in a game. The organizational face of knowledge in a game results from the systems of interactions between the actors, which are governed by the rules, and impact on the available resources.

The corpus of assertions are embedded in a game in three ways. Assertions express that and how cause-effect relations operate in a certain culture. They may have the form of laws of nature, codes of conduct, rules of law, customary law included, that prescribe how to behave, beliefs about how things relate to one another, etc. As discussed in Chapter 2, the first place to look for assertions is in the rule-base of the game. The second place in the resources and the way they are mediated in the game. In a computer-supported game, based on a set of algorithms (and hardware & software procedures), a variety of assertions are built-in into the game in the form of causal relations, if-then inference schemes, etc. Often a game player is not aware of many of rules in computer games, unless the game needs to be loaded on the computer following a set of instructions on how to handle them. All these instruction are part of the rule-base of a game. Last but not least, assertions are embedded in the participants in the form of the four kinds of knowing as expressed in Figure 3.4. They are part of the competency of the players. The actors constitute systems of interactions. They draw upon rules and resources while functioning in the game. By changing the interactions, the rules and/or the resources, they either transform the social system – represented via the game – or produce a completely new one. They can also mentally change position, from inside participant (actor) to outside observer of the magic circle. That could help to develop strategies for the maintenance or transformation of the social system, in this case, the game. Such a transformation will impact on all three faces of knowledge: the social organization, the substantive corpus of assertions, and the range of media of representation.

Emotional Intelligence

Although emotional intelligence (EQ/EI) is a term that still conveys "work-in-progress", it is worthwhile to take it on board in relation to gaming, especially gaming involving several actors that interact to achieve their competitive or common goals. I will use as the following working definition of EQ: the ability, or capacity to perceive, judge, and manage the personal feelings, the feelings of others, and of groups (Goleman, 1995; Mayer et al., 2001). For those reasons, it is a basic ingredient of playing games to raise self-awareness, and for building Emotional Intelligence in a learning community. The key to emotional intelligence is *self-directed learning* that is, intentionally developing or strengthening an aspect of who you are and who you want to be.

Four basic competencies of Emotional Intelligence are:

- *Self-awareness*: the ability to read your own emotions and to understand the linkages between emotions, thought and action; the capacity to use emotions to facilitate thinking.
- *Self-management*: the ability to keep disruptive emotions under control, to be trustworthy, flexible, to shift undesirable emotional states to more adequate ones, and to enter willfully into emotional states with a drive to achieve.
- *Social awareness*: the ability to empathize with others' concerns, and to read, to be sensitive, and influence other's emotions.
- *Relationship management*: the ability to inspire, persuade, and resolve disagreements, and to sustain interpersonal relationships.

The following aspects of steering self-awareness are relevant for becoming effective game players/learners: figuring out who you are: your strengths and weakness; uncovering who you want to be; creating a learning agenda for building on your strengths and coping with your weaknesses; experimenting with and practicing new behaviors (action repertoires), and their impact on thought and feelings; developing supportive and trusting relationships that make change possible.

Problem solving

In the rationalist tradition, explicit knowledge is composed of abstract, context-independent, formally interconnected concepts. Knowledge is mainly related to the way in which something operates (i.e., its functionality). In the nominalist tradition, knowledge is context dependent. It is formed by processing meaning and sharing the interpretive schemas of the persons involved. It is not accumulative per se, because historical conditions change. This implies that the facts and their context change. As both scientific traditions have different conceptions about knowledge, they pursue different objectives in knowledge transfer.

In the rationalist tradition problems are generally well-defined, related to a specific knowledge domain that is, a particular body of disciplinary knowledge such as mathematics, chemistry, physics, cognitive psychology etc. Staying within the rationalist tradition, entering the realm of ill-defined problems, well-articulated task-environments are created, where no single answers to the problem at hand are available. In the nominalist tradition, multiple realities are recognized. Learners bring order to their world while processing meaning.

In the nominalist tradition, the term knowledge has a connotation which is different from its meaning in the rationalist tradition. The interpretation of what constitutes a problem differs as well. In the rationalist tradition, problems are defined as situations where one has a good idea about what to accomplish, but no clear idea about how to accomplish it (Prawat, 1989). Problem solving then implies, applying the right scientific knowledge. In the social realm however, the key question is: What is the right and just knowledge? Many situations, in terms of the rationalist definition, hardly qualify as problems because in our pluralistic society we tend to disagree on what to accomplish and what resources to allocate. This applies to health care, crime, education, environmental degradation and numerous other issues. Apparently, in such a context the word problem connotes a meaning which is different from its meaning in the rationalist tradition.

Rein (1976) has stated that knowledge presupposes a framework to interpret it, but in a pluralistic social system there are competing frameworks. They are conveyed and defended by interest groups or stakeholders, in general by institutional actors. Actors are persons or groups of persons with roles and interests, carrying out one or more activities in a social system. Actors:

- Engage in meaning processing and frame problematic situations through multiple circular, recursive interactions;
- Construct knowledge;
- Produce a collective structure (social system), which can easily go beyond their comprehension;
- Find themselves in a complex situation with its ambiguous and uncertain outcomes.

Instrumental problem solving, applied in algorithmic approaches such as in agent-based simulation, being part of the rationalist tradition, is not well suited for dealing with problematic situations generated by multiple actors and multiple realities. That would presuppose one common definition of reality. Therefore, instrumental problem solving is too limited in scope to address meaning production. A framework for social problem solving, as represented in Figure 3.4, is more suitable. Game facilitators should keep in mind the following guidelines for making such playful settings productive (Moore & Anderson, 1975).

- Learners should be given the opportunity to act from various perspectives. They should not just be a recipient of information, but should be capable of acting, at times be referees.
- Activities should contain their own goals and sources of motivation, not just represent means to some end such as grades. In an effective learning environment, their activities are autotelic: goals are valued for themselves.
- Within the magic circle, learners should be freed from a dependence on authority and allowed to reason for themselves; they are thus made productive in the learning process.
- The environment should be responsive to the learner's activity. Not only should they be given feedback, they should be helped to be reflexive, evaluating their own progress, and whenever needed, provided information that helps them make sense of the situation.

Zone of proximal development

The initial capabilities and competency of the players are a precondition for effective situated learning as depicted in Figures 3.1 and 3.2, and meaning creation illustrated in Figures 3.3 and 3.4. If the game is too easy, they will not be motivated to take part. If it is too complicated they are not able to hitch on, they may disconnect and become frustrated. As regards digital games for kids, usually several stages of complexity are offered. Once a kid has mastered the first level, it can level up to the second skill level, etc. Such procedures show that games offer a range of options to develop skills. They vary for age groups and levels of expertise of the players. In the context of professional training, games need to be tuned to the capacities and learning potential of the participants. It is the main task of the designer and facilitator to ensure that the game is tuned to the needs, the initial skills, and the potential for learning of the players.

The term of *zone of proximal development* captures very well this concern for a learning environment tuned to the current qualities of the learners (Vygotsky, 1978). In terms of learning through gaming, I will phrase it as follows. The zone of proximal development of a game is the distance between the actual development level of the individual participants, at the beginning of the game, and the level of potential development as determined through playing the game under the qualified guidance of the facilitator, and in collaboration with more capable peers (fellow players). It refers to each person's and each group's range of potential for learning in the settings of Figures 3.1, 3.2, 3.3, and 3.4. That range is illustrated in Figure 3.5.

Game sessions should stay between the lower and upper levels of proximal development. It is the task and responsibility of the game facilitator to select the right game, and to assess the related zone of proximal development of the participants. The facilitator should know where to pick them up in their development, and where to bring them. That is not an easy task. Most important is to watch the initial competence motivation, as mentioned at the beginning of this chapter.

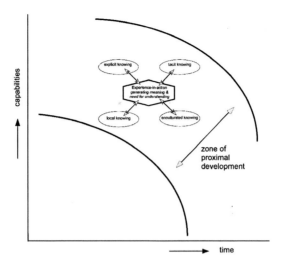

Figure 3.5. Zone of proximal development within the magic circle
(see Figure 3.4)

ACTION LEARNING

The ideas presented above, relate to the debate on innovations in Education, revolving around the theme of *action learning*. Action learning is a process of learning and reflection that happens through gaming. It is however not limited to the domain of gaming. It integrates the four sources of knowledge; explicit, local, tacit, and enculturated knowledge, described above and summarized in Figures 3.4 and 3.5.

Current questions in education

Many schools are dealing with motivation and dropout problems of pupils, and as a consequence with problems of discipline in class. Enforcing discipline, attention and learning is more difficult with the younger generation than it used to be with older generations. This all requires that the teachers need more capacities and skills to get and hold the pupils' attention. Research in educational psychology has provided theoretical and empirical evidence on various learning styles of children. Pending the outcome of discussion on the terms, I will distinguish the following modalities of learning:
- visual (preference for learning by seeing)
- verbal/auditory (preference for learning by hearing)
- reading/writing (preference for learning by processing text)
- kinesthetic or practical (preference for experiential learning: learning by doing).

Pupils in class represent a mix of these preferences. Some *multi-modal learners* show more than one strong learning style, which is an advantage if it includes the reading/writing learning style. The visual, verbal/auditory, and kinesthetic learning styles do not fit well in traditional education and learning environments with the teacher in the role of expert, transferring knowledge in highly structured fashion. The related emphasis on the reading and writing learning style treats knowledge as an integral, self-sufficient substance that can be split up in pieces. In terms of Sfard (op. cit.), the learner's mind – in the view of the acquisition metaphor – is seen as a mental container of knowledge, and learning is a process of concept development, of filling up that container. Such knowledge is a capacity of the individual mind. It is a process of gaining possession over some commodity. Learning, in this view, is a matter of acquisition, construction, and application of new knowledge in new situations. The teacher's role is to help the learner to construct and internalize the material, to become owner of it. The related learning environment presumes a learning style tuned to that educational frame: reading and writing.

Increased accessibility of education results in a high diversity of children in class, some are very intelligent, some are very slow, some very motivated, some are impossible to motivate in the school setting. If it is the goal of education to keep all pupils on board to do justice to all of them, than teachers will have to offer learning environments on various levels of competency of groups, as well as more individual attention and coaching. In traditional classrooms, this causes a teacher's dilemma, because of the limited facilities of teachers. It leaves the pupils too little space for individual guidance. Moreover, such learning conditions would require that the teacher would need to control that range of learning styles top down. That is too much to ask from the teachers, providing the strict rules and regulations of the educational system.

The generation of youngsters is bombarded with a wide variety of information sources. They range from TV, radio, the Internet, mobile phones, and last but not least video games, surrounded by their particular game cultures. These youngsters enter the educational system with a mindset, which is different from the one of the older generations. Playing digital games requires kinesthetic and multi-modal learning styles. The educational system has to deal with such learning styles, and the connected youth culture, and it should take advantage of such opportunities. A new generation of teachers, more familiar with the Internet and home PCs than the elder generation, will bring with them as well a fresh outlook on learning, more tuned to the abilities and needs of the current pupils.

Core ideas of the new approaches to action-learning include the recognition that students enjoy learning more, and learn more when they themselves experience the need to know something. This observation is closely linked to the meaning of the zone of proximal development (Vigotsky op. cit.), as presented above. The precondition for the effectiveness of this approach is that children learn-while-doing. If the underlying assumptions sound reasonable, then it would not make sense to transfer knowledge in measured portions in a predetermined schedule to "fill up the mental containers". Such a teaching mode can always be used to complement the action-learning mode. To ensure variety in learning environments, these modes should not be considered "either-or." They should be utilized to enrich each other. Another core idea for action-learning is to make education problem oriented. The task of the teacher then will be to structure the (interactive) learning environment to facilitate this sort of learning. Problem-oriented learning, interpreted this way, matches with Dewey's notion of *ideas* and *learning communities* (Dewey op. cit.), and the role of schemas and situated learning, discussed above. To make knowing usable for children, action-learning should take on board the frame-of-reference expressed through Figure 3.5.

One precaution, often expressed by critics of action-learning, should however be considered. They mention that action-learning may be a disadvantage for pupils with learning leeway when they enter school. Critics stress that it is crucial that people – through knowledge – gain control over their lives, and are not being confined to practical experiences per se. Providing the discussion on situated learning – presented above – the idea that such kind of learning is confined to the situation per se, may incriminate on the critics themselves by implicitly presenting themselves as advocates of the acquisition metaphor. It would enhance the quality of the debate if they would be explicit about their theory of knowledge. They endorse that the pedagogical relationship between teacher and learners, which offers opportunities for knowledge acquisition in a learning environment in education, is the key to learning. That line of reasoning is misleading and demagogical for it implies that action-learning disregards that pedagogical relationship as valuable. Situated learning, taking into account the dynamic interrelationship between explicit, tacit, local, and enculturated knowing, offers suitable learning conditions and ways to understand major aspects of the world, ways to think and feel about the world, and ways to act on it (Barth op. cit.). Considering Vygotsky's notion of the zone of proximal development, it would help the debate when we would differentiate between three different learning environments: the *reproductive, the heuristic, and the self-organizing learning environment* (Klabbers, 1996). To help young children to adapt to the school environment, the reproductive learning environment will help them to reproduce basic knowledge such as reading, arithmetic, etc. Still that reproductive learning environment would need to include the different learning styles of youngsters. Once they have mastered those basic routines, in addition they can learn to master viable search strategies and critically examine adequate intellectual resources in the heuristic learning environment. When they finally have matured enough, they may in addition engage in the self-organizing learning environment, taking Moore and Anderson's (1975) guidelines on board. Gradually they will learn to handle context-independent (explicit) knowledge, and context dependent tacit, cultural, and local knowledge to enhance their interpretation of the overwhelming amount of data and information available for example through TV, the Internet, and mobile phones. Those types of knowledge will become increasingly accessible to them. One approach I have been applying in linking gaming to traditional knowledge transfer via head-on teaching has turned out to be productive. By first inviting students and professionals to play a selected game, I have provided them with a common experience, a common understanding of the four types of knowing in a meaningful interactive learning environment (see Figure 3.4). Following the framework of the gaming macro-, and micro-cycle (see Figures 3.1, and 3.2), they together entered the magic circle, at the end sharing a common history. The outcomes of the gamed experience, and lessons learned, shared during debriefings 1 and 2 (see this chapter), made them aware of lacking knowledge, and motivated them to know more about the subject matter at stake (see for example Chapter 11). That motivation I have used for head-on lecturing, concentrating on explicit knowing. Subsequently, I selected another game – suitable to the overall learning goals, requiring additional skills, and invited them to playfully enter the magic circle again. Gradually and increasingly, they started to engage themselves in knowledge debates and shape local learning communities with their built in momentum.

Interestingly, in such learning communities, learners with different learning styles added variety to the learning process. On one occasion I acted as game designer, on another occasion as game facilitator and coach, still on another occasion I was "head on teacher".

Four examples will illustrate action-learning approaches, emphasizing heuristic and self-organizing learning environments. The intended audiences were university students and members of organizations. The gaming approaches the authors have designed and used, fitted with the zone of proximal development of the participants.

Kriz (2003) in his paper "Creating effective interactive learning environments and learning organizations through gaming simulation design", described the way he used simulation games to teach about organizational learning and change and to apply the underlying principles to design a comprehensive training course as driver of change of the educational system at the university. This training course embeds several layers of gaming: experiential learning, debriefing, train-the-trainer, train the designer, and meta-debriefing. Those, who have participated in the course become practitioners and change agents in the educational system. His main focus was bridging the gap between academic knowledge (explicit knowledge) and professional action, and through action learning, the transformation of knowledge.

Romme and Putzel (2003) in their paper "Designing management education: Practice what you teach", took the theory and practice of how to create experiential and interactive learning environments seriously when designing a curriculum that was organized and run according to the management and organization principles being taught. Basically, they used theories about organizational behavior, to set up an organization that manages itself. It is a form of experiential learning about the management and organization principles being taught. They discussed five precepts for experience-based and interactive learning environments in (undergraduate) education in organization and management subjects: (1) design education as an authentic organization, (2) exploit benefits of peer mentoring and assessment, (3) give students both management and learning roles, (4) act and delegate as a senior manager, and (5) program to create constructive tension-to-learn. Romme and Putzel used their interactive learning environments as forms of real time simulation games to convey new ideas on the educational system.

Ruohomäki (2003) in "Simulation gaming for organization development", made use of knowledge domains adjacent to organizational behavior. She paid attention to the following approaches to change: organization development (OD), which is concerned with incremental, long-term organizational improvement, emphasizing participation of organization members, and business process reengineering (BPR), which stresses fundamental, radical and rapid organizational design by top-managers and experts. She and her team have developed the WORK FLOW GAME, and used it as part of organizational change processes in various organizations such as, the administration of a university, the labor administration and the administration of an industrial company. Although she relied on the ability of an organization to learn, her major interests were in improving work processes from a socio-technical, OD and BPR perspective.

García-Carbonell, Rising, Montero, and Watts (2001) showed the potentials of simulation and gaming to enhance communicative language acquisition. They addressed the theoretical and practical meshing of simulation and gaming methodology with theories of foreign language acquisition, including task-based learning. They told a story both about gaining knowledge and skills to speak a second language, and its impact on the educational discourse. It is about communicative competence as such, taking into account the subject matter that is relevant for their students. By using computer-assisted and computer-based simulations, they relied on types of interactive learning environments, as presented above. They argued convincingly that theory development in communicative competence moves consistently into the direction of simulation and gaming, which enable the linking of several types of competence with cognitive and affective skills. The results of their empirical study are very convincing, and in support of their thesis about "declassrooming" the classroom.

The reader should be aware that during the design of games and simulations, explicit, enculturated, and possibly, local knowledge are embedded in these artifacts, which become available to the participants while they play. In line with Figure 3.4, they are complemented with tacit understanding resulting from playful gaming. Within the magic circle, the interactive learning environment provides the necessary conditions for making sense, and producing meaning about the subject matter. For example, business games are designed on the basis of micro-economic theory (explicit knowing). Those games are calibrated with data and information about a certain sector of the economy of one or several countries (e.g. manufacturing printers) (local knowledge), and based on fiscal accounting rules that apply to those sectors of the economy. These accounting rules, as well consumers' behavior modeled in the game, are expressions of the prevailing business culture (enculturated knowledge). During a game session, following the framework of Figures 3.1 and 3.2, the participants are put in the driver's seat of running "their companies" in the competitive market. They give meaning to the data, information, and knowledge becoming available during the dynamics of play, and interwoven in the game setting. A similar story can be told about MONOPOLY, and other games. It shows the meaning of Figure 3.4 at work. Therefore, framing the magic circle, presumes a well-defined and well-designed interactive learning environment.

In elementary, and the early years of high school, dedicated games should be tuned to the characteristics of the reproductive learning environment, enhancing the capacities of young children to playfully learn to read text, to do arithmetic, to perform group tasks, to interpret geographical maps, and to develop a sense of history. It all will enhance their enculturation in terms of their growing awareness of time and space, particularly with respect to their positioning game in physical, mental, private, and public space in our modern, tool rich, societies. Games frame playfully apprenticeship environments to experiment with behavior. Especially for youngsters, they should be valued for themselves.

Chapter 7, and more particularly the section on artifact assessment, provides more illustrations for underpinning the ideas on action learning, discussed above. In Chapter 7, I also discuss methodological questions related to assessing interactive learning environments from the design science viewpoint. The debate about the scientific underpinning of action-learning revolves around the feasibility of evidence-based research on learning applying textbook-style laboratory experiments with experimental and control groups, based upon the *principle of control, randomization, and comparison* (see also the ongoing discussions with respect to the What Works Clearinghouse (WWC): http://www.whatworks.ed.gov) I will argue that the related limited technical rationality does not correspond with the preconditions for meeting these three principles – both methodologically and technically – and therefore should be abandoned. Evidence-based research for learning in educational institutions is a form of flawed analysis. I consider upholding the requirements of evidence-based research on learning in (interactive) learning environments, under such conditions to be unscientific. As I will underpin my line of reasoning in Chapter 7, it is an example of applying the *analytical science* methodology to the realm of the *design science*, a wrong cross over of research methodology, and a weak basis for making causal inferences. Action learning should be assessed from the design science and not from the analytical science perspective. Being explicit in advance about the positions of the debaters would clarify key questions in the currently unfruitful debate, which seems to be more politically than scientifically driven.

Each learning environment requires specific and partially distinct capacities of the learners and the teachers corresponding with the qualities of the games. Teachers need to be well qualified as regards knowledge content of the games, the forms of knowledge in which it is framed, and the styles of reasoning that are practiced by the professionals involved. Connected to gaming sessions, and based on the debriefings, the pupils, understanding the knowledge content from the game experience, will have a chance to deepen their knowledge through the more traditional setting of lecturing and studying the subject matter at hand. Such alternating learning environments offer a broad spectrum of learning conditions. They presuppose school settings and school organizations that are tuned to the various learning goals of the reproductive, heuristic, and self-organizing learning environment (Klabbers, 1996). Questions about the suitable school organization as precondition for making the three learning environments effective go beyond the learning process as such. They condition it. They relate to the domain of educational policy and politics. That however is out of the scope of this chapter.

CHAPTER 4

A THEORY OF GAMING

INTRODUCTION

To grasp gaming is an important goal for a variety of disciplines, each of which uses different theoretical backgrounds and methodologies. This diversity of approaches results in a many-sided image of gaming and makes bridge building between particular perspectives both necessary and difficult. One possible solution is to explore specific domains, where different fields of study converge. Such an approach can provide a more detailed characterization of the common problems, as well as highlight the interpretative limitations of the specialized areas of research. That is, defining and investigating the existing points of convergence promotes establishment of foundations for a more coherent understanding of what gaming is. In Part II, I will present such a common and converging perspective. It goes beyond the specific knowledge domains of (mono-) disciplines and enlightens gaming from the viewpoint of social systems, more particularly social systems as complex adaptive systems. It offers a meta-disciplinary view, connecting various levels of organization.

This chapter addresses a theory of gaming. I will not discuss (mathematical) game theory for two reasons. Firstly, mathematical game theory (see chapter 1) is a special case of the more general theory that I will present here. In the next chapter, I will argue why it is a special case. Secondly, I have made a distinction between a game as a form of play, an artifact, and the dynamics of play. While using the term "gaming", I emphasize the activity of playing games in relation to forms of play. It is the interconnection between forms of play, and the evolving process – within the boundaries of the magic circle – that is the focus of my attention. An overarching theory is needed to encompass the total experience of game play. By definition it should be interdisciplinary, and as I will argue in the following chapters, meta-disciplinary. Those who are dealing with digital games play with the term *gameology*. I interpret that term to mean a design theory for digital games. It is an instrumental theory for those special artifacts. That also is not what I have in mind with gaming theory.

Whenever players enter the magic circle to play a game, they shape a real as well as an imaginary world. Therefore, games are both social systems and images or models of social systems. If being models that are used to study a real reference system, then the validity of the rules of correspondence between the model and the reference system is vital for developing and testing theories, and for implementing lessons learned from the exercises with the model. If games are used for entertainment, then the resemblance with a reference system such as, a particular city, neighborhood, building, etc. may help the player to enter that imaginary, virtual world, just for the fun. Like in science fiction, totally new worlds in outer space may trigger imagination. Also such virtual communities refer to social systems with their peculiar actors, bound by curious rules, and utilizing all sorts of interesting resources. Therefore, the central thesis of this chapter is: *games are social systems,* and moreover they represent social systems – real or imagined. They are also *models of social systems.* It is crucial to keep that dual position in mind. Even if a game involves one actor, that actor will always enter the magic circle with a social system, real or imagined, in mind. A player does not enter a social vacuum. For example, in the game GRAND THEFT AUTO, the individual player forces the avatar to move in a virtual city, engaging many other characters, and using resources such as cars, guns, the infrastructure of the city, roads, buildings, street signs, etc. Any game represents a symbolic world.

Actors that inhabit a social system constitute systems of interactions. They draw upon rules and resources while performing tasks. Through confirming each other's roles, and making use of the rules and resources, they produce and reproduce the social system concerned (Klabbers, 1986; Giddens, 1993). By changing the interactions, the rules and/or the resources, they either transform the system or produce a completely new one. They can switch position, from inside participant (actor) to outside observer (Klabbers, 1996). In this case, they can question their motives and personal efforts, the rules and/or the resources, to develop strategies for the maintenance or transformation of the social system. Underlying this approach to social systems are notions about autopoiesis (self-reproduction), self-reference, and reflexivity (self-awareness). Classical systems science, when applied to social systems, fits into the scientific tradition of rationalism, or positivism. It is called first-order systems theory. Current social systems theory builds on concepts such as, voluntarism (Parsons & Shils, 1951), autopoiesis (e.g., Maturana & Varela, 1980), structuration (Giddens, 1993), second-order systems theory (von Foerster, 1984), and constructivism (e.g., Dewey 1960; Piaget 1980; Kuhn 1962; von Foerster 1973; von Glasersfeld, 1991). Concepts such as *system, organization,* and *structure* play an important role in these approaches. I will discuss key concepts of complexity science as a frame-of-reference for gaming theory covering the notions expressed above. Complexity science offers an integrative framework for addressing the diversity of gaming artifacts, approaches, and processes. The reader is invited to use the terms *social system* and *game* interchangeably. For that reason, it may help to keep in mind games such as, INTERNATION SIMULATION, various business games, and massively multi-player online role-playing games (MMORPGs).

ON COMPLEX SYSTEMS

Complex Systems comprise interacting parts with the ability to generate a new quality of macroscopic collective behavior through self-organization. They have the capacity to produce the spontaneous formation of temporal, spatial or functional structures. The collective behavior of the whole system cannot be simply inferred from the understanding of the behavior of the individual components. To take this understanding on board, new concepts and sophisticated tools are needed. Key concepts and tools – with sometimes overlapping contents and methodologies are: self-organization, complex systems, adaptive systems, co-evolution, turbulence, catastrophes, instabilities, nonlinearity, and chaos. Gaming offers adequate tools for the study of social systems.

With respect to the study of complex adaptive systems one should recognize that playing the game changes the game. Earlier I have presented the basic structure of a game, consisting of the interrelationship between actors, rules, and resources. That structure is *recursive*: it repeats itself across hierarchical scales, and it is self-similar at the various levels of aggregation.

To grasp the meaning of complexity theory in the social and human domains, it is worthwhile to distinguish between *algorithmic, organizational and organized complexity*. *Algorithmic complexity* refers to calculability and reproducibility of systems (Stewart, 2001). It relates to the quantity of information to describe a system (Cohen & Stewart, 1995), to the minimal precursor pattern, the minimal templet, to (re-)construct the pattern (Katz, 1986). Moreover, algorithmic complexity is based on a systematic theory of models, relating the observer to the observed (Casti, 1994). The community of observers, dealing with this type of complexity, dons the lens of complexity through a variety of mathematical, systems-theoretical, cybernetic approaches. Focus is on a mechanistic, functionalistic approach to systems. It excludes organizations that observe themselves, rather than being observed. Therefore, algorithmic complexity as such is out of the scope of this book.

Organizational complexity relates to organizations in transition (Stewart, 2001). Complexity is explored as it emerges through far-from-equilibrium *dissipative, autopoietic,* or *self-organizing systems* in evolutionary space. This branch of complexity theory has its roots in evolutionary biology and the study of ecosystems, which increase or decrease in complexity as their component systems co-evolve (Kaufmann, 1993). It refers to the explanations of phenomena in which an a priori indeterminable number of microstates are narrowed down to a few biologically or socially relevant ones (Küppers, 1995). This is the case when no general explanations, or algorithms can adequately describe the relevant process, and a specific causative configuration is needed, but not yet available, to explain its unique history and further evolution. For example, general scientific explanations are not available, or are of less relevance to describe the particular circumstances that led to the attack on the Twin Towers in New York, the 11th of September 2001, or to describe the circumstances that caused a disease on the basis of a particular arrangement of DNA and living conditions. One might question the relevance of a scientific explanation of the particular sequence of microstates in a game of CHESS, or GO, providing the huge game space of both games. The game space of the simple board game AWARI contains 889.063.398.406 positions. CHESS and GO grow exponentially more complex. A simplified version of GO – a five by five game board – has recently been solved. Applying intelligent search- and learning techniques, van der Werf (2004) needed to search only 1.5 billion end positions instead of the theoretical 10^{25} end positions (complexity 25). These numbers give an indication of the dimensions of the term "game space". The processes involved select a unique and specific course through unimaginable large sequence spaces. Specific organization, structure and process produce order within such space. That order is understood and explained through knowledge of structural, systemic, and environmental histories and knowledge of the extent of information and means of interpretation (Stewart, 2001). This could be possible by grasping the context, or boundary conditions that lead to a unique history, and requires knowledge of local circumstances (local knowledge).

These distinctions do not take into consideration basic features of organizations that are self-observing, as they primarily pay attention to the perspective of the observer, who is positioned outside the system of study. Therefore, with respect to complexity of reflexive social systems, it is important to distinguish between the perspectives or positions of the outside/observer and inside/participant. From the observer's position, organizational complexity refers to the number of components, the degree of differentiation or diversity (variety) of these components, the degree of interdependence (connectedness) among these components, the emerging dynamic state space in connection with the swift and unpredictable changes (turbulence) of the environment.

To properly deal with gaming (read: social systems), in addition a third type of complexity is needed, which emerges through the self-awareness of the internal actors who cope with high levels of complexity of the internal organization of the social system vis-à-vis the environment. To a large extent this complexity emerges through the co-production of the actors involved. It is a form of negotiated order resulting from the strategic utilization of rules by competing interest groups in favor of certain forms of institutionalization. To distinguish this form of complexity, which is a social construction, from organizational complexity, which presupposes an outsider's and functionalist viewpoint, it is appropriate to speak of *organized complexity*. While organizational complexity is relevant for the study of gaming − from the viewpoint of the outside observer − organized complexity should be mainly understood from the perspective of the internal participants of a social system: the actors. This distinction requires a mental as well as an epistemological switch.

The distinction between on the one hand algorithmic and organizational complexity, and on the other hand, organized complexity becomes complicated when one recognizes the complexity of the human and social realms. Classifications in the human and social sciences are more difficult to handle than in the natural sciences. The classification "quark" or "ant" is indifferent in the sense that calling a quark a quark, or an ant an ant, makes no difference to them (Hacking, 1999). It does not influence their behavior. This is not the case in the social and human realm. Taking an example from the world of international relations, the classification "terrorist" (as a kind of classification) is an interactive kind because it interacts with "things" of that kind, namely people, including individual terrorists. They become aware of how they are classified and modify their behavior accordingly. They form an interactive, self-referential kind. Quarks in contrast do not form an interactive kind; the idea of quark does not interact with quarks (Hacking, op. cit.). The classification "quark" is invariant, while the classification "terrorist" changes with fluctuating political contexts. It is fruitful to study organizational complexity when dealing with indifferent kinds. However, referring to games, it is too limited a view when considering interactive kinds. In such case, I argue that organized complexity is a more fruitful idea. In the study of gaming, both organized and organizational complexity should be linked as they complement one another.

Organizational and organized complexity mingle in the study of social systems, as actors both observe themselves and are being observed by the other actors. Organized complexity refers to the subjectivity of perspective and relative position of actors within the social system, while they act and as a consequence self-reproduce the internal organization. Emphasis is on local, tacit, and enculturated knowledge. Organizational complexity refers to knowledge developed by a community of observers. Their emphasis is on inter-subjective explicit knowledge. Therefore, complexity theory of social systems has to take on board notions such as, *incentives, reflexivity, identity, opacity, particularity, uniqueness, locality,* and *incondensability*. In practical terms, views on organized complexity are translated in existing social systems through organizing on the basis of dialogue, commitment of members, agreeing on rules, and codes of conduct. While focusing on organizational and organized complexity of gaming, algorithmic complexity is out of the scope.

KEY CONCEPTS RELEVANT FOR GAMING THEORY

Whenever a new frame of organization is introduced it is worthwhile to dwell upon its basic views, and on the background of the ideas that are articulated. *Complexity* is associated with epistemic processes: discovering the rules underlying the universe in its diversity, from atoms to galaxies, from living systems to societies. The interpretation of complexity is closely linked to the idea of organization, which is a fundamental way of thinking about our world in an organized way.

The terms *complexity* and *complex systems* refer to particular behavior of systems far-from-equilibrium. It will not be easy to demonstrate the usefulness of complexity theory for the study of gaming. Adequately developing, experimenting with, and validating gaming models of for example business organizations, face considerable theoretical and practical difficulties. The risks of real-time experimenting with far-from-equilibrium systems are too high from ethical and practical viewpoints. It may for example lead to bankruptcy of companies involved, to hazards of social security and health of the people involved, even before the experiment is over. If this type of experimenting is out of the question, what next best option is available?

Organization & system

I will first address basic views on organization. Its idea refers to qualities of interrelated parts that form a whole. It relates to the universe in its diversity such as atoms, molecules, our planet, stars, living organisms, humans, business organizations, institutions, and societies. These different entities are not reducible to each other. They have in common that each is made up of organized elements that form a whole. Terms that convey the meaning of that whole are *system, organization, network,* and *interrelation.* Systems operate within well-defined boundaries. Networks have limits that vary. Both represent interconnections of elements and form an organized whole. Organization connects parts to each other and parts to the whole. Pascal has expressed the circular reciprocity between parts and the whole by pointing out that it is impossible to know the parts without knowing the whole, or to know the whole without knowing the parts (Pascal, 1897). The terms system, organization, network and interrelation, although they are inseparable, can be distinguished from each other. Morin (1999, p. 115) argued that the term system, as in living systems, scatters the quality of being and existing. It diverts attention from living beings and their existential dimension by focusing on the way they function. The meaning of organization implies that attention is paid to the inside to understand a particular combination of parts and their interrelationships with the whole. This implies that we should talk about "the system," and "this organization." The notion of organization, as in living systems, is related to understanding the internal composition of the whole. It pays attention to local circumstances. The notion of system refers to generic qualities of all systems, social systems included.

Ashby (1968) has pointed out that the concept of organization is related to the treatment of *conditionality* between entities or parts. The essential idea is the product space of *possible* interactions between parts and some subset of points, showing the actual interactions. This implies that conditionality is a constraint in the product-space of possibilities. Through different degrees of conditionality various forms of organization are established. This implies that conditionality refers to linkages between the entities that is, their interrelationships. The peculiarity of the product space is "that it contains more than actually exists in the physical world ... The real world gives the subset of what is: the product space represents the uncertainty of the observer" (Ashby, 1968, p. 109). Ashby continued by saying that a substantial part of the theory of organization is concerned with properties that are not intrinsic to the entity but are relational between observer and entity.

Emergence

Morin (1999) mentioned that all organizations produce something beyond their components:
- the organization itself;
- the global unit constituting the whole;
- the new qualities and properties that emerge from the organization and global unit.

These new qualities or properties are called *emergences*. Emergences have an innovative character with respect to the qualities of the components taken separately or structured differently in another type of system. The properties of the whole are not the sum of the parts. The whole behaves differently in all circumstances. For example, the living cell has emerging properties unknown to macromolecules outside its biological organization: it feeds, metabolizes, and reproduces. Similarly, a company cannot be regarded as the sum of all the individuals that compose it. It is an entity with specific and unique qualities. This applies as well to playing a game. It generates more than the sum of actions by individual players. Moreover, it is a shared process and experience.

Emerging qualities feed back on the parts and give them qualities that they could not have if they were isolated from the organizing whole. The whole is not only more than the sum of the parts, but the part of that whole is more than a part by virtue of the whole (Morin, 1999). This applies especially to games with actors as parts of a special kind: parts that reflexively interact in the construction of the social system.

Emergence is a basic property of organization. It has a new quality that arises once the organization is formed. The idea of emergence connects *quality, product* (the emergence is produced by the organization of the system), *totality* (because it is indissoluble from the global unit), and *innovation* (because it is a new quality with respect to previous qualities of the single elements). Emergence sometimes seems to be an epiphenomenon, a product or result; at other times it is the main force constituting the originality of the organized entity (Morin, 1999, p. 119). For example, group identity is a global outcome of people interacting and interfering, inseparable from the interactions and interferences resulting from that identity on the individual. It is possible to conceive it as an epiphenomenon. Group identity can also rightly be viewed as a superstructure, resulting from within the organization that manifests itself in a superficial and fragile way, like all that is secondary and dependent. This description ignores the feedback of group identity on ideas, behavior and being of individuals, and the revolution it causes i.e., identity of us against them. This description ignores the completely new and sometimes, decisive dimension that the self-critical attitude of group identity can bring to personality, as is shown within-group dynamics. The very irreducibility of the concept of emergence either to superstructure, epiphenomenon, or totality makes it a complex whole. This assertion is illustrated in the example of the outdoor gaming exercise, sketched in Chapter 1.

Morin warned of reducing organization to *structure*. He said that organization means structure, relation to wholeness, specific characters, relations between the whole and the parts, unity-multiplicity, and emergences. Therefore the notion of structure becomes inadequate to capture the notion of organization. That notion opposes *dissociation*, which breaks up the complex unit, and *reduction to holism*, which suffocates the micro-levels of the constituent parts. Organization establishes a circular relation, an understanding from the whole to the parts and vice versa. The whole produces qualities unknown to the isolated parts, namely emergences, and at the same time establishes constraints that suffocate qualities (by a specific treatment of conditionality between parts) and renders virtual certain possibilities of the parts. Hence, the whole is not necessarily superior to its parts (Morin, 1999).

To illustrate this point, the bureaucratic regime of a company may inhibit qualities of its employees that are richer than those of the whole. The richer emergences belonging to the employees, as for example noticed through group identity, may emerge in individuals but not in that company. Such a company would not live up to its potentials. To demonstrate inhibiting forces of a bureaucratic regime, emergent qualities are not simply built into games. It would imply that the designer could mechanically define them in advance. That would contradict by definition the emergent qualities.

Social insect behavior offers another interesting example. It sheds light on rule-driven behavior of individual ants and its effect on the organization of ants. Ants, bees and bacteria display sophisticated kinds of cooperative behavior as a survival strategy. Based on a few and simple rules, ants self-organize and show *swarm intelligence* (Bonabeau et al., 2000). It is an emergent property of organization, not available to individual ants. That rule-driven behavior of single ants results in collective intelligence, which produces the mechanical outcome of swarm behavior.

Related to complexities of organization, and the non-reducibility of emergence, is the concept *dialogic*, a principle of knowledge that conceives that antagonistic forces complement one another (Morin, 1999). Before addressing this issue further, let me first illustrate how it works by raising the following question: How can large, complex organizations solve the problems of normal functioning that is efficient operations, reduction of complexity, control, and governance, and still embody the tensions which power innovation? Complex organizations have difficulty with innovation. They have to perform a delicate balancing act between opposing forces and coalitions. For effective product innovation the following sets of dialogic activities need to be taken into account (Dougherty, 1996):

1. Conceptualizing the product to enable the integration of market needs and technological potential (market-technology linking): balancing the tension between outside and inside;
2. Organizing the process to accommodate creative problem solving: balancing the tension between old and new;

3. Monitoring the process: balancing the tension between determination and emergence; and
4. Developing commitment to the effort of innovation: balancing the tension between freedom and responsibility.

The complementary antagonistic forces are clearly demonstrated via these steering dilemmas. They demonstrate the more fundamental of forces of organization and disorganization. Weick and Westley (1996) have captured this tension as well by pointing out that organizing and learning are essentially two antithetical processes. They state that to learn is to disorganize and increase variety. To organize is to forget and reduce variety. This notion implies that through organizational learning, the parts, their interrelationships, the whole, and emergences will change. Organizing implies freezing contingencies between the parts by means of inducing particular sets of constraints. Due to the complex meaning and volatile features of organization, the outcomes of emergences over time are difficult to comprehend, especially when the system is not isolated and exchanges information and energy with its environment. *Attractors* may limit the variety of emergences. They are behavior patterns to which the system tends to recur.

Attractors

Gharajedaghi (1999, p. 51) has presented four attractors that determine the nature of recurring patterns:
1. *Point attractor* – drawn to or repelled from a particular and single activity or goal;
2. *Cycle attractor* – oscillation between two or more activities: see dialectic of four tensions mentioned above;
3. *Torus attractor* – a certain form of organized complexity repeating itself (goal-seeking);
4. *Strange attractor* – unpredictable complex patterns emerging over time (self-organizing).

Applying his notions to the four dialogic activities, pointed out above, several attractors can be observed. For example, a company may be drawn to or repelled from a certain set of forces, for example by clinging to one narrow-minded goal. In such case, a *point attractor* is dominant. Such a company will have difficulty with facing innovation. In another organizational configuration, the dynamic equilibrium between the dialogic set of activities may show an oscillation, a periodic shift of emphasis from one set of forces in the policy arena to another. The emergent property of that system is a *cycle attractor* when the opposing forces keep each other in a balanced gridlock, limiting further growth. When the dialogic set of activities moves out of such a mutual inhibiting situation and results in a growth pattern, than a *torus attractor* is at work. Suppose, it is fruitful to redesign the system, a new choice of ends and means may lead to unpredictable growth patterns, emerging out of new preferences of purposeful actors. Such type of self-organization creates a *strange attractor.* No two steering measures or outcomes are ever the 'same', thus ruling out simple mechanistic models of steering.

So far I have paid attention to parts, wholes, their interrelationships, organization and system, to gather the idea of emergence. What can be said in systemic terms of the direction of emergence?

As mentioned above, classifications in the human and social sciences are more difficult to handle than in the natural sciences. If the distinction between *indifferent and interactive kinds* (Hacking, 1999) is excluded from the conceptual design, than game theory will be reduced to a purely mechanical, functional approach, leaving out self-referential characteristics of the actors. Roles need to be checked for their looping effect that is, the interaction between an idea or category and the persons playing the related role. This observation is particularly relevant as games evolve through the interactions between the actors. Social order emerges continuously from the interactions between human actors, which to a certain extent are viewed as cognitive agents. Social structure is constituted by human agency, and it is the medium through which it is constituted (Giddens, 1993). It is self-referential and based upon reflexive social actors. Therefore, attractor models of social systems should take into account the duality of structure as well as the looping effect of role descriptions as classifications of a certain kind.

Here, I will pay attention to the *qualitative articulation of complexity* while focusing on attractors within social systems. The high dimensionality and dynamic flux of events, uniqueness of circumstances, and self-referential features – to a large extent intangible – hamper a straightforward application of formal, mathematical models to social systems (Klabbers, 2000, 2001, 2002). One should realize that especially new conceptual frameworks in the natural and social sciences ultimately rely on ordinary language (Bergstein, 1972). Schrodt (1988) mentioned that the mathematical chaos theory describes systems whose general behavior is predictable but whose specific, micro-level behavior is not. Rigorously applied to social systems whose general behavior is not predictable, the conclusion is that such the quantitative articulation of complexity for two reasons not (yet) feasible: (1) It is not possible to formalize key qualities of social systems, and (2), in case it would be feasible, the data and information, necessary to validate it are usually not available. Moreover, in order to understand how co-evolution between actors within a social system works, focus of interest should be the micro-level behavior of the constituting actors. In a game, global behavior emerges from the co-evolving actions of the actors. That awareness influences the ongoing game, and will be a topic of conversations during the debriefing and further assessments. For these reasons, I emphasize a conceptual approach to complexity of social systems. Sallach (2000, p. 251) suggested that such conceptual models include identification of:

1. The existence of an attractor pattern: a certain social order,
2. The origin and termination processes of the attractor pattern (if any),
3. The field boundaries of the attractor influence,
4. The attractor basin(s), and
5. Possible control parameters.

Open systems

Social systems are thermodynamically open. According to the Second Principle of Thermodynamics, they can progress only because they interact with their environment. Therefore, social systems are *open systems*. They survive because they reproduce their organization. That is to say, they keep their organization invariant (autonomous and stable) by replacing destroyed elements. They do it through interactions with their environment. They draw boundaries to distinguish the system from its environment. Such form of closure is needed for its reproduction. Thus, social systems are both operationally closed and thermodynamically open. The material resources obey the laws of thermodynamics. They use energy and other resources to survive. Therefore, social systems are as well *dissipative systems*. The social organization as such reproduces the system of meaning via the systems of interactions between the actors. To preserve its identity, that part of the system is operational closed. Accordingly, *closure* is a basic property of open systems. It enables the system to maintain some form of identity – stability – in its environment.

A consequence of these notions is a linking of natural systems that are matter and energy-connected and obey laws of physics, with human systems that are idea-connected. Therefore, social systems are *hybrid systems*, drawing attention from widely different knowledge domains.

The laws of thermodynamics are viewed as constraints on the development of ecosystems. Only processes that follow the conservation principle and consume *exergy* are possible (Jørgensen, 1999). Jørgensen notes that a flow of exergy through the system is sufficient to form an ordered, *dissipative structure*.

Exergy is defined as the work the system can perform when it is brought into equilibrium with the environment or another well-defined reference state (Jørgensen, 1999, p. 320).

A dissipative structure brings forward the emergence of organization in terms of its total performance, considering the conditions of the environment. Ecological and social systems have many possibilities for moving away from thermodynamic equilibrium. Evolution has been toward organisms with many genes that are actually used (information genes) and more types of cells i.e., emergence of more complex wholes with more information content. In line with this argumentation, evolution of social systems moves toward collective networks with increasing information carrying capacity and more diversity of competence through complex wholes such as teams, business units, companies, and institutions, bringing forward a more differentiated organization. Information technology is an important driving force in this regard.

The essence of a social system as an open system is the necessity to invoke an outside, or an *environment*, in order to understand what takes place in the inside of the system, that in its turn expels it to look outward. What takes place inside the system can be understood in correspondence and comparison with the outside (Rosen, 1991). This understanding implies that the outside is constructed and enacted from the inside. The environment is not simply "reality out there" to which the social system re-acts.

To account for what an open system is doing, the linkage between 'inside' and 'outside' forces us to look at the larger systems' perspective. The idea of open systems requires us to accept levels of scale in understanding their behavior. This is why reductionism, or analysis, which only permits us to decompose a system and its behavior into subsystem behavior, fails for our understanding of open systems (Alvarez de Lorenza, 2000). The inside-outside linkage implies that, inside the system, means are available to observe both the outside and the boundary. Alvarez de Lorenza and many others pointed out that open systems, in order to relate to the environment, construct images of their environment. Such modeling is to be understood as a semiotic process. Closure is the active, self-referential process from the inside to distinguish the system from the outside.

Semiotic processes – semiotically closed systems – involve perception, interpretation, decision, and action with the environment. As I have argued, the environment is enacted, based on the characteristics of the inside. It is a social construction. These semiotic processes involve a *reference* and an *interpretation of sign tokens,* maintained in coding relation with their interpreters: the actors. Use and interpretation of symbols, representations, and internal models by the actors (whether explicit or implicit) are keys for understanding social systems. In addition, we should focus on the syntactic, semantic and pragmatic relations among sign tokens, their interpretations, and their use and function for the system in question. The coding nature of symbol systems is arbitrary – the symbol refers to its referent when interpreted by an actor, acting within the constraints of the symbol system (Joslyn, 2000).

Closure

The idea of open systems leads to *levels of scale* in understanding their behavior. The inside-outside linkage implies that the inside of the system has means available to observe both the outside and the boundary. Alvarez de Lorenza (2000) and many others have pointed out that the system, in order to relate to its environment, models that environment. That expression in itself is confusing, as long as it is not made clear what such modeling is all about. Model theory offers a wide variety of types of models and approaches to modeling. In addition, it should be clear what is meant with the system, "modeling its environment". Is such a model merely a mirror or image, or is it a symbol, that enacts the environment. Related to this notion of a model is the meaning of 'knowledge'. How complete should be a model of and our knowledge about the system? The inside-outside distinction is relevant when considering the limited resources the system has available to model its environment. For the "birth" of an open system, what type of model or knowledge of the environment is necessary and sufficient to make it happen?

The inside-outside linkage implies also that we can speak of a difference, an interface, a distinction in terms of space and time between the system and its environment. Will temporal, and spatial integration suffice for a model to be adequate? Can sequences of action by the system be explained through successions of external stimuli, mirrored or symbolized by the system? Will integration exclusively be found in language in general, or in the modeling language in particular? Is it the system that makes the distinction, or is it some outside observer?

Based on these questions on open systems, Joslyn (2000) recognized two types of scaling: *spatial scaling,* running from subatomic particles to astronomical objects, and *complexity scaling* evolving from subatomic particles through chemical to social systems. Both are characterized by the same concepts: wholes and parts, insides and outsides, and alternating levels of variation and constraint. Joslyn (op. cit.), while looking for a general descriptive language to cover these concepts, proposed the term *closure,* and a *typology of closures.* Closure concepts relate to *boundaries, hierarchy,* and *system identity.* Joslyn (op. cit.) aimed at synthesizing general notions of systems, and distinguished two approaches to systems definition:

- *Structural definition*: comprising parts, attributes, relationships, and whole with new properties at a level hierarchically distinct from the parts.

- *Constructivist definition*: viewing a system as a bounded region of some (abstract) space that functionally and uniquely distinguishes it.

The last definition emphasizes distinctions between system and environment drawn by people (Goguen & Varela, 1979). It relates to constructivist epistemology, nominalism, and second-order cybernetics (Von Foerster, 1981) with as its objects first-order cybernetics (Atmanspacher, 1997). Joslyn noted that this understanding is also used in classical physics, more particularly in thermodynamics, where a system is "any quantity of matter, any region of space, etc., which is selected for study and set apart (mentally) from everything else, which then becomes the surroundings" (Abbot & Van Ness, 1972, p.1, cited in Josly, 2000, p. 68).

Joslyn remarked that (physical) constructivists such as Kampis (1991) and Rosen (1991) emphasize open-ended systems that frame their own elements and universes of discourse through the emergent processes of their own self-modification and self-creation. These systems are not *composed of* objects – as in the *realist epistemology*. They are *defined on* objects – as in the nominalist epistemology.

The term *closure* only makes sense, if there exists a boundary between system and environment, consisting of boundary elements that belong to the system, and yet are influenced by the environment. Joslyn further distinguished two forms of relations (entailments, forces, influences) that flow through a system-environment boundary:

- One-directional input-output relations (linear input-throughput-output sequences);
- Circular relations (feedback-loops) (reciprocal simultaneous flows across boundaries).

Circular relations identify closures that are the mechanism for system formation. Joslyn noted that circular relations at the system's boundary strongly connect the system with its environment, creating a new system at a next higher level of aggregation. The closure of the former system-environment coupling becomes the interior of the new system at meta-systems level, forming a new boundary with the environment. It is distinct from one-directional system-environment relations that still exist with the former system. This idea is applied in System Dynamics (SD) modeling in the sense that an SD model includes for example both the circular relations between a company and its market, which together form the "newly closed system" represented in the model. Boundaries distinguish processes that are included (inside), from those that are excluded from the closure (outside). Based on these notions, Joslyn pointed out that each form of closure introduces a form of hierarchical scaling. Spatial scaling is smaller, and temporal scaling is faster on the inside as compared to the outside. These forms of scaling provide the system a temporary stability, autonomy and identity. Simon (1969) used these ideas on scaling while discussing *nearly decomposable systems*. Through closures, boundaries, and hierarchies, open systems establish (temporary) stability and identity.

In terms of closures and throughputs, Joslyn distinguished two extreme classes of systems: *totally closed and totally open systems*. An example of a totally closed system is an idealized adiabatic isolation leading to thermodynamic equilibrium. In thermodynamics, an *adiabatic process* is a process in which no heat is transferred to or from working fluid. The term "adiabatic" literally means an absence of heat transfer; for example, an *adiabatic boundary* is a boundary that is impermeable to heat transfer. The system is said to be adiabatically (or thermally) insulated. An insulated wall approximates an adiabatic boundary. A transformation of a thermodynamic system can be considered adiabatic when it is quick enough so that no significant heat transfer happens between the system and the outside. In totally open systems, all objects are in the boundary, none in the interior, only throughputs of linear flows, leading to loss of identity. Such open systems cease to exist as distinct systems. A transformation of a thermodynamic system can be considered *isothermal* if it is slow enough so that the system's temperature can be maintained by heat exchange with the outside. With respect to heat exchange, it is totally open.

Real complex systems are in between these extremes, constituting degrees of balance between one-directional and circular processes. This frame of reference enabled Joslyn (op cit.) to distinguish four types of closure:

- *Control systems* – causal closures stabilizing controlled variables (semiotic closure);
- *Self-referential systems* – closure of reference within a system via a formal language or a natural linguistic community, bringing forward referential autonomy;
- *Self-organizing systems* through:
  - o *Mechanistic rules* – autocatalytic processes, attractors of dynamical systems;
  - o *Modifying rules* – reframing (re-arranging) organization;
- *Self-reproducing systems* (autopoiesis) – creation of self-producing systems.

The term *closure* includes one crucial property that is, *scalar hierarchy*, which denotes discrete levels in complex systems. Havel (1996) argued that *scale* is a dimensional unit similar to space, time and mass. Following this line of reasoning, discrete levels of hierarchy are represented as discrete entities along the scalar dimension. These discrete levels are absent with fractal structures. Their self-similarity is smeared to different extents across a wide range of scalar values. Objects can participate in multiple kinds of relations, possibly existing in multiple closures simultaneously (Joslyn, 2000). Scalar hierarchy brings forward multiple, hierarchically nested levels of systems and control relations.

Open systems – in their capacity of semiotically closed systems – involve processes of *perception, interpretation, decision,* and *action* with their environments. Joslyn said that these semiotic processes involve the reference and interpretation of sign tokens, which are maintained in (contingent) coding relations with their interpretants. This gives rise to issues such as, the use and interpretations of symbols, representations by the system, and the syntactic, semantic, and pragmatic relations among sign tokens, their interpretations, and their use or function for the system (Josly, 2000, p. 72).

This style of reasoning about open, semiotic systems brings forward a frame of reference for gaming and simulation, particularly for their design. It is summarized in Table 4.1.

Semiotic relations are contingent, meaning that the symbol and its referent share no properties in common. The symbol refers to its referent (reference system) when interpreted by an agent acting within the constraints of the symbol system. Purely physical systems – in contrast – are characterized by necessary functional entailments (Joslyn, 2000).

Co-evolution

Complex social systems (games) evolve through:
o   A medium number of actors, with
o   The ability to change rules i.e., demonstrating self-reference and intelligence,
o   While acting on local information.

The actors shape systems of interactions: the social organization. They draw on rules and resources while performing tasks. Through their actions, they produce and reproduce the social system. By changing the interactions, rules and/or resources, they either transform the system or produce a completely new one. Through their actors, social systems sustain *intentionality*, *expectancy*, and *memory*.

As has been pointed out above, *emergence* is a basic property of organization. Emergence is being shaped through *co-evolution within* the social system in combination with its *adaptation to the environment.* Evolution of one subsystem (actor) depends partially on the evolution of the other. In other words, each actor changes in the context – the local environment – of the other.

Table 4.1. Design & analysis options of open systems: games and simulations

Open Systems	Design & Analysis Options			
	Non-reflexive systems: Mechanistic application of rules		Reflexive systems: Construction of rules	
	Referential systems: Machines	Self-referential systems: Robots	Self-Organizing systems: Self-arranging	Self-reproducing systems: Self-creation
Perspectives	Structural tradition		Constructivist tradition	
	Linear relations	Circular relations: -Autocatalytic cycles; -Attractors	Circular relations: Self-modification	Circular relations: Self-creation
	Types of closure			
Outside Observer & Signifier	Transitive Spatial Causal Syntactic	Organizational Topological Time	Semiotic Semantic	Semiotic Symbolic
Inside Participant & Signifier		Time closure	Self-closure; Linguistic operational closure	Psychic closure

Co-evolution takes place via interacting actors that change in terms of internal dynamics during the same time span. In social systems, there is always a tension between short-term adaptation and long-term adaptability. Co-evolution in social systems expresses itself through the evolution of the system of interactions between actors, which shapes the emerging organization.

When reflecting on the actors, it is appropriate to distinguish between two positions: the position of the outside observers and the position of the inside actors. This distinction implies two types of closure, the closure drawn by the outside observer and the closure enacted by the inside actor. The observer has to deal with two types of models: the observer's model of the actor and the actor's internal model. The observer can only approximate the actor's internal model through the indirect experience of it by the observer. Therefore, the articulations of the truths of the observer and actor's models must be partial and circumstantial. It is a situation of double undecidability (Boxer & Cohen, 2000).

A social system is shaped through an interrelated collection of actors that in concert enable the system to achieve its purposes. Actors, through their system of interactions, are the essential forces of social regularities, forces that structure and restructure social systems and the conditions of human activity. Actors produce social systems as historically located, under the conditions of their own choosing. The idea of *organization* should not be conceptualized as simply placing constraints upon human agency, but more as enabling. Duality of structure means that organization is constituted through action, and reciprocally, action is constituted structurally. Processes of structuration involve the interplay of meanings, norms and power. Through the idea of duality of structure, social structure is both constituted by human agency and at the same time the very medium of this constitution (Giddens, 1993). Here the term "agency" refers to actors of a certain type: institutions.

Boxer and Cohen (2000) considered agents to be systems with the following properties:

- *Composite* − relying on the capabilities of other agents − they act on local knowledge;
- *Emergent* − not being a mere static aggregate of those capabilities;
- *Purposive* − having their own goals and seeking to achieve them − they are action oriented;
- *Anticipatory* − capable of choosing among possible actions on the basis of their own internal model (image, idea) of its world − based on limited information processing capacity;
- *Adaptive* − capable of learning and thereby modifying both their organization and their internal model with a view to improving their performance.

In complex adaptive systems, actors never possess a perfect model of their environment, which contains other actors that are continuously changing. They acquire information about it only through interacting with it, never having total information about its current state. The actors co-evolve. They have limited knowledge and resources, such as matter, information and funds. Therefore, they cannot hold a large group of potential models of their environment, including models of the fellow actors. Through increasing synergy, system's behavior can far exceed the capacity of single actors. Through decreasing synergy, the system may collapse, ceasing to be adaptive, or to exist.

Coordination (steering)

"Coordination" is a key concept to manage organized complexity. It deals for example with balancing over time the four tensions, mentioned above. To relate and compare actors and resources, a form of equivalence between signs and technological tools is needed. However:

> A form of equivalence, which implies the realism of signs (logo, trademark, etc.), does not offer the same possibility of calculus as the one based on the realism of technical and functional tools. The comparison of these forms of equivalence demonstrates that time and space take different configurations in each of them, with significant consequences on judgment (Thévenot, 2001, p. 408).

Signs are social constructs, appealing to conventions, and are by their very nature arbitrary. In order to deal with different configurations of coordination, or steering in social systems, Thévenot presented a principle of evaluation via the following three orders of *worth*, enabling various modes of coordination.

- An elementary form of attachment between human beings and their environments, which include humans and material. Their attachments with material enhance human capacities, and are considered resources. Via these attachments, human beings relate to the world. New configurations of links emerge through identification and development of new equipment such as for example information systems.
- The extension of the attachment via specialization and development of this equipment, complementary to human abilities. For example by improving visibility with proper equipment of visibility (microscope, spectacles, etc), or building airplanes to be able to fly.
- The systematized attachment between human beings and animals requires a reflection on justice that is, about just and unjust power. It corresponds to the political and moral requirements of public space, and nature.

By emphasizing equipment, complementary to human abilities, Thévenot (2001) ignored the role of technology as competitive to human abilities. The related technological imperative should not be neglected in understanding current forces of economic development and innovation.

One important order of worth is still missing. It relates to the attachments among human beings as members of an organization. It is an attachment that gives shape to the system of interaction between actors.

- An additional attachment related to market and industrial order is needed especially in the case when a market good is a service. It refers to the attachment between institutional agents and the way they construct and disseminate explicit and tacit knowledge within their internal organization, and convey it to the environment that is, the market. This form of attachment is increasingly mediated through information technology, creating a virtual world, which for many people is real.

Complexity results from these forms of attachment. Through compromises, the critical relationships between the resulting modes of coordination can be made compatible, both temporarily and spatially. Social systems are arrangements that have to deal with such an organized complexity, based on distinct coordination conventions. Members of such systems engage in different modes of coordination, depending on the configuration of the situation in which they find themselves, and which they enact. All socials systems have to cope with critical tensions between these different orders of worth.

THE EMERGENCE OF ORGANIZED COMPLEXITY

Collective networks – communities of practice

Weick (1979) has introduced the term, *interlocked behavior* to link the individual behaviors of persons. He used the term *double interact* to describe contingent action and response patterns. A *double interact* is a sequence in which an action by individual actor A evokes a specific response in actor B (A and B interact), which is subsequently responded to by actor A. Actor A may affirm, accept, modify, reject, revise, abandon, deny B's response. That sequence constitutes a double interact. When this sequence of interactions between both actors continues over time, behaviors become interlocked, shaping a double interact that shows dynamic stability. Actors A and B are sustaining a relationship. The idea of double interact does not refer to the kind of relationship between A and B; to the content and context of each interact. It also does not tell us anything about the incentives of people involved, their interests, needs, norms and values to shape or glue the interact into a double interact. Their meaning can only be established in concrete social settings with real actors.

If more than two persons – individual actors – become involved in mutually building and maintaining double interacts, collective structures emerge that rapidly go beyond our comprehension. In such networks, simultaneously many interacts are happening that we are not aware of. People do not invest all their time and effort in one double interact and one particular collective structure. Commitments to double interacts are dispersed among several collective networks. Individual actors are partially included in each of them. They allocate their efforts over various networks dependent on their shifting interests, motives, needs, etc. Some interacts stay within one network, and simultaneously the actors look outside the network for significant persons who respond to some of their actions. Viability of those networks depends on the degree of commitment to preserve and perpetuate the system of interactions.

Allport (1962) has suggested that people give shape to collective networks by first converging on shared ideas of forming an organization i.e., on common means. Subsequently, they activate a repetitive series of interlocked behaviors. First people converge on diverse means rather than on common goals (Weick, 1979). People create organization, which subsequently forms the basis of contingencies on the actions of all participating actors. Individual human beings through empathy are capable of joint attention. Such ability makes human beings pre-eminently social. This implies that they simultaneously focus on surrounding objects and each other. As a consequence human beings engage in mutually referential triangles encompassing each other and the surrounding abstract and concrete objects. Such referential triangles are embedded in the double interacts. In a wider scope, this understanding is part of the play element of culture. In the growth and transfer of culture from one generation to another, *mimicry* plays an important role. Interlocked behavior, so understood, always refers to the natural environment and the social constructs, images that are relevant in a culture. In computer games, as in every game, such referential triangles are a basic part of the game design, while the players may not be aware of them.

Collective networks, based on double interacts, resemble communities of practice. Wenger (2002) has addressed this issue in great detail. Competent membership of such communities includes:

- *Mutuality of engagement* – participating through building and maintaining double interacts,
- *Accountability* to the common enterprise – responsibility taking – and,
- *Negotiability* of the repertoire of practice – the (inter-) action repertoire of the members; in other words, the rules of the game.

The notion of emergence of collective structures based upon interlocking behaviors of individuals allows the scaling up from individual to institutional actors.

Duality of structure

Groups become institutionalized, double interacts become ritualized, and the resulting actors are being treated as abstract objects to which we attribute independent existence. They become reified. This is expressed in terms such as "democracy", "the economy", "the invisible hand", which have become abstractions that we treat as substantially existing. Their emergent properties are not reducible to the behaviors of individuals. Although democracy is socially constructed, as an abstract object it is real. Democracy may be ontologically subjective. It is epistemologically objective. Giddens (1993) speaks in this regard of duality of structure.

> Interaction is constituted by and in the conduct of subjects; structuration, as the reproduction of practices, refers abstractly to the dynamic process whereby structures come into being...Social structure is both constituted *by* human agency and is at the same time the *medium* of this constitution (Giddens 1993, p. 128).

Institutions exist through the reproduction of practices of its members and by doing they produce a certain collective structure. That structure is also the medium for reproducing the organizational structure. It brings forward the codes of conduct and the navigation system for the members to understand the meaning of communication and to confirm that same structure.

Actors constitute systems of interactions. They draw upon rules and resources, and thereby reproduce them in the course of their day-to-day activities. They may distance themselves from the rules and resources, in order to question them, or to build theories about them, or even more importantly, to devise strategies for either their maintenance or their transformation (Giddens, 1993). The related idea of duality of structure includes the option that actors confront rules and resources as 'objects' in the social environment.

By changing the interactions, the rules and/or the resources, they either transform the system or produce a completely new one. Underlying this approach to social systems are notions about autopoiesis (self-reproduction), self-reference, and reflexivity (self-awareness).

Enduring patterns

To reflect on enduring patterns of social systems, the emphasis on structure and organization, initiated in action, interaction, and double-interaction, needs further elaboration. Archer (1995) mentioned that humans, engaging in social activity, produce structures and cultures that have emergent properties of their own. Such properties, as pointed out above, are sustained by and reproduced by human activity. She noted that the related temporal dimension is not explicit in the structuration theory of Giddens. Archer has made her point explicit through the concept of *morphogenetic cycle*, representing cycles of social interaction of actors. Archer was interested in constructing analytic narratives, which implies that she has taken the position of the outside observer, emphasizing the social realist position. I prefer to focus on the social construction of structures as collective networks, taking a nominalist position. Accordingly, I have adjusted her line of reasoning as follows. The morphogenetic cycle is represented in Figure 4.2.

Tn^1 Structural conditioning

    Tn^2 Social interaction Tn^3

        Structural (re-)framing Tn^4

            $Tn+1^1$ Structural conditioning

For n, the cycle number, 1,2, etc.

Figure 4.1. The morphogenetic cycle (adjusted from Archer, 1995)

Archer (1995) argued that in observing any series of social interactions, we must not start at T^2, that is, when the social interaction takes place, but rather at T^1, when the structural conditioning – the process of organizing – was formed through interlocking behaviors. It is the initial stage of organized complexity. She argued that Giddens was not explicit about this distinction. Such structural conditioning happens through institutions, markets, or sets of ideas by for example political parties. They form the *medium* constituting the interactions. The participants in this process of structural conditioning are not just be recipients of information, at times they are agents, referees, and reciprocators. Therefore, at T^4 the participants seek to understand the relationships between the structural conditions and the actions that take place, and consider the structural elaborations that then take place. For the observer, the series of interactions are a reference system, for the participants they form a self-referential system that triggers their reflexivity. The participating actors may decide to develop strategies for the maintenance or transformation of the social system and its specific form of structural conditioning. Through this linking of action and structure the traditional dichotomy is being resolved. Actions refer to processes in a network, and structure to the intermediate states of those processes. Actions, and in the context of gaming inter-actions, shape organization with emergent properties, based on intended and unintended consequences of those inter-actions. This raises the question of the durability of networks. Mutch

(2002) proposed two valuable notions: *inscription* and *irreversibility* to support sustainability.

> The construction of networks that are durable involves the inscription into material form of the assumptions that underpin the interests of particular actors in the network. In many organizations, for example, particular ways of working (notably within functional boundaries) are inscribed into software, inscriptions that subsequently make other forms of action difficult. The degree of difficulty depends on the irreversibility of such inscriptions, of unraveling the enrolments that happened to construct such inscriptions (p. 490).

The term *inscription* is similar to Wenger's use of the term *reification*. It is certainly the case that, due to progressing use of Information Technology, particular ways of working are inscribed into software. More generally speaking, in social systems, behavior becomes increasingly interlocked through rules and procedures embedded in the hard- and software: see for example the Internet. The inscription into material form, although important to notice, fits into that wider form of organizing. Inscriptions are particular forms of reification.

Previously I have introduced attractors that indicate behavior patterns of complex systems. On a higher level of abstraction, on the level of *organization*, or *system*, *structure attractors* can be distinguished that describe the tendencies of organizations to maintain contingent forms, configurations, or structures. They enable the classifications of organizations.

Since the first Industrial Revolution, we have witnessed the emergence and proliferation of different forms of organization (with their particular reifications and inscriptions) such as the machine bureaucracy, the divisional form of organization, the professional bureaucracy, the simple structure, the adhocracy, the open systems form, the matrix and project organization, the mechanistic and organic organization, the learning organization, etc. (Taylor, 1911; Weber, 1947; Burns & Stalker, 1961; Kast & Rosenzweig, 1973; Mintzberg, 1979; Senge, 1990). New forms of organization show an increased fluidity in their external appearances. They are known as chains, clusters, networks, alliances, and virtual organizations (Clegg & Hardy, 1996; Handy, 1995). Some of these forms are not mutually exclusive. Structure attractors shape forms of organization with their embedded rules of communication. They implicitly convey conventions on how people will deal with one another.

This diversity of configurations covers a wide variety of management paradigms that have been in use during the twentieth century, especially during its last decades. Each of them inscribes different ways of working and communicating into procedures, and rules, and partly into hard- and software. Dependent on the rigidity of behavior codes, or on the efforts it took to construct such inscriptions, it may be very difficult to unravel them. Ways of working become embodied in the members and therefore they become inscribed in their mental software. Therefore, an information system, once designed and implemented, will be difficult to change or replace.

Combining Weick's views on interlocked behavior, double interacts, and collective networks with Archer's morphogenetic cycle, it should be stressed that the individual in modern democratic societies is not a completely free agent. The psychology of individual freedom collides with the sociology of structural conditioning, limiting the variety of social interactions.

Weick, Allport, Archer, and Giddens' basic themes provide the frame of reference for giving the idea of organized complexity the necessary underpinning. Game designers and facilitators should take them on board. In social life as well as in a game, the participating individual actors may not be aware of the conditions under which they are acting. That leaves open the question whether the players anyhow should be (made) aware of it during the game, or during the debriefing. That depends on the purpose of the experiential learning exercise.

As mentioned earlier, social systems are forms of organization, consisting of actors (agents), rules and resources. In a layered setting of actors, such as in society, these building blocks are being treated as abstract objects to which we attribute independent existence. Such abstract objects are for example institutions, companies, markets, sets of ideas (classifications), laws and regulations, and resources such as capital, equipment, time, information, etc. These objects belong to different classification systems. They are mediated through various interrelated categories of actors. As actors are formed during the process of social interaction, individual actors possess tacit knowing through their embodied nature. They belong both to collective networks if they have the freedom to act as members of voluntary associations, and to groups that are predetermined such as, age and gender. Many times, based on previous structural conditioning, individuals don't have the freedom to switch between classifications and often they belong to predetermined groups while not being aware of it, or of the consequences. Therefore, linkages between structural conditioning, social interaction, and structural elaboration need special attention while designing and facilitating games.

Reflexive actors in social systems

Actors are socially constituted. Through structural conditioning, people belong to collective networks of their own choosing. They also belong to groups that are predetermined. The latter groups do not emerge as a result of interlocking behaviors by the persons belonging to that group. They do not emerge from the inside, but are established by the set of ideas, or classification schemes defined on them by society. These classification schemes are other examples of inscriptions to sustain the durability of networks. Examples are age, gender, social class, income, race, immigrant, refugee, terrorist, etc. People belong both to groups that express their ideas (classifications), and to predetermined groups, based on classifications mainly used for socio-economic and political purposes. As participating individual actors may not be aware of the conditions under which they are acting, both types of classification can easily get mixed up during social interaction. Therefore, it is worthwhile to elaborate on the type of objects that emerge from social interaction in collective networks and their impact on knowledge frames. This question relates to the stability of classifications within the context of structural conditioning. This awareness should impact on the specifications of game design.

Above, I have discussed the emergence of collective structure, based on interlocking behaviors and double interacts. Emphasis has been on their formal aspects. The idea of double interact does not refer to the kind of relationship between persons A and B, to the content, context, and meaning of their interacts. Once collective networks have been established and related structural conditioning is shaping the conditions for structural elaborations, actors have available both their explicit and tacit knowing to mutually engage in their practices.

Since social systems emerge through the interrelationships between actors, rules and resources, the key concepts on social systems, elaborated above, are not limited to the structural elaborations between the actors. In a triangular process, they also stretch out to the world in 'objects' such as 'money', 'raw material', 'manufactured products', 'time', and 'space'. The way actors relate to one another – within the context of structural conditioning – needs further reflection. The resulting knowledge will impact on the design and usability of games.

SUMMARIZING COMMENTS

Complexity science and complex systems theory provide the frame of reference for the design, facilitation & debriefing, and evaluation of games and simulations. The reader should keep in mind the more elaborate games that are being used in professional practice such as business & management games, disaster management games, international relations simulations (virtual diplomacy) etc. In case of games for entertainment, massively multi-player online role-playing games (MMORPGs) are good examples as well. They are my reference when reflecting on games and complex systems. One should however keep in mind that what may look simple games on the surface, may turn out to be complex games from the perspective of the terminology presented in this chapter. The very large game space of the simple game AWARI should remind us about this. For the player it will be simple to understand and play. Its organized complexity is a major part of the fun of playing. For the researcher it is mind-bending to study. The organizational complexity of games – finding and explaining the particular sequence of microstates in their game space – may very well be the cause of a researcher's headache.

It is worthwhile to draw attention again to the dual position of outside observer and inside participant. Both positions as such are necessary but insufficient conditions for understanding gaming. They need to complement each other. The game designer has to be especially aware of this. Dependent on the purposes of a game, the designer has to build into the game the parts of the social system: actors, rules, and resources, in such a way that on the global level – the whole – they shape a form of organization that behaves according to the specification of the design. Yet, on the local level of the interacting parts, the participating actors should have the freedom to construct the social system according to their goals and incentives. If the game is designed for entertainment purposes, then the game's verisimilitude may be helpful, even in case of a "Star Wars" game. If the game is designed for learning purposes, then it should resemble the generic qualities of the social system involved without the need to be precise in the outcomes. In case the game is designed to simulate a well-defined reference system to implement changes, then the internal organization of the parts needs to be calibrated in such a way that it generates valid outcomes on the global level. In addition to the verification of the internal processes, it is required to explain the system's behavior on a more global level. The rules of correspondence between a game, as model, and the reference system need to be accurately defined and tested. Due to the emergent properties of games those requirements have turned out to be a major difficulty. Shaping proper conditions for the inside participants to be reflexive actors – and not merely mechanistic robots such as avatars – who generate adequate emergent behavior on the global level, is one of the major bottle necks in the design, as well in the evaluation of the game in accordance with the criteria for success of system's change.

The dual position, necessary to deal adequately with gaming, complicates research and practice to change existing situations into preferred ones. I have started with stating that games are social systems as well as models of social systems. They are simultaneously real and imagined. To be able to adequately perform their task as change agents, game designers and facilitators need to tune the reality of the gamed world to the multiple reality of the reference organization "in real life". This requirement goes beyond the rational procedures of (fully) estimating the game as a model. Two factors complicate meeting those requirements: the emergent properties of the complex adaptive system, which makes it difficult if not impossible to predict their behavior, and the many intrinsic intangibles related to the behavior of the actors. Both factors mingle in the dynamics of play.

In the following chapters, I will address these issues in more detail.

CHAPTER 5

GAMING METHODOLOGY:
VIEWS ON MODEL BUILDING

INTRODUCTION

Games are both real and models of reality. In this chapter I will pay attention to game design as a particular form of model building. Starting with discussing the scientific method, and introducing the model cycle, gradually I will open boxes and add new boxes to the modeling scheme to be able to take on board the basic qualities of game design. I will present different types of models to demonstrate similarities and differences between simulation and gaming models.

THE SCIENTIFIC METHOD

The core competence of the analytical sciences is the ability to perform controlled, repeatable laboratory experiments by which theories can be tested. This procedure is called the scientific method. The ability to perform such experiments is particularly the domain of the natural sciences. That approach is less straightforward for the social and behavioral sciences. The major barrier to bringing the "social" under the umbrella of the analytical science is the understanding that the scientific method in the creation and testing of theories of individual and social behavior encounters complicated epistemological puzzles related to *classifications* and *causality*. Even as the laboratory to perform controlled experiments is available in the form of gaming laboratories, supported by the digital computer, major bottlenecks still need to be resolved.

The core scheme of the scientific method is the so-called model cycle, represented in Figure 5.1. A researcher starts with selecting a reference system that is relevant for the intended study. That choice depends on the knowledge domain of the discipline involved. One just needs to skip through the numerous scientific journals to get a good impression of the great diversity of reference systems. The structure of scientific research forces knowledge to be extracted from a fully integrated world into disciplinary knowledge domains and inference schemes. Such knowledge becomes des-integrated by disciplinary research. Therefore, reference systems convey the prevailing disjointed scientific perceptions of the world, and by definition are constructs of the human mind. They are moreover selective, ignoring many qualities of the world that are beyond the reach and capacity of current scientific research. Reference systems run from galaxies to elementary particles in physics, from large organic to inorganic compounds in chemistry, from ecosystems to single insects in biology, from societies to individual human beings in the social sciences, from languages to single phonemes in linguistics.

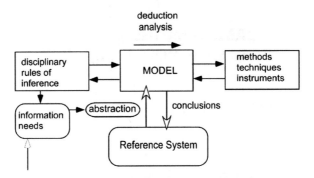

Figure 5.1. Representation of the model, or empirical cycle

Starting with disciplinary rules of inference, a shared notion of knowledge – supported by the related disciplinary community – generates a continuous flow of information and data needs. It is framed into a form of knowledge that fits into the predominant style of reasoning of a particular discipline. That common understanding guides the process of abstracting from the reference system the relevant data and information needed for a specific research project. They are input to the prevailing model frames of disciplines. Once the model is ready for use, it will enable the researcher(s) to carry out the experiment, perform data analysis and to draw conclusions. The explicit knowledge gained will increase the knowledge base about and understanding of the reference system. This applies as well when experiments falsify theories. Such theories can subsequently be excluded from further inquiry.

The term *model* is abstract. To give the term model, and the model cycle more meaning, I will discuss types of models, and steps taken during the model cycle to illustrate the scope of Figure 5.1.

Typology of models

When starting a project, researchers begin with conceptualizing the issues at stake. They can further develop existing theories, or envision completely new ones when the project is purely scientific. They can also start asking questions to practitioners – people involved – if the project aims at studying real life systems. People dealing with such systems are knowledgeable about what goes on, and they will tell about their experiences, about things that work well and are nice, things that need improvement, because they cause frustration etc. In general, when asked, people start telling stories that express their experiences and views. In doing so, they give meaning to the situations they encounter. They may illustrate their points by using examples, often phrased as metaphors. These theories, stories, and metaphors are examples of conceptual models: concepts and their interrelationships. In science as well in daily life, we make use of a variety of models to express our ideas, and to learn how things work. A journalist covering a story is applying a conceptual scheme (model) to address the issue at hand. Table 5.1 depicts a classification scheme that covers in broad terms the variety of available models. It is one of the many schemes available, and it suits the purposes of this chapter.

Table 5.1. Typology of models

Models		Examples
Qualitative	*Typological*	ideal types; extreme types
	Conceptual	concepts or attributes and their interrelationships; theories; scenarios;
Quantitative	*Iconic*	scale models; replicas; mock ups
	Analogue	identical behavior/different form: e.g. laboratory animals
	Mathematical	mathematical, symbolic systems with the following characteristics: <ul><li>descriptive – normative</li><li>deterministic – stochastic – fuzzy</li><li>dynamic – static</li><li>linear – non-linear</li><li>state-space with/ & without feedback</li><li>conditional if-then algorithms</li><li>etc.</li></ul>

Below I will discuss the distinction between quantitative and qualitative models. Here it will suffice to know the differences between typological and conceptual models, and between iconic, analogue, and formal, mathematical models. Scientific research favors quantitative models, and especially formal models, to explain why systems operate the way they do. However, building mathematical models starts with ideas and concepts, and moves on during an iterative process, to become formalized in mathematical terminology. Formal languages provide abstract inference schemes with no explicit reference to content. Those *abstract models* represent *forms of knowledge*. They are lenses for observing reference systems from a particular point of view. They form the basis for developing *empirical models*: abstract models loaded with content abstracted from the reference system. I will not elaborate the great variety of mathematical models. The literature provides sufficient details for the interested reader.

With these notions of the variety and richness of models in mind, I will describe the model cycle of Figure 5.1 in more detail, using the *System Dynamics* (SD) approach as a good example. In SD the formal model is a set of differential, or more precisely difference equations. SD models represent dynamic, deterministic, non-linear feedback systems. In Chapter 8, I will describe the SD approach in more detail.

Steps in model development

SD distinguishes two phases in model development: framing the conceptual system of feedback loops, and subsequently mapping the conceptual system into the flow diagram of the mathematical model.

For designing games and simulations, conceptual models, also called conceptual systems, are suitable to start with. Most theories in the behavioral and social sciences are conceptual models. A multidisciplinary project team will first start figuring out what every team member has in mind with regard to the questions that need to be addressed. When dealing with a concrete reference system, they also will talk to the people involved. Together they will start framing the system. In terms of Schön (1983), they interactively, name the elements and attributes to which they will pay attention, and frame the contexts in which they will pay regard to them. Gradually, while sharing knowledge, and ideas, they co-construct a *cognitive map*, or *Gestalt* of the reference system. That map conveys basic *attributes* and their relationships. Once they have agreed that the conceptual map covers reasonably well the reference system, they move to the next phase. They map the conceptual model into a formal, mathematical, system with variables and equations. Once the formal model has been completed, it will be tested with empirical data. Usually not all data needed to load the model are available. To cover that deficiency, the model behavior is tested for its sensitivity to the parameters, and key parameters are tracked that have great impact on the system's behavior. They will influence the quality of conclusions to be drawn from runs with the model. These steps in model building are illustrated in Table 5.2. Steps 1–7 represent the design of the conceptual model, steps 8–11 the quantitative modeling, and step 12 is the feedback from the model into the reference system (Klabbers, 2000). Table 5.2 illustrates the abstract meaning of Figure 5.1.

Table 5.2. Steps in building an SD model

1.	Formulate the issue;
2.	Make a verbal description of the dynamics of the reference system;
3.	Define the time horizon (i.e., time scale);
4.	Choose system boundaries;
5.	Choose level of aggregation;
6.	Develop the **conceptual map** that is, draw a (flow) diagram of causal relationships;
7.	Verify conceptual model – check verisimilitude with reference system;
8.	Design the **formal system** of equations;
9.	Make an **operational model** by loading the formal system with empirically estimated parameters;
10.	Analyze the system via simulation runs – do sensitivity analysis;
11.	Verify or validate the model behavior – compare model behavior with available knowledge about the behavior of the reference system (calibration);
12.	Draw conclusions, wrap up lessons learned, and implement results.

SIMULATION METHODOLOGY

The terms *model* and *system* are keywords for model building and game design. Therefore, I first will present working definitions of both terms.

Definition of a model

If *Im* is used as an image of *O*, than *Im* is by definition a model of *O*.
Symbolically:

M = {Im, Rc}

M = model
Im = image
Rc = Rules of correspondence, on how to interpret the image in terms of the original: the reference system.

This open definition implies that anything can be used as an image or model to symbolize an original, under the precondition that the rules of correspondence are made explicit. A model so defined is an *abstract object* with a number of interconnected *attributes*, which shape its internal *structure*. To be able to describe that structure in more detail, I will introduce the terminology of systems theory.

Definition of a system

To convey the basis idea of a system, I will restrict this description to *binary relations* between sets. A relation between two sets is called *binary*. A relation between three sets is called *ternary*, etc. A relation between set A and itself is called a *binary relation on A*.

A system as a set of ordered pairs (a_i, b_j) is represented as follows:

$A = \{a_1, a_2, \ldots a_n\}$
$B = \{b_1, b_2, \ldots b_m\}$

The *elements,* or *abstract objects* of both sets are: $a_1, \ldots, a_n$ and $b_1, \ldots b_m$.

The binary relation between the two sets R(A,B) is defined as follows:

$$R(A,B) \subseteq \{(a,b): (a,b) \in A \times B\}$$

Qualitative and quantitative systems

In *qualitative systems*, the *nominal, ordinal, or interval measurement scales* define the properties of the values of the attributes. When attributes are measured on a nominal scale, then the sets, and their elements can only be distinguished from each other: A is different from B. Classifications as presented in Chapter 2 are examples of nominal scaling. An ordinal scale allows in addition to rank order the attributes according to some criterion such as, high, low; larger, smaller; more, or less, etc. An interval scale adds to the ordinal scale information about the distance between the values of the rank order. In *quantitative systems* the attributes are defined by *ratio scales* that is, by absolute values such as temperature, weight, distance, etc. In such a case it is useful to apply the term *variable* for the attributes, to indicate the possibility to measure precisely its change over time on a ratio scale. Changes over time of qualitative values are either less relevant, or can only be made with much less precision. Consequently, the outcomes or assertions resulting from qualitative studies leave more room for multiple interpretations, then the outcomes of quantitative studies, based on ratio scale measurements. It is out of the scope of this chapter to discuss this matter in more detail.

Input-output systems: black boxes

One way of specifying the behavior of general systems – whose variables are classified as *inputs, throughputs* and *outputs* – is the **input-output** (causal) **specification**, see Figure 5.2.

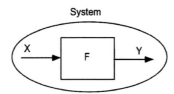

Figure 5.2. Illustration of input-output system

The system's behavior is explicitly specified as a binary relation, a Cartesian product of two disjoint families of abstract sets X – the input set – and Y – the output set, see Table 5.3.

Table 5.3. Cartesian product of sets X and Y

XxY	y_1	y_2	...	y_n
x_1				
x_2				
...				
x_n				

The illustration of the Cartesian product plays an important role in model building.

The input X, the transfer function F, and the output Y define together the properties of the system, depicted in Figure 5.2. The transfer function F transforms the inputs into outputs. The internal structure of the box F is either unknown to or is of no relevance for the researcher. For that reason it is called a *black box*. The inference scheme, that is, the invariable relationship F between X and Y is widely used in science in a whole variety of contexts. The following list of terms of Table 5.4 summarizes commonly known terms.

As soon as the x-y correspondence through F is established, any **x** will generate a specific **y**, independent of time. Consequently those systems are predictable, history independent, synthetically deterministic, and analytically determinable. For that reason von Foerster (1984) called this type of system a *Trivial Machine* (TM).

The Trivial Machine reproduces a causal relationship between X and Y through F. Science, through the application of the scientific methods, is particularly focused on establishing causal relationships between variables in the form of laws of nature. Therefore, the term *causality* is a keyword in science.

Table 5.4. *Examples of input-outputs systems*

X	F	Y
input	operation	output
input	system	output
input	black box	output
independent variable	function	dependent variable
cause	Law of Nature	effect
minor premise	major premise	conclusion
stimulus	Central Nervous System	response
goal	system	action

Causality

A causal (cause-effect) relationship between x and y implies:
- a time dependent controllability of x over y
y follows x in time, and
- x is a necessary and sufficient condition for y
- an asymmetric relation between x and y: if x is the cause of y, then y is not the cause of x.

This last criterion implies that y can only cause x through a third (auxiliary) variable z. Causal relations can either be positive ($\rightarrow$ +) or negative ($\rightarrow$ −). A relation between x and y is positive, when both change in the same direction. If x increases, then y increases. If x decreases, then y decreases. A negative causal link is an inverse relationship. If x increases, then y decreases and vice versa. To start conceptualizing a system it is worthwhile to start with framing a binary relation on the set of attributes. As mentioned above, a relation between set A and itself is called a binary relation on A. Researchers can frame binary relations, if they have sufficient knowledge about the reference system. In case that reference system is not well understood, drawing attributes from various disciplines and also from less known territory, then it is fruitful that the project team recruits colleagues and practitioners to jointly create an explicit image, or *schema*, of the reference system. I have used the *interdependence* or *contingency matrix*, see Table 5.5, to support such shared conceptualization process,

Table 5.5. *Representation of the interdependence or contingency matrix*

A $\rightarrow$ A	a_1	a_2	...	a_n
a_1		+		−
a_2			−	
...				
a_n		+		

In this matrix, attribute a_1 is causally linked to a_2, and the relationship is positive. Attribute a_1 is the cause of a_n, and the relationship is negative, etc. Empty cells mean that no cause-effect relationship exists, or that the researcher is not (yet) aware of it.

Participative model development

When a project team meets to start building a model, the interdependence matrix is a suitable tool to engage the participants in a mutual conversation about the key qualities of the reference system. The result may look like the matrix in Figure 5.3. To make explicit the cognitive map, embedded in an interdependence matrix, the matrix is subsequently transformed into a causal loop diagram, which shows the system's attributes (a, ...x), and the way they are causally linked to each other.

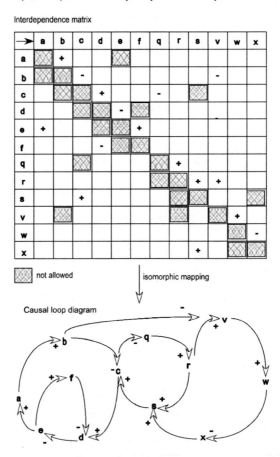

Figure 5.3. Mapping the interdependence matrix into a causal loop diagram

That diagram visualizes the qualitative, conceptual system of attributes and relationships. These notions are basic to building models. They are explicitly used in the System Dynamics (SD) approach. In scientific research a great variety of formal models are in use. It is up to the project team to decide which formal system addresses best the qualities of the causal loop diagram. Various formal systems will simultaneously apply.

Next I will describe two generic systems that are being used in simulation methodology: the descriptive and normative system.

DESCRIPTIVE AND NORMATIVE SYSTEMS

The general systems approach makes a distinction between two classes of dynamic systems: descriptive and normative systems. Descriptive systems are basically input-output systems with a throughput defined by a parameter, decision vector, and state vector, completed when appropriate with an auxiliary vector – representing supporting variables.

Descriptive systems

Generic Structure of a Descriptive System

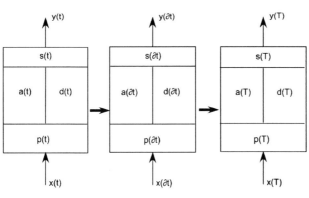

x(t) = input vector
p(t) = parameter vector
a(t) = auxiliary vector
d(t) = decision vector
s(t) = state vector
y(t) = output/criterion vector

initial condition t = 0
final condition t = T

Figure 5.4. Illustration of a descriptive system (adjusted from Hanken & Reuver, 1973)

The dynamic system consists of the input vector $x(t)$ and output vector $y(t)$, similar to Figure 5.2. In addition the transfer of the input is defined by a built in decision vector – an algorithm – a parameter vector for both the decision and auxiliary vectors. The internal state needs more clarification. The state function S is defined by both the input x at time t and state s at time t-1:

$$s(t) = S(x(t), s(t-1))$$

s(t-1)   = S (x(t-1), s(t-2)), etc.

Therefore, S represents the memory or history of the system. Table 5.6 explains the meaning of the system variables.

Table 5.6. Key system variables (adjusted from Hanken & Reuver, 1973)

	System variables				
	Independent variable	Internal causal network			Dependent variable
type of variable	Input variable	Decision variable	Auxiliary variable	State variable	Criterion variable
symbol	x(t)	d(t)	a(t)	s(t)	y(t)
# of components	k	l	m	n	q
meaning	Number of inputs	Degrees of freedom	Supporting attributes	Memory	Number of outputs, behavior criteria
distinctions	k = 0 - the system is not connected to an environment	l = 0 - throughput, cascade system l ≠ 0 - the system allows decision making		n = 0 - the system is without memory n ≠ 0 - the state space represents the memory of the system	q=0 by definition trivial
related to	other subsystems	linking rules and resources	conceptual bridges in causal network	memory	problem definition and purpose of system
product space	X input space	D decision space	A auxiliary space	S state space	Y output or behavior space

The auxiliary vector a(t) refers to variables (attributes) that help to explain the causal linkages between the decision and state functions. The dynamic system evolves over time via small time increments ∂t from the initial state t to the final state T.

Normative systems

Normative systems include an internal mechanism to steer the system dynamically towards a well-defined goal. In current practice, that mechanism or algorithm is called an *agent*. Agent-based simulations are used to search for satisfying strategies for improving systems' performance. I will use the term agent for such a mechanical devise, and the term actor for human players. In the world of computer games, the players are the actors, controlling the avatars – digital characters – moving through virtual space. Figure 5.5 conveys the structure of a normative system.

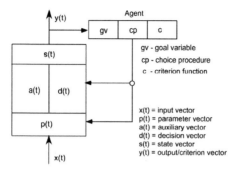

Figure 5.5. Representation of a normative system (adjusted from Hanken & Reuver, 1973)

Compared with the structure of a descriptive system, an agent is added, which is composed of a goal variable, a choice procedure, and a criterion function. That agent is rule driven. The *goal variable* selects from the output vector y(t) those variables that are related to the goal of the system. Those variables are input to the *choice procedure*, which compares the output y(t) with the preferred output, which is defined by the *criterion function* c. The choice procedure triggers an algorithm for finding the best option at time t. Pending any discrepancies between the actual and desired output, the choice procedure triggers an action, which impacts on the decision vector d(t), and parameters p(t), adjusting them to move the system in the right direction. If the action of the agent does not change the decision vector d(t), it will only adjust the parameter vector. If it changes the decision vector, then the normative system will show adaptive qualities. The normative system, represented in Figure 5.5, is the frame-of-reference for *multi-agent-based modeling*. Subsets of goal variables, choice procedures, and criterion functions can be allocated to several agents performing their different algorithms. Phrased in this way, the frame of the normative system with its built in formal decision algorithms, contains also the frame of mathematical game theory. It is one specific example of the various model frames that are depicted through the scheme of Figure 5.5.

The parameter vector p(t) is needed to tune or calibrate the descriptive or normative system in accordance with the behavior of the reference system. This is firstly done through sensitivity analysis, and subsequently by estimating the parameters with empirical data. This procedure is a precondition for experimenting with the model, see steps 9–11 of Table 5.2.

Model verification

Fully estimating a simulation model is not simple. Bekey has listed difficulties of mathematical model building that particularly apply to social systems (see Table 5.7). Most of these difficulties have not yet been resolved. Thus, the question whether a certain simulation model works cannot be answered straightforwardly. The test of the model lies in whether it can be used in accomplishing the client's purpose (Churchman 1970). Sometimes a conceptual map satisfies a client's purpose, sometimes a formal system will do the job. On other occasions, a (partly) estimated operational model will give the answers needed. Key question is: Are simulation models to be viewed as "truth machines" or as tools to explore different sets of assumptions and values? Answers to this question define the kinds of learning environments that can be expected from such modeling.

Following Bekey's observation it is useful to distinguish between the degrees of similarity – the validity of the rules of correspondence – between the model (artifact) and the reference system.

Table 5.7. Difficulties in mathematical modeling (Bekey, 1971)

Inadequate knowledge of the state of the system.
System identification techniques may not be useful.
The data which are required to validate a mathematical model of a large system are difficult, if impossible, to obtain.
Data, when available, are noisy.
Control of poorly defined systems is in its infancy.
Criterion functions are hard to obtain.
In large, interconnected, complex systems the separation of input and output may be very difficult, and the application of controlled specific inputs nearly impossible.
In many cases, decomposition is by no means obvious and models of individual components are not all suitable for a resulting synthesis.
On many levels of a given large system entirely different time scales may be encountered.
Also the physical scale may fall into a series of hierarchies.
State variables in the system may not have compatible dimensions, a problem for multi-disciplinary research.

Randers (1972) distinguished four classes of models:
- Class 1: *Common sense models* – Model assumptions are based on the modeler's intuition and general knowledge about the system.
- Class 2: *Expert opinion models* – Model assumptions (hopefully) represent the consensus of the existing knowledge – as found in the literature and among experts. They also satisfy the requirements for class 1 models in being basically reasonable.
- Class 3: *Partially estimated models* – Model assumptions satisfy the requirements for class 2 models. In addition, formal techniques are used to demonstrate the capability of the individual assumptions to reproduce real world data.

- Class 4: *Fully estimated models* – Besides satisfying the class 3 requirements, the full system can be shown to reproduce the reference system's behavior through formal techniques such as simultaneous equations estimations, or by regression techniques.

Taking Bekey's observations into consideration, I argue that trying to achieve fully estimated models of social systems is an ideal that cannot be reached both for methodological and practical reasons. Especially financial constraints to fully estimate simulation models should be taken seriously. In general, we should settle for partially estimated models as the next best option.

This description of models and systems refers to *deterministic systems*, which univocally convey causal relations. With respect to *stochastic systems*, the same variables, as described above, are represented through chances extracted from chance distributions.

The process, described above is a well-known procedure of building a mathematical model to simulate the behavior of a reference system in the real world. For several reasons it may not be necessary or suitable to go all that way, and to decide that the conceptual model, or a class 1 model suits the purposes as well. In the social sciences, a theory – expressed in the terminology of a conceptual model – is tested via the deductive hypothetical method. A theory leads to framing hypotheses that need to be tested. In such a case the model cycle has the meaning of an empirical cycle, with the hypotheses representing the conceptual model. They need to be tested in an experiment. A simulation model of a system represents a mini-theory of that system. Testing and validating such a theory is very difficult for reasons expressed above.

These ideas on model building demonstrate the working of the scientific method, and more particularly, the model or empirical research cycle, as sketched in Figure 5.1. Figure 5.5 represents a closed agent-based simulation model. It shows the mechanics of such normative systems. Opening the loop between the descriptive system and the agent, and replacing the agent with real actors, sets conditions for open models, and interactive simulation and gaming (Klabbers, 1974), see Figure 5.6.

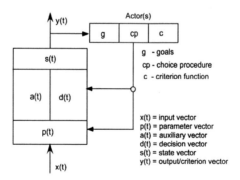

Figure 5.6. Representation of an actor-based system

Including the actor(s) in the simulation frame implies an important epistemological switch from a functionalist to a constructionist approach, from principles of allopoietic to autopoietic steering. Figure 5.6 represents the core idea of gaming. Its framework can be used to develop computer-based games as well as other fully-fledged games characterized in Chapter 2.

GAMING METHODOLOGY

Gaming methodology builds upon simulation methodology discussed above. It offers a broader scope, and takes in addition on board other theories of knowledge. It requires an appropriate knowledge frame to include the basic ideas, presented in Chapters 2, 3, and 4. These basic ideas revolve around the terms organized complexity, complex adaptive systems, co-evolution, emergent behavior, and reflexive actors: actors demonstrating self-awareness. I consider it worthwhile to sketch historical and social dimensions of the gaming approach. Therefore, I will insert an intermezzo.

INTERMEZZO

The field of simulation & gaming that emerged during the 20th century has been developed and practiced by professionals from a variety of disciplines. In the 1960s and early 1970s several international and national societies and associations in systems science, cybernetics were founded. They had a common interest in the trans-disciplinary growth of knowledge, and the study of complex organized systems. This institutionalization was the result of a crystallizing process that started at the end of the 19th century with scientific management, and since the 1930s with the advancement of general systems theory, and cybernetics, gaining momentum in the 1950s with the development of computers. These changes were part of the so-called Second Industrial Revolution.

General Systems Theory, Cybernetics, and Scientific management

Characteristic of the *First Industrial Revolution* was the transformation of energy from one form to another. Through artificially constructed engines such as the heat engine, a whole new complex technology emerged, replacing natural (physiological) engines (animals and human beings) as sources of mechanical work. Heat engines became the slaves of those industrial societies. Human beings were responsible for their maintenance, for tending them and steering their work through routine control operations. The increasing complexity of the industrial enterprises through mass production, and the resulting auxiliary social and political organizations, required a new way of thinking about the efficient organization and management of work. The counterpart of the complex technology became scientific management, advocated by Henri Fayol, F.W. Mooney, Lyndall Urwick and Frederick Taylor. They saw management as a process of planning, organization, command, coordination, and control, while drawing on a combination of military and engineering principles. The classical management theory with its emphasis on designing bureaucratic organizations, combined the way the machine routinized production with the way the bureaucracy routinized the process of administration (Morgan, 1986). The resulting mechanistic organization is a product of the First Industrial Revolution.

The *Second Industrial Revolution* emerged from the appearance of machines (artifacts) designed to process information rapidly. The needs of military technology during World War II stimulated the development of rapid automatic computing machines to support antiaircraft guns as major weapons of defense. Devices were developed, which were able to adjust their performance on the basis of the observed difference between a preset goal state and its current state. Such technological artifacts exhibited the principle of purposefulness in a way, which resembles the behavior of living systems. This principle is central in cybernetics: the science of communication and control. The appearance of complex information-processing machines – computers – and the new concepts from cybernetics influenced views on living organisms and social organizations. The concept of purposefulness of behavior of living systems and social organizations as such was not new. What was new was a set of concepts susceptible to mathematical operations from which the purposeful aspects of those systems could be derived. Systems that are living in the common, or biological and social sense of the word, share many features with artificial systems. *They relate to the way such systems are organized.* This commonality between non-living, living, and social systems led to broadening the idea of organism to the concept of *organized system.* Related core concepts are: *structure* (being), *function* (acting), and *evolution* (becoming). They form in the broadest sense of the word the scope of General Systems Theory (GST) (Von Bertalanffy, 1968).

The term *organized system* resulted from new views on industrial organization supported by advances in science. Advances in technology were a driving force.

I consider this historical and social setting important for understanding the meaning and potential impact of gaming. Gaming in its contemporary form emerged from these societal developments. Therefore, I will start with some general notions extracted from organization and management science, and mapped into social systems theory.

Characteristics of social systems

Based on the frame-of-reference presented in Chapter 4, I will further enlighten the gaming framework. Social systems are boundary-maintaining entities. This implies that they make distinctions between 'us' and 'them'. In complex adaptive systems, each actor establishes local boundaries, which separate the internal actors from each other and from their environment. Boundaries serve as interfaces. Jointly, the internal actors establish interfaces with the common environment. Social systems are anchored in the attitudes, perceptions, beliefs, motivations, habits, and expectations of human beings (Katz & Kahn, 1966). They are partially open. Boundaries are demarcation lines or regions for the definition of system activity. They set the domain of activities of the social system. Where the boundaries are drawn is a matter of convenience and strategy. Within companies, functional management areas such as, production, marketing, and finance are responsible for distinct activities. Faculties and departments at universities deal with different domains of activities related to the disciplines involved. Boundary regulation is a key function within any social system. The concept of *interface* is useful to understand boundary relations between social systems and their environments. It ensures closure (see Chapter 4). The interface is the area of contact between one (sub-) system and another. At the interface many transactional processes across systems boundaries take place, involving the transfer of energy, materials, money, and information. Information technology (IT) offers many new kinds of interfaces. For example, mobile phones, the Internet, the computer screen, the typical computer keyboard, the mouse, etc. represent a whole range of interfaces. In the Information Society, interfaces are becoming increasingly adaptable to people's needs in time and space. They are gateways for citizens to connect to the vast and evolving IT-infrastructure, and enable them to interact with each other in cyberspace. These notions are embedded in the general scheme of a multi-actor system (see Figure 5.7).

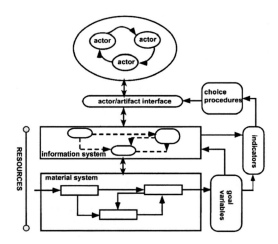

Figure 5.7. Representation of a multi-actor system

Take for example a chemical plant. The material flow represents the flow of chemicals, and the chemical reactions that take place in the reaction chambers. Raw material flows in and chemical products flow out. The control of the throughput of these processes is automated, and the information flow − including the control algorithms − is embedded in the information system. The control panel is the interface between operators and the semi-automated system. The feedback control loop between the material and information systems is semi-autonomous. As long as the plant's behavior stays within the bandwidth of the control variables, the system will run on its own. In other circumstances, the operator intervenes. The scheme of Figure 5.7 applies as well to manufacturing, to banking, in general, to the whole variety of social systems. The information system represents a valid model of the material system. That model resembles the models depicted in Figure 5.4, and 5.5. The human operator receives information about the state of the process via a list of indicators (goal variables). These data and information are perceived via the interface of the operator with the information system. The indicators inform the operator continuously about the state of the process. The operator may need to intervene and change the parameters of the material flow to steer the system, or may decide to adjust decision rules. The medium of intervention is the human computer interface (HCI), which shows the information and control panels at hand. Also here a feedback control mechanism is operational. If intervention is not necessary, the automated feedback-control system with its in advance built-in control algorithms operates independently of the human operator. In Figure 5.7 both the material and the information system represent the system's resources. Through information technology, real time, on-line control of such industrial infrastructures has become standard procedure since the 1950s. I have chosen the example of a chemical plant as a metaphor, because it demonstrates in a transparent way the basic structure and mechanisms of a social system. A similar line of reasoning applies to running a family, managing a hospital, or a university, and other kinds of social systems. Basic differences between the form and content of multi-actor systems depend on the purposes of such systems, on the prevailing management regimes, the meaning of the processes, and the capacity to deal with intangibles such as attitudes, beliefs, norms and values.

With the frame of Figure 5.7 in mind, it is sufficient to map the material resources in the information system when building a model of a social system. One option is to describe the material flow in mathematical terms. Another option is to symbolize them through pieces, being moved on a game board. The designer will choose which medium of representation is most suitable for the occasion.

The ideas, underlying Figures 5.5, 5.6, and 5.7, provide the frame-of-reference for multi-actor, multi-agent modeling, and digital gaming. Figure 5.8 integrates these ideas. Agents are entities in a model-base that take action, make decisions, that impact on their task environment (resources). They are rule-driven algorithms in the decision-information network of the system involved. In computer games, such agents become characters that populate the virtual game space. The players (actors, 'puppeteers') – via the human computer interface – directly control some characters in the virtual environment. Those are called avatars, the heroes of the game.

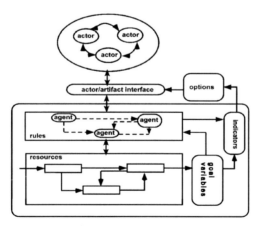

Figure 5.8. General model of a multi-actor, multi-agent system

Classifications and looping effects

From the viewpoint of theories of knowledge (epistemology), the information system and the system of actors of Figure 5.8 encompass distinct disciplinary styles of reasoning. Hacking (2002) pointed out that each scientific style of reasoning introduces a new class of objects to study and the very criteria of truth. Game designers and facilitators need to be aware of this, to prevent them from making serious mistakes during the facilitation, debriefing and assessment of games. I will explain the styles of reasoning that are at stake.

In Chapter 4, I have pointed out that actors are socially constituted. They belong to collective networks of their own choosing, and to groups that are predetermined. They are classified for many reasons. One main reason relates to public administration and its need to bring administrative order to society for legal, fiscal, and political reasons. These classifications provide the concrete context of structural conditioning (see Chapter 4). Developing classifications is a basic human quality. Classifications in society are produced and supported by scientific research. Psychology and sociology – through the classifications they developed – are having a great impact on the way policy makers and the media frame society. Therefore, let us take a closer look at the way science develops classes of abstract objects.

The construction of objects by science. We face two existential questions: What is it that we create, and how much is fully determined in ways that are totally independent of ourselves? As science has a special position in addressing these questions, I will pay attention to the scientific project to enlighten the construction of objects in scientific communities.

Looking into the history of science, Hacking (2002) observed that in ancient times men studied, observed and speculated about phenomena. In modern times we make phenomena, or isolate and purify them. Torricelli made a vacuum by filling a glass tube with mercury. Boyle improved on it by using an air pump. In chemistry, physics, and biology many artifacts have been created, that subsequently have been used in engineering. Hacking (2002) pointed out:

> Undoubtedly the most powerful style of reasoning, that which has made possible the modern world, that which has permanently changed the world, large and small, that which is altering and engineering the world at this moment, is what I call the laboratory style, which was emerging four centuries ago (p. 3).

This laboratory style is the driving force of change. It stresses instrumental reasoning with the implicit view on the controllability of nature. In laboratories, certain phenomena can be isolated and purified, especially phenomena in chemistry and physics. In biology, it is less straightforward to isolate and purify them without risking the destruction of some basic features of the organism. Isolating a cell from an organism to study its anatomy may kill it. Recent advances in biology enhance the study of cells "on line and in real time" without destroying them. Isolating and purifying phenomena in a laboratory is part of the analytical approach of science. We should be cautious by keeping in mind however that for example, the properties of water are not derived from analyzing the properties of oxygen and hydrogen. The properties of an organism cannot be gathered from the properties of its constituating parts. The properties of a collective social network cannot be inferred from the properties of its members. In such cases the laboratory style of reasoning – based on a reductionist approach to science – meets its boundaries.

Hacking pointed out that each scientific style of reasoning introduces a new class of objects to study and criteria of truth. Are these objects real; are electrons and quarks real, or only instruments for thinking and experimenting? He argued that the essence of each style of scientific reasoning is classification. "Classification is at the core of the taxonomic sciences ... Disputes about the truth of classification precede anything we now call science ... Today, they (*classes*: note author) are discussed as a product of society and human history" (Hacking, 2002, p. 5).

Classifications, developed in science, have been disseminated into society. They have percolated into society to become part of every day language. It is not worthwhile to debate whether they are real, or merely social constructions. Hacking stated:

> You cannot escape classifications by maintaining that they are historical, social and mental products. We live in a classified world which might be deconstructed in a playful way, but whose structures we will need in order to think until they are altered not by deconstruction but by construction, by creation (Hacking, 2002, p. 8).

Names exist in institutions, practices, authorities, and interactions with things and interactions among people, connotations, stories, analogies, memories, and fantasies. Hacking (1999) called the related social setting the *matrix*, a concept very much similar to the term *structural conditioning*, described in Chapter 4. Accepting that we live in a classified world, we realize that we use classifications in shaping collective networks, classifications, which form the basis for structural conditioning. In the context of game design it is important to be aware of two different types of classificatory fields. Through these types fundamental differences between the natural and human and social sciences are recognized. They impact on the intrinsic qualities of social systems, and thus on games.

Indifferent and interactive kinds. Hacking has distinguished *indifferent and interactive kinds* (Hacking, 1999). Classifications such as sticks, stones, plutonium and quarks are *indifferent* in the sense that calling them by that name makes no difference to them. They are not aware of themselves. The classification *enzyme* is indifferent, but not passive. It works in chemical reactions. However, an enzyme does not interact with the classification of enzyme. The classifications *cat* and *dog* also do not interact with the animals so classified. I can call my dog "cat". It will not influence his behavior.

There is a big difference between enzymes, cats, and dogs, and people. People are self-conscious, aware of themselves, and of their social environment. They are *actors, acting under descriptions.*

> The course of action they choose, and indeed their ways of being, are by no means independent of the available descriptions under which they may act (Hacking, 1999, p. 103).

> Names affect people in many ways. Calling a person a genius, a terrorist or a refugee makes a difference in terms of the relations between external descriptions and internal sensibilities. It can affect people so classified, and change them. Our knowledge of those individuals must be revised as they

change, and our classifications themselves may have to be modified. ... In fact the classifications in the social sciences aim at moving targets, namely people and groups who may change in part because they are aware of how they are classified (Hacking, 2002, p. 10).

Classifications of this kind are *interactive:* the classification and the individuals or social system – so classified – may interact to fit or get away from the classification that may be applied to them. Hacking called this the *looping effect* of human kinds. With new names, new objects come into being. As we participate in various collective networks, we experience ourselves as being persons of various classifications. These interactive, self-referential kinds, become manifest when during the game design process, roles are defined, and during a game session, when players/actors assume those roles.

Wrapping up these notions on classifications, it is important to realize that in social systems both types of classificatory fields – indifferent and interactive kinds – exist simultaneously. When dealing with systems of indifferent kinds, I will use the term *referential systems*. Referential systems are indifferent to the classifications that apply to them. It will not change their behavior by being classified. When dealing with social systems, I will use the term *self-referential system*. Self-referential systems relate to interactive kinds through the looping effect. They are a basic ingredient of the system of interactions and structural conditioning. Actors through self-referencing are aware of themselves, observe themselves. They are reflexive actors, continuously in dialogue with external classifications and internal sensitivities, adjusting their behavior accordingly, and as a consequence spurring the need to modify classifications. Understanding that looping effect both on the level of the individual and collective network is a prerequisite for game design.

GAME DESIGN CYCLE

Taking these views on social systems and games into consideration, then the model cycle, represented in Figure 5.1 needs to be adjusted. It is no longer sufficient to speak of reference system, presuming that it is based on one type of classification, which by implication means, a referential system of interrelated indifferent kinds.

We need to decompose the reference system in two interconnected systems: a referential (indifferent kinds) and a self-referential (sub-)system (interactive kinds). In terms of Figure 5.8, it looks as follows (see Figure 5.9). The social system, depicted in Figure 5.9 is from epistemological perspective a hybrid system. It consists of interconnected referential and a self-referential systems. Each of these systems requires different theories of knowledge for a proper use of the embedded classifications. With these understandings in mind, I have adjusted the scheme of the model cycle of Figure 5.1 (see Figure 5.10).

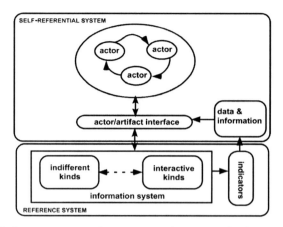

Figure 5.9. Representation of connected referential/self-referential system

The reference system of Figure 5.1 is decomposed into the interconnected referential and self-referential systems. Games are not confined to one discipline. They cross disciplines, and therefore transdisciplinary or interdisciplinary styles of reasoning are required to be able to take on board relevant qualities of the referential and self-referential systems. A game designer, who is not aware of these key qualities, will make serious mistakes in the design and assessment of games. If it is common practice – in applying the scientific method – to speak of analyzing the model (see Figure 5.1), in terms of gaming, it is more worthwhile to use the term *exercise*.

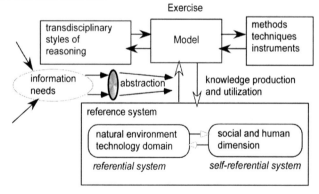

Figure 5.10. Representation of the game design cycle

Suppose the designer disregards the self-referential system, and only selects the referential system as the basis for building the model, in that case the whole effort is similar to the meaning of Figure 5.1. The designer may also on purpose disregard the self-referential qualities of the social and human domains. That would strip the social system from its reflexive capacities, and reduce human capabilities of self-

125

awareness to merely functional qualities. Such a reductionist approach implies that the designer makes a value judgment.

Performing exercises with games – running game sessions – will enable the participating actors to gain knowledge, and to learn about their individual and group behavior and its impact on system's behavior. They will learn about the emergent qualities of the complex adaptive system they are part of. That knowledge produced, those lessons learned, will impact on the social system of which the game is a model. In Chapter 2, I have introduced the framework, which encompasses the basic ingredients of any game; see Figure 2.2 and Table 2.10. I have introduced it to demonstrate how it can be used to deconstruct the architecture of existing games. Here I will elaborate that framework from the perspective of game design.

GAME DESIGN

Game design passes through the following stages:
- Specifications of the design
- Conceptual design
- Instrumental design
- Testing and implementation
- Training of facilitators
- Maintenance.

More in detail it looks as follows (see Table 5.8).

Table 5.8. Illustration of the iterative design process

Iterative design process	
Designer:	Client:
• *Feasibility study - design specifications;*	• Cost-benefit analysis;
• *Visions on current and preferred situation;*	• Processes + data + information;
• *Conceptual design of new situation;*	• Models (+ transactions at HCI*)
• *Technical design specifications;*	• Feedback on requirements
• *Actual design of the artifact by game designers, programmers;*	• Organizational preparations for implementation;
• *Transfer, implementation & training;*	• Checking of users documentation& training;
• *Evaluation (assessment);*	• Evaluation (assessment);
• *Maintenance*	• Maintenance

* HCI: Human Computer Interface

During the stage of preparing the specifications of the design, the designer will address the following questions:

- Who is the client?
- What are the purposes of the game?
- What will be the subject matter?
- Who are the intended audiences?
- What will be the context(s) of use?

To answer these questions, keep in mind the frame of Table 5.9 – see below.

- **Who is the client?**

  To understand the context of this question, it is important to answer it from the position of the designer, who develops the game for a client, even if the client is fictitious. The iterative design process provides a transparent path into the future of the design, and a vehicle for continuous conversations between designer and client. In case of the design of a digital game for the entertainment business, the client is the person who will pay the bill. With respect to games for purely educational purposes, the client is the teaching staff, backed by the controller who is responsible for the school budget. In all these circumstances, it is worthwhile to make the distinction between the person who is (financially) *accountable* for the project, and the *problem owner* who needs the game (artifact) to achieve well-defined goals. In connection with the person who is accountable, and the one who owns the problem, the designer should also include the person who will eventually be responsible for the maintenance of the game. This question applies particularly to computer-supported games dependent on new releases of hard- and software. If the game will be used to enhance the capacities of the related social system and competency of managers or policy makers, then the client is well known. If the game is being designed for reasons of research, then usually the client, who is accountable, is the agency sponsoring the project. The problem owners of a research design project are more diffused among the scientific community. An advisory committee may represent the peer group involved. In the following, I will focus attention on the design of a game mainly for practical purposes.

- **What are the purposes of the game?**

  The intended game may be used as part of a teaching or training program to raise awareness about general issues. The game may also be designed for specific purposes, to improve the competency of a well-defined group of people, to enhance decision or policy making, to support change processes, or for testing theories. Dedicated games are usually tailor-made models of the social system involved. Under these circumstances, the game is intended as an *intervention medium*. In any case, the purposes need to be well defined in advance to enable proper preparations for assessments.

- **What will be the subject matter?**

  While discussing the subject matter with the client it is fruitful to be aware of the distinction between game form and content. For example, a board game is one of many forms available. That form may be used to embed highly diverse contents. That applies to all forms of games, and especially to computer-supported games. Forms are conveyed through media of representation. They come in all conceivable shapes. Form and content are tuned to the purposes of the game, taking into consideration the (financial) constraints of the client. The subject matter, the content in connection with the problem, should be embedded in the most suitable form of the game. The designer should be aware that the client's needs are often triggered by complaints, or bottlenecks. For a proper approach it is crucial to track the causes and processes underlying a felt gap between "what is" and "what should be". Usually it is a pretext, a certain phrasing of a symptom, referring to causes that need to be brought to the surface. It is the designer's task to bring them forward during conversations with the client (problem owner). Generally, the designer should not take the initial phrasing of a problem on face validity. Other actors involved might frame the issue differently, because of multiple interests and positions that are at stake. The client finally needs to confirm what really is at issue before the actual design can start.

- **Who are the intended audiences?**
  The intended audiences define the level of competency, abilities, and skills of the players at the start of the game session. They also define the language and language use – jargon – of the manuals, and the information and text provided during the game. The symbols used in the game should convey the images, familiar to the people that will play the game. Youngsters use other language and symbols than managers of a large company. The designer should take into account Vygotsky's idea of *zone of proximal development* and the prevailing schemas of the players, when referring to the intended audience (see Chapter 3).

- **What will be the context(s) of use?**
  The intended game may be used to address a general concern, a general issue, or topic. Usually such games are generic. They may be used as a stand-alone game to convey a general message, or to function as "ice-breaker." They can also be used for in-company training to raise the level of awareness about team building, communication, leadership, etc. Most games delivered off the shelf are generic, stand alone games. The game may also be designed for specific purposes, to improve the competency of a well-defined group of people, to enhance decision or policy making, or to support change processes. Such dedicated games are usually tailor-made models of the social system involved. The purposes of such games need to be explicit. Under these circumstances, the game is intended as an *intervention medium*. As part of the contexts of use, the designer needs also to prepare the training of facilitators. This should not be considered an incidental circumstance. Finally, it may define the success or failure of the project.

Answers to these questions will define the *design specifications*. They also include the feasibility study in terms of the game concept and the financial constraints. The answers also provide the context and therefore the meaning of the concepts used in Table 5.9. Once agreement has been reached about the specifications of the design, the most important stage starts: the conceptual design. During the conceptual design, Table 5.9 will provide the framework for the architecture of the artifact. It provides a common frame-of-reference for conversations among members of the project team, and consultations with the client. In Chapter 2, I have introduced this framework to deconstruct existing games. Here I propose to use it to construct new games. It will help the designer to be aware that the actors, assuming possibly more than one role, will shape the system of interactions: the social organization as such. To frame the rules of the games, it is suitable to first decide whether the game will be open or closed. In a closed game, all information and data pertaining to the form, content, and goals need to be built-in in advance. Usually such games are rule-driven. Open games provide a frame – a free form – inviting the players to self-organize the game process on the basis of information and data provided. They are open-ended self-constructing narratives. Such games provide the actors with suitable conditions for co-constructing complex adaptive systems with interesting, and often surprising emergent properties. These considerations impact on the phrasing of the rules. When the designer is preparing a computer-supported game, it is very important to realize that hardware, and especially software, are based upon multiple built-in rules (manuals/instructions) that stay implicit while playing a computer-based game.

Being knowledgeable about those rules is a precondition for playing the game. A person who is not familiar with these rules – instructions on how to handle the equipment – will not be able to play related games.

With respect to digital games, the designer will use nested rules for the avatars and other characters that pop up at the screen, and move according to those rules. The media of representation reflect the game resources, and the game space. They can be boards, simulation models, spreadsheets, information systems, databases, paper and pencil, whatever is convenient from the viewpoint of purposes, audiences, and contexts of use.

The gaming literature covers many publications that describe in detail the technicalities of the design. As I emphasize here methodological questions, technicalities of the design are out of the scope. In Part III, I will present some case studies to illustrate the methodology at work.

Game dramatic effects

While participating in a game, every player (actor) constructs an individual and sometimes unique narrative. From the perspective of the design of digital games, Rollings and Morris (2004) distinguished five elements of a model of drama: *style, plot, character, setting, and theme.* For digital games that are based on a narrative structure these elements are relevant. They do not apply to gaming in general because for most games the plot is not specified in advance. CHESS has three potential end states: player A (white) wins, and the black kings falls, player B (black) wins and the white king falls, or the game ends in a draw. In MONOPOLY the plot cannot be defined in advance, the outcome depends on how the players engage during the game. A similar line of reasoning applies to most non-digital games. It is also not straightforward as regards MMORPGs (massively multi-player online role-playing games) to speak of a plot. A plot presupposes a stop rule, and a predefined dramatic end-of-the-story. I would not call one of the outcomes of a game of CHESS a plot, a secret plan, or conspiracy. The end states are well defined in advance. Rules and resources uniquely define characters in digital games. They are rule-driven agents as in a virtual puppet show. Actors in a game are self-aware, and they have the freedom to interpret their roles in various ways, and to engage in the gamed drama the way it fits their goals. Even actors in a

Table 5.9. Game architecture (see Table 2.10, Chapter 2)

Architecture of games			
Design Specifications	1. Client 2. Purpose 3. Subject matter 4. Intended audience 5. Context of use		
Social System	**Syntax** *Form*	**Semantics** *Content*	**Pragmatics** *Usage*
Actors	Number of players Number of game places of actors	Roles Composition of roles in social organization	Learning context: types of steering Learning goals: Kinds of knowing
Rules	Game manipulation set: Preparatory rules; Start & stop rules; Rigid-rules; Principle-based rules; Free-form. Initial game positions; Allowable moves; Final game positions	Relationships between roles, communication rules, procedures Evaluation of places for resource allocation, and relative position within team of players	Team of game facilitators Format & instructions for rigid-rule vs. free-form Assessment functions
Resources	Game space; Set of game positions; Set of pieces	Positioning of pieces: meaning of cultural, socio- economic situation Set of occupied & available positions	Materials: Equipment Paraphernalia Facilities

theater or movie shape their personal views on the roles. Therefore, I will rephrase the game elements of a model of drama: *style* (medium of representation*), strategy, actor, setting* (context of use), and *theme* (subject matter). These elements are included in the game architecture of Table 5.9 in similar ways a building provides the space for people to move around and create the drama of human encounters according to social rules and conventions. A building is a resource. A game is a symbolic space with particular rules, conventions, and resources. The players move around in that semiotic game space.

ACTOR-ARTIFACT SYSTEM DEVELOPMENT

Driven by advances in computer and information science, modern digital games are very sophisticated. The players need progressive levels of competency to win. *Policy exercises* specifically designed to enhance policy development in the political arena also need broad expertise of the professionals that take part. They will deal with a broad range of advanced support systems such as information systems, decision support systems, and planning systems to engage in policy dialogue. It is important to tune these gaming artifacts to the (potential) qualities of the players, otherwise they do not address the intended audiences properly, and money will be wasted. In this section, I will discuss these issues from the perspective of actor-artifact design and social system development. Games are examples of actor-artifact systems.

In our tool rich societies we use artifacts such as computers, mobile phones, cars, airplanes, bicycles, baby buggies, and industrial plants as extensions of our capacity for dealing with the environments in which we live. One could grasp their usability as singular tools to store and use information, to communicate over long distances, to increase parents' mobility with children, to move heavy loads, and to manufacture equipment to produce artifacts. A narrowly technical view on these artifacts would hamper understanding their social impacts or consequences, the way they are embedded in societies. Such artifacts have become basis ingredients of social systems. Integrating them in daily practices is part of social systems development. Computers, and mobile phones are part of the global information and communication infrastructure; airplanes and cars are ingrained in national, regional, and global transport systems. The wider implications of the meaningfulness and impact of the world of artifacts are especially relevant for their planning and design in relation to the human users. A proper design methodology would envision those artifacts as extensions of our capacities in a great variety of contexts of use, and would help to prevent developing poorly designed artifacts, eliminating costly and wasteful modifications, retro-fittings that would delay smooth operation.

Even the design of artifacts with "concrete handles" such as in cars, airplanes, etc., is not straightforward. The system of requirements to build them has to take into account capacities of the potential users to handle them. For artifacts such as, information systems, decision support systems, man-machine simulations, and games, an appropriate design methodology is even trickier and risky, because they are ingrained in multiple work and management streams in a variety of forms of organization such as, machine bureaucracy, divisional form of organization, professional bureaucracy, adhocracy, matrix and project organization, and new and more flexible forms such as networks and, virtual organizations. Each of these organizations are structured in different ways, which impacts on their internal horizontal and vertical communication rules, and on the role of information-based artifacts that support such communication. For those reasons, their design should place special emphasis on the Human Computer Interface (HCI) design as an integral part of the actor-artifact development. It should be linked to the training of the users to improve their abilities, and to prepare them to handle the system properly. Therefore, the design of the actor-artifact system (AA-system) as such, should be understood from the broader scope of total system development. These notions are depicted in Figure 5.11.

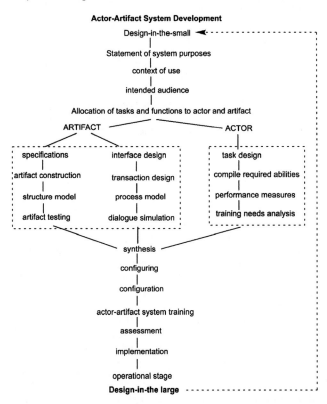

Figure 5.11. Representation of actor-artifact system development

The meaning of the terms "design-in-the-small" and "design-in-the-large" will be explained in Chapter 6. Lessons learned from the design-in-the-large may be feedback into the next cycle, or next version of design-in-the-small. This development scheme is relevant for the design of computer-supported artifacts as for example, information systems, and digital games for entertainment purposes, as well as for developing such artifacts for training personnel in virtual learning environments ("flight simulators"). In digital games for entertainment, the leveling up of the skills of the players should be included both in the task and the interface design.

A GAMING APPROACH TO AGILE SOFTWARE DEVELOPMENT

The representation of the iterative process of actor-artifact system development, as illustrated in Figure 5.11, and Table 5.8, indicates that the methodological considerations of game design – discussed above – need to be embedded in development project organizations – game design studios – to design and market games. Digital game development is strongly based upon software engineering methods. The effectiveness, efficiency, and timing of software engineering are a cornerstone for video games for entertainment, as well as computer-supported games and simulations (virtual worlds) for research and education. In this section, I propose to use gaming methodology for software development on computer-support and -driven games and simulations, carried out by those design studios. What will gaming methodology have to offer to software development projects? What is the state of the art of software development?

Although the software development process is incompletely defined, various detailed development methodologies have been developed. The waterfall model was one of the first systems for software development. It was a response to the need to better organize and manage such complicated processes. This model focused on linearly connected development phases, starting with the requirements and analysis phase, continuing with the design, implementation, and testing phases, and finally with the transition phase to business (clients and users). The underlying idea was that the output of each phase should provide all necessary information to smoothly perform the next phase. It soon became clear that the linear input-output process – envisioned by the waterfall model – did not allow for intermediate feedback between the subsequent phases. Consequently, alternative approaches such as, the spiral model (Boehm, 1988) appeared, which addressed this shortcoming. During the 1990s, iterative object-oriented methodologies matured into what today is called the Unified Process (Jacobson et al., 1999), which has many adherents in the software community. These methodologies pay attention to the management of software development and to the qualities of deliverables for clients and other customers. They convey a bureaucratic, mechanistic view on the software development organization. People in those organizations have distinct and well-defined roles with specific responsibilities such as, project manager, requirements managers, analysts, designers, programmers, and testers. Each of them is responsible for delivering standardized documents including textual descriptions, graphical models or programs. These formal documents should provide the necessary input to the other roles. In addition, an ideal bureaucratic organization should continuously monitor, measure and assess its work processes to be able to improve its productivity and quality. For various reasons this bureaucratic model is becoming less suitable to deal with volatile market conditions, and rapid advances in Information Technology (IT). Through its interplay with computer hardware, software development plays a key role in advancing IT-applications such as, digital games, and virtual game worlds.

Configuration of the information business

The value chain of a company consists of all activities it performs to develop, produce, market, deliver, and support its product or service. This applies to manufacturing as well as to information processing such as in the service industry. The value chains of companies that supply each other and buy from one another collectively make up an industry's value chain. It is a particular configuration of competitors, suppliers, distribution channels, and customers. The value chain should not be visualized as a linear flow of activities, as it includes all the information that flows within a company and between a company and its suppliers, its distributors, and its existing and potential customers. It is a collective network, glued together by information. Advances in Information & Communication Technology (ICT) such as the Internet and Intranets cause a breaking down of the traditional links between the flow of the product- or service-related information and the flow of the product or service itself. Such business configurations shape networks, driven by collaborative arrangements with producers and their customers.

Managing complex technology

The economics of information is fundamentally altering the competitive landscape of business. Fast and cheap information exchange force protected regional companies into battles with distant rivals. The ICT industry is in the leading position with regard to the rate of innovation. The core concept for its advance is *modularity* – building a complex product or process (system) from smaller subsystems that can be designed independently, yet function together as a system (an integrated whole). Modularity is achieved by partitioning information into *visible and hidden design rules* (Baldwin & Clark, 1997). Visible design rules refer to three categories: *architecture, interfaces* and *standards*, which are communicated to the parties involved. Hidden design rules refer to the degrees of freedom of software design teams to frame software systems according to the specifications of the visible design rules. Modularity has helped designers, producers and users to gain enormous flexibility inside and outside the computer industry. It enhances the development and use of software engines for building virtual worlds. Modularity heightens the competitive pressures among suppliers. It also transforms relations among companies. Module designers, as they compete in the race to innovate, easily move in and out of joint ventures, technology alliances, subcontracts, employment agreements, and financial arrangements. Companies can compete in their roles of architect or designer of modules.

Modularity within the project organization

In order to create superior modules, leaders in companies need the flexibility to move quickly to market and make use of rapidly changing technologies, ensuring that the modules conform to the overall architecture. Project managers can speed up development cycles for individual modules by splitting the work among independent teams, each pursuing a different sub-model or different path to improvement, thus shaping a modular approach to design. These managers must provide adequate leadership by delineating and communicating a detailed operating framework for each of the teams to work. The framework has to extent into the work of teams themselves by establishing principles for matching appropriate types of teams to each type of project. It must specify the size of teams and make clear what roles senior management, the core design team, and support groups should play in carrying out the project's work. The organizational framework establishes an overall structure within which teams can operate. It provides ways for different teams and other groups to interact, and defines standards for testing the merits of the team's work.

Flexible product development

The World Wide Web and open source software provide one of the most challenging environments for product development. The market needs that a product intends to satisfy and the technologies required to satisfy them can change radically – even as the product is under development. In response to such factors, project teams have to modify the traditional product development process in which design implementation begins only once a product's concept has been determined in its entirety. The traditional development processes pass through the following sequential stages: design, development, production, and market. Functionally integrated teams do the work. In turbulent business environments, such a sequential approach to product development is inefficient by running the risk of creating an obsolete product once it enters the market. What is needed under those circumstances is a flexible development process with the ability to manage jointly the evolution of a product and its application context. Needed is continuous feedback about the interactions between technical choices and market requirements, allowing a design studio to timely respond to changes in markets and technologies during the development cycle. Dedicated project teams play a key role in integrating such flexible processes.

Team based organization

Learning in organizations can primarily take place through experimenting to see if and how ideas work. In doing so, people get to know each other, and shape communities of practice (Wenger, 2002). Under rapidly changing market conditions, it is important that processes are linked to a purpose. Such a purpose is instrumental at changing people's behavior because they can see what they are aiming for. Consequently, a project needs to be organized in a way that lets everyone see clearly how things are done and understand what each person's role is in getting it done. Such a project organization is based on processes (hyper-archies), not on tasks or hierarchies (Evans & Wuster, 1997).

To be able to see the impact of people's actions on project performance – and to encourage intellectual ownership – team based flat organizations, allow people to have many face-to-face interactions and to form personal relationships. Thus, they can develop the kind of embedded knowledge that is needed to continuously improve performance and to create new future options. The successful strategy for the design studio is about finding the right options for the design-game to play.

Impact on project management: agile programming

Advances in ICT are having a great impact on software development projects. Traditional linear value chains such as the waterfall model are being replaced by value networks, which require new forms of organization. These emerging new forms show an increased fluidity in the external appearances of projects such as, clusters, networks, (strategic) alliances and virtual organizations. Consequently, the internal organization of a software engineering project has to mirror the fluidity of the external appearances. On the inside, formal compartmentalization needs to be broken down into an empowered, flat, flexible organization. By maintaining, modifying and transforming inter-organizational relationships, project organizations can construct their own environments, their own markets, as they seek allies to which they can bond for periods of mutual benefit.

It is interesting to note that new software development methodologies are emerging, focusing on activities in the development process rather than on deliverables as such. These methodologies are named *agile methodologies* and include *extreme programming* (Beck, 2000), *crystal clear* (Cockburn, 2002), *scrum* (Schwaber et al., 2002), and others. A common basis for these methodologies can be found in the agile programming manifesto (Cunningham, 1995), which favors:

- Individuals and interactions over processes and tools
- Working software over comprehensive documentation
- Customer collaboration over contract negotiation
- Openness to changing circumstances over following a plan.

The proponents of agile programming claim that software companies engaged in the new agile methodologies inevitably experience that the software engineers develop new channels for communication in addition to the prescribed ones. Moreover, they develop new work practices to minimize workload to better deal with documentation and other methodological issues. The agile movement claims that many of the practices of standard bureaucratic development methodologies are counterproductive. They give lower product quality. They run the high risk of generating a mismatch between the final product and customer needs, and they make the software engineers less satisfied with their work (Beck, 2000). They argue that in a team-based organization, people perform better and learn more when using all modes of communications available as part of the new work conditions, where people have the opportunity to immediately communicate with each other. They also consider it important that customer representatives participate actively in the development process to make sure that the final product is close to the customer's evolving wishes and goals. They also propose design and programming techniques that ensure high quality while avoiding unnecessary complexity, continuously performing elaborated tests, and rigid compliance to standards for writing programs.

Enhancing process management of software engineering through gaming

I have argued above that, designing software systems under volatile market conditions requires new ways of organizing work and new approaches to process management. To become more effective, design studios need to be both highly flexible, and well focused. To be able to deal with the emerging requirements of flexible product development and team based organizations, management of software engineering projects needs support to make the organization more visible to itself, without jeopardizing the quality, the tuning of the project to clients' needs, and the time-to-market the product. Therefore, using gaming techniques to software development is a promising approach to address these issues. It links gaming with ideas on agile programming. During digital game development projects, applying agile programming, key members of the project organization need support to learn to work together on tasks and issues while at the same time helping them to become more aware of and skilled in dealing with the project dynamics. Action and reflection are needed to help both project management, the software engineers, and the client to adequately elicit explicit and tacit knowing, solve complex problems, work on redesign, determine goals and priorities, and tune product requirements to evolving market needs. Cockburn (2002) compared agile software development to rock climbing, which he views as a finite, cooperative game. An agile programming approach includes:

- Load bearing
- Team work
- Individuals with talent
- Skill sensitivity
- On the job training
- Tools
- Dealing with limited resources
- Planning
- Improvisation
- Fun
- Challenge
- Risk taking.

However, an important difference between an agile programming project and the rock climbing metaphor lies in the more or less clear view on the target. The top of the mountain is well defined, although the way to reach it may be open for debate, requiring good leadership. The goal of an agile software development project is poorly defined as compared to rock climbing. Many intangibles play tricky roles. In addition, shifting interests and growing awareness of the qualities of the deliverables by the client may cause the "top of the mountain" to shift over time. Therefore, shared reflection-in-action between all stakeholders (actors) is vital to an effective, and flexible game on agile software development.

Cockburn (2002) views the software development process as a cooperative game of invention and communication. The developers cooperate to reach the goal of producing a piece of software within a fixed period of time and with a fixed amount of resources. The gaming approach may contribute to a better understanding of the design process, and consequently enhance the software development processes both from the perspective of project management, and the quality of the product. Abrahamsson et al, (2002) used another gaming metaphor for agile programming by introducing the *scrum* as one of the agile methods. It refers to the game of rugby, and happens when an out-of-play ball is put back into the game again. The scrum requires good, tight, adaptive, quick, and self-organizing teamwork.

Take extreme programming (XP) – one of the agile programming approaches – as an example. An extreme programming project usually consists of 12 or 14 activities carried out simultaneously and in parallel by the design studio. Some activities refer to performing the basic software design and programming activities as such. Others focus on communication, guided by evolving rules about how and when to interact. The team members have to take into account constraints on work practices or even on the workspace. This XP-framework is similar to the setting of a game session, based on the interconnected macro-, and micro-cycle (see Chapter 3). A typical and vital activity of XP is *pair programming*, a technique where two programmers use alternatively one keyboard, one mouse, and one monitor. Another important part is the so-called *planning game*, a term, which already has its gaming connotation. Within the "pair programming game", each member is involved in programming, testing, refactoring, integration. Pair programming challenges the team members to express what they think, and to elicit to each other their embedded knowledge about, and experience with programming. Pair programming, together with code sharing, sets the stage for tapping and utilizing the joint intellectual capital of the programmers. *Refactoring* is a change to the system that leaves its behavior unchanged. It enhances nonfunctional qualities of the design such as, simplicity, flexibility, understandability, and performance. Thus, the extreme programming practice can be viewed as a set of games, each set with actors, rules, and resources, each game tuned to a particular activity level.

For example, the level of the code base contains all code made for the particular project, and all code is checked out when starting a task and the new version checked when the task is done. The code base includes micro-level modules in the form of object-oriented classes. XP provides an alternative to the handling of modules, using collective ownership, so that anybody can change any code. This is in contradiction to the approaches chosen in bureaucratic methods where each module is considered to be the responsibility of one or few programmers. At the next level of aggregation, software components are much more complex and can be seen as pieces of software with thousands of classes. Components may be off-the-shelf or especially designed for a particular project, maybe as the result of a subproject. Agile methods have yet to address the problem of agile development of software that is so complex or large that many teams are needed, each team building one or a few components. The risk of poor communication between teams may lead to the design and use of formal documents to communicate between teams to ensure well-defined code ownership. Would this happen then bureaucratic routines may slip into the work procedures. To prevent that from happening, Rollings and Morris (2004) proposed that – for each team member – the codes of each programmer needed to be understood by all members. Therefore, coding standards (rules), stylistic edicts that affect various aspects of the code, are needed. They too refer to modular design that can be used over the course of a number of projects. This requires that the style of the programming interface should be consistent for all the modules released to the project teams. This will prevent confusion about the modules that support similar functionality. They mentioned the following coding priorities: *speed, size* – on space-limited platforms code size becomes an important consideration, *flexibility* – where re-use is an option, flexibility of code is important, *portability* – the platforms targeted must be broadly similar in capabilities, and *maintainability* – readability and ease of modification. These rules of the game, these common resources and their common interfaces, should help the programmers (actors) to perform well.

There is another correspondence between XP and gaming. The iterative approach to program development and the macro-cycle of a game session are very similar (aee Chapter 3). The micro-cycle encompasses the iterative phases of the game process. It focuses on learning-by-doing and knowledge-in-action. One cycle in XP development is one cycle in a game session, briefing and debriefing included. Viewing XP programming as a self-organizing game, is consistent with the ideas underlying agile programming methods.

Gaming has the potential to provide a suitable framework for agile programming that is useful for formulating and documenting the work processes. It may thus be used to make agile-project teams more visible to themselves (helping the team members to become more reflexive actors), to facilitate learning and mutual understanding, and even to enhance the co-evolution of the teams, and project management. The gaming approach therefore supports the internal organization of the design team to become more reflective about its steering of the project. Added advantages of the gaming approach to agile programming are to make it easier for newcomers to enter the programming team, and to sustain a common understanding of the development practices.

SUMMARIZING REMARKS

In this chapter I have reviewed the scientific method to make it appropriate for game design and system development. I have elaborated the model or empirical cycle, and steps in model building. Distinguishing between qualitative and quantitative models, I have argued that model building starts with a conceptual model, which then can be mapped into various formal mathematical or quantitative models. Estimating such models is not easy. Subsequently I have made the distinction between descriptive and normative systems, allocating games to normative systems. With that frame-of-reference in mind I switch from close mechanistic systems – used for simulation modeling – to open actor-based systems – used for gaming. That switched implied a transition from a functionalist to a constructivist approach. While discussing multi-actor systems, and referring to Hacking (1999), I have argued that as regards social systems, we should keep in mind the different sorts of classification in the natural and social sciences. This led to differentiating reference systems into referential and self-referential subsystems. Based on these understandings I have presented the game design cycle.

Methodological aspects of game design take on board the conversations between the designer and the client to tune the artifact to the client's needs. The resulting design specifications are input to the actual design, based on the architecture of games presented in Table 5.9. That table offers a common frame for the design team as well as a common medium for conversations with the client about the qualities of the game. Complex sophisticated games – actor-artifact systems – need a special approach to systems development in order to include the important features of the human computer interface vis-à-vis the actor. Finally, on the basis of the methodology presented, I have argued why it is worthwhile to use the gaming approach for software development of digital games.

The methodology presented here takes on board the gaming theory discussed in Chapter 4, with special emphasis on the study of organized complexity. Both Chapter 4 and 5 transcend the particular domains of disciplines. So, it is worthwhile to ask what kind of science we are actually dealing with when we engage in gaming.

GAMING: WHAT KIND OF SCIENCE IS IT?

Reflecting on the bewildering variety of games and simulations, the versatility of their interactive learning environments, the intricacies of gaming theory and methodology, presented in the previous chapters, one stressing question surfaces: What kind of science is it that we are talking about? The reader, after having read the previous chapters, will not expect a simple and straightforward answer. To position gaming as a science, it is worthwhile to wrap up key qualities that provide a general view on this challenging field of enquiry and practice. I will argue that the landscape that unfolds is actually a garden state, although some might consider it a mentally impermeable labyrinth.

THE POSITIONING GAME

The origins of the academic field of gaming and simulation go back to advances in the General Systems Theory and cybernetics of the 1930s and 1940s, management science of the 1950s, and the applied computer science studies of the 1960s. Its aim has been systematizing the design of applications in social systems such as companies, cities, and public institutions dealing with education, health care, and ecosystems. Most recently the field has been enriched with the design and study of digital games for entertainment. Nowadays gaming studies are hosted mostly in business and management schools, faculties of social sciences (economics included), computer science departments, and humanities faculties. Mathematical game theory, a branch of mathematics and econometrics, has gained academic fame with several Nobel prizes.

Gaming has proven itself to be influential on practice for the following reasons. It has developed close links with professional practitioners, who use the approach to deal with the complexities of social systems. Apart from mathematical game theory, the gaming field has not yet attained a prominent position within academia. The object of study does not fit easily within the categories of conventional scientific disciplines. It addresses questions of human behavior in the context of organizational action and social change that do not fit easily in the limited knowledge domains of the various disciplines involved. Within the setting of academia, it draws among others from the social and behavioral sciences, information and computer science, and engineering, each of them pursuing their particular disciplinary interests. Therefore, the added value of gaming is questioned by all of them. It does not come as a surprise that gaming is still conquering its position in the science policy arena. It challenges the existing explicit and tacit subdivision of disciplinary territories, and the related procedures for allocating research budgets. Disciplinary peer reviews have difficulty in gaining authority in multi- and inter-disciplinary research questions. Crossing knowledge domains implies taking the risk of entering less known or even un-known territory. The resulting feelings of insecurity are aggravated by features of the gaming field such as, variety of research topics and approaches, cross- and inter-disciplinary theories, methodological pluralism, and a very large area of enquiry and practice. This diversity and pluralism is a force in addressing multifaceted processes in contemporary social systems. It is a weakness in academic organizations that are compartmentalized along disciplinary lines. Thus, an interesting question is: Is academia the norm, and the one prevailing norm to judge the field of gaming?

The objects of gaming studies are diverse. To name a few, they vary from testing behavioral and social theories such as, the endowment effect, the mere ownership effect, group information sharing, the social presence theory, media richness theory, and normative and informational influence (Noy et al. 2006), to evaluating pedagogical content knowledge and the transfer of simulation technology from R&D into school settings (Blasi et al., 2006), improving cross-cultural communication and language learning (Garcia-Carbonell et al., 2001), international relations (Starkey & Blake, 2001), utilities deregulation (Wenzler et al. 2005), business and public management (Thorelli, 2001; Cecchini & Rizzi, 2001), and to improving global environmental policies (Meadows, 2001).

Gaming, in connection with complex adaptive systems theory, could enhance the capacities of policy makers by providing them with suitable multi-actor platforms to experiment with and assess viable action repertoires in political arenas. It could teach them that complex adaptive systems require a new mode of steering. The conventional control mechanisms of bureaucratic regimes are becoming rapidly obsolete.

Promising thematic areas of gaming are: supporting the functioning of organizations; enhancing social systems development and organizational learning to improve the organizational value of knowledge; assessing the societal impact of current cultural and socio-economic changes; performing participative assessments on the impact of digital games on the youth culture; and setting up educational systems in relation to various learning styles. All these examples show the potential and richness of the gaming approach. In Part III I will discuss several cases in more detail.

In Chapters 4 and 5, I have elaborated theoretical and methodological foundations, paying attention to complexity science as the currently most compelling meta-disciplinary area of enquiry of high relevance for gaming. In gaming, various theoretical platforms are already crossing conventional boundaries of academic disciplines with serious methodological implications. The following list give an idea of the diverse inference schemes that meet in this multi-disciplinary game studies arena: structuration theory; critical theory; semiotics & linguistics; logical positivism; schema theory (educational sciences); realism vs. constructionism, management science & behavioral science, functionalism vs. constructivism, etc. Choosing between these and other theoretical frameworks will have methodological implications. In chapter 5, I have discussed methodological questions related to simulation and game design. I have not yet discussed evaluation, or assessment methodology: running games in diverse contexts of use for different audiences. Some evaluation studies favor the positivist research methodology, laboratory experiments and quantitative methods. Others stress surveys, qualitative interpretive or critical methods, case studies, or action research. Therefore, evaluation methodology is a field with many flowers representing a broad range of disciplines and professions.

In Chapter 1 I have presented a random list of disciplines and departments of fellow scholars globally involved in gaming: *architecture (& building); biology; business administration; cognitive economics; cognitive engineering; communication; computer science; computing arts and design sciences; design & environment; economics; education; environmental information; information science; information systems; integration of technology in education; interactive arts; international relations; language; linguistics; management; marketing; mathematical economics; media studies; natural resource management; policy studies; organizational behavior; political science; project management; psychology (leadership/work & organization); public administration; research methodology and methods; social psychology; social sciences; sociology; systems agronomics; systems management; teacher studies; technology education; telecommunication; urban planning; etc.* Each of these disciplines and departments pursue their specific styles of gaming, mixing their particular scientific approaches with domain specific knowledge, with their art and craft of designing games. In Chapter 4 I have presented a meta-disciplinary gaming theory aimed at bringing the great variety of disciplinary approaches under one integrative scientific umbrella. Meeting this challenge is a prerequisite for advancing gaming theory and methodology. Without a coherent frame-of-reference gaming will stay fragmented in the scientific realm. It is not sufficient that those disciplines, mentioned above, have in common that they use gaming for instrumental reasons. Underlying those gaming methods and techniques are methodological and theoretical issues that need to be addressed, and that require crossing disciplinary lines.

CROSSING THE LINE

Envisioning the potential influence of gaming in academia requires a thorough review of its current position. Reviews of a field of inquiry are considered forms of knowledge accumulation and generation, synthetic perspectives on inquiry that allows a discipline to share a common understanding of its current state, and directions to go. Those involved in advancing gaming – performing such reviews – will face severe obstacles. They need to take into account disciplinary reviews, which with regard to gaming are of limited scope. In addition, while linking disciplinary perspectives, they need to master conceptual, technical, and discursive competence to assess each of the supporting disciplines. Moreover they need excellent communicative competence that is, cross-disciplinary, cross-cultural competence to link disciplines. Conquering these obstacles is not a purely scientific – "academic" – effort. One major obstacle is the academic structure.

A disciplinary review is a process and product that serves as an assessment of already published work to (re)define a given knowledge domain. Disciplinary knowledge domains are constructed according to social and epistemological commitments and conventions of the discourse community in which such a review is situated. Moreover, it is political as the terms of the material conditions underlying research and practice – its social utility – and the power relations out of which it is produced, are framed in a political context. Knowledge thus produced is a form of cultural capital (Apple, 1995). The kinds of knowledge that are recognized as legitimate or of high status enable universities to use this recognition as a form of social capital (Apple, 1999). Disciplinary knowledge is a form of power. It operates as a regulative mechanism, which is expressed by the meaning of "discipline." Following Bourdieu (1993), I argue that scholars and their research institutions exist in determinate and overlapping fields of power. Markets of social capital exist in structured ways, in contexts. A particular kind of knowledge can only be a valued form of capital, if the knowledge itself is recognized within the relevant field of power as important. In addition, it should be recognized by more powerful fields, connected with that specific field, as of high status as well (Apple, 1999). Knowledge is a covert and implicit form of power and it operates through discourses (Foucault, 1979). Popkewitz (1991) argued that such power is embodied in the ways that individuals construct boundaries for themselves, define categories of good/bad, and envision opportunities. Power, phrased in this way, is intricately bound to the rules, standards, and styles of reasoning by which individual scientists speak, think, and act in self-reproducing their community of research and practice. The traditional form of power, adhering to organs of the state, is explicit. Scientific knowledge as a form of power is embedded in the language of a discourse, and in the instrumentation of research. Discourse, according to Foucault (1972), is a system consisting of rules of formation and volitions that control what can be said within a particular field. It defines which inference schemes are valid, and which ones are of less value. Such a straightforward view on disciplinary knowledge and its status in the form of social capital is for several reasons more difficult to capture when dealing with the trans-disciplinary field of gaming.

In the trans-disciplinary field of gaming the discourse is not similar to the one used within one particular mono-discipline. One reason is that which constitutes knowledge and social capital is less straightforward. By crossing knowledge domains, gaming is challenged to link multiple and potentially incompatible knowledge domains into one framework. In crossing disciplinary lines gaming scientists come across and will have to be competent in using two kinds of knowledge: *declarative and procedural knowledge.* Declarative knowledge refers to facts, concepts, principles, and laws of the related disciplines. It is disciplinary "knowing that". Procedural knowledge concerns procedures and strategies. It is disciplinary "knowing how". Procedural knowledge develops while playing the game of crossing disciplinary lines. Procedural tacit knowledge involves knowing how the system functions in which one is operating.

The great variety of disciplines and research topics, and the methodological pluralism in gaming demonstrate a serious need for cross-disciplinary theories, and eventually a meta-disciplinary perspective such as presented in Chapter 4. Such a commonly felt need is missing. The field is suffering from insecurity regarding its position in academia. The body of knowledge is not in the form of a cohesive structure. The diversity and pluralism of gaming are an advantage when addressing multi-faceted processes of social systems. They are a weakness in academic organizations that are compartmentalized along disciplinary lines. Table 6.1 wraps up current strengths and weaknesses of gaming.

For the following reasons, gaming has not yet attained a prominent position within academia (except mathematical game theory). The object of study does not fit easily within the categories of conventional scientific disciplines. Nonetheless, mathematical game theory fits nicely in economics departments. What are reasons for its success?

The broader field of gaming addresses questions that go beyond the limited scope of game theory. It addresses organizational action and social change that easily cross knowledge domains. It draws from the social sciences, humanities, and engineering (in particular information technology), faculties that for various reasons question its added value. The paradox is that the weakness of gaming in academia is its strength in practice. Gaming is influential in the development of knowledge and experience, dealing with practical issues. It has a strong record in the development of various types of interactive learning environments, increasingly with computer support, to help actors to improve their capacities in a great variety of social settings.

Table 6.1. Strengths and weaknesses of the field of gaming

Strengths	Weaknesses
• Pragmatism: responsiveness to the needs of government institutions, the industry, and individuals vis-à-vis institutions; • Cross-disciplinary approach, including a range of professions; • Gaming depends on its own potential as well as on organizational and social action that shape it.	• Pragmatism makes the field issue-oriented; • Slow to appreciate the significance of building theories; • Body of knowledge not in the form of a cohesive structure; • Thematic diversity, and theoretical and methodological pluralism are weak credentials within academia. • Within conventional academic settings, gaming faces serious limitations. As a trans-disciplinary field, it is positioned in different departments and faculties.

Above, I have assessed the position of gaming in the academic arena, and come to the tentative conclusion the major sources of its weakness are thematic diversity, and theoretical and methodological pluralism. They are weak credentials in academic organizations that are compartmentalized along disciplinary lines. It is interesting to note that exactly those weaknesses are the source of its strength in the societal context. So, the assessment of weakness of gaming depends on the current academic structure, which I have presented as the temporary "norm". Here, a basic question arises: Should that compartmentalized academic organization be the norm? To address it properly, the following second-order question should be answered. What is the norm about that norm? Whose interests are at stake to uphold that norm? So far I have used the following terms: *multi-disciplinary, cross-disciplinary, trans-disciplinary, inter-disciplinary*, and *meta-disciplinary* to locate the realm of gaming, and to embed the dual position of gaming – vis-à-vis the question of what is real, and what is imagined – in scientific research. Is it that only gaming is suffering from that "academic norm", or do we bump into a more fundamental question that applies to all scientific endeavors that dare to cross the disciplinary lines? In order to properly address that question, it is worthwhile to further elaborate key characteristics of interdisciplinary research.

INTERDISCIPLINARITY

The various approaches to play, game, and simulation in Chapter 1 did not produce a coherent image of the field. A leitmotiv was missing. Moreover, as argued above, the way scientific research is organized aggravates this lack of coherence. In scientific research, play- and game-studies are scattered over various disciplines. I have noticed an interesting similarity with the development of the play-concept in languages in general. Huizinga (1985) pointed out that some of the so-called primitive languages have words for the different species of a common genus, as for eel and pike, but none for fish. He argued that the abstraction of a general play-concept has been tardy and secondary in some cultures. This is surprising as the play-function itself is fundamental and primary. He noted that the absence of a common Indo-European word for play points to the late conception of a general play concept. Even the Germanic group of languages differs widely in the naming of play. Paraphrasing this assertion for academia, I argue that disciplinary languages have different words for the different species of a common genus, as for play, game, role-play, simulation, policy exercise, experiment, etc. These various indications convince us that the abstraction of a generally agreed gaming concept has been tardy and secondary in disciplinary cultures. This is surprising as playful gaming itself is fundamental and primary to human life in social and institutional settings, academic settings included. The main reason for such tardiness lies in the mono-disciplinary inference schemes that hamper the development and use of an appropriate – read interdisciplinary – theory of knowledge on gaming. Academic rigor faces difficulties with the ambiguity of play (see Chapter 2). It seems that it excludes playfulness of research cultures. The structure of scientific research forces knowledge to be extracted from a fully integrated world into disciplinary knowledge domains and inference schemes. Such knowledge becomes des-integrated by disciplinary units called departments in universities. Playing a game is a total event of being involved in a temporary, provisional, and integrated world. Through scientific studies that total event is cut into disciplinary pieces. For example, psychologists don the lenses of cognition, and group dynamics, sociologists extract various social theories of information sharing, communication, and power relations, economists focus on rational decision-making, language departments view games as text or mimetic art, computer scientists approach games as dedicated software systems and algorithms, etc. The resulting scientific stories emanating from one singular game become disjointed in time and space as they are based on distinct styles of reasoning performed by the variety of university departments. How can scientific knowledge from gaming be assimilated, re-integrated and disseminated? A fruitful theory of knowledge is lacking.

Many things come to mind to address that question, some related to promising epistemological and methodological approaches, some to making arrangements for cross-fertilization in new organizational settings for research and education, and some to the re-allocation of funds for interdisciplinary research. The conceptualization of a suitable theory of knowledge (a common scientific language) dealing with gaming is a prerequisite for constructive conversations and connections that lead to new knowledge and understanding of the world. Conditions for a productive rhetoric on interdisciplinary research are currently lacking in academia.

Interdisciplinary inquiry and education are inspired by the drive to answer complex questions and deal with problems, whether generated by scientific curiosity or put forward by society. They lead researchers in different disciplines to meet at the interfaces and frontiers of those disciplines, and even challenge them crossing frontiers, to form new disciplines. Popper (1963) has argued that we are not students of some subject matter, but students of problems, which may cut right across the borders of any subject matter or discipline. The laboratory, hypothetic-deductive, statistical, taxonomic, and evolutionary styles of reasoning underpin experimental and empirical research, and as such, they are not confined to one discipline. Thus, there should be other reasons and mechanisms for dividing knowledge to be extracted from a fully integrated world into disciplinary knowledge domains and inference schemes. In academia for historic reasons we are talking about university and not multiversity. As noted above, knowledge as a form of power is embedded in the language of a discourse, which is a system consisting of rules of formation and volitions that control what can be said within a particular field (Foucault, 1972). A discourse defines the rules of inference and the styles of reasoning of a particular discipline, and the knowledge produced by it depends on the assumptions underlying prevailing paradigms and the types of inquiry. At the interface between adjacent disciplines, at the unexplored fields of research, those paradigms, and the underlying assumptions are called into question. The resulting debates are often competitive games for at least two reasons. They are contests about claims of validity and reliability of existing disciplinary knowledge, and criticism about flawed research methods. Moreover, vested interests and academic status of prominent scientists are at stake. Playing such power games could be, and should be both constructive, and rhetorically enjoyable, however high the science policy stakes. Most of these discussions happen when project proposals are judged among peers through "blind" peer reviews, which hamper face-to-face communication. The setting of this game is not an open science policy arena. This also applies to peer-assessed paper presentations during conferences with time slots of 10 minutes or less for paper presentations. I do not question that science should apply its inherent polemic qualities in a playful manner. I question the tacit epistemology that drives the peers that judge project proposals. I question the myopic perceptions of disciplinary peer reviews with regard to across disciplinary questions. As long as government funds are allocated along disciplinary lines, it will enforce the universities to act as nation-states, faculties as kingdoms, and departments as counties. They form formidable obstacles for interdisciplinary research and education. For example, in the Netherlands, interdisciplinary research questions emerged during the 1960s and 1970s from advances in systems theory. During that period, available funds provided sufficient redundancy to financially support a number of interdisciplinary pilot studies. Initiatives also received support for establishing interdisciplinary research groups. In order to become productive, such groups, and even some small institutes, needed time to construct a common interdisciplinary platform for research and teaching. In order to become sustainable such settings needed several years to establish a research tradition.

Interdisciplinary research is a mode of research that integrates perspectives, concepts, theories, data, information, methods, techniques, tools, from two or more disciplines or bodies of specialized knowledge to advance fundamental understanding or to solve problems whose solutions are beyond the scope of a single discipline. It is not just edging up of two or more disciplines in one facility for research and education to create an integrated outcome. It is a linkage and synthesis of ideas, vocabularies, methodologies, and methods. Interdisciplinary research requires the researchers to learn the principles and practices of the other disciplines. Such a setting requires openness of mind, and appropriate rhetoric. As a rule of thumb, a culture re-shaping in professional organizations to establish an interdisciplinary sustainable research facility takes between 5−10 years to become effective. Due to governmental budget cuts, starting in the late 1970s and pursued vigorously since then, that time was not granted to many interdisciplinary research facilities in the Netherlands. The first actions taken by the disciplinary units that financially supported those interdisciplinary initiatives were to cut those funds, to strengthen disciplinary trenches. This was an interesting and informative example of conditioned reflexes along disciplinary lines that destroyed most interdisciplinary initiatives in the 1980s. Recently, the Dutch government, stimulated by research funding policies of the European Committee, has taken initiatives to stimulate and financially support multi- and inter-disciplinary initiatives. Times seem to be changing. Whether these initiatives will be sustained over the next decade remains to be seen.

Multi-disciplinary, cross-disciplinary, and trans-disciplinary research is less far reaching than inter-, and meta-disciplinary research. They may borrow methods and techniques from one another. They tend to stick however to their particular ideas, styles of reasoning, vocabularies, and methodologies. They represent slightly different ways of dealing with a common problem, and do not change their discourse during the period that they work together. The differences between these three forms are mainly organizational. Once that incentive to work together is over, everyone goes his way. They may borrow from each other styles of reasoning, methods, skills, or instruments, and may assimilate them in their practice without considering the underlying principles. With interdisciplinary research, the system of interactions between members of a project team may shape a new research field or discipline. These forms of research are collaborative and involve people of disparate backgrounds. The joint outcome is more than the separate contributions of each discipline. It takes extra time and effort to build a new research facility through learning new languages, styles of reasoning, and methodologies. The authors of the US Committee on Facilitating Interdisciplinary Research (2005) recommended continuing social science-, humanities-, and information science-based studies of the complex social and intellectual processes that could make interdisciplinary research successful. I consider this naïve. These disciplines need to resolve first and for all their own interdisciplinary research problems, breaking through their disciplinary traps themselves before they can add value to other interdisciplinary initiatives.

The US Committee on Facilitating Interdisciplinary Research (2005) mentioned four powerful drivers for interdisciplinary research: the inherent complexity of nature and society, the desire to explore problems and questions that are go beyond a single discipline, the need to solve societal problems, and the power of new technologies (p. 40). I would argue that all non-trivial societal problems surpass the domains of single disciplines. Interdisciplinary research is one of the most productive and inspiring of human pursuits. The common frame-of-reference produced and reproduced in such organizational settings provides a format for conversations and connections that lead to new knowledge, unforeseen from a mono-disciplinary viewpoint. As a mode of discovery and education, it is delivering much already and promising more. Examples are a more sustainable environment, healthier and more prosperous lives, new discoveries and technologies, and a deeper understanding of our place in space and time. To prosper, academic and business institutions should explore adequate leadership and management styles, experiment with suitable administrative structures tuned to professional organizations, moving away from bureaucratic forms of organization, and adopting more fluid forms that stimulate collaboration and reward communication.

FRUCTIFICATION

The focus of the US Committee on Facilitating Interdisciplinary Research is mainly on research of the natural sciences and engineering. Wayne Booth (1987) carried the idea of interdisciplinarity a step further in his Ryerson Lecture at the University of Chicago. He discussed the lack of understanding between scholars of all disciplines, a lack that undermines the very idea of a *uni*versity. Booth was very explicit while stating that for people to understand one another is the sine qua non of a genuine university. To appreciate his views, I will start with some of his main conclusions. Booth abandoned, once and for all, a Unified Language of All the Sciences. So, he is not a Unity of Science supporter. His idea of a "*uni*versity" does not ever hope to exhibit, a single language applicable to all worthwhile inquiries. Instead, he advised that we should proliferate, multiply, and rejoice in variety, without discarding Occam's razor entirely. He proposed that the law we should most celebrate is no longer the law of parsimony. It is instead the *law of fructification*. Pursue a problem with at least two hypotheses--and don't despair when they all survive your tests or are rejected by them. He also warned that we should never forget that all human problems resist reduction to any one formulation or method of inquiry (Booth, 1987). His concerns relate especially to the following groups of people who tend to suffer from the disciplinary jargon, the non-specialist undergraduate, graduate students, policy makers and executives who are in charge of awarding research funds. Booth proposed that all faculty members should be required to teach each year at least half of their courses to graduates or undergraduates, concentrating on the question of what kinds of argument are defensible, in one or more of the four rhetorics, see below. A precondition for such open mindedness is curiosity. Therefore, and in addition, he proposed that at tenure and promotion times the primary decision is to be made by departmental representatives – joined by a larger group from outside the department – on the basis of one test only: Is this candidate now still curious, still inquiring into one or more of the four rhetorics, and is it probable that this candidate will continue to stay curious at the age of forty, fifty, or sixty-eight?

Based on that position, he proposed three kinds of rhetoric, leading to three kinds of understanding to enhance communication between scholars at universities.

Rhetoric-1

This first rhetoric applies to front-line research. Small groups of experts rely on special topics of persuasion. Booth (1987) argued that these persuasions are the *tacit convictions* shared by all involved in advancing disciplines or bodies of specialized knowledge. Based on those convictions they construct arguments within that field that should help to reach conventional (and often non-verbal) agreements between peers. Rhetoric-1 concerns those assertions that for example rely on statistical reasoning, and instrumental reasoning. The underlying tacit assumptions may shift over time, due to new research findings. However at any given moment in time, the peers rely on that common understanding. This notion of rhetoric-1 resembles quite well the idea of a paradigm, and related paradigm shifts as discussed by Kuhn (1962).

Rhetoric-2

Rhetoric-2 is common-sense rhetoric, which we share as members of the various social systems such as, family, club, business, university, and society we participate in. It concerns those assertions that are included in everyone's notions of common sense: "trust is not blind", "loyalty matters", "it is wrong to cheat", etc. They make sense in any argument. Rhetoric-2 is thus the set of assertions available in the functioning of all social systems, not just of universities.

Rhetoric-3

This kind of rhetoric is neither as special as rhetoric-1, nor as general is rhetoric-2. It is rhetoric proper to all within a university, not to any one special group. Booth (1987) called it the *rhetoric of inquiry*, or of *intellectual engagement*. He mentioned that we learn how to judge whether the arguments in fields beyond our full competence *somehow* make sense. Whether that style of reasoning *somehow* accords with standards we recognize. We sense whether a colleague, even in fields that are quite remote to us, *seems* to have mastered the tricks of that particular trade, and moreover the tricks of this whole trade we all share, the trade of learning and teaching for the sake of learning and teaching.

All three of these rhetorics are highly fallible, rhetoric-1 through paradigm shifts, and rhetorics-2 and 3 through their more fuzzy assertions. Booth referred to informants who have told him that it is "not really very hard to tell competent work from incompetent, even if you know nothing about the details and cannot replicate the argument or experiment." Those informants – in Booth's terms – use rhetorics-2 and -3. Editors of journals use them to judge manuscripts. Research boards use them to reward grants.

Booth (1987) noted that without rhetorics-2 and -3 the University would have "to surrender to total balkanization or even tribal warfare." The university would disintegrate to a multiversity, a mere collection of research institutes warring for funds. I observe that such tribal warfare is very common, especially when financial constraints are increasingly tight and ongoing budget cuts become a way of university life. It is experienced as a zero-sum game.

The three rhetorics, and especially rhetorics-2 and -3 seem to fail when interdisciplinary research is at stake and conflicting interests foul the science policy arena. The three rhetorics work properly when they preserve the vested interests of the collection of research institutes, and the related faculties. Booth (1987) implicitly supported this thesis by pointing out that each individual scientist survives as scientist by virtue of indeterminately large networks of critical trust, based largely on the sharing of rhetoric-3. He referred to Polanyi (1964) who stated that we are all inherently "convivial," the way we live and work together. He argued that we live in "fiduciary" structures that we have not constructed and could never construct on our own. Exactly, these existing fiduciary structures hamper interdisciplinary initiatives due to a lack of necessary collaborative arrangements to change and innovate them. To conquer such impediments Booth proposed that we should use another picture of how to relate to specialists, and referred to Donald Campbell (1969), who suggested the following way to combat the "ethnocentrism of disciplines," the "tribalism" and "nationalism" of specialties, by pursuing the "fish-scale model of omniscience" (Campbell, 1969, pp. 327-329, in Booth, 1987). Campbell presented a network based on connecting the interests and competencies of each group of specialists as one scale in a total fish-scale. That scale is overlapping and overlapped by the interests and competencies of adjacent specialties. The total network or fish-scale contains whatever is known. Each node in the network knows a little. Together they form a knowledge organization with emerging properties that go beyond the qualities of each individual node.

Rhetoric-4

To be effective, such a collective network requires a fourth type of rhetoric, in Booth's terms, rhetoric-4. It deals with the inter-translation of the rhetorics-1, 2, and 3 to non-specialists. Booth (1987) pointed out that successfully engaging non-specialists such as, business executives and government officials in the inter-translation of rhetorics is a prerequisite for serving public needs. Universities should become centers for the study of the four rhetorics. They are linked to each other, serving however different audiences, and different needs. Regarding gaming, rhetorics-1 and 3 play a definite role during game design. Rhetorics-2 and 4 are vital during game sessions, and transferring the outcomes to users.

Wrapping up these notions, a successful investment in these four rhetorics will conquer the balkanization and tribal warfare between the academic compartments. It is a precondition for interdisciplinary initiatives to prosper. Reflecting on the structural impediments from which gaming is suffering in academia (see above), the cross-fertilization, which results from these four rhetorics, will also shape fruitful conditions for gaming research. Games might as well take on board those four rhetorics as preconditions for cross-fertilization of knowledge among stakeholders (actors).

META-MODELING

Each of the disciplines involved in gaming uses a particular set of images, or models, as media of representation for conveying their ideas, theories, and methods. In Chapter 5, I have presented methodological questions, related to model building. However, to preserve a high diversity of models, and prevent falling into the trap of pursuing a unified language of all the sciences, and in addition to be able to bridge the specific modeling languages, a meta-modeling perspective is needed. A modeling of models that incorporates three levels of discourse: the *philosophy of science level*, the *science level*, and the *application or practical level* (Van Gigch, 2002). At the philosophy of science level, we need to take on board the relevant theories of knowledge – epistemologies – that apply to gaming. I have presented them in Chapters 3 and 4. At the science level, we need to include the disciplinary and interdisciplinary rhetorics, mentioned above. At the science and practical levels, we should be aware of the intricacies of game design as discussed in chapter 5. Also here the four rhetorics should be included, with a special attention to rhetoric-2 and 4. Interdisciplinary research is usually limited to a few adjacent disciplines. Gaming is used in many separate disciplines. Therefore, the idea of the interdisciplinary research is too limited to capture the broad scope of gaming. Game design and use implies dealing with multiple realities. They can only fruitfully be addressed from a meta-scientific perspective.

Understanding, but not accepting the current structure of scientific research – for reasons argued above – I have come to the conclusion that particular applications of gaming can be traced over a *continuum* that at one end starts with (mono-) disciplinary approaches, moving towards multi-, cross- and trans-disciplinary approaches, subsequently towards interdisciplinary approaches, and moving on to the other end of the continuum, characterized by meta-disciplinary approaches.

TWO COMMUNITIES

As mentioned earlier, the Committee on Facilitating Interdisciplinary Research (2005) mentioned four powerful drivers for interdisciplinary research: the inherent complexity of nature and society, the desire to explore problems and questions that are go beyond a single discipline, the need to solve societal problems, and the power of new technologies (p. 40). Booth (1987) proposed the four rhetorics as prerequisites for serving public needs. The common incentives of both authors that transcend the confinements of single disciplines are to serve public needs, and to solve societal problems. Although clear in their purposes, they do not discuss the impact of these statements on the attitudes and incentives of the research communities involved when dealing with the related pure and applied research, and "engineering" in its broadest sense. To enlighten the distinction between kinds of research, I will present two different scientific communities: the analytical and the design science community. Both are of high relevance for gaming, however for distinct reasons. To understand the differences and communalities of the analytical and design sciences, we need to be aware of the way we construct objects by science. Therefore, we need to face two existential questions: What is it that we create, and how much is fully determined in ways that are totally independent of ourselves? The collective networks of analytical and design scientists tend to answer these questions differently.

ANALYTICAL SCIENCE COMMUNITY OF OBSERVERS

In Chapter 5, I have discussed the laboratory style of doing research, which is one of the most powerful innovations in doing science (Hacking, 2002). In ancient times men studied, observed and speculated about phenomena. In modern times we make phenomena, or isolate and purify them. In chemistry, physics, and biology many phenomena have been created, that subsequently have been used in engineering, generating current industrial societies. Contemporary science – chemistry, and biology – constructs artificial objects that do not exist as such in nature. Nevertheless, they still obey basic laws of nature. This laboratory style is the driving force of scientific discovery in physics, chemistry, and biology. It can also be applied to social reality, for example by designing experiments to test theories about cognitive behavior, the social psychology of leadership, group dynamics, sequential decision making in experimental economics and game theory, etc. Against this background, gaming and simulation provide appropriate methods for conducting a laboratory style of enquiry in individual and social behavior, using the hypothetic-deductive method. They enhance developing and testing behavioral and social sciences theories, which is basic to the laboratory style of reasoning. Those involved in the related analytical science view themselves implicitly and explicitly as observers, independent of and neutral to the objects of inquiry. They eventually see themselves as referees to judge the world from their observatories. When they group themselves to study certain knowledge domains such as in mono-disciplines, they rely on distinct styles of reasoning. Consequently, the various analytical science disciplines form different and separate *communities of observers*. Communities such as psychology, sociology, international relations, economics, biology, chemistry, and physics are operationally closed, as they construct and re-construct their different, and sometimes mutually exclusive rules of inference. Those who apply the laboratory style of reasoning enjoy a high status in academia. They pursue paradigms in the so-called normal science tradition (Kuhn, 1962).

NATURAL SCIENCE MODEL OF ANALYTICAL SCIENCE

The scientific method of natural sciences is based upon experimental and empirical research, which produces and validates knowledge, while applying the scientific method as discussed in Chapter 5. Rigid rules are necessary that isolate and protect phenomena from flawed analysis. Table 4 illustrates the inquiry scheme of analytical science.

Table 6.2. Inquiry scheme of analytical science (adapted from March & Smith, 1995)

Research outputs	Research activities	
	Theorize Why and How? *Understanding and explaining*	Justify Testing
Domain-specific & grand theories		
Models Mini-theories Hypotheses		
Methods Techniques		
Predictions Explanations	Novel ideas; new paradigms;	

Researchers accept the following methodological features of inquiry:
- Researcher objectivity and distance;
- Environmental control of independent variables;
- Hypothetic/deductive reasoning;
- Explanation & Prediction.

Within the scheme of Table 6.2, gaming and simulation fit into "domain-specific theories", "models", "mini-theories", and "methods/techniques", both for theorizing and testing. A game can be designed to explicitly encompass and express a certain theory. In that case the research output is both a mini-theory and a research tool. Subsequently, such an artifact can be used as a tool or method to test that theory through some experimental design. Finally, when the embedded theory has been confirmed, the artifact can be used first to explain its behavior, and secondly, to make predictions. It is also plausible to select an existing game and use it as a tool or technique for testing theories, because the game allows the proper handling of the relevant independent and dependent variables in a controlled laboratory setting. The first approach of specifically designing the artifact − driven by a clear-cut theory that is to be tested − is the most pure form of the analytical science approach to gaming and simulation. It is most pure, because form, content and meaning of the theory involved fit together in the frame of the game. In the latter case, the game is a more of a tool to test formal aspects of a theory.

Applying the scientific method implies that theories are justified or falsified via historic data. The analytical sciences are based upon "re-constructing the past." If that re-construction has been confirmed empirically, or experimentally, then the theory is used to predict the future.

To keep the big picture, the term *community of observers* refers to all disciplines that apply the analytical science approach. Pending my line of reasoning, I will not make distinctions between the various disciplines, although in practice we should talk about communities of observers with each discipline representing a particular community.

DESIGN SCIENCE COMMMUNITY OF PRACTICE

The design style of enquiry does not produce general theoretical, or universal, context-independent knowledge, which is the purpose of the analytical science. It is a science, an art, and also a craft. Design scientists produce and apply knowledge for unique circumstances in order to create usable artifacts. Design science consists of constructing artifacts for special purposes and for assessing their impact under the well-defined circumstances of use. A basic question that needs to be addressed is: How well does the artifact perform, considering the specifications for the design, including the goals to be achieved? Contrary to the theory-driven approach of the analytical science, *the design science is issue driven*. It addresses human needs, conquers bottlenecks, and capitalizes on opportunities. Research activities of design science include among others, developing and assessing artifacts, developing meta-artifacts, models, methods, processes, and procedures.

Professional communities of practice have gained high esteem in society, while they usually have a lower position on the academic ladder. They address questions that fit into the realm of *post-normal science*. Funtowicz and Ravetz (1993) used the term *post-normal science* for issue-driven research in a context of hard political pressure, high economic interests, values in dispute, high decision stakes and high epistemological and ethical systems uncertainties. They use the term *post-normal* to indicate that the puzzle-solving exercises of normal science (that is: analytical science in the rationalist (Kuhnian) sense) are no longer appropriate when society is for example confronted with the need to resolve policy issues regarding tricky trans-national and trans-generational social issues (Klabbers, 2004).

The scope of the design science is much broader than purely instrumental. It propagates that everyone designs who devises courses of action aimed at changing existing situations into preferred ones. To be able to distinguish between purely instrumental design, and the broader scope of design as a form of social change, I have distinguished between two levels of design: *design-in-the-small* (DIS), referring to game design as such, and *design-in-the-large* (DIL), referring to changing existing situations into preferred ones, if possible based on lessons learned from design-in-the-small (Klabbers, 2003). Both levels of design are closely interconnected. Simon (1969) argued that everyone designs who devises courses of action aimed at changing existing situations into preferred ones, and that the intellectual activity that produces material artifacts is no fundamentally different from the one that prescribes remedies for the sick patient, or the one that devises a new sales plan for a company or a social welfare policy for a state (Simon 1969). The idea of design – so understood – is the core of all inquiry that creates artifacts that serve human purposes. It is also an approach that is used in professional training. It is the principal mark that distinguishes the design science from the analytical science. Schools of (social) engineering, as well as schools of architecture, management & business, education, law, and medicine, are all concerned with the design style of reasoning.

As discussed in Chapter 5, gaming centers on the design, deployment and use of artifacts that represent tangible solutions to real-world problems. It has much in common with engineering, architecture and other fields of design such as information science. March and Smith (1995) argued that whereas natural science tries to understand and explain reality, design science attempts to create artifacts that serve human purposes to change real world situations. These artifacts are assessed against criteria of value or utility for the user/client, who will ask: Does the artifact work? Does it provide an improvement, a better way of handling processes? Does it improve existing human and social capacities, or trigger new skills and knowledge?

Table 6.3. Inquiry scheme of design science (adapted from March & Smith, 1995)

Research outputs	Research activities	
	Build Develop ways to achieve human & social goals	Evaluate, Assess
Constructs (Formal) languages Meta-artifacts		
Models Local theories		
Methods Procedures: a set of steps		
Artifacts		
Implementation; Interventions;		

Design is a key activity in fields such as architecture, engineering, urban planning, sustainable development, information science, and in gaming as approaches to problems in those fields. Here again, I refer to the dual position that games are both models, and real. March and Smith continued with the observation that rather than producing general theoretical knowledge, design scientists produce and apply knowledge of tasks or situations in order to create effective artifacts (March & Smith, 1995, p. 253).

They distinguished four types of products (see Table 6.3):
- Constructs – a basic language of concepts (meta-languages);
- Models – higher order constructions;
- Methods – ways of performing goal-directed activities;
- Implementations – instantiations intended to perform certain tasks.

Basically, the design science is involved in *building and assessing artifacts*. *Usability* is the key criterion.

A significant difficulty in design science results from the fact that the performance of the artifacts is related to the environment in which they operate. March and Smith noted that incomplete understanding of that environment can result in inappropriately designed artifacts or artifacts that result in undesirable side effects. Evaluation is complicated by the fact that performance is related to intended use, which can cover a range of tasks. They argued that the assessment criteria should be determined for the artifact in a particular environment: its context of use, and its intended audience(s). Progress is achieved in the design science when existing methodologies, technologies, and procedures replace less effective ones.

If the artifact is a new product such as, a mobile phone, a car, or an airplane, then the evaluation criteria are well defined as compared to the more intangible evaluation criteria of a game in its context of use for various audiences. In order to address this question from the perspective of game design, I will elaborate the interplay between design-in-the-small, and design-in-the-large.

DESIGN-IN-THE-LARGE AND DESIGN-IN-THE-SMALL (DIL AND DIS)

As mentioned above, to be able to distinguish between the broad scope of the term "design" as pointed out by Simon, and the more limited instrumental perspective of game design as implied by March and Smith, I have made the distinction between design-in-the-large and design-in-the-small (Klabbers, 2003). Design-in-the-small (DIS) refers to the design of simulation games as artifacts, while design-in-the-large (DIL) deals with the impact of those artifacts on changing existing situations into preferred ones. In Chapter 5, I have pointed out that games – as artifacts – are designed with explicit goals in mind. Moreover, the goals of such goals – the meta-goals – refer to the objectives of the design-in-the-large that are, social change, and social innovation. Design-in-the-small produces artifacts in the capacity of support systems that enhance those processes of change. Those support systems allow the actors opportunities for experimenting, and playfully constructing viable options with all parties involved. In such circumstances, the magic circle is a safe place for testing options and working out strategies. Once a game has been designed it can be used for dual purposes. It can be both used as input to the design-in-the-large, and as a method or model in the analytical science tradition to develop and test theories. When the artifact is intended as input to the design-in-the-large to enhance social systems development, then the two levels of design need to be connected, see Table 6.4. The framework presented in Chapter 5, gaming methodology, and especially Figures 5.3, and 5.11, and Tables 5.5, 5.8, and 5.9, provide a suitable basis for the actual design-in-the-small. I have discussed the core ideas of design-in-the-large and social systems development in Chapter 4. Table 6.3 is primarily focused on the instrumental design. It does not provide clues about the use of the artifact, as intervention in an ongoing process with the purpose to change its course. Such change or organizational development processes presuppose a frame-of-reference as presented in Chapter 4. Without the related notions about social systems, design-in-the-large could be viewed as a form of social engineering.

Table 6.4. Linking two levels of design: DIS & DIL (adjusted from Klabbers, 2006)

Design-in-the-small (DIS) (Ch. 5)	Research inputs/outputs	Research activities		
		Build Develop ways to achieve human goals	Evaluate, Assess	
	Constructs (Formal) languages, meta-artifacts			
	Models Local theories	Conceptual design		
	Methods & procedures (a set of steps)	Actual game design (instrumental)		
	Instantiation	Calibration & testing		
Design-in-the-large (DIL)	Constructs, meta-artifacts (see Klabbers, 2003-b)	System's development program		
	Social context and arena for action on the basis of the artifact	Education & Training program		
	Institutional conditions of interaction with the artifact	Actual use of gaming artifact		
	Institutional consequences of interaction with the artifact	Implementation lessons learned		
	Stakeholder-based assessment			Participative assessment

Such a narrowly technical approach would not do justice to the inherent qualities of complex adaptive social systems, and would deny them basic properties such as, emergent behavior resulting from their self-referential, self-organizing characteristics. Gaming artifacts, if improperly used in the context of design-in-the-large, would easily run the risk of becoming alien to the users, out of touch and context. If that would happen, then all efforts to tune the game design process to the needs of the actors in the social system, according to the guidelines discussed in Chapter 5, would be in vain. The levels of design, as depicted in Table 6.4, refer to two different, however closely connected, realms of inquiry. They represent different knowledge domains, and theories of knowledge. In addition, we should be aware that both scientific communities pursue different goals and apply different standards of success. Increasingly we realize that in order to be effective, the design science has to carry out research especially aiming at designing meta-artifacts, constructs and languages that enhance and facilitate both levels of design. In many cases, the design science produces new knowledge and abilities, and generates new ideas that otherwise would not have surfaced. These opportunities are usually out of the scope of the analytic science with its emphasis on re-constructing the past. The scientific underpinning of the design process not only impacts on a design theory, it influences and improves as well, artifact development in the sense of product development, research management and research policy, and assessment procedures of design-in-the-large.

LINKAGES BETWEEN THE SCIENCE OF ANALYSIS AND DESIGN SCIENCE

Relating the continuum that runs from (mono-)disciplinary via interdisciplinary to meta-disciplinary approaches to the communities of observers and practice, I present the following scheme (see Figure 6.1). In the field of gaming people from the analytical and design sciences meet each other. This is causing confusion, misunderstanding, and sometimes frustration, due to the fact that the positions from which they speak and write stay often implicit. In the silent language they use when they debate and talk − referring to the tacit understanding of rhetorics-1, 2, and 3 − the representatives of the analytical science assume that their kind of research is the norm that applies unequivocally to the design science. As long as both communities are not aware of their different epistemologies, and methodologies, they run the risk of judging each others on the wrong terms, using criteria of success that apply only to their particular domain. Such a situation is hampering the exchange of ideas. Moreover, members of both communities may not understand how they can benefit from one another. Generally, analytical scientists, while pursuing universal, context-independent knowledge (laws of nature), have difficulty with post-normal science questions that are so relevant for the design science. Here, rhetoric-3, and 4 could be beneficial for improving the quality of the conversations between the two communities. I will discuss this matter in more detail in the next chapter.

Members of both communities are well aware of the many efforts it takes to successfully accomplish a simulation/gaming project. Once the *artifact* has been designed it may be used to enhance changing existing situations into preferred ones. However, there is always the other option. The artifact generates qualities and outcomes that can be studied by the community of observers in a similar way as *natural objects* are studied. They can develop theories to be tested through the gaming artifact. The field of agent-based modeling is a clear example of using an artifact − a multi-agent-based model- to test theories about economic behavior, while applying the laboratory style of reasoning, and taking the position of an outside observer. The communities of observers, while obeying the rules of inference of their disciplines, pay mainly attention to reconstructing the past, the communities of practice engage in shaping multiple futures. They may use knowledge from the analytical science as input into their design as long as it contributes to the quality of the artifact. If they do so, they need to translate universal concepts into specific, and sometimes, local circumstances.   Building artifacts is a science, a craft and an art. It is a process not fully understood. Gaming as a design science deals with embodied artifacts, embodied in their forms, and in their utilization by the players (see Chapter 3).

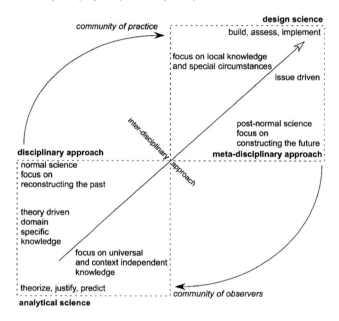

Figure 6.1. Framework for interconnecting two gaming communities (adjusted from Klabbers, 2006)

The analytical science is focused on disembodied objects, dealing primarily with the purely conceptual. As the ultimate drive of science is to generate knowledge to help solving societal problems, and to address public needs, that drive is symbolized in the straight arrow in Figure 6.1 that runs from the analytical to the design science domain.   Both arcs indicate the way both communities may influence one another. Theories, techniques, and tools from the analytical science domain are used as input for the design science domain. Artifacts and their use may raise fundamental theoretical questions that the analytical science may judge relevant for further inquiry. However, the following problem may arise with testing theories about certain computer-supported games (IT-artifacts).   Taking into account the rapid advances in information technology (IT), a particular artifact may have become obsolete once a theory that explains the functioning is being presented. This risk will bear specifically on digital games and their rapid evolution to new updates and new versions.

We belong to multiple communities of practice: family, school, work organization, institutions (Wenger, 1998). They are integrated in our lives and life styles. All are forms of design. Engaging in such communities involves a continuous process of (social) learning. Wenger noted that such learning presumes active participation in the practice of social communities, and constructing of identities in relation to these communities. He distinguished several kinds of practice: practice as the social production of meaning, practice as a source of coherence of a community, practice as learning process, practice as boundary, forming complex social landscapes and peripheries, practice as locality (configuration of communities of practice), and knowing in practice (learning as an interplay of experience and competence). Practice as social learning produces communities with emergent structure, characterized by continuity and discontinuity. A community of practice includes the explicit and silent language, what is said and written as well as what is unspoken, tacit. The idea of practice – in Wenger's view – includes language, documents, images, symbols, well-defined roles, specified criteria, codified procedures, regulations, contracts, (artifacts). Wenger referred to tools, a term, which I consider too limited in view. Referring to Chapter 1, particularly to Huizinga's notion of play, I argue that engaging in a community of practice resembles participating in the "magic circle". It is participating in a game, framed by actors, rules, and resources. The development of artifacts in a process of design-in-the-small, and its interplay with design-in-the-large, is at the core of the communities of practice.

With the frames-of-reference presented in this chapter, it is now appropriate to answer the question: Gaming, what kind of science is it? The answer is: Gaming is both an analytical and a design science. As an analytical science, it ranges from disciplinary, to multi-, cross-, trans-disciplinary, and inter-disciplinary approaches. As a design science, it moves on from inter-disciplinary to ultimately, meta-disciplinary approaches. Design projects are subject to many resisting worlds that need more explicit attention.

RESISTING WORLDS

The designer, while developing a game (artifact) for a client, or user, will run into multiple and connected intricacies, into resisting worlds. Reviewing gaming and its position in academia and potential in society, I will discuss some of them in more detail.

Multiple theories

Suppose that in designing a game more than one theory may be valuable to address the pluralistic social domain, characterized by multiple realities, in which more perspectives compete for dominance. Various conflicting inference schemes from natural sciences, economics, political science, sociology and psychology may come into question. As shown by Club of Rome projects in the 1970s, or Global Climate Change projects in the 1990s, scientists disagree about how to interpret results from model exercises. I will illustrate this with the following example. It refers to handling risk in contemporary societies.

Beck (1992) argued that risk and the perception of risk condition each other. A problem of risk is not an objective fact. Facts and the significance of facts through valuations by people imply that risk problems are social constructs (Hoppe & Peterse, 1993). Risk and the perception of risk are the same. Only from the viewpoint of a narrowly technical rationality, is there a difference. Such rationality is driven by the statistical style of reasoning, which relates risk to the chance of occurrence of an event, and its impact when it occurs. This analytical science approach to risk enforces a division between experts and non-experts in the public debate, with the analytical sciences representing the experts. The resulting debate is about the dominance of one particular definition of reality: the dominant view of the expert. Beck articulated that the 'irrationality' of the 'deviating' public risk 'perception' lies in the fact that, in the eyes of the technological elite, the majority of the public behaves like engineering students in their first semester. Once the public is stuffed full of technical details, they will share the experts' viewpoint about the assessment of the technical manageability of risks, and thus of a lack of risk in society. Those experts are convinced that protests, fears, criticism, or resistance in the public sphere are a pure problem of information. This perception and viewpoint is wrong. Even in their highly mathematical or technical terminology, statements on risks contain statements about how we want to live – statements, that is, to which the natural and the engineering sciences *alone* can provide answers only by overstepping the bounds of their disciplines (Beck, 1992). He continued by arguing that the origin of the critique of science and technology lies not in the 'irrationality' of the critics, but in the failure of the techno-scientific rationality in the face of growing risks and threats from civilization. This failure is systematically grounded in the institutional and methodological approach of the risk sciences. A failure constituted through their concentration on analytical science based methodology and theory, which puts them in the position of outside observers. The analytical sciences are – according to Beck – entirely incapable of reacting adequately to civilization risks, since they are prominently involved in the origin and growth of those very risks. They become the *legitimating patrons* of the global industrial pollution and contamination of air, water, foodstuffs, as well as the related generalized sickness and deaths of plants, animals and people (Beck, 1992). Thus, institutions of science and technology find themselves in a double bind. On the one hand they represent a major force in generating first-order scientific knowledge to increase productivity and related second-order risks and threats. On the other hand, they are the lenses that make those hazards and dreads visible. (See Chapter 10 for more details.)

On the surface, this example shows the tensions between different conceptions of risk in society. Underlying these differences is a more fundamental one: the tension between the analytical science and design science approach, and the conviction that representatives of the analytical science methodology are the very experts.

The designer of a game on risk in society will have to deal with these tensions and the related resisting worlds. I will address this question in more detail in Part III.

Indifferent vs. interactive kinds

The picture sketched above becomes even more complicated when one recognizes that the realm of the natural sciences is simple compared to the human and social realms. Classifications in the human and social domains are more difficult to handle than in the natural sciences. Referring to Hacking (1999) – discussed in Chapter 5 –

the classification "quark" is indifferent in the sense that calling a quark a quark makes no difference to the quark. Take for example the multi-cultural Western-European societies, and the classifications "Jesuit", "Muslim" or "Jew" (as a kind of classification). It is an interactive kind because it interacts with things of that kind, namely people, including individual Jesuits, Muslims and Jews. They become aware of how they are classified and modify their behavior accordingly in a good or bad sense. They form an interactive, self-referential kind. Through those classifications, they become aware of the group (class) they belong to, and aware of themselves as members of that group. Quarks in contrast do not form an interactive kind; the idea of quark does not interact with quarks. The classification "quark" is indifferent, while the classifications "Jesuit," "Muslim," and "Jew" fluctuate in the national debates.

Therefore, we should not be surprised that games do not behave as expected. They resist in two ways. Those parts referring to the natural world – matter and energy – representing resources, and those parts, referring to actors and rules, representing the human and social realm, may not behave as expected for very different reasons. In both cases, it may be a lack of knowledge. Moreover, interactive kinds may obscure the picture due to shifting classifications, enacted by the players themselves. Such inadequacies cannot be solved through the theoretical models and speculative conjectures of the analytical sciences. Such a reductionist epistemology would limit gaming to a narrowly technical rationality, to a purely instrumental tool, denying the players actions whose values do not refer to themselves but solely to their functionality. They would leave out one important intrinsic characteristic of a game: play that is valued for its own sake.

Instrumental vs. intrinsic values of games

Casti (2000) described a study by W. Brian Arthur, and John Holland about creating an artificial stock market inside a computer. With that electronic stock market, they could manipulate among others, trader's strategies, and market parameters. Each trader – acting as a rule driven agent – has a set of if/then rules, and acts in accordance with only one rule at a given time period. The agents can evaluate their different rules by assigning a higher probability to a given rule that has proved profitable in the past, and/or by combining successful rules to form new ones that can be tested in the "market". The agents in the model are "individual traders". The model applies a genetic algorithm, which mimics the way nature combines the genetic pattern of males and females of a species to form a new genome, which is a combination of the genomes from the two parents. The surrogate stock market generates random fluctuation about its fundamental value. Casti described two other business simulations, referring to the insurance world, and a super market. All three examples have in common that the agents are modeled by applying simple, invariant rules. To my knowledge, the model of the stock market has not yet been validated and applied. The computer experiments, which follow the scientific method, are controlled and repeatable.

Another example is provided by studies, conducted in social insect behavior. They shed light on rule-driven behavior of individual ants and its effect on the organization of ants. Ants, bees and bacteria display sophisticated kinds of cooperative behavior as a survival strategy. Teamwork of social insects is largely self-organized, and coordination arises from the different interactions in the colony. These singular interactions are primitive, combined they result in efficient solutions to difficult problems. Based on a few and simple rules, ants self-organize and show "swarm intelligence." It is collective behavior that emerges from a group of social insects (Bonabeau et al., 2000; Bonabeau & Meyer, 2001). It is an emergent property of organization, not available to individual ants. That rule-driven behavior of ants results in collective intelligence, which is the mechanical outcome of swarm behavior. Calling an ant an ant does not make any difference to an ant. That property exactly enables the use of simulation modeling to test rules and observe the resulting crowd behavior, which is an aggregate of individual ant behavior. Such ants do not need to work under supervision. They are completely pre-programmed by genetic rules.

These studies, based on advances in complexity science, are impressive and promising. They enlarge our understanding of complex (social) systems. Such scientific research should proceed with caution when applied to the human and social realm. Implicitly, images of social order creep in that have an ideological meaning. Those scientists, who apply such approach, should be explicit about their view on (virtual) society and governance. Thinking that rule-driven swarm behavior is good reason to abandon command-and-control management, however worthwhile in itself, would be simplistic. It neglects the human drive to not only play by, but also play with the rules, to transform the social system on the basis of self-referential actions. Such simulation studies convey an image of totalitarian human societies of the types we have experienced in the twentieth century. Which human being would want to live in *ant colony*?

In game design we should be keen on distinguishing between the instrumental and intrinsic value of the artifact.

Troubles at the science/policy interface

To add even more equivocality, I will leave the domain of science as such, and address the puzzle of utilizing scientific knowledge for practical purposes. I will restrict myself to the science/policy interface. Without proper knowledge about the intricacies at that interface, utilization of scientific knowledge will remain limited due to lack of understanding by scientists about their role in the public debate. The example on dealing with risk supports this case. The international debate on *global climate change* provides an interesting example. It illustrates the type of policy questions that need to be addressed, based on adequate support from scientific studies.

Policy makers in governments and industries as well as individual consumers base their response to the climate change issue on the balance between three types of considerations: the perceived risks of climate change, the socio-economic and technological feasibility of response options, and the ethical aspects of an equitable distribution of responsibilities amongst different societal actors. Especially in industrialized countries, they are overwhelmed by a profusion of complex and sometimes contradictory information from the scientific community. Although the greenhouse metaphor has been introduced by the natural sciences, the subsequent linkage of the results of scientific research with policy making implied a broadening of the scope and thus of the interpretation of problems, causes, impacts, and options. The rationalist approach of the analytical sciences became less predominant in the debate. Because of the complexity of the problem and the existing scientific uncertainties, a variety of competing reality definitions existed, which were based on the different perceptions and positions of the major policy actors involved. This made clear that policy makers' appreciation about what science can do in such an arena is not straightforward and not self-evident. The perceived controversy about climate change among scientists appeared to be a main stumbling block for the public at large and policy makers to decide on the urgency of preventive measures. It was also noted that communication between the science and policy communities should be improved considerably (Klabbers et al., 1996-a). Due to the complexity of the issue, many ambiguities and uncertainties are involved.

Wynne (1992) noticed that the discussions about uncertainty seemed to rely implicitly on the naive notion that inadequate control of environmental risks is due only to inadequate scientific knowledge. He criticized this idea, and added the concept of indeterminacy as a category of uncertainty. Indeterminacy refers to the open-endedness (both social and scientific) of the processes of environmental damage caused by human intervention. Indeterminacy introduces the idea that contingent social behavior, including decision and policy makers' behavior, has to be related to the analytical and design science frameworks. It also acknowledges the fact that many of the intellectual commitments, which constitute our knowledge, are not fully determined by empirical observations. The latter implies that scientific knowledge depends not only on its degree of fit with nature, but also on its correspondence with various social constructions of reality. The richness and reach of knowledge transfer depends on its success in building and negotiating trust and credibility for science. In addition to Wynne's comments on knowledge construction, it is worthwhile to realize that different scientific disciplines define knowledge differently, and that these differences play an important role in the debate about Global Climate Change (Klabbers 1996-a; Klabbers et al., 1995). Referring to the term *post-normal science* (Funtowicz & Ravetz, 1993) for issue-driven research in a context of hard political pressure, values in dispute, high decision stakes and high epistemological and ethical systems uncertainties, the puzzle-solving exercises of normal science (that is: analytical science in the rationalist (Kuhnian) sense) are no longer appropriate when society is confronted with the need to resolve policy issues regarding unquantifiable trans-national and trans-generational environmental risks. Climate risk assessment exhibits many features of post-normality (Klabbers et al., 1998). Again, questions at the science/policy interface show the tensions between the analytical and design science with respect to their roles in society, and their different rhetorics.

Limitations of rationalist knowledge

Advances in industrial societies are science and technology driven. So evidently, science, including the engineering sciences, plays a vital role in producing new knowledge. Science is associated with innovation and progress. Knowledge and knowledge management are viewed as key success factors in industrial societies. Consequently, professional knowledge and professionals are held in high esteem. Traditional professional knowledge claims are being questioned for a variety of reasons.

In the practice of the industrial society, *explicit* and *tacit knowledge* play a vital role. From the cognitive science perspective of knowledge, in a variety of ways the mind creates inner representations that correspond to reality. In this view, knowledge is considered to mirror reality (von Krogh & Roos, 1996) (see Chapter 3 for the discussion on schemas). Since the Enlightenment, the public debate stresses a rationalist, view on scientific knowledge. General assumptions about that kind of knowledge are:

- Knowledge represents a pre-given world.
- Knowledge is explicit.
- Knowledge is universal and objective.
- Knowledge is context independent.
- Knowledge results from information processing.
- Knowledge is cumulative.
- Knowledge is transferable.
- Knowledge enables instrumental problem solving.

This type of knowledge is explicit, articulated and can be packaged and transferred easily between agencies with the use of information and communication technology (ICT). The branch of the analytical science called "applied science," while sticking to the observer's position of the analytical sciences, and putting itself in the chair of the expert, implicitly and explicitly applies this conception of knowledge. This view on knowledge is a prerequisite for knowledge management in industry. It conveys however only part of the story on knowledge (see Chapter 3).

Local knowledge, which is embedded in the culture of companies and institutes, is a unique combination of explicit and tacit knowledge. Tacit or embedded knowledge is highly situation specific and less diffusible across groups or institutes than explicit knowledge. It resides in individual and social relationships. It can only be revealed and communicated via close and interactive relationships with the ones possessing it (von Krogh & Roos, 1996). The scientization of the industrialized world and the related proliferation of professional knowledge of the type described above, have become vital for the functioning of the industrialized society. Traditional professional knowledge – based on the analytical science approach – is not well suited to coping with complex and unique situations. Problem solving as encountered in mathematics and physics brings forward a technical rationality, emphasizing a rationalist framework for interpreting knowledge. The related problem solving strategies are too limited in scope for the design science. They disregard competing frameworks based on multiple perceptions. In practice, the rationalist conception of scientific knowledge hampers dealing adequately with local and tacit knowledge.

Schön (1983), in addressing the crisis in confidence in professional knowledge – based on the notion of knowledge, sketched above – observed that the expression of lagging understanding, unsuitable remedies, and professional dilemmas have become the norm. Practitioners – representing the design sciences – are confronted with conflicting values, goals, and interests. In professional education, knowledge that is general, theoretical, and propositional enjoys a privileged position. While teaching professional knowledge, many methods of didactic education assume a separation between knowing and doing. Knowledge is treated as an integral, self-sufficient substance, theoretically independent of the situations in which it is learned and used (Brown, Collins & Duguid, 1989). Accordingly, professional activity consists of instrumental problem solving made rigorous by the application of scientific theory and technique (Schön, 1983, 1987). From a practitioner's point of view there is a growing crisis of confidence in this type of professional knowledge and consequently in this type of knowledge transfer by our educational institutions. Schön stated that professionally designed solutions to public problems have had unanticipated consequences, sometimes worse than the problems they were designed to solve. Newly invented technologies, professionally conceived and evaluated, have turned out to produce unintended side effects unacceptable to large segments of our society (Schön, 1983). It is axiomatic that complexity, uncertainty and value adjustments regarding a problematic situation are not resolved by transforming an ill-structured problem into a well-articulated learning task (Klabbers, 1996-b).

Considering these bottlenecks in the design of gaming artifacts, the following conclusion and warning are worthwhile. Game designers use ideas, theoretical and conceptual models, and speculative conjectures about rules that are couched in terms of those models. They also refer to media of representation for crafting those models. Designers have views about how gaming (the artifact) works and what you can do with it: how games can be designed, modified, adapted. Typically, the game does not behave as expected. Above I have presented resisting worlds. Designers have to accommodate themselves to that resistance. They can do it by correcting the major theories and conceptualizations involved, they can revise beliefs about how the game works and they can modify the game itself. The end result is a robust fit between all these elements. Coping with these puzzles makes game design (artifact design) a science, an art, as well as a craft.

Building gaming artifacts is one part; assessing their usability, and developing and testing theories about them – is another part of the story.

CHAPTER 7

EVALUATION METHODOLOGY

In the previous chapter, I have positioned the field of gaming both in the design and analytical science tradition. Both domains pursue different research objectives. The analytical sciences develop, test and justify theories. Empirically grounded theories are the basis for success. The design sciences build and evaluate artifacts for well-defined contexts of use, and intended audiences. *Usability* is the key to the success of the design sciences. Following my line of reasoning of the positioning game in academia (see Chapter 6), I argue that whenever "design science" spaces for gaming in academia exist, they risk marginalization, as long as they are not considered either a " stand alone interdiscipline," or an established research method of a discipline. As part of a traditional discipline, gaming maintains both a concern and a methodology that function under a *centripetal force* (disciplinary unification) whereas the quality of its design and use requires a *centrifugal force* (an inter- and a meta-disciplinary approach) that defines the quality of the design in a way that is as multifaceted as possible. In current academic practice, the resulting tensions are difficult to handle. Gaming, from that viewpoint, needs at least a cross-disciplinary dialogue between all relevant disciplines of the design and analytical sciences, in order to enlighten and enhance the conversation over quality. Such a constructive dialogue is lacking. More importantly, the analytical sciences wrongfully stress their research methodology as the standard to evaluate progress in the design sciences. In Chapter 4, 5, and 6, I have presented a frame-of-reference for gaming that meets the requirements of dealing with complex social systems, their duality of structure, as well as their emergent properties. *Openness* and *closure* of social systems as discussed in Chapter 4, are key qualities that need to be addressed in the design and use of gaming artifacts.

The scientific method requires that a theory encompass all the elements to explain the relevant behavior of the reference system, that the experiment to test that theory will control all independent variables, and keep constant all confounding parameters that may influence the dependent variables. Therefore, in the analytical science approach *control* and *closure* are key terms. Similar to building simulation models, analytical science requires that all relevant information and data are included in the model, which acts as a mini-theory. Via a suitable research design it is tested and justified. The analytical science aims at explaining observable phenomena. A key for understanding scientific explanation lies in the concept of *causality*. A simple way to explain a phenomenon is to look for its cause. Explanation and causal linkages are closely related. The requirements of the analytical science should not straightforwardly be applied to the design science. An important quality of artifacts is their openness for use under varying circumstances. Cause-effect relations have different connotations in the analytical and design sciences. Therefore, it is worthwhile to first discuss in more detail the concept of *causality*. It is the pivot for the revolving discussion on evaluation methodology in both branches of science.

CAUSATION

The analytical sciences distinguish two approaches: the theoretical, which is ultimately formal and mathematical, and the experimental approach. They progress by a continuous interplay between theory and experiment. Developing and testing games and simulations are notoriously difficult, because they contain many freely adjustable parameters. As a result it will be very difficult, and maybe impossible to predict valid outcomes. In case that the predicted effects are not visible, researchers may keep the theory alive by changing the value of one or several parameters, to make it easier to see the expected effects during the experiment. In Chapter 5, I have argued why fully estimated simulation models of social systems are the exception to the rule. In addition, a fully estimated game seems a contradiction in terms. The ambiguity of play ducks out of experimental control. In addition to these methodological difficulties, we should keep in mind that social systems consist of reflexive actors. Their behavior is contingent and emergent. Classifications might change due to looping effects between classes and people classified in a certain way. Establishing valid and stable linear cause-effect relationships as regards social systems is exceptional. This understanding expresses doubt about the rigor and narrowness of the concepts *causality* and *causation* with respect to social systems. Compared with the analytical sciences, cause-effect relations have a different meaning in the design sciences. I will elaborate further that establishing causal relations in the design sciences serves other goals.

In gaming and simulation we should first be motivated by epistemological and methodological questions. Performing calculations through experimentation is secondary to a deepening of our conceptual understanding of social systems. As pointed out in Chapter 3, that understanding is not limited to explicit knowledge in the rationalist tradition. It includes as well local, tacit, and enculturated knowledge. The added value of gaming, points in two directions. Both the game researcher and the players learn to conceptually understand the dynamics of the social systems involved: the researcher from the observer's position, the players from the "driver's position", as active insiders, who are engaged in making sense of the dynamic situation. For the analytical scientist, the players are abstract objects defined by a composition of traits. For the design scientist, they are real people with abilities, capacities, and needs.

In Chapter 5, I have introduced the following definition of causality. A causal relationship between 'x' and 'y' implies:

- a time dependent controllability of 'x' over 'y';
- 'y' follows 'x' in time, and
- 'x' is a necessary and sufficient condition for 'y'
- an asymmetric relation between 'x' and 'y': if 'x' is the cause of 'y', then 'y' is not the cause of 'x'.

Empirically confirming that a causal relation between the objects *x* and *y* exists is not simple. Under the auspices of a laboratory, theories can repeatedly be tested under highly controllable circumstances. For field researchers, or in general empirical researchers working outside the premises of laboratories, it is often very difficult to find evidence for causal relations. By paraphrasing Hacking (1999), I have said that game scientists have theoretical models, and speculative conjectures couched in terms of those models. They also have views about how gaming works and what you can do with it; how games can be designed, modified, adapted. Typically, a game does not behave as expected. The world resists. Scientists have to accommodate themselves to that resistance. They can do it by correcting the major theory under investigation, they can revise beliefs about how the game works and they can modify the game itself. The end result is a robust fit between all these elements (Klabbers, 2001). In Chapter 6, I have described various resisting worlds. Finding scientific evidence in those worlds is tricky. Therefore, the methodological requirements for empirically establishing causal linkages in gaming need further attention.

THE EPISTEMOLOGICAL STATUS OF CAUSATION

Popper (1979), referring to Hume (1739), discussed the following traditional philosophical problem of induction. The key question he raised is: What is the justification for inductive inferences? The phrasing of this question is based upon two assumptions: there are inductive inferences, and there are rules for drawing inductive inferences. Popper argued that both formulations are uncritical. He used the term "bucket theory of the mind", referring to Hume's commonsense theory of knowledge, which says that we strongly believe in certain regularities that govern our lives. Popper (1979) noted that belief in regularities is justified by those repeated observations, which are responsible for their genesis. He referred to such believes as optical illusions. There is no such thing as induction by repetition. He addressed Hume's two problems of induction, distinguishing a logical and a psychological problem. The logical problem (H_L) reads as follows: Are we justified in reasoning from repeated *instances* of which we have experience to (the probability of) other *instances* (conclusions) of which we have no experience? Popper's answer is: No, however great the number of repetitions. While referring to the psychological problem (H_{PS}) Popper raised the question why do all reasonable people expect, and believe, that instances of which they have no experience, will conform to those of which they have experiences? Why do we have expectations in which we have great confidence? Popper mentioned that Hume described processes of inference and looked upon these as rational mental processes. Popper disagreed and translated all psychological terms such as, *instances, beliefs, and impression*, into objective terms. He rephrased Hume's problem of induction by introducing terms such as, *statement, explanatory theory, test, observation statement, and observation*. He restated the logical problem in an objective, or logical mode of speech by replacing Hume's *instances* – of which we have experience – by *test statements*: singular statements describing observable events. He also changed *instances of which we have experience* by *explanatory universal theories*. Popper applied that style of reasoning to the logical and not to the psychological problem, arguing that, once the logical problem is solved, the solution is transferred to the psychological problem, following what he called the *principle of transference*: What is true in logic is true in psychology, in the scientific method, and the history of science. Popper underpinned his views with the following statements:

Lemma 1: Can the claim that an explanatory universal theory is true be justified by *empirical reasons*, meaning that the truth of certain test statements or observation statements are based on experience? Popper's answer is: No, it cannot.

Lemma 2: Can the claim that an explanatory universal theory is true, or that it is false be justified by *empirical reasons*, implying that the assumption of the truth of test statements justifies either the claim that a universal theory is true or the claim that it is false? Popper's answer is, yes, the assumption of the truth of test statements sometimes allows us to justify the claim that an explanatory universal theory is false. To deal with competing explanatory theories that address the same scientific problem, Popper introduced a third reformulation of the problem of induction.

Lemma 3: He asked whether a preference, with respect to truth or falsity for some universal theories over others could ever be justified by such empirical reasons?

Popper stated that in the light of his answer to L2, the answer to L3 becomes obvious: Yes, sometimes, if we are lucky, it can be justified. While searching for a true theory, we should prefer that theory whose falsity has not yet been established. Statements L1, L2, and L3 form the basis for causal explanations in experimental and empirical research. Only a formulated theory – based on the L1, L2, and L3 formats – can be objective.

Popper argued that induction – the formulation of a belief by repetition – is a myth. In order to survive in evolutionary terms, animals and human beings may need to seek regularities. It may improve adaptation to their habitats. At the same time, that very search may hamper their adaptability, the capacity to adapt to fundamental changes in the environment. Regularities that we try to impose are psychologically a priori. There is however not the slightest reason to assume that they are a priori valid. Repetition presupposes similarity, and similarity presupposes an invariant nature, as well as a point of view, a theory, or an expectation that, to survive, needs to be tested. Popper pointed out that we can reason rationally, and we can act rationally, not upon repetition or habit, but upon the best tested of our theories, which are the ones for which we have good rational reasons. They are the best sources available for action. Popper's strong position in the debate on objectivity may be productive in research in physics. In the human and social domain, that assumption for reasons expressed in previous chapters, is less straightforward. Popper observed that the psychological mechanisms of association forces people to believe, by custom or habit, that what happened in the past will happen in the future. As Richard Tarnas (1991) has pointed out, cause is being recognized as merely the accident of a repeated concatenation of events in the mind. Tarnas viewed it as the reification of a psychological expectation, apparently affirmed by experience but never genuinely substantiated. This perspective offers a biologically, and evolutionary useful mechanism without which we could not live. However, as said before, even such associations, based on regularities in our natural environment need to be tested in practice. Tested theories form a path of adaptation, and adaptability in evolutionary space. From the viewpoint of scientific inquiry, mechanisms of association have no rational basis whatever. Frege (1892) understood by a thought not the subjective act of thinking but its objective content. Popper (1979) concluded that human knowledge is utterly irrational. That normative statement may be valid within Popper's frame-of-reference: the laboratory style of reasoning. If in general that assertion would be true, then it would also apply to Popper's conclusion.

Providing the incompleteness of theories, it seems to be utterly irrational to wait for and rely on valid theories before humans can act "rationally" on the world. Human decision making, purely based on rational thought, would come to a stand still due to the fact that such decisions can only be made after all options have been collected, weighted, and tested. In evolutionary terms, this does not seem to be adequate, because guaranteeing a tested and justified reproduction of the past may take much time, and even if successful, it will not guarantee a similar continuation into the future.

The instrumental scientific method, which follows from Popper's epistemology, proceeds through isolating some central, specific fact, and then through experimenting using that fact as a basis for further deductions concerning a well-defined set of phenomena. Such an approach implies that the success of the scientific method is based upon a strict procedure, a recipe. Hypothetic-deductive reasoning is the core of that approach.

Popper warned about psychological and philosophical determinism, which followers of Hume have substituted for the problem of physical determinism. Hume referred to the *doctrine of necessity* or the *doctrine of constant conjunction* (Hume, 1739, cited in Popper, 1979, p. 219). Hume's interpretation of determinism listens to the statement: like causes always produce like effects, and like effects necessarily follow from like causes (Hume, 1739). He argued that a spectator (observer) could commonly infer our actions from our motives and character. Even where he cannot, that observer concludes in general, that he might, were he perfectly acquainted with every circumstance of our situation and temper, and the 'most secret springs of our disposition'. This is what Hume called the very essence of necessity. Popper remarked that Hume's successors rephrased it as follows. Our actions, or our volitions, or our tastes, or our preferences, are *psychologically* 'caused' by preceding experiences ('motives'), and ultimately by our heredity and environment" (Popper, 1979, pp. 219-220). Popper questioned this. He argued that physical determinism demands complete and infinitely precise physical determination and the absence of any exception whatever. He related this notion with physically closed systems: systems of physical entities, such as atoms, molecules, physical forces, which interact with each other, and only with each other, leaving no room for interaction with, or interference by anything outside that closed system. Psychological and philosophical determinism by Hume's successors is very different from such physical determinism. Popper said that a physical determinist would not take them seriously because assertions such as 'like effects have like causes' are so vague that they are incompatible with physical determinism. To appreciate these questions from the perspective of gaming, and more particularly including the ideas expressed in Chapters 3 and 4, I will put them in the broader context of theories of knowledge.

VIEWS ON KNOWLEDGE

Gill (2000) noted that the 19th century was dominated by a basic belief in the notion of progress. It was coupled with a deep confidence in the ability of human thought to comprehend the essential structure and meaning of human existence and reality. This modernist thought was expressed by Hegel's philosophy that saw reality as fundamentally a matter of mind and ideas, and knowledge as a function of strict rationality (Gill, 2000, p. 2). Kierkegaard, Nietzsche and others rejected Hegel's rationalistic idealism based on the assumption that objective knowledge is possible within human existence. Kierkegaard stressed the limited character of our cognitive capacities and the vital role of our volitional commitments in human knowing (Gill op. cit., p. 3). Their criticism on modernism eventually started the postmodernist movement gradually getting hold in the 20th century. During the 20th century thinkers such a Bertrand Russell, the early Ludwig Wittgenstein, and Rudolf Carnap – representatives of what is called, *logical positivism, logical empirism,* or *analytical philosophy* – were involved in refining modern philosophy. They restricted the definition of knowledge "to include only those ideas and claims that can be grounded in sensory experience and tested by empirical methods. Thus, the so-called verifiability criterion of meaning and truth became the order of the day" (Gill op. cit., p. 4). Popper is an exponent of this line of thought. He and his colleagues made the distinction between facts and values absolute. The claims of science and logic were considered the ultimate source of knowledge about the natural and social worlds. In Chapter 3, I have referred to this kind of knowledge as *explicit knowledge.* In Chapter 6, I have used the term *rationalist knowledge.* In the setting of a game – the magic circle – this limited view on knowledge excludes local, tacit, and enculturated knowledge from scientific inquiry. From the gaming theory presented in Chapter 4, one may gather too that this rationalist knowledge excludes as well current understanding of complex adaptive systems. As I have pointed out, in complex adaptive systems, actors never possess a perfect model of their environment, which contains other actors that are continuously changing. They acquire information about it only through interacting with it, never having total information about its current state. The actors co-evolve. They have limited knowledge and resources, such as matter, information and funds. Therefore, they cannot hold a large group of potential models of their environment, including models of the fellow actors. In games it becomes clear that assertions (rules) and actions are a function of the actors' intentions in conjunction with certain social and linguistic conventions. Gill (op. cit., p. 9) noted that Popper sought to eliminate entirely the personal element in knowledge claims, and to make such claims wholly explicit in nature. Popper (1979) had expressed these views in the chapter "Epistemology without a Knowing Subject." Gill (op. cit., pp. 28-29) has summarized the related shortcomings of modernism.

- The modernist epistemology is atomistic by dividing up reality and knowing into simple units. To be understood, these units must be simple. It leads to reductionist analysis. Atomism and reductionism aim at controlling and manipulating both reality and the reasoning process, denigrating the role played by imagination and feeling in cognitive activity.
- Modern philosophy treats reality dualistically. Dualism such as mind and body (Descartes), the knowable and the unknowable (Kant), fact and value percolate through every aspect of contemporary life and thought, from the reductionism approach to medicine to the dealing with risk society.
- Modernism forces us to choose between an indubitable grounding and open-ended relativism, between objectivity and subjectivity. It is its chief epistemological dilemma. Pure objectivity is impossible. The latter yields no knowledge.
- Modern thought is excessively intellectualist. It treats knowledge as if it were an exclusively mental – cognitive – activity. The role of the body – interacting with the surrounding environment – is conceived of incidental at

best. The mind is treated as not inextricably interwoven with somatic activity.

Playing a game is an embodied experience. Popper's epistemology strips the study of games from its basic qualities. Polanyi (1964) stressed that knowledge is basically a human enterprise. It cannot exist independently of humans. He proposed to reconstruct modernism to take on board human cognition and values. Gill (op. cit) criticized postmodern thinkers for throwing away the banana and eating the peel in their efforts to dismantle the presuppositions and arrogance of modernism. Polanyi (op. cit.) set aside the 'cult of objectivity' without setting aside the possibility of and need for criteria of meaning and evaluation in our search for knowledge. He introduced an understanding of knowing as grounded in the body, the society of knowing agents – communities of observers and practice (see Figure 6.1) – and the affirmation of our cognitive powers of judgment (Gill, op. cit., p. 30). In Chapter 3, I have elaborated Polanyi's ideas (see Figure 3.3). The debate about modernism in Chapter 3, when discussing the meaning of schemas and the various roles of cognition, was a prelude to this criticism on modernism.

Science is inherently democratic in the sense that scientific evidence must be verifiable in public space (falsifiable in Popper's terminology). The processes of scientific inquiry must be transparent to others, open to public scrutiny. I support these requirements. What is at stake with respect to gaming are the kinds of questions asked, their framing, the dreaming up of arguments and counter-arguments and the rhetorics used to persuade fellow scientists and the public. Awareness about the epistemological questions raised in this section will prevent games from being judged on the basis of a narrowly technical – read reductionist, logical positivist – rationality, and the related view on causality.

OPENING THE BLACK BOX

Popper's scientific theory of knowledge – is predominant in experimental and empirical research. The drive to develop testable theories has led to a practice to unravel the world scientifically by reducing complex phenomena to isolated, manageable pieces through controlled experimentation. The inference scheme of such research design is the sequence: independent variable – black box – dependent variable, see Figure 5.2 and Table 5.2. The scientific method – linking the independent and dependent variable – has proven to be very fruitful. Main focus of this inference scheme is on the "how" question, for it is required to empirically confirm empirical correlations and tangible causes. Such a predominant scientific approach, encompassing all aspects of scientific endeavor, asks for a critical review, especially because the resulting scientific practice has brought to the surface serious limitations in theory development and justification. These limitations should be understood to be in connection with the questions of interdisciplinarity and the four rhetorics, discussed in Chapter 6. Tarnas (1991) noted that modern science's mechanistic and objectivist conception of nature is not only limited, it is also fundamentally flawed. He referred to major theoretical inventions, and mentioned among others Bateson's "ecology of mind" (1972), the theory of dissipative structures, complexity science, and chaos theory. I would like to add to this list, "fractal geometry", and "autopoiesis." All these approaches point to new views on nature and open possibilities for a less reductionist scientific world conception. They invite researchers to open the black box. New empirical approaches are needed to deal with these theoretical insights.

A major reason why a narrowly rational approach should not be pursued in social domains is based on the following observation. To be experimentally or empirically feasible that is, controllable, the study of social systems needs to be fragmented in small, disconnected pieces. The resulting domain specific mini-theories – unlike the more elaborate theories of the natural sciences – cannot cover the human and social domains comprehensively. Even in case people would use such a – not yet falsified – mini-theory as a basis for 'acting upon the world,' they cannot take the risk of applying it straightforwardly, because that would imply that reality definitions outside the scope of the (incomplete) mini-theory are not only being neglected, they are moreover considered of less relevance. Such a value statement goes beyond the domain of the theory involved. In pluralist democratic societies such a myopic judgment would be tricky. Mini-theories in the human and social domains are not like the more encompassing theories in physics. They shed light only on very limited details, moreover based on weak empirical (correlational) evidence. One should also be aware that experimenting with existing social systems runs the risk of being unethical. There are in addition other fundamental reasons for being uncertain about scientific evidence, and for being cautious about acting upon the world, based on such evidence.

Theories and paradigms are not only incomplete they are also limited in scope. They are lenses donned to make sense of part of the world for a certain period of time. The classical Cartesian-Newtonian cosmology broke down under Einstein's special and general theories of relativity, and by Bohr's, and Heisenberg's quantum mechanics. Alvin Toffler (1984) remarked that the notion that the world is a clockwork, the planets timelessly orbiting, all systems operating deterministically in equilibrium, all subject to universal laws that an outside observer could discover – this model has come under fire ever since it first arose. Einstein put the observer back into the system. The machine, the clockwork, looks different, depending on where the observer stands within it. Yet, Einstein's universe is still a deterministic machine. Following quantum mechanics, at the subatomic level, matter and energy are interchangeable, observable both as particles and as waves. The position and momentum of a particle cannot be precisely measured simultaneously. This so-called Heisenberg's uncertainty principle replaced Newtonian determinism. In quantum mechanics, non-local connections between particles contradict mechanistic causality. The notion of substance in hard discrete objects such as, atoms as solid, indestructible, and separate building blocks of nature, has given way to formal relations and dynamic processes. It has become evident that scientific observation and explanation affect the nature of the object observed. The physical world of Newton represents a scientific universe of mechanistic and materialistic determinism. The quantum world opens completely new, and unexpected intellectual possibilities very much different from the strict mechanistic causality of phenomena, and the possibility of object observation of nature. By stating that human observation and interpretation influence the observed object, quantum mechanics has placed humans again within the scientific universe of the analytical science. However, the revolution in physics has not resulted in comparable theoretical transformations in the other natural and social sciences (Tarnas, 1991). The core transition in thought relates to the interpretation of the concept of *natural object*. In Newtonian physics natural objects are solid, indestructible, and separate building blocks of nature. In quantum physics, they are not really things at all. They are processes or patterns of relationship. Quantum phenomena do not take decisive shape until observed. Particles seem to affect each other at a distance with no known causal link. Fundamental fluctuations of energy happen in a total vacuum, and connected to this, the 19th century puzzle of 'ether' seems to be back again in the scientific debate. Natural objects in quantum physics are mathematical abstractions, great thoughts − to be tested − through the scientific method. As elaborated above, induction can never bring forward general laws. Tarnas denoted that scientific knowledge is a product of human interpretive structures that are themselves relative, variable, and creatively employed. Because the act of observation in some sense produces the objective reality that science attempts to explicate, the truths of science are neither absolute nor unequivocally objective (Tarnas, 1991). Through quantum physics, we have come to acknowledge that reality is both a product of human imagination, a scientific construction that needs to be tested, and it may need to be structured in a way the human mind is not yet able to discern. Without being explicit about it, Tarnas (1991) stressed interdisciplinary research, because in virtually all contemporary disciplines, it is recognized that the complexity, subtlety, and multivalence of reality far transcend the grasp of any one intellectual (read domain specific, *note author*) approach, and that only a committed openness to the interplay of many perspectives can meet the extraordinary challenges of the postmodern era.

IRREVERSIBLE SYSTEMS AND THE ARROW OF TIME

In addition to quantum physics, another fundamental view on nature has radically undermined the machine conception of nature: complexity theory, building upon thermodynamics and far-from-equilibrium open systems (dissipative systems). Open systems exchange matter, energy and information with their environment. Biological and social systems are good examples of open as well as dissipative systems because they require energy to sustain, and to move to higher levels of order. They contain continuously fluctuating subsystems. Fluctuation at a certain moment in time can become so powerful that it shatters the preexisting organization. Prigogine and Stengers (1984) called this revolutionary moment a *bifurcation point*. It is inherently impossible to predict or to determine in advance which direction that change will take. The system can become *chaotic*, or move into a higher level of order. They raised two basic questions to which until recently no answer was provided. The first one refers to the relation between disorder and order. The law of increase of entropy describes the world as evolving from order to disorder. Contrary to that closed systems theory, biological and social evolution show how complex systems emerge from more simple ones. How can structure and organization arise from disorder? Prigogine and Stengers (1984) have addressed this question, and they argued that nonequilibrium in the flow of matter and energy might be a source of order. The second question is more basic. Classical and quantum physics describe the world as *reversible*. In this description there is no evolution, neither to order nor to disorder. The information (the algorithmic complexity, see Chapter 4) needed to describe the dynamic system remains constant in time. Here rises a contradiction between the static view of dynamics and the evolutionary view of thermodynamics. Key questions are: What is *irreversibility*? What is *entropy*? Prigogine and Stengers pointed out that order and disorder are complicated notions. The units involved in the static description of dynamics are not the same as those that have to be introduced to achieve the evolutionary paradigm as expressed by the growth of *negentropy*. This transition leads to a new concept of matter, matter that is *active*. Matter leads to irreversible processes, which as such organize matter (Prigogine & Stengers, 1984). They aimed to unify dynamics and thermodynamics, bringing out in clear terms the radical novelty of the entropy concept in respect to the mechanistic worldview. According to Prigogine and Stengers, time and reality are closely related. For human beings, reality is embedded in the flow of time. The irreversibility of time is itself closely connected to entropy. They argued that to make time flow backward, we would have to overcome an infinite entropy barrier. Each initial condition of the system corresponds to a certain quantity of information. All initial conditions for which this quantity is finite are permitted. Reversing the direction of time, we would need an infinite quantity of information. Therefore, we cannot produce situations that would evolve into our past (Prigogine & Stengers, 1984).

Classical laws of motion lead to trajectories that the particles follow. The dynamic laws are expressed in terms of the characteristics of trajectories. The basic characteristics are: *lawfulness, determinism, and reversibility*. I add another characteristic, called *closure* (see Chapter 4). In order to calculate a trajectory, in addition to our knowledge of laws of motion, an empirical definition of a single initial state of the system is needed. The general law then deduces the series of states the system passes through as time progresses. All states are defined equivalent. The structure of the equations implies that if the velocities of all points of such a system are reversed, the system will go backward in time. It is reversible. Prigogine and Stengers (1984) argued that the property of reversibility in dynamics leads to a difficulty that surfaced with the introduction of quantum mechanics. They stressed that manipulation and measurement are essentially irreversible, and that active science is by definition extraneous to the idealized, reversible world it is describing. This assertion weakens the precondition of logical empirism requiring a disconnected neutral observer, who does not interfere with the system. In line with Heisenberg's uncertainty principle, manipulation and measurement (observation) influence the pure state of the system in irreversible ways. The observer – by interacting with the system through measurements – becomes embedded in the object of research. Popper (1979) mentioned that Compton (1935) was one of the first to examine the human and biological implications of the quantum physics' indeterminism. Compton was at that time not only dealing with problems of physics. He also was addressing biological and philosophical problems, including ethical ones. He formulated the fundamental question of morality: Is man a free agent? If the atoms of our bodies follow physical laws as immutable as the motions of the planets, why should we try to be free? What difference can it make how great the effort, if mechanical laws predetermine our actions? (Compton, 1935, quoted in Popper, 1979, p. 217). Popper called this the nightmare of the physical determinist. A deterministic physical system is closed. It is completely self-contained. Everything that happens in such a world is predetermined, including all human actions, which can only be epiphenomena (superfluous byproducts) of physical events. Both Compton and Popper were worried about the problem, which arises from physical deterministic theory, which describes the world as a physically closed – self-contained – system. Popper defined a physically closed system as a set or system of physical entities, such as atoms or elementary particles or physical forces. They interact with each other – and *only* with each other – in accordance with definite laws of interaction. Those laws do not leave any room for interaction with, or interference by, anything outside that closed set or system of physical entities. It is this 'closure' of the system, according to Popper that creates the deterministic nightmare" (Popper, 1979).

Once preconditions of *closure* and physical *determinism* are abandoned, the powerful criteria of *lawfulness, and reversibility* – as seen from mechanistic viewpoint – are being undermined. The new characteristics that should be taken into account are: *indeterminism, open and dissipative systems, irreversibility, and emergent properties.* The notions underlying these terms exclude the ideas of causality as inferred from modernist thought.

In addition to irreversible processes in nature, Eddington (1958) introduced a distinction between primary and secondary laws. Primary laws control the behavior of single particles, while secondary laws are applicable to collections of atoms or molecules. A consequence of this view is that each level of aggregation generates its particular laws. Eddington emphasized that insisting on secondary laws implies that the description of single particles is not sufficient for understanding the system as a whole (Eddington in Prigogine & Stengers, 1984, p. 8). That statement removes the fear expressed by Compton's deterministic nightmare, which is an example of a reductionist theory of knowledge. Eddington considered the second law of thermodynamics as an outstanding case of a secondary law. He referred to it by introducing the term *arrow of time.* Science should not restrict itself to a microscopic dissection of objects. It should pay more attention to the evolving relationships between objects. The arrow of time conveys the idea of becoming, a manifestation that the future is not given. It is constructed, designed. To summarize the views that undermined the Newtonian notion of the world, as clockwork, a machine:

- Einstein put the observer back into the system. The machine, the clockwork, looks different, depending on where the observer stands within it.
- Following quantum mechanics, at the subatomic level, matter and energy are interchangeable, observable both as particles and as waves. The position and momentum of a particle cannot be precisely measured simultaneously. This so-called Heisenberg's uncertainty principle replaced Newtonian determinism.
- Prigogine and Stengers argued that irreversible processes are the source of order. Processes associated with randomness, and openness lead to higher levels of organization, such as in dissipative systems.

Together these views on nature are very much different from the foundations of Newton's mechanics, and the concept of causality. They require a fundamentally new scientific approach.

CAUSALITY REVISITED

Despite all these fundamentally new views on nature that have radically undermined the idea of causality of the machine paradigm, Prigogine and Stengers (1984) observed that this paradigm is still the reference point for physics. It is the core idea of establishing cause-effect relations through the scientific method. It is so influential that the social and behavioral sciences, and especially economics – with its closed equilibrium systems approach to macro-economic modeling – remain under its spell. The machine concept of searching for simple causes and effects, pursued through the linear sequence of independent-dependent variables, and statistical reasoning, hampers the social and human sciences in assimilating the new ideas, expressed above. Contrary to natural science, which deals with universals and grand theories, the social and human sciences deal with particulars, and fragmented and disconnected theories. A big picture is missing. The lack of epistemological coherence in the social and human sciences aggravates the current situation. It seems that they are still suffering from psychological and philosophical determinism, hidden under the coat of statistical reasoning.

Popper, while maintaining the rationality of logic statements, underpinned the rigorous testing of theories, and the strong neutrality in the search for truth. His reformulation of Hume's statements about induction, stressed the claim of an explanatory universal theory, based on the truth or falsity of test statements. As demonstrated by Kuhn (1962), the practice of scientific research, particularly through its institutional setting, undercuts such a rigorous commitment. He argued that 'normal science' presupposes a conceptual and instrumental framework – a *paradigm*, which is accepted by an entire scientific community. Within the natural sciences relativity theory, quantum physics, and complexity science are examples of different paradigms, which are supported by different scientific communities. These paradigms provide interpretive structures – particular notions of causality included, that allow researchers to develop elaborate theories, isolate data, and solve the resulting problems (puzzles). Flaws in those structures, generated through the resulting mode of scientific practice of normal science, inevitably evoke crisis, which cannot be resolved within the existing framework. Subjecting the paradigm itself to constant testing, as would follow from Popper's views, normal science tends to avoid internal contradiction by routinely reinterpreting conflicting data and facts in ways that support the existing paradigm, or by neglecting awkward data. When this happens, a paradigm shift is needed. Only after that transition, when the related scientific community accepts a new conceptual structure, will it move to a new 'normal science' scheme, which again governs research for well-suited theories and novel facts. Each paradigm acts as a lens through which every scientific observation, and measurement, is filtered. It maintains an authoritative bulwark by common convention that disciplines the thinking and inference schemes of individual researchers, faculties, universities, and agencies that finance research. It disciplines academia. Conventions are arbitrary. As such, paradigms are temporary social constructions, and the communities that adhere to them not only follow the related inference scheme, they moreover become actors in the political arena, to ensure and strengthen their social, political, and financial interests to secure research budgets. The resulting science wars, which are typical between paradigms, cannot be resolved with the scientific methods per se.

CAUSATION IN THE HUMAN AND SOCIAL DOMAINS

The views on causation, expressed above, apply predominantly to advances in the theory of knowledge, which is relevant for the natural sciences. Based on these growing insights, indirectly I have commented on related research questions in the behavioral and social sciences. In reference to Figure 5.10 (see Chapter 5), I have focused attention mainly on referential aspects included in the reference system. Here, I will pay attention to self-referential aspects that relate to causation. They build upon the gaming theory presented in Chapter 4.

Boulding (1956) distinguished in the universe two opposing forces, one eliminating differences in potential and thereby generating a uniform soup of high entropy, the other producing organization, far from equilibrium. The tendency towards entropy is represented by the second law of thermodynamics of closed adiabatic systems, systems with no heat transfer to their environment, with tendency to maximize entropy with high probability. The tendency of open, dissipative, systems is to give rise in organization through input of energy to maintain them and to move in the direction of far-from-equilibrium systems. On the basis of the second tendency, the universe evolves in continually increasing complexity of organization, culminating in societies. Boulding distinguished nine levels of theoretical analysis, ranging from static structures such as, in geography and anatomy of the universe, and arrangements of atoms in a crystal, to transcendental systems. The major proposition of Boulding is that each level of organization includes characteristics of the lower levels. The key question Boulding addressed from systems' theoretical viewpoint referred to the interconnections between distinct levels of discourse to form a hierarchical system representing the universe. He pointed out that the concept of *image*, which is another term for the *subjective knowledge structure* of human beings, begins in a very rudimentary form at the third level of organization. That level covers homeostatic control systems, which presuppose a "device" that has an image of the environment in the shape of the information about its current state – received through a sensing mechanism (for example, temperature) – and a value system indicating a desired state (desired temperature). The image has fully developed at the seventh level of discourse, the level of organization of the human being. It is the capacity for organizing information into large and complex images, which can be expressed and recorded through our capacity for language (Boulding, 1956). I add that at the highest levels Boulding's notion of the image should be complemented with the notion of *self-image*.

Boulding (1968) argued that the most valuable uses of the hierarchical systems theory is to prevent us from accepting as final, a level of theoretical analysis, which is below the level of the empirical world which we are investigating. He criticized economics, for instance, for being still largely based upon mechanics of utility and self-interest. Its theoretical and mathematical base is drawn largely from the level of simple equilibrium theory and dynamic mechanisms. It has hardly begun to use concepts such as information, which is appropriate at the third level of analysis, and still makes little use of higher-level systems.

Building upon Boulding's hierarchical systems theory, and exploring the distinct levels of systems' evolution, Joslyn (2000) distinguished two types of scaling: *spatial scaling* from subatomic particles through astronomical objects, and *complexity scaling* from subatomic particles through chemical, and biological systems to social organizations. Both are based upon similar concepts: wholes and parts, insides and outsides, and alternating levels of variation and constraint. Needed is a descriptive language, a discourse, for dealing with such features of complex systems. Joslyn pointed out that within such a discourse the concept of *closure* takes an important role. That term relates to *boundaries, hierarchy*, and *system identity*.

From an epistemological viewpoint two approaches to hierarchical systems theory are distinguished: the *realist* (structuralist) and the *nominalist* approach. The realist conception refers to existing entities with objective attributes, which – structurally linked together – form a whole that operates as a unity. In this view, systems are *composed of* interrelated elements (entities). The nominalist tradition emphasizes that people draw distinctions. They are not inherent to natural entities as such. Classifications, the making of distinctions, are the most significant act of science and therefore of systems theory (Hacking, 2002; Goguen & Varela, 1979). The nominalist views a system as a bounded region of some (abstract) space that functionally distinguishes it from its environment. In the nominalist tradition, the idea of system is *defined on* entities or (abstract) objects, on system's properties. Joslyn (2000) observed that logically we could recognize only two forms of relations that flow through the system-environment boundary: the *linear input-output relations*, and the *circular, reciprocal influences* that flow in both directions simultaneously across the boundary. In the *linear input-output relations*, subsystems represent *throughputs*. The *circular, reciprocal influences* identify *closures* of the corresponding subsystems. The term *circular, reciprocal influences* in relation with closure needs further clarification otherwise the notion of closure may stay fuzzy. If closure is a key term, central to hierarchical systems theory, because it enables us to distinguish between levels of system's evolution, then we should be explicit about its meaning.

Autopoiesis

Maturana and Varela (1980) had to change drastically their epistemological view on vision to underpin their experimental findings. They started with the implicit assumption that, as regards animal vision, they were dealing with a clearly defined cognitive situation. They assumed that there was an objective (absolute) reality, external to the animal, independent of it, and not determined by it. The animal could perceive (cognize), and use the information obtained in its perception, to compute a behavior adequate to the perceived situation. The epistemology that guided their thinking was that of an objective reality independent of the observer. That approach to vision could not account for the manifold chromatic experiences of the observer by mapping the visible colorful world upon the activity of the nervous system. Maturana and Varela concluded that a different approach and a different epistemology were necessary. They tried to correlate the activity in the retina with the color experience of the subject. They had to deal with two difficulties. Firstly, the new approach required them to treat the activity of the nervous system as determined by the nervous system itself, and not by the external world. Accordingly, the external world would only have a triggering role in the release of the internally determined activity of the nervous system. Secondly, and more fundamental was the discovery that one had to close off the nervous system to account for its operation, and that perception should not be viewed as a grasping (mirroring) of an external reality. In their views, perception is the specification (enactment) of one external reality, because no distinction was possible between perception and hallucination in the operation of the nervous system as a closed network of interacting neurons. Therefore, perception is a constructive activity. This understanding is supported by psychological studies of *apparent movements*. In physical space two objects – a dot, a line, an illuminated area – which are separated from each other in time and location, alternate in the way they are depicted. Physically, they are disconnected. Perceptibly these alternating objects give an impression of movement of the objects between both positions. The experience of apparent movement is constructed (enacted) by the nervous activity of the brain, it does not exist in physical space (Graham, 1964).

Maturana and Varela (1980) needed a new language to clarify the idea that circular organization is sufficient to characterize livings systems as unities. They coined the term *autopoiesis*, meaning continuous self-reproduction of the organization (*autos* = self, *poiein* = to produce, remake, conceptualize). Another term for *circular organization* is *self-referential system*. Maturana and Varela

(1980) remarked that linking circular organization with causal relations is both *inadequate* and *misleading*. It is inadequate because the notion of causality is a notion that pertains to the *domain of descriptions*. That notion it is only relevant in the metadomain of the outsider, in which the observer makes his commentaries. It cannot be deemed to be operative in the phenomenal domain, the object of the description. Linking circular organization with causal relations is misleading because it obscures the understanding of the phenomenal domains as determined by the properties of the brain that generate them. Following their line of reasoning, Maturana and Varela introduced a key concept: *structural coupling*. To understand the term, it is worthwhile to make a distinction between the *composite unity* (nervous system), composed of the internal organization of components (components of the nervous system), and the *medium* or environment in which it operates. Both the unity and medium interact as independent systems that trigger in each other a structural change. More precisely, they select in each other a structural change. This notion of structural coupling is very much different from the notion of input-throughput-output as expressed in the *linear input-output relations* in open systems theory. In autopoietic systems, the environment and the composite unity interact via reciprocal perturbations, which trigger structural change in both domains. The *organization* of a system is defined as the set of relations between its components that define it as a system of a particular class. Maturana and Varela (1980) defined *structure* as the composition of the actual components (all their properties included) and the actual relations holding between them. Structure concretely realizes a system as a particular member of the class of composite unities to which it belongs by its organization. The composition of the actual components and their interrelationships may change, and consequently, the structure will change. Therefore the particular organization of a system is a subset of the relations included in its structure. A particular organization can be realized by systems with different structure. This can be illustrated in chemistry by isomers, which are compounds with the same chemical formula and molecular weight, only the atoms (components) are arranged differently in the molecule, giving them different properties: same organization, different structure (code). Organization gives the composite unity, or entity, autonomy and stability within certain limits. If in the history of interactions of a system with its environment, the organization of such a composite unity remains invariant while it undergoes structural changes triggered and selected through its recurrent interactions in its medium, then adaptation is conserved. If it would not be conserved, then the outcome for the composite unity is disintegration.

From the reflection on self-referential, self-organizing, autopoietic systems I gather that they screen, shield, or mask themselves from their environment, which makes them operationally closed. Such closure happens in the boundary area between that composite unity and its environment. The boundary element or component, although contained within the system, receives influence from the environment. The boundary between a composite unity and its medium is then the collection of boundary components. They take part in the structural coupling between the entity and its medium or environment. Joslyn (2000) referred to *semiotically closed systems* that maintain cyclic relations of perception, interpretation, decision, and action with their environments. In terms of Maturana and Varela I should say that such semiotically closed systems influence one another through reciprocal perturbations. The boundary components that take care of shielding the composite unity from its environment perform an act of closure.

One important property of closure is the recognition of discrete levels of operation, which form hierarchies in complex systems such as the one described by Boulding (see above). Through closure the entity establishes a form of autonomy with respect to its medium or the environment in which it operates. Both the entity and its medium give shape to a system at a certain level of aggregation, which results in the formation of a new boundary region. That new region therefore shapes a system at a higher level of aggregation. Gradually and recursively such composite entities form a hierarchical system that evolves over space and time. Composite systems entail interconnected components or subsystems, which recursively entail sub-subsystems until the most elementary element – or building block – of the unity is reached. Building on these notions, Joslyn (2000) distinguished the four types of closure, which I rephrase as self-reference, self-organization, autopoiesis, and allopoiesis. Self-referential and self-organizational forms of closure frame conditions for *spatial closure* such as, national and geographic borders, biotopes, regional ecosystems, and *temporal closure* such as observed in the subsequent administrations of democratic societies, in general systems that evolve through subsequent phases of development.

Advances in the natural sciences during the 20th century have opened up new horizons. Their visiting cards no longer refer to the idea of simple mechanistic causality, so dominant in the 19th century science. It seems that empirical positivist research in the social and behavioral sciences is still confined to psychological and determinism, even when applying statistical reasoning.

EVALUATION METHODOLOGY

The basic notions on causality, discussed above, mesh with the gaming theory presented in Chapter 4. Empirically, or experimentally, establishing causal links highly depends on the underlying frames-of-reference. If *irreversibility* is the key term for the natural science domain, then *(semiotic) closure* is the key term for the human and social sciences. If *indeterminism, irreversibility, closure,* and *emergent properties* are fundamental notions of gaming, then they should apply both in the analytical and design science domains. They should reflect on the development and justification of theories, as well as on the building and assessment of those artifacts. In this section, I will discuss related current methodological questions in more detail, and observe that the search for *linear input-output relations* is still the most important driver in evaluation studies. Advances in science such as presented here, still resound only weakly in the study of the human and social domains. This condition is not beneficial for the study of gaming. Whatever the richness of various (local, read, disciplinary) theories, as soon as the behavioral and social sciences start empirical research, they regress to methods and techniques that are based on simple, mechanistic cause-effect relations, even when applying highly advanced statistical techniques.

EVALUATION METHODOLOGY IN THE ANALYTICAL SCIENCE TRADITION

Chatterji (2005) summarized the core ideas underlying the scientific method by sketching the simplest experiment. It involves a 2 x 2 research design: two variables (the independent (treatment) and dependent variable (expected outcome), and two groups. One group is randomly assigned to the treatment condition, while the other (the control group) receives no treatment (an alternate or placebo). This design is recommended as one of the better research designs for addressing questions about cause and effect, because it upholds *the principle of control, randomization, and comparison* (Campbell & Stanley, 1963; Cook & Campbell, 1979; Shadish, Cook, & Campbell, 2002; Spector, 1981, *cited in* Chatterji, 2005). Chatterji listed a number of variations to this basic experimental design: multiple group, longitudinal designs or split plot designs.   When randomization is problematic, quasi-experimental designs are considered the next best option for addressing cause-effect questions (Shadish, Cook, & Campbell, 2002 cited in Chatterji, 2005). Examples are matched group comparisons, interrupted time series designs, and regression discontinuity methods.   The various experimental designs offer trade-offs among the principles of control, randomization, and comparison. The core question of the textbook-style laboratory experiment concerns dealing with the following tensions. Chatterji (2005) noted that to different degrees, such trade-offs threaten the internal validity of the experiment, preventing conclusive causal linkages to be made between the treatment and outcome variables, or to the external validity (generalizability) of the findings. Highly controlled experiments are so closed (sealed of) that they reduce the external validity because they create unrealistic laboratory-like conditions that cannot be replicated in actual settings where an intervention is eventually implemented. More loose controls, on the other hand, diminish internal validity, permitting inferences only about the *gross effects* of the intervention rather than its *net effects* (Rossie, Freeman, & Lipsey, 1999). Dealing with those tensions means acting on practical constraints such as, available time, financial and other resources, and subjects. Documented threats to textbook-style experiments are: subject selection biases, different history of subjects, problems with outcome measures (poor validity, reliability, or instrument reactivity), subject attrition, non-representative samples, and poor operationalization of variables or lack of treatment fidelity in the experiment (Chatterji, 2005).

Basically, textbook-style experiments pursue the inference scheme of the Trivial Machine (Von Foerster, 1984). He defined a machine as a conceptual device with well-defined rules of operation.   The TM is defined as a black box **F** processing input **x** to output **y**, see Figure 7.1 (see also Figure 5.2 and Table 5.2).

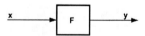

Figure 7.1. Representation of the Trivial Machine

The inference scheme that is, the invariable relationship **F** between **x** and **y** provided by trivial machines, is widely used in science (see Table 5.2). As soon as the x-y correspondence through **F** is established, any **x** will generate a specific **y**, independent of time.   Consequently TMs are *predictable, history independent, synthetically deterministic,* and *analytically determinable*. On the conceptual level, this inference scheme represents philosophical determinism. On the level of instrumental reasoning it presents a linear-mechanistic kind of causality, even when attributing to the input and output variable probability distributions, which is common research practice in the social and human sciences. The underlying view conveys a world consisting of connected trivial machines – based on linear mechanistic causality. The methodological features of inquiry are:

- Researcher objectivity and distance by an impartial and passive observer;
- Environmental control of independent variables;
- Control of all moderator variables;
- Hypothetic/deductive reasoning;
- Statistical reasoning; and
- Prediction.

The related rigid rules of enquiry are necessary to isolate and protect phenomena from flawed analysis.

The principle of *control, randomization*, and *comparison* is a precondition for establishing valid cause-effect relations between treatment and outcome. All processes in between treatment (cause) and outcome (effect) are captured in a so-called black box. This approach is only adequate for textbook style laboratory experiments. If the three conditions for various practical reasons cannot be met, meaning that researchers are not in control of the experimental setting through isolating the discretely defined variables, ensuring that everything else will remain unchanged, they may try to justify their lack of robust outcomes by arguing why they could not meet the standards of the "scientific method," represented through TMs. They should also question the basic flaws in their thinking about the research methodology.

Beyond the confines of a laboratory experiment the preconditions of control, randomization, and comparison usually are not met for very good reasons. One important reason may be that at a theoretical level, characteristics such as, *indeterminism, irreversibility, closure*, and *emergent properties* conflict with the principle of *control, randomization*, and *comparison*. Trying to meet those requirements in field studies, that principle of control may very well be unrealistic because governmental programs, policy initiatives, or design-in-the-large projects (system development) do not obey principles of mechanistic causality based upon reversible processes. Thus, we have to look for a more adequate methodology that justifies that we are dealing with complex dynamic systems. In those systems with emergent properties, the internal structure and processes as such do matter. We need to open the black box to understand "what works" under which conditions, because actors intervene and construct knowledge, suitable to their needs. Next, I will illustrate with a simple example why the Trivial Machine is conceptually too limited to deal with *indeterminism, irreversibility, closure*, and *emergent properties*.

State-space feedback system

Above, I have argued that researchers should be aware of theoretically simple, linear, and mechanistic causality. The Trivial Machine is within analytical science research the most obvious and predominant inference scheme for establishing linear chains of causal relations. The internal characteristics of the black box do not matter, or are ignored, and it is assumed that they do not interfere with the verisimilitude of the treatment-outcome causality. Above, I have seriously questioned that assumption. By presenting the inference scheme of the Non-Trivial Machine (NTM), Von Foerster (1984) however, has demonstrated that the internal structure, and processes within the black box do matter – see Figure 7.2.

Suppose we were to ignore the internal structure of the Non-Trivial Machine by considering it a black box as depicted in Figure 7.1. Trying to establish causal relationships between x and y would provide us with some surprises. The reader should keep in mind that Figure 7.2 represents a deterministic system. What can we learn from Figure 7.2? The Non-Trivial Machine is a powerful construct for understanding complex dynamic systems. NTMs provide an interesting terminology such as, *recursive processes* and *autological, self-referential* and *second-order concepts* (i.e., concepts that are embedded in their own domain).

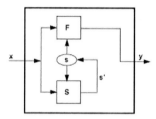

Figure 7.2. Representation of the Non-Trivial Machine (adapted from von Foerster, 1984)

As can be inferred from Figure 7.2, the driving function y = F(x,s) is similar to the TM of Figure 7.1. The state function s' = S(x,s) is new and is recursive: s' is defined by s at an earlier stage. Suppose NTM is a discrete system. In that case the state function can be represented by:

s(t)   = S (x(t), s(t-1))
s(t-1)   = S (x(t-1), s(t-2)), etc.

S represents the memory or history of any NTM. The internal state generated through S influences the processing of subsequent inputs (x) to outputs (y). This means that the output **y**, not only depends on the input **x**, but also on the internal state **s**. Von Foerster (1984) has shown that identification of a large class of NTMs is impossible (trans-computational) because the machine's driving and state functions cannot be inferred from observed sequences of input/output pairs (x,y) from outside the black box.

NTMs are characterized as *synthetically deterministic* (constituted by deterministic driving and state functions), *history dependent, analytically indeterminable*, and *analytically unpredictable*. Suppose we arrange an experiment based on NTM scheme and put researchers in the position of observers/ experimenters. This will teach them that the simple notion of causality inferred from prior experiences with the TM no longer holds. Pending the shifting internal state of the system, an outcome (response) **y** once observed for a given treatment (stimulus) x may *not* be the same for the same stimulus one time step further in time. Behavior of an NTM depends on its internal state, which depends recursively on the system's history.

Adapting the representation of the NTM (Figure 7.2) to the framework of a game broadens the scope of the discussion about evaluation methodology even further. Figure 7.3 represents the generic model of a game. The actors shape a system of interactions − influenced by the rules of the game. Both the system of interactions and the rules represent the morphogenetic cycle, discussed in Chapter 4 (Figure

4.1), and consequently the internal state of the system. Similar to the NTM of Figure 7.2, that dynamic internal state impacts on F, which accordingly processes the input vector X, producing the output vector Y.

Therefore, by definition, games are characterized as *synthetically indeterministic* (constituted by the emerging properties of the morphogenetic cycle), *history dependent, analytically indeterminable,* and *analytically unpredictable.*

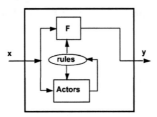

Figure 7.3. Generic model of a game

These simple interventions in the internal structure of the black box, depicted in Figure 7.2, and 7.3, require drastic changes in the style of reasoning about causality. They demonstrate the conceptual limitations of the textbook laboratory experiment, which conveys an image of a world, consisting of linear causal links between treatment and outcome variables. With regard to feedback systems and games, such textbook laboratory experiments do not fit. Investigating a non-trivial machine, or a game, as if they were trivial machines, is an example of flawed analysis within the analytical science domain. It is an example of choosing a wrong research methodology.

DESIGN SCIENCE EVALUATION METHODOLOGY

As pointed out above, the analytical sciences favor the *regularity conception of causality,* derived from David Hume, elaborated and further developed by John Stuart Mill, Carl Hempel and Ernest Nagel (Maxwell, 2004). That conception is primarily interested in the question whether **x** caused **y**, rather than how it did so. It refers to the notion of the Trivial Machine (TM) (von Foerster, 1984; Klabbers, 1996) – see above.

Mohr has related the regularity assumption, underlying this notion of causality, to "variance theory," which deals with variables and correlations among them (Mohr, 1982). Scientific rigor is established through formulating precise statements of the underlying theory, generating well-specified hypotheses, and employing subsequently (quasi-)experimental designs, quantitative measurements, and statistical analysis for testing hypotheses. The resulting causal relations are defined by their invariance in space and time. This is the *gold standard* of the scientific method of the analytical science. Knowledge generated through this methodology is disembodied and decontextualized.

In contrast to the *variable approach* of the analytical sciences, stands the *process approach* of design sciences, which needs a different mode of explanation, rooted in the comparative and observational richness of data and information from designers and users. Maxwell (2004) argued that process theory deals with events and processes that connect them. Applied to gaming, and the related levels of design: design-in-the-small, and design-in-the large, I rephrase it as follows. Process theory deals with actions, events, and processes that interconnect them. In the design science, causal processes are defined on the actor-artifact system. They are built-in into the working of that system. When I drive a car from A to B, then − as driver − I steer causal processes, take on board events that happen on the road, and if all goes well, I will reach B in due time. It is a process fundamentally different from variance theory as a way of thinking about scientific explanation. In terms of Maturana and Varela (1980), variance theory would be inadequate because that notion of causality is a notion that pertains to the *domain of descriptions*. That notion it is only relevant in the metadomain of the outsider, in which the observer makes his commentaries. It cannot be deemed to be operative in the phenomenal domain, the object of the description. It would be insufficient and inadequate to capture the story, motives, and experience of the driver-and-his-car (actor-artifact unity) while driving from A to B. I would argue that the differences lie in the position of the researcher. Following the variable approach, as a member of the community of *observers*, research is focused on establishing the *x-y correspondence through F*. Following the process approach, as a member of the community of *practice*, assessments involve designers and users, and the way they *construct meaning about the artifact in its context of use*. The users are actors in public and private space. Process causality refers to linkages between actions and events, and the way they unfold simultaneously and sequentially in time and space. These actions and events are designed in into the utilization of artifacts. When driving a car from A to B during the night through a hilly region while it is raining heavily, the series of actions by the driver to steer the car, to get feedback about the grip of the wheels, to avoid collisions with animals crossing the road, etc. demonstrate process causality at work. It is an embodied experience. This understanding is similar to understanding the working of a game in terms of an actor-artifact system.

The process approach enables observing causality through evaluation studies of artifacts, operating in unique circumstances – as single cases, or unique events. It allows for the study of temporal and spatial chains of events, and for looping effects. Meanings, beliefs, and intentions held by users of the artifacts are essential parts of the causal mechanisms operating in their use. They are causes that help understand and explain human action in relation to the artifact. Utilization of artifacts is context-dependent, and embodied. Variance theory of causality is dis-embodied. Actors interact with the artifact, or as in games, are embedded in the artifacts, and they generate a dynamic actor-artifact system. Practices, which emerge from using artifacts, the rules, and roles, influence their meaning for the actors. Causes are not restricted to physical entities. They include as well mental states. The relationship between causal mechanisms, embedded in the use of artifacts, and their effects is not fixed but contingent, emergent, and irreversible. They depend on the context within which the artifact operates. Using the scientific method, derived from the analytical sciences, and applying its special causal explanation to assessing the usability of the actor-artifact system, would fail to incorporate the interpretive character of our understanding of human thought and action vis-à-vis the artifact. Therefore, it needs to be abandoned as a viable approach to design science, especially as regards the interplay between design-in-the-small and design-in the-large.

EVALUATION METHODOLOGY: BLURRED BOUNDARIES

Although numerous in-depth evaluation studies on gaming have been performed, a comprehensive framework for evaluating simulation games is still missing. Either results are inconclusive, or various evaluation studies produce contradictory results. One of the main reasons for this lack of evidence is the ambiguity of the researchers' position vis-à-vis the analytical and design science. It makes quite a difference for an evaluation study whether researchers are explicit about their membership of either one of both communities. If they position themselves either in the analytical or design science domain, they should be aware of the conceptions of causality that underlie their styles of reasoning. Numerous evaluation studies confuse methods that are adequate for the analytical science with the prevailing methodology of the design sciences. Many evaluation studies of games – as artifacts – are implicitly based upon the variance theory, and the variable approach of causality – as pursued in the analytical sciences, while ignoring the process approach, based upon interconnected actions and events that happen under unique circumstances. They take methods from analytical science and apply them to the design science, without questioning the underlying methodological and epistemological assumptions elaborated above. If they aim at developing and justifying theories, being the major objective in the analytical sciences, up front, they should explicitly convey that to the reader. In addition, they should be explicit about the theory they want to test, and also underpin their approach by demonstrating that they have upheld *the principle of control, randomization, and comparison*. If on the other hand, they aim at building artifacts to change existing situations into preferred ones, they should make that clear as well. For either justification or assessment studies, they should use the appropriate methodology, and be very cautious about using analytical research methods as *inadequate crossovers* for assessing artifacts-in-use. It would blur the methodological boundaries between the design and analytical science.

Most games – artifacts – can be used as tools to test simultaneously various domain specific theories such as educational theories, individual and social cognition theories, group dynamics, decision-making theories, etc. Each specific theory will enlighten certain characteristics of the game-artifact, while ignoring other ones.

Evaluating games (and simulations) from the viewpoint of an analytical scientist is distinct from assessing games (artifacts) from the position of a design scientist. Design scientists (game designers) build their artifacts to function in well-defined contexts of use for intended audiences. The artifact should be assessed from that viewpoint, in principle taking on board the options of *causality from single cases*, and/or *causality under unique circumstances*. Those types of causality emerge through interconnected actions and events, set in motion by the actors involved. They are the insiders who know. Both realistic options go beyond the preconditions of developing and testing context-free, and universal theories. Key questions in the design sciences are: Does it work? Is it usable in this context of use for this audience? Analytical sciences test theories context-free, as theories need to be universal. Key questions in the analytical science are: Is this a valid theory? Is this the right conclusion?

PRACTICE OF THEORY TESTING AND ARTIFACT ASSESSMENT

In this section, I will discuss several examples of theory testing and artifact assessment, keeping the framework of Figure 6.1 in mind. It is out of the scope of this chapter to discuss them in detail. I will frame and summarize them in such a way that they enlighten issues presented above.

Theory testing

Noy, Raban, and Ravid (2006) have positioned themselves in the analytical science domain by testing social theories in computer-mediated-communication. For these purposes, they have selected two games: LEMONADE STAND and HULIA, and one simulation: AUCTION SIMULATION. Although these artifacts are based on particular mini-theories, they have decided to use them solely as methods – research tools – for testing several social theories: the *endowment effect*, the *mere ownership effect*, *group information sharing*, the *social presence theory*, *media richness theory*, and *normative and informational influence*. They attempted to untangle the technological determinism limitation by examining the broad and complex interconnecting effects of various factors on information sharing. The theories that have been tested are not restricted to one particular mono-discipline in the social and behavioral sciences, and therefore, I consider their approach cross-disciplinary.

The three artifacts (LEMONADE STAND, HULIA, and AUCTION SIMULATION) enable Noy et al. (2006) to manipulate the following independent variables: online social cognition level of the players, online interaction level, type of agent: human (actor) or computerized (agent), the dimension of single vs. group participation, and the role of the participating parties: competition vs. collaboration. The artifacts have not been designed specifically to incorporate those theories. They have been designed for more general purposes, among others to educate people in the working of certain economic processes. Consequently, their content is different, and the meaning of the interactions – communication – between the actors is different from the content of the theories to be tested. In addition, the rules and resources are different. For the research purposes, all three artifacts have been used as tools to test social theories, taking on board managerial dilemmas, with a focus on access to and sharing of information. They share interactive use of computers by human participants, the use of models to simulate either some of the participating parties and/or the business and process environment. In case a participating party was simulated, the artifact became an actor-agent-artifact system.

Through their design specifications, the artifacts were different with respect to the dimensions of single vs. group participation, the role of the participating parties: competition vs. collaboration, the level of social cognition of the players, the type of agent, and the level of interaction among agents. Applying different research designs for testing the theories with the three artifacts, the outcome showed that some results confirmed the causality hypothesized while some results did not support the hypothetical causal relationships between the independent and dependent variables. For example, the LEMONADE STAND, used to manipulate information sharing, ownership showed a statistically significant effect on the willingness to share information, again lending support to the causal relations between ownership and subjective value. The supply chain management game,

HULIA, was used for testing various aspects of information sharing. Noy et al. (2006) tested the hypothesis that the amount of communication between group members (independent variable) will enhance group performance (dependent variable), measured by net group revenue. That causal relation between the independent and dependent variable – amount of communication and performance – was justified by being statistically significant. The AUCTION SIMULATION was used to test the effects of virtual presence and interpersonal information as the independent variables on bidding behavior, the dependent variable. The experimental results confirmed that, with higher level of virtual presence, the bidders lowered their bids, and posted fewer bids during the auction session, while interpersonal information did not cause such a clear effect. Causal relations were also found for virtual presence and only partially for interpersonal information and their effect on bidding behavior. This study is a clear-cut example of the analytical science approach, applying the scientific method, and the variance theory of causality. From a theoretical perspective, one should understand that the theories to be tested are still disconnected, and through the use of three different artifacts – based on distinct mini-theories – they cannot be integrated in one nomological network. Nevertheless, Noy et al. (2006) offered two frames for linking the artifacts and the theoretical concepts. A fully integrated theory can only be achieved when only one game is being used, specifically designed to incorporate the relevant theories, mentioned above. Through changing the parameters of that game, the independent variables for the experiment, various dependent variables (criterion variables) can be measured, and causal links can be tested. Such a specifically designed game would present a pure case of theory development and testing. The added value of such an effort will be that form, content, and meaning of information and knowledge are uniquely related to one another. The end result will be a more robust theory.

The second example of the analytical science approach concerns Rouchier and Robin's (2006) study of rational behavior of individuals in a market environment by combining two methodologies: experimental economics and agent-based simulation. Their research combines two approaches: the theoretical, which is formal and mathematical, and the experimental approach. Rouchier et al. progress by the continual interplay of theory and experiment. The mini-theory is embedded in the agent-based model, which allows them to make predictions that they experimentally can test. The experiment is used to validate the theory, included in the artifact. It allows them to study both predictive and content validity, as the variables in the theory and experiment have similar meaning. The artifact, in its turn, helped explaining experimental outcomes. Rouchier and Robin have shown that the experimental and simulation approaches are complementary to each other. The observations made during a series of experiments helped them to formulate assumptions about procedural rationality of individuals, by identifying which variables could be important for subjects to influence their decisions. While performing simulations, they were able to test their assumptions. The various experimental runs with the agent-based model enhanced the calibration and validation of the theoretical model.

The third example of the analytical science approach refers to Mallon and Webb's phenomenological approach to games analysis (Mallon & Webb, 2006). They expressed a need in computer games literature for intrinsic evaluation methodologies and workable operational research procedures, designed to evaluate subjective game-play experiences and judgments and other user pay-offs. The phenomenological methodology, they presented, provides a bottom-up, subject-centered, inductive and empirically driven research approach. The first example by Noy et al. (2006) followed a top-down approach (deductive), while the second one by Rouchier and Robin was a mixed approach, partly top-down, partly bottom-up (deductive & inductive). Mallon and Webb developed and tested evaluation criteria for four narrative adventure games. Through this study they developed a series of preliminary evaluation criteria, which were tested and refined in a subsequent study of three games from the closely related narrative role-play genre. Their evaluation approach offers bridges between the design and analytical sciences. Their research contributes to the analytical sciences by identifying theoretical principles for evaluating quality in narrative adventure and role-play games. It contributes to the design sciences by supplying findings expressed as design principles. They initiated a design theory of those types of games in terms of meta-artifacts, and questioned the uncritical use of analytical tools such as, film theory or narratological theoretical approaches to games research. The core of their criticism is that literary scholars fail because they try to fit their subject of study to their particular theoretical frame. They should instead frame inductively a suitable theory from the game experiences. The debate revolves around two issues: the uncritical application of *narrative theories and analytical tools* to games research, and the *place of narrative* within games. This distinction is relevant for the use of narrative analytical tools for investigation and usage of narrative elements within the games themselves. The first one refers to the meta-domain of descriptions, the second one to the players' experiences. A second argument concerns a sentiment in the game-development community about the importance of story – its narrative. Some game designers suggest that the play starts when the story stops. Mallon and Webb warned that such a sentiment risks that the narrative will be sidelined in games. Through their phenomenological approach, they developed and tested proposition statements or guidelines, which summarize lessons learned, and evaluation criteria from the reported experiences and critiques of the "experimental" players.

Mallon and Web proposed a linkage between analytical-science descriptions and design-science prescriptions for good narrative in computer games. Implicit in their approach has been the conviction that narrative theory testing should begin with game artifact testing. Their study illustrates how a phenomenological methodology can establish such relevance, using a variance theory of causation.

Artifact assessment

Dugdale, Pallamin, and Pavard (2006) have performed an assessment of a mixed reality environment, using an ethnomethodological approach to training firefighters. Training firemen is a difficult, and a time consuming process. Close to reality exercises are often used to simulate emergency incidents such as, hotel fires, and ship fires, under realistic circumstances. During debriefing sessions the firemen reflect on and assess their performance. The advantages of such training are well documented. They provide the firefighters a good sense of immersion into handling the incident. Dugdale et al. noted that such close to reality simulations are expensive to organize, difficult to design, time-consuming to perform, and complicated to assess. Therefore, they have been developing a cost effective and efficient training tool, enabling the trainees to sufficiently immerse in the situation, allowing them to exhibit the usual social and emotional behaviors, and to communicate and interact naturally with other participants. They have used virtual reality technology for training purposes, providing the firefighters with an immersive learning environment and intelligent virtual agents – avatars – through which they operate in virtual worlds of fighting fires. In their approach, several of the firefighters communicate with each other through the virtual environment, and utilize their own problem solving capabilities, including the influential emotional and cultural aspects. They place the control of the virtual agent – avatar – in the hands of the human actor – the trainee firefighter. The avatar acts as the extension of the actor in virtual space. They designed the artifact, based among others on field studies, which showed that the firefighters rely heavily on the non-verbal behaviors of other firefighters in order to assess the current situation and to manage the emergency incident. Reading those non-verbal behaviors is a critical aspect in communication, and therefore a critical success factor. Dugdale et al. (2006) have implemented that option by having trainees communicate with each other through the virtual environment. In particular, they have focused on the role of *indexicality*, which highlights the fact that in our everyday activities we are constantly using external references to structure our discourse.

The analysis of their field studies data suggested a design specification, which focused on non-verbal behaviors, the role of contextual information, and inter-agent communications, including cultural, social and emotional aspects of human communication. In order to assess some of these aspects they conducted an empirical study consisting of three phases:

- Verifying the communicative acts of the virtual agents as such, in order to gauge their expressiveness. The goal of these experiments was to assess if the virtual agents were conversationally equivalent to a human actor. Thus, the virtual agent should seem believable to the firefighters by exhibiting meaningful non-verbal behavior (use of gestures, body positioning, head movements, etc.).
- Verifying the contextual virtual environment, providing the same decision making support as that found in the real world, Dugdale et al. analyzed the decisions or actions taken in the real world and then checked if it was possible to make the same decisions in the virtual world.
- Thirdly, they addressed the problem of how to establish the collaboration and coordination of activities in the virtual world with indexicality. The limits imposed by a virtual world made the indexicality of the virtual objects sometimes problematic. Thus, they compared the performance of users in both the real and virtual worlds in order to identify how the virtual world influenced the communicative style chosen by the firefighters.

The first question for the participants of the group, watching the video of the virtual agent, concerned the realism of the agent. The results showed that more than half of the participants considered the virtual agent to be realistic. Concerning the elements, which played a role in making the virtual agent realistic, almost all of the subjects commented on the importance of the gesture as well as the natural posture of the virtual agent. Looking in more detail at the comments, those, who expressed a negative opinion about the realism of the virtual agent, attributed the lack of realism mostly to the general 'cartoon-like' aspect of the related character.

To assess phase 3, they developed a scenario dealing with an emergency incident, during which the firefighters needed to coordinate their response. The following situations needed to be assessed: A group of firemen discussing the situation around a map. The firefighters must first be able to see the map and each other, to communicate verbally with others, to point at, and write and draw, on the map, and to gain each other's attention by physical contact in the real world. The avatars, writing and drawing on the map were a problem. The question was whether this information was available in the virtual world. The actor, through direct control of his avatar had a direct visual perception of the other agents, since they can be maneuvered in their virtual environment. Concerning the verbal communication, the trainees can communicate directly via real headsets. Embedding non-verbal communication such as, making gestures, was more difficult to frame. The actor can consciously control the gestures of the virtual agent, for example, to make the avatar point to the map. However, it is problematic for the virtual agents to write and draw on the virtual map. Finally, exchanging tactile information – the firemen gaining the attention of others via touch – was not possible, because the virtual world did not support this medium of communication. In this respect the virtual world was not logically equivalent to the real world. So, the designers had to look for a substitute modes of communication, for writing, drawing and the exchange of tactile information. Interviews with firefighters showed that using maps is the best way for them to communicate and consolidate information. Regarding tactile information, the idea that the trainees could wear a tactile suit configuring that when the virtual fire fighter – the avatar – touches a colleague, the corresponding pressure would be felt on the recipient via the suit. That option was considered to be outside the scope of the project. Regarding the problem with the map, a possible solution was to provide the trainees with a specific interface (e.g. an electronic whiteboard), which they all can see. A suitable substitute for the transfer of tactile information was not yet available. Thus a tactile communication facility in virtual space was lacking in the design of the artifact. This hampered the indexicality in the virtual world.

From all of the experiments conducted in the real world, Dugdale et al. (2006) extracted a general set of interaction strategies. They noticed a strong mirroring effect of the body positions of the actors, allowing both actors to see each other's gestures and the referred object. In addition, the majority of interactions seemed to obey a strict set of communication rules. For example, the character describing the location will always look at the face of the listener in order to assess whether the description has been understood and confirmed. This confirmation is expressed verbally, via gestures, or by facial expressions. These interaction rules were not built into the behavior of the virtual agents. However, through driving the actions of the virtual agent, the trainees were able to perform these modes of communication. Dugdale et al. mentioned an interesting puzzle at the actor-avatar interface. Due to the limited range of vision and the time needed to make a visual inspection of the environment, the actors chose to take a position that allowed them to share the most similar view of the scene. It facilitated the task of identifying the referred objects instead of respecting the social rule of looking at the interlocutor. The main communicative strategy occurred via direct verbal expressions between the actors, as the virtual agents did not directly look at each other for confirmation.

For example, when two actors were using the virtual environment, one actor (controlling his avatar) was continually asking the other one (also controlling an avatar) if she understood the location of the referred object, rather than waiting for feedback from the behavior of her virtual agent. That fellow actor confirmed her understanding by pointing at the screen and not by moving the arm of her virtual agent. This suggests that it is still unnatural for the user to express his or her opinion using the gestures of the virtual agent. Dugdale et al. (2006) concluded that more work is required in developing more "natural" human computer interfaces. I disagree with this conclusion for the following reasons. Looking from the

193

perspective of the actors-artifact system, and especially considering the actor-artifact interface, the design question that is at stake is where to define the boundary between the actors and the virtual environment. It seems more natural to allocate the tactical communication task and gestures – indicating direct communication to the actors. Putting it this way, I propose that the actors and avatars should be complementary to each other, and not be in competition with one another. If they complement each other, they can perform the total task more "naturally." If their tasks are designed to be in competition with each other – a traditional engineering approach – then it will be very difficult to develop adequate software to ensures that the artifact, and in particular the avatar's behavior will mimic the real world sufficiently. Thus, Dugdale et al. should question their design principles, and adjust the specifications of the design. They should embed the artifact with its virtual characters in the setting of a computer-assisted game with the real actors shaping the social organization in charge of fighting fires. From design viewpoint it would be easier, and more natural, and more in line with the adaptability of the real actors, referring to their tacit understanding of the situation. Those characteristics cannot be captured in the logic of software design. Thus, it is worthwhile to look again at the allocation of tasks between artifact and actors, and consequently at the design specifications for the human-computer-interface (see Figure 5.10). Dugdale et al. (2006) illustrated in clear terms the iterative character of the design process, in close cooperation with the client (see Table 5.8). Moreover, through the design process, they demonstrated the initial stages of the interplay between design-in-the-small (DIS) and design-in-the-large (DIL). They designed a *mixed-reality game*. One part included the virtual reality of firefighting. It was embedded in the real world of the firefighters, who interacted directly with each other in the real world, and indirectly through their avatars.

Blasi and Alfonso (2006) describe the transfer of simulation technology from research and development of the artifact – THE VIRTUAL LAB – into school settings. They discuss the development process and the formative evaluation, drawing on a usability study. Blasi and Alfonso offered a four level assessment, including, verification of the artifact, variation check of content, verification in context, and valuation in the field of education. They also addressed barriers (resisting worlds) to the use of formative evaluation. Taking into account the two levels of design: design-in-the-small (DIS) and design-in-the-large (DIL), Blasi and Alfonso started with the concern for the DIL in the early stages of the development of THE VIRTUAL LAB. They noted that the design of the artifact (DIS) is evident in the world of the simulation. They asserted that the design-in-the-large of the THE VIRTUAL LAB, was their major concern. It is not sufficient to design the artifact and to hand it over to the users. The concern for DIL implies that the artifact is also later shaped by the end user's prior knowledge, assumptions, and conditions for learning. The designers should have in mind a clearly articulated purpose at the beginning of the development of the artifact, which can be extended or subverted by the users in their context of use. Blasi et al. conducted the usability study to explain the effectiveness of the design in use, the assumptions and experiences that shape student use, and the potential use alongside the needs within the classroom, in relation to the overarching goals in education. The usability study provided them clues about the context and the conditions for implementation. They observed that access to classrooms and resources for this kind of studies is limited, which presents a barrier that remains unaddressed in the design sciences. It is an unrecognized need in the analytic sciences. Organizations that issue grants seldom include usability studies within the design process. The development process does not always provide the time needed to build and maintain working relationships within the schools to tune the design to the user's needs. They argued that without consideration of the context, the process of design will produce functional artifacts that are less than optimal in terms of their accessibility and applicability for instructors and learners, and accordingly there will be less than optimal outcomes and impact. They elaborated the idea of causality, embedded in the artifact and in its use, and pointed out that causality extends beyond limited cause and effect within the interactive learning environment of the THE VIRTUAL LAB. It encompasses the developers, the learners, and the conditions within which they create and use the technology. Aspects of the design-in-the-large (DIL) are inherent in the designers' assumptions about their own work. They range from their assumptions about users to their unspoken goal for effecting change through the design of the technology. Blasi et al. presented six questions that provide a systematic approach to the analysis of an artifact when outlining causality within the design:

- Epistemology: Where is knowledge generated in the design?
- Ontology: What is the purpose of the design?
- Teleology: What are the end goals of the design?
- Causality in the design: Where is cause and effect configured in the design?
- Causality in the actual use: How are cause-effect chains and loops embedded?
- Causality for the evaluation: What are the theoretical models for attributing cause-effect?

They acknowledged that evaluators might focus on variables, processes, or a combination, while attributing cause and effect in the evaluation. So, in practice, it might be fruitful to interconnect the three types of causality, included in the design, in the actual use. These choices can vary at each level of the evaluation in line with the assumptions of causality in the design itself. They can also vary from the verification of the artifact as such to its valuation in relation to larger educational goals. Based on the VIRTUAL LAB as an example, the authors used four levels of evaluation building on distinctions between DIS and DIL: functionality and fidelity of the artifact (DIS), efficacy, the impact on learners specific to the content (DIS), usability, the accessibility for learners specific to the context (DIS), and synergy, the contribution of the artifact to larger goals within the field (DIL). The research methods they applied, both quantitative and qualitative, needed to be appropriate in the evaluation across these four levels. They included: verification (of the artifact), variation check (of the content), verification (in the context of use), and valuation (in the field of education). The authors viewed the design process as a potential agent for change.

What is most interesting in this research is the mingling of the concept of causality of the analytical science – included in the scientific method applied by THE VIRTUAL LAB, with the concept of causality – interconnected actions events (processes) – of the design science. It offers interesting opportunities for cross-fertilization.

Kriz and Hense (2006) reflected on theory-based evaluation of gaming, using *logic models*. They claimed that the main aim of theory-oriented evaluation approaches goes beyond testing the outcomes of gaming simulations in respect to meeting their learning goals. The goal of assessing gaming simulation is not only to prove *whether* a simulation works but also to show *how* and *why* it works in a given context. They discussed logic models, also called, program models, program logics or program theories. Through logic models the authors outlined the linkages between the simulation game, its participants, and its environment, and generated desired outcomes. In evaluation studies, these logic models are primarily used to support the planning of the evaluation of the artifact, and to provide a framework for interpreting the evaluation results. Thus, theory-oriented evaluations go beyond mere outcome-evaluations of assessing the effects of a gaming session into consideration. They moreover identify the crucial factors, which cause or moderate such effects. For this purpose, Kriz and Hense position theory-oriented evaluation in the design science domain. They discussed their approach, using SIMGAME, a simulation game for business education in secondary schools, as an example. Their research incentives are to change and improve existing dysfunctional educational and organizational situations (design-in-the-large) through the design and use of simulation games (design-in-the-small). On the basis of the program model, they developed a list of 50 criteria, which supported and guided the design and use of SIMGAME. In their theory-based approach they used knowledge from analytical science, which added practical value to the design-in-the-small of the game and later contributed to the design-in-the-large of the educational systems involved, by applying SIMGAME in the classrooms.

In their approach they aimed at bridging the gap between design and analytical science. They argued that game designers should use knowledge from the analytical sciences as input into their design practice, because this knowledge will contribute to building and using the artifacts (the games). To do so, they have to translate the universal context-independent knowledge of analytical science research into their concrete local circumstances. Kriz et al. noted that the term *theory* should be understood as *meta-artifact* (see Table 6.2). Due to the intensive use of theoretical considerations, their approach has great potential for producing results, which can be transformed and accumulated into generalized experiential knowledge.

While reviewing their research, they addressed some of the tensions within the analytical sciences, and the tensions vis-à-vis the analytical and design sciences, which I have addressed in Chapter 6. To cope with these tensions, they have chosen to play a dual role in the academic debate especially with their colleagues from the analytical science community. They are using the research terminology of the analytical science, for example when talking about input and output variables, to underpin their theory-based approach of the design sciences. They are aware that this might lead to the criticism that disparities between both domains may become blurred, due to existing different methodologies and terminologies of both communities. As a matter of fact, they are of opinion that by staying with the theory-oriented approach within the standards of the analytical science, they stay recognized and more visible by their peers in the analytical science community. Because of the social pressure of their peers from the analytical sciences, they accept that style of reasoning as the norm, accepting as well to be hostages of the analytical sciences.

Kriz and Hense argued that while performing evaluation studies, it was definitely important to them to examine classical theory driven problems, using the classical quasi-experimental research method, based on the variable approach of causality and statistical techniques, and interpreting the results by the scientific standards of their peer group. At the same time, within the framework of formative evaluations in real issue-driven projects such as with SIMGAME, in practice their approach yielded concrete results with regards to the usability of the artifact. This was their way to convince the participating stakeholders to accept the parallel use and development of the logic model along with the simulation model. Kriz and Hense are aware of their double role. They are researchers who claim to develop generalized concepts, which are part of the analytical science tradition. They are also change agents in the design science tradition, offering domain specific knowledge and expertise in their context of use. They are only accepted in their academic environment if they adhere to the rituals of the analytical science. They are only accepted in practice, if they can meet the expectations of the sponsors, regarding practical outcomes. Thus they find themselves in the splits, or one might observe a double-bind. They pointed out that the logic model, which emphasizes theory-based evaluation, suits them well to link to both communities and their different research traditions in the field of gaming simulation. Based on my line of reasoning in Chapter 6, I argue that Kriz, Hense, and other professionals, operating under similar circumstances, can live with such ambiguity for a short while. Those working conditions are not sustainable as long as the related epistemological and methodological questions are suppressed, or are ignored in the academic conversations. Developing and applying skills of rhetorics-1, 2, 3, and 4 (see Chapter 6) might help.

Recapitulating these examples on artifact assessment, the main questions for testing the usability of the artifacts deal with meaning processing. Does the utilization of these artifacts make sense to those who are involved in the design, and its use in practice? The resulting style of reasoning is different from the style of theory testing, which is more detached. Artifact design and assessment convey the nitty-gritty of making science work, including the ambivalence of the policy arena that shapes more or less beneficial conditions for the design-in-the-large. Each of the authors, dealing with artifact assessment have, based on their local circumstances, different stories to tell. They enlighten the tensions between institutional actors, each with their different research agendas. Design science not only requires high quality scientific skills, in addition, and crucial to its success, it requires social and rhetorical skills.

SUMMARY

In this chapter I have discussed methodological questions about testing theories and assessing artifacts. Both forms of evaluations aim at establishing causal links. As causality is a core concept in evaluation studies, I have elaborated its meaning in contemporary science, and illustrated that various paradigms offer different views on causality. While searching for an appropriate evaluation methodology for gaming, I have questioned the textbook research method of the analytical sciences, and the related variance theory of causality. The related inference scheme of the Trivial Machine (Figure 7.1) does not do justice to irreversible processes that are so characteristic of games. I have presented the Non-Trivial Machine (Figure 7.2) and the generic model of games (Figure 7.3) as more suitable alternatives to capture the internal dynamics of what happens while playing games. The conception of causality in the analytical sciences is a notion that pertains to the *domain of descriptions*. That notion is only relevant in the metadomain of the outsider, in which the observer (researcher) makes his commentaries. It cannot be deemed to be operative in the phenomenal domain, the object of the description: playful gaming.

As demonstrated so eloquently by Noy et al. (2006), theory testing through gaming is generally limited to local theories. They pointed out that by using different games and simulations for testing different theories, they were not yet able to present a coherent theoretical network, linking those local theories. From the perspective of gaming theory, presented in Chapter 4, these local theories shed light only on particular and limited aspects of social systems. They are singular particles in theoretical space. Evidence is based on occasional viewpoints, and the application of the *Trivial Machine*. The resulting theory development is disjointed, and incremental. Would they have been developed within the broader framework of complex adaptive systems, using properly designed games, then the outcomes of these local theories should become interconnected. Such a meta-disciplinary view on gaming is currently lacking in academia and national science policies.

One general conclusion should be drawn. Gaming deals with irreversible processes and game sessions demonstrate in Prigogine's terminology the working of "the arrow of time". Indeterminacy, which is the social science equivalent of Heisenberg's uncertainty principle in physics, is a basic ingredient of playing games. That understanding should be conveyed in the term *causality*. The variance theory of causality applied in the analytical sciences is only relevant in the meta-domain of the outsider, the domain of descriptions. It is not able to capture process causality that evolves from playing games and that produces a network of cause-effect linkages based on simultaneous and sequential chains of actions-interactions-events. That insider's understanding of organized complexity is a prerequisite for assessing the usability of gaming artifacts.

CHAPTER 8

SYSTEM DYNAMICS & INTERACTIVE SIMULATION

SYSTEM DYNAMICS

System Dynamics (SD) is an experimental, quantitative approach for designing structures of social systems and policies that are compatible with a social system's growth and stability objectives. The experimental model approach for the design of large-scale systems is the key for improving system's performance. SD models comprise aggregate behavior of social systems.

Due to advances in information technology and software design, simulation modeling has become increasingly accessible to the general public. These advantages necessitate additional responsibility of model builders with respect to the impact of knowledge transfer through such models. Especially policy makers and managers tend to extract more certainty from simulation studies of social systems than scholars generally think to be justified. Policy makers and managers as well as the lay public tend to ignore ranges of uncertainty of model output. Assumptions underlying models, which are based on insufficient theoretical and empirical evidence, are important sources of uncertainty. So, while the model generates quantitative outcomes, the underlying foundation may be conceptually weak. Decision makers either may not be aware of this or choose to ignore such weaknesses, or if they disagree with the outcomes, they may choose to play off stakeholders, the model builders included, against one another. When this happens, the model becomes part of the meta-game. SD model building is not a neutral process. It takes place in a policy arena and that awareness should be reflected in the knowledge elicitation and utilization activities. Therefore, before elaborating on the various interactive learning environments, which are based on System Dynamics (SD) modeling, key features of SD need to be understood.

CHARACTERISTICS OF SYSTEM DYNAMICS

System Dynamics started in the late 1950s with Jay Forrester's Industrial Dynamics (1961). It analyzes management processes through evaluation of realistic models that incorporate decision-making policy and the interactions of information, money, orders, material, personnel, capital equipment, natural resources, etc. During the late 1950s, Industrial dynamics has grown out of four major advances: theory of information-feedback systems, the study of policies guiding decision making, the experimental model approach to the design of large systems, and the availability of the digital computer for simulation studies of systems that are too complex to be handled via analytical solutions such as differential equations modeling. During its development the early scope on Industrial Dynamics broadened to Urban Dynamics

(Forrester, 1969), World Dynamics (Forrester, 1971; Meadows et al., 1974), and finally to System Dynamics. These varieties are all based on principles of non-linear feedback systems (Forrester, 1968). Rapid advances in information technology and SD-software packages improved availability and accessibility of computers dramatically. In the 1960s SD models ran on mainframe computers, based on the DYNAMO computer program. Experimenting with those models was cumbersome. Nowadays various software packages enable the development and use of large-scale models on the personal computer, local area networks and Web-based learning environments. In the 1990s System Dynamics went back to basics, paying mainly attention to business dynamics (Sterman, 2000). Via the idea of the *learning organization*, the spirit of Industrial Dynamics has been disseminated outside the community of SD specialists (Senge, 1990).

The basic building blocks of SD models are two different *causal loops*, the negative and the positive feedback loop. The behavior of the negative loop is directed toward a goal defined outside the loop. Behavior of the positive loop is not goal directed. It represents exponential growth or decline, departing from some initial focal condition. SD models are state-space models, linking material and information flows within and between loops. Built-in decisions connect information flows with material flows. Shifting the dominance of loops can explain how levers for change may vary over time, and which policies are beneficial or detrimental to the system concerned.

The experimental model approach is a powerful means to learn to understand and change system's behavior. Through SD models, experts and practitioners have available a communication vehicle, a common language, for mapping social system's resources that is, a reference system and its behavior. Building an SD model progresses through an iteration of steps (see Table 5.2).

In particular circumstances it may be worthwhile to stop the model building exercise with the development of a conceptual map. The related knowledge elicitation and representation process finishes in this case with a system of concepts and their interrelationships, based on the framework of positive and negative feedback loops (Figure 5.3). Such an approach has much in common with Checkland's soft systems methodology (Checkland & Scholes, 1990). The question whether a certain SD model works cannot be answered straightforwardly. The test of the model lies in whether it can be used in accomplishing the client's purpose (Churchman 1970). Sometimes a conceptual map satisfies a client's needs, sometimes a formal system will do the job. On other occasions, an (partly) estimated operational model will give the answers needed. Key questions are:

- Are SD models to be viewed as "truth machines" or as tools to explore different sets of assumptions and values? Answers to this question define the kinds of simulation environments that can be expected from SD modeling.
- Which constraints of SD modeling tools should be considered with regard to the *learning organization*? Which learning metaphor is stressed by the five disciplines presented by Senge (Senge, 1990, 1994)?

It is out of the scope of this paper to elaborate on validation in System Dynamics. Among others, Barlas (1996), and Barlas and Carpenter (1990) have extensively covered this topic. I will wrap up some of the basic issues Barlas has raised.

SD models belong to the class of quantitative, non-linear mathematical models. When they are used for practical purposes, such as improving social systems' performance, all model builders are aware that those models are incomplete, relative, and partly subjective, and that model validity means usefulness with respect to a purpose. Consequently, model validation is more a matter of social conversation than of objective confirmation (Barlas & Carpenter, 1990). SD models are causal models with a transparent structure. For that reason Barlas refers to them as white boxes. Validation studies cover primarily judging the validity of the internal structure, parameters included, and subsequently the validity of structure-oriented behavior (Barlas, 1996). Based on these ideas, I have raised two fundamental questions about SD models of social systems (Klabbers, 2000):

- Since validity of an SD model means adequacy with respect to a purpose, who are the judges or problem owners of such a purpose?
- Since structure of social systems is a social construct, knowledge about it is not a product of merely mirroring 'reality'. Moreover, structure evolves over time on the basis of systems of interactions, through various perspectives and interests of the stakeholders (actors) involved. So, who are the owners of a particular structure?

Referring to the distinction between the design science and analytical sciences, an even more fundamental question should be discussed. Providing that the purpose of SD models is to improve social systems' performance, including the awareness of model builders that those models are incomplete, relative, and partly subjective, and asserting that model validity means usefulness with respect to a client's purpose, I argue that SD is a design science. Barlas confirmed this indirectly by stating that model validation is more a matter of social conversation than of objective confirmation. An SD model is an artifact that is to be used to change current conditions into preferred ones. Design-in-the-small, according to the steps in model building (Table 5.2), is directly coupled to design-in-the-large: intervening in, and improving social system's performance. Assessing SD models should therefore be carried out through the design science evaluation methodology, presented in Chapter 7.

For that reason it may be more suitable to use the term *model adequacy* instead of the term *model validity*, which is confusing because of its analytical science connotation. Model adequacy refers to its usability. As we do not speak of the validity of a bike, a car, or an airplane, we should not use that term either for SD models. That would only be appropriate if we would use a particular SD model for theory testing.

These questions underlie issues related to modeling social systems. They need to be addressed prior to the start of the actual modeling process and should provide additional conditions for either artifact adequacy or theory justification, strengthening the case of usability via conversation. In line with the notion that SD models serve a purpose, I would like to stress that every model is for improving understanding and enlarging the action repertoire of decision makers.

System Dynamics has its roots in feedback control theory, which is mainly applied in the field of engineering and automation. Cybernetics is the formal science in which control systems in electronic and mechanical devices are studied and compared to biological systems. Both represent different communities of scholars and practitioners. I consider them to be a part of classical systems science.

CLASSICAL SYSTEMS THEORY AND SOCIAL SYSTEMS

System Dynamics is based on information-feedback control theory. Simulation plays a vital part in SD. It provides the conditions for the experimental approach to understanding system behavior (Forrester, 1961) and thus for reflecting on learning about organizations. The concepts *organization* and *model* play a basic role in understanding SD in the broader context of management science.

Model building is a central feature of System Dynamics. Its core construct is the feedback loop, based on circular causality. I have elaborated the various meanings of causality in Chapter 7. In the context of this paper it is sufficient to consider one aspect of causality namely that a causal relationship between 'x' and 'y' implies a time dependent *controllability* of 'x' over 'y'; 'y' follows 'x' in time, and 'x' is a necessary and sufficient condition for 'y'. Controllability is an appropriate concept for denoting causality in human organizations, which are the empirical basis for SD modeling. Organizational concepts are not entities such as particles in physics. They partly denote tangibles by design or due process, and intangibles due to tacit knowing, and the mental equipment of the people involved. In other words, they are social constructs. With regard to social systems, model building does not refer to mapping of ontological processes, but to constructing a system of meaning in the form of feedback loops.

Ashby (1968) has pointed out that the concept of organization is related with the treatment of conditionality between entities or parts. Causal feedback loops are particular forms of conditionality. The essential idea is the product space of *possible* interactions between parts or entities and some subset of points, showing the actualities. This implies that conditionality is a constraint in the product-space of possibilities. See for example the interdependence matrix of Figure 5.3. Through different degrees of conditionality various forms of organization are established. The peculiarity of the product space is "that it contains more than actually exists in the real physical world." From an ontological point of view, "the real world gives the subset of what is: the product space represents the uncertainty of the observer" (Ashby, 1968, p. 109). Ashby continued by saying that a substantial part of the theory of organization is concerned with properties that are not intrinsic to the thing but are relational between observer and thing. When 'things' belong to the domain of physics, chemistry, or technology they can objectively be studied as parts of the physical world. Two observers eventually will agree on the same product space. When 'objects' belong to the human and social domains, two observers legitimately can use different product spaces within which they record the same subset of actual events. When applied to companies, it is worthwhile to take into account the position of observers, to understand their potentially different perceptions of 'organization', based on different interests. Functional and general managers for example will not only observe different product spaces, they moreover will experience different conditionality between observer and 'thing'. To bring these different perceptions together in one coherent conceptual system belongs to the art and science of SD modeling, and gaming.

Another essential component of the concept of organization is the assumption of a whole composed of parts. Form the viewpoint of a theory of dynamics; a system can both be seen as an unanalyzed and analyzed whole. Ashby mentioned that one observer of a material system may see entities interacting in some 'organized' way while another observer may only see trajectories of different states. He concluded that any dynamic system could be made to display a variety of arbitrarily assigned parts, simply by a change in the observer's viewpoint. This notion refers to the level of aggregation of a model in combination with the time horizon of the model, and the viewpoint of the observer.

Ashby (1968) subsequently introduced the concept of a *machine*: a device of which the internal state and the state of its surroundings, define uniquely the next state it will go to. Therefore, an SD model is a machine. Machines bring forward a mechanistic view of reality.

Ashby further made an interesting distinction between *organization*, which is noticed by the actual observer, and *mapping*: the act of recording who will represent system's behavior in mathematical or other symbolism. This observation leads in principle to two communities of observers: the community of observers, involved in the system's performance, and the community of model builders, as a special kind of observers, who make representations. If the observer and model builder – the one who performs the mapping – are different persons, then both are potentially facing a communication problem.

The abstract concepts of *product space, conditionality* and *organization* sketched above, refer to material systems, to the system's resources. For social systems, such as companies, institutions and nations, this approach is too limited. One of the reasons is that, compared with purely material systems, some key objects of social systems are less identifiable. As discussed in Chapter 2, in social systems three interrelated strata are distinguished for describing different types of objects and processes: culture (systems of interactions), (communication & coordination) structure, and technology (resources). These strata are the building blocks of any social system. They represent distinct knowledge and action domains. They help observers to structure the constraints on the product space of a specific social system.

Applying this stratification to SD, the technology stratum represents the material flows as input, throughput and output. The structure stratum contains all information and decision flows, controlling the material flows. The culture stratum represents the goals, or set points, and decision rules. In SD models those decision rules are fixed. Closed SD models are not self-organizing in the sense of generating new model structures to cope with new circumstances. In other words, within one product space only one type of conditionality, and thus one interpretation of organization, is allowed. The group dynamics between the model builders, to achieve agreement on a specific interpretation for shaping the model, depends however on the influence (power) of the people involved. That perspective is beyond the scope of the technicalities of model building.

THE ROAD TO INTERACTIVE SIMULATION

In SD models all information to explain the system's behavior should be included in the model. Such models are *closed*. This implies that only those aspects of the social system that can be formalized are accepted. These restrictions hamper the mapping of vital social processes into SD models, because important aspects of the structure and particularly the culture stratum cannot be formalized. These characteristics of SD modeling limit the reach of the experimental learning environments, based on SD models. Traditionally, SD stresses mechanistic aspects of social systems. In cybernetic terms, structure defines functional relations, which are statements of circular causal connections. Functions explain causation and define the reproduction of structure. While building an SD model both conditionality between observer and object, and the product-space of possibilities need to be considered both by the observers and model-builders. They are the common basis for reflection. This implies that the system's structure should be the outcome of an ongoing negotiation process between inside actors and outside observers.

These views relate to two presuppositions for modeling. First, models are representations of a reference system, based on *invariant relations* between the entities. Second, that reference system is stationary or in steady state during the modeling study. This means that relationships during one period of time are of the same nature as any other following period. If this precondition does not hold as for example in World Dynamics (Forrester, 1971), the SD model may initially convey an exact image and increasingly a wrong one over time. Over a period of decades, the structure of the global socio-economic system – the reference system – changes drastically, implying that the assumption of invariant relationships over time is easily violated. This observation is relevant as SD models use time horizons that extend the 'natural' cycle time of the systems involved.

Considering the major goals of SD and its relations with learning in and about organizations, (see Senge, 1990), these basic assumptions generate the following dilemma. Organizational learning links two antithetical processes. To learn is to disorganize and to increase variety. To organize (to manage) is to forget and reduce variety (Weick & Westley, 1996). Organizational learning in the SD tradition means organizational change based on SD tools and methods. The objective of companies engaged in organizational learning is to improve management practices to better cope with heavy pressure, looming crisis, and accelerated change. If improving those management practices implies changing the structure of a company, that is, to disorganize and to increase variety, SD tools and methods are of limited use because of their mechanistic approach, stressing historic conditions. Emphasis is on reconstructing the past as a basis for constructing the future. As a reference for creating future options, Senge's five disciplines, that is, personal mastery, and mental models, building shared vision, team learning based, and systems thinking do not provide sufficient conditions for voluntary structural changes in social systems. The type of reflexivity needed to disorganize, to question conditions that govern the existing social system, do not fit into the SD approach. Therefore, learning environments based on traditional SD tools and methods are limited in scope regarding organizational change and development, to fully capitalize on organizational learning. They are too mechanistic.

To overcome the shortcomings of classical systems theory and the related traditional SD approach, I will introduce another perspective. With this other lens, I will re-arrange the concepts of social systems, mentioned above, to offer a coherent basis for organizational learning in combination with SD.

A system is self-organizing when it changes from separated to joined parts. It is self-connecting. It is also self-organizing if it changes from bad organization to a good one. Ashby stated that "good organization" implies that a number of parts interact to achieve some given "focal condition". There is no good organization in any absolute sense. An organization that is good in one context may be bad under another. Ashby made clear that no machine is self-organizing. Ashby's abstract view on self-organizing systems bears on living and social systems. For the study of self-organization of social systems, additional notions about the duality of structure and reflexivity are needed to couple self-organizing with self-reproduction. I will rephrase Ashby's definition, taking on board Giddens' notion about the duality of structure (see Chapter 4). *A social system is self-organizing when it changes from separated to joint parts through the actions of participating actors. They may confirm each other roles, while making use of rules and resources, and thus reproduce the social system. They may question the roles, rules and resources and devise strategies for the transformation of the social system.*

Applying the framework of Figures 7.2 and 7.3 (Chapter 7) to the instrumental use of SD, I distinguish two configurations.

- *Traditional simulation with closed models* according to the frame of an NTM. During the simulation run, it is not possible to make intermediate adjustments in the parameter setting. The researcher sets the parameters of the model at the beginning of the run for the period t=0 to t=T. This type of zero-actor simulation is depicted in Figure 8.1. It is called zero-actor, because the researcher is an observer, who does not interfere with the internal dynamics of artifact, and only observes the outcomes of experimenting with the model. In practice, this distinction between researcher and actor/stakeholder is not so clear-cut.

- *Interactive simulation with open models.* With interactive simulation, some loops of the SD model are opened, and one or more actors are included in those loops. The resulting configuration of multi-actor simulation, incorporating SD models, is presented in Figure 8.2.

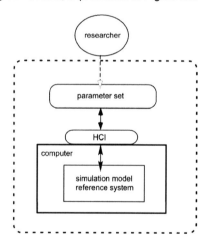

Figure 8.1. Representation of standard simulation with an SD model

In both cases, the researcher and the actor(s) connect to the computer and interact with the model through the human computer interface (HCI), usually a keyboard and screen.

In a multi-actor simulation set up, actors communicate, share knowledge and information to gain influence in the internal dynamics of the artifact: the simulation model. They make intermediate adjustments in the parameters, during run-time. They draw upon rules and enact a system of interactions through these rules. In doing so, they develop strategies for steering the resources, mapped in the simulation model. The actors have distributed access to the model, which means that they are only able to influence parts of the (integrated) model. They have the possibility to intervene in the behavior of the system of resources. These intermediate interventions allow for adapting the strategies as the social system develops over time. The actors can only adjust the model parameters, not the model structure.

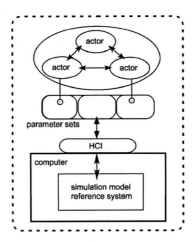

Figure 8.2. Representation of multi-actor simulation

Both types of simulation represent *heuristic learning environments* (Klabbers, 1996). They deal with searching for satisfying strategies in relation to organization's objectives. Parameters are adjusted within the existing structure. However, to use simulation in a *self-organizing learning environment*, interventions in interactive learning environments have to deal with the design (production) of new structures (Klabbers, 1996).

SD models can be used in heuristic as well as self-organizing learning environments. The instrumentalities of both simulation formats are different. Therefore, the software specifications for running those simulations are different.

For the design of self-organizing learning environments, existing software packages need to allow for taking on board the duality of structure and the related self-reproducing features of social systems (see Chapter 4). Instead of adjusting parameters within a model, self-organizing systems need to specify structural parameters about the model. This requires a higher level of competency of the actors, and the model builders. In the next section I will further structure those research and learning environments.

SIMULATION MODES: CONNECTIVITY – INTERACTIVITY

Building on the two varieties of simulation described in the former section: simulation with closed and open models, I will present a framework for categorizing SD models according to the type of interactive learning environment they provide. For that reason, in addition to open and closed models, I will distinguish between *connectivity* and *interactivity*, and *common and distributed access*. The term common access means that the researcher and the actor have all information available about the model. This situation is similar to the games with common access such as in CHESS (see Chapter 2). The term distributed access means that the actors (users) will only see part of the model and its outcomes. The form and especially the content of their interfaces with the model vary. I will pay less emphasis here on the instrumentality of those simulation environments and more on methodological questions.

As mentioned above, a model is *closed* if it contains all information to explain the system's behavior. A fully estimated model is an example of a closed model. It is *open* if additional information from outside the model (or system) is needed to describe and explain system's behavior. One reason for choosing interactive simulation is the lack of sufficient theoretical and/or empirical evidence about causal relations, to close the model. Another reason is to use the interactive model to study the adaptive behavior of the system through the interventions of the actors.

Connectivity refers to the mode of linking a user or client to the computer (the physical artifact). In case of a so-called closed model, it is the model builder, the SD expert, who is responsible for the connection with the model. The interface allows only *common access* to the model. As regards closed models, it is the researcher or simulation operator who conveys the results of the simulations. With respect to interactive simulation with real actors, they all have access to the model via the same interface. As 'interactivity' refers to the interactions between the users in their role of actors, in the case of closed models, the users do not directly interact with the computer. The simulation operator is the go-between. *Distributed access* enables the actors to directly connect and interact with parts of the model at different locations. In educational sciences connectivity and interactivity refer to the *locus of control*.

Simulation mode I – closed models

With pure simulation runs, carried out by the model builder, there is no specific actor to address. This is the zero-actor option (see Table 8.1). For example, results from studies such as Industrial Dynamics, Urban Dynamics, World Dynamics, and Limits to Growth are published in books to reach a broad audience. In a second option, a user-group, acting as one client system or actor, develops interactively strategies to be tested with the model. The expert is go between with the model. This is the one-actor option. A third option offers the possibility that more than one user group develops strategies, while interacting within teams. The expert – the go between with the model – receives the decisions made, implements them in the computer model, runs the model, and distributes the outcomes. This is the n-actor option. So, when a management team jointly uses an SD model of their company, it is viewed as one team actor, consisting of several interacting individuals.

Simulations require the initial setting of run time. It is not possible to stop the run, make intermediate parameter adjustments, and continue stepwise during the rest of the run. So, only at the beginning of each run is the parameter set defined. This is the 'single access' mode of connectivity. Even when different actors provide different sets of parameters, the expert, in the role of intermediary, combines them into one parameter set for the whole run.

Table 8.1. Simulation mode I: closed models

Simulation Mode I	Connectivity	Interactivity	Examples
Closed models	Common access via simulation-operator,	1. Zero-actor	Industrial Dynamics[i]; Urban Dynamics[ii]; World Dynamics[iii]; World3[iv]
	Common access via simulation-operator - facilitator	2. one-actor	Simulation mode BEER GAME[v]
	Common access via simulation-operator - facilitator	3. n-actor	STRATAGEM [vi]; FISH BANKS LTD.[vii]

Simulation mode II − open models

Actors may have the opportunity to have direct access to the (integrated) model. If they can only change the parameter set at the beginning of the simulation run, they use the option of single access. In addition, they may have the option to make a *stepwise* simulation run, during which they can adjust their strategies based on the intermediate results. It gives the actors the opportunity to adapt their strategies, while the system evolves over time. Although this option can be used by one actor it is more interesting to use it in combination with several actors, having access to parts of the (integrated) model. This is a frame of reference for multi actor, multi level simulation (Klabbers et al., 1980) (see Figure 8.2). It is in line with management structures of social systems. Decision makers have only control of parts of the system. This option is called the *distributed access* option of connectivity. In such a case, the client can connect directly with the computer. Dependent on the communication rules within an organization, teams may directly interact with each other. They can use this option to reach agreement on how to shape a comprehensive strategy that is to be carried out and tested via the model. So, linked to the distributed access option is the step-wise progress of the simulation over time. To catch the meaning of the framework, some characteristic examples are chosen.

Tables 8.1 and 8.2 represent different types of functionality of mathematical models, and thus offer different (interactive) learning environments. Simulation mode I resembles best the frame of the Non-Trivial Machine (see Figure 7.2). Simulation mode II, especially interactivity level 2 and 3, bear resemblance with the actor system (see Figure 7.3). The users are able to make intermediate parameter adjustments to make the model adapt to advancing understanding, and/or progressing clarity of goals.

Table 8.2. Simulation mode II: open (interactive) models

Simulation Mode II	Connectivity	Interactivity	Examples
Open models	Common access via simulation operator	1. zero-actor	See simulation mode I
Step wise progress in time	Common access for user	2. one-actor	World3-91 EXPLORER [viii]
Step wise progress in time	Distributed access for multiple users	3. n-actor	DENTIST[ix]

The examples given in Table 8.2 only provide changes in the parameter specifications of the underlying SD models. Participants cannot make intermediate adjustments in the structure specifications of the models: transform the model over time. This implies that the potential for experimenting is bounded by the model structure, which is fixed. The actors are confined to the fixed structure of rules and resources that cannot be transformed. The simulation is rule-driven. Simulations of this type map operational processes. They cannot catch the flavor of the fuzzier, and less structured sort of work of the upper level of management, involved in long-term strategic, normative decisions and entrepreneurship. Because of these limitations, all interactive learning environments presented in Tables 8.1 and 8.2, are heuristic. They enhance searching for satisfying answers within the given model structure.

PARTICIPATIVE DESIGN OF INTERACTIVE SIMULATION

Simulation mode III

In the foregoing sections the idea of interactive simulation was based upon the experimental use of available closed and open SD models. I have pointed out the limitations and opportunities of such simulations with respect to the frameworks of the Non-Trivial Machine and the Actor System (Chapter 7). Current SD related learning environments put learners in a situation where they may adapt the model structure to newly emerging views. This implies that they have to learn to cope with the dilemma about organizational learning: linking two antithetical processes: learning as a way to disorganize and to increase variety, and learning as a way to organize, to forget and reduce variety (Weick & Westley, 1996). Consequently, interactive simulations that are based on simulation modes I and II (see Tables 8.1

and 8.2), cannot deal with disorganizing and increasing variety to transform the existing system. They merely allow the learners to organize and to forget and reduce variety. So, the next logic step is to re-arrange interactive simulation and provide the actors with the opportunity to interactively build their own system of resources and rules that is, to build their model of the reference system, and when understanding advances, change and adjust the model structure. This simulation mode provides conditions for experimenting with the self-reproduction capacities (adaptability) of social systems. Dependent on the instrumentality of the programming software, various types of connectivity may allow more or less flexibility in the design process. The simulation environment that is related to participative model building is shown in Table 8.3. Increasing level of interactivity means also increasing opportunities for transforming the existing structure of the social system. Simulation mode III requires a higher level of competency of the actors that simulation modes II and I.

Table 8.3. Simulation mode III: participative model building

Simulation Mode III	Model	Connectivity	Interactivity
Participative model building	Closed	Common access via simulation operator	1. one-actor
	Open	Common access via single users	2. one-actor
	Open	Distributed access for multiple users	3. n-actor

Interactive simulation based on mode III, views the system as autopoietic. It is not structured by external information it receives, but by its system of interactions between the actors involved. Therefore, the actors internal to the social system construct (produce) the (meta-) cognitive structures. Interactive simulation based on simulation mode I (see Table 8.1), stresses allopoietic steering. Emphasis is on control from the outside. Those who are in control do not view themselves as part of the system they want to control. Simulation mode I emphasizes the use of the following terms: *knowledge, concepts, conception, notion, misconception, meaning, sense, schema, fact, representation, material, and content.* The actions to become owner of such knowledge are: *reception, acquisition, construction, internalization, development, accumulation, and grasp.*

Designers of simulation mode II (see Table 8.2), have the option to balance different views on learning (see Chapter 4). They can offer learners the possibility to use terms such as, *practice, discourse, communication, interaction, and improved participation in interactive systems.* They should however keep in mind the limitations of such rule-based simulations. That restriction hampers the actors from distancing themselves from the rules and resources to devise strategies for their transformation. That option would provide the conditions for interactive simulation to become self-organizing as described with simulation mode III. Truly self-organizing learning environments stress that the ideal of objectivity, that is, universal knowledge, and knowledge as accumulation by mental containers, need to be replaced with inter-subjective agreement within a historic community (see Chapter 3).

DENTIST: A CASE

For several decades the Netherlands have been witnessing an ongoing restructuring of the health care system, the dental health care system included. The political debates mainly focused on two issues: keeping control of the costs, while at the same time maintaining and improving the qualities of the service. Many policy measures have been taken, and since January 2006, the Dutch government has implemented a complete new health care system. On the one hand it aims at stimulating the development of a healthcare market with competition among providers, hoping that the market discipline will control costs. On the other hand its purpose is to make citizens (consumers) more aware of the costs. In good bureaucratic tradition, all kinds of medical treatments have been split up in discrete classes that define in clear-cut terminology the treatments included and the time allocated. These classes are called diagnosis-treatment combinations (DTC). The medical bills for covering the costs describe in great detail the application of these DTCs. The classification system does not (yet) cover all treatments, particularly the ones that cross the functional boundaries between medical specialists – the multi-disciplinary treatments. Also in good bureaucratic tradition, for such cases 'phantom' treatments' are devised to satisfy the bookkeeping requirements of the accounting departments. The basic goal of the new system is to balance 'supply and demand' in the health care business with government watching at a distance. Thus, the Dutch government is implementing a huge bureaucratic control system to liberalize that public domain from government interference and to stimulate the development of a commercial health care market: an interesting political and social paradox with many unforeseen consequences. It is complex adaptive systems theory with emerging properties at work. Hospitals are becoming limited liability companies with insurance companies, and specialists, their shareholders. Orthopedic surgery – potentially being outsourced by hospitals in the near future – designed according to the principles of production lines in the car making industry (NRC, April 22, 2006). The human body, considered a machine, and hospitals acting as service centers to replace spare parts. During the first phase of this industrial revolution of health care, emphasis will be on mechanization, the next one on will pursue automation through business process re-engineering practices.

During the late 1970s and 1980s, we have dealt with that social issue from the perspective of dental health, which in retrospect has been a test case of government interference with health care. That political struggle during the 1980s was a foreshadowing of the evolving political treatment of the Dutch health care system to its current form, a development sketched above. We were asked to develop a model that would help to understand the behavior of the dental health care system. The client was the faculty of dentistry of Radboud University in Nijmegen, the Netherlands. It provided us – the model builders – with inside knowledge about the organization of dental health care. The project has been carried out by the Social Systems Research Group (SSRG), which had been developing and applying the *method of interactive simulation* since 1974. The end-result of the project was a multi-actor simulation (a computer-supported game) called DENTIST (Klabbers et al., 1980). SSRG had designed a specific software system for multi-actor simulation to deal with questions such as the health care system. DENTIST evolved through three phases:

1. Phase 1: development of the SD model;
2. Phase 2: development of the interactive simulation;
3. Phase 3: development of the multi-actor simulation (game).

I will not describe the three phases in detail, and merely enlighten the approach.

During phase I, we applied the steps in model building as described in Table 5.2. The related SD model structure was depicted in Figure 5.4 and Table 5.6. We were able to partly estimate the model. Input to the modeling exercise was the question: How will supply and demand of dental care evolve over time, taking into account various opinions about the concept *dental health*, and alternative policies aimed at improving overall care delivery? Providing the time cycles of key processes such as, the education and training of dentists, and the duration of professional careers, we considered a time horizon of 25-30 years adequate. The client presented a list of 90 attributes that were relevant to develop a conceptual system – a network of cause-effect relationships. We applied the mapping of the system in line with the frame of Figure 5.3.

During phase 2, we embedded the simulation model into the framework of interactive simulation, opening some loops for intervention by the actors. Phase 3 covered the design of the multi-actor simulation: the DENTIST game. Figure 8.3 illustrates its structure, including the aggregated causal network of the SD model, and the location of the actors' intervention

The switch from the closed simulation model to interactive simulation implied as well a switch from a descriptive to a normative system, as depicted in Chapter 5, Figures 5.2 and 5.4. If the agent would have been an algorithm – a rule-based decision model – then we speak of agent-based modeling. That agent could have been modeled according to rules of inference used in Artificial Intelligence (AI), or in neural networks. Those 'intelligent' actors act mechanically, according to prescriptions developed by the designer. The problem however is that such valid prescriptions for DENTIST are not available.

A next step to visualize the formal images could be the configuration of the agent(s) into characters (avatars), and the simulation model into connected systems, operating in virtual space. On the instrumental level, such a move will add visual cues to the medium of representation of the simulation.

The structure of the DENTIST multi-actor simulation (game) is depicted in Figure 8.4. In the game, four groups of players – actors – are distinguished:

- The government & insurance companies;
- The profession of dentists (practitioners);
- The parliament;
- The public opinion.

Parliament and public opinion cannot directly intervene in the system of care. They can only observe how the system operates, and based on that information, they can try to influence the government/insurance companies, and the profession of dentists. The public opinion actor is able to observe which decisions are implemented, and thereby can check whether the government/insurance companies, and/or the profession do not cheat, pending the mutual agreements reached during the consultations. Only the government and the profession can directly intervene in parts of the system, and monitor the resulting performance partially. The game operator has full knowledge about the system's state, and is able to trigger events that impact on the health care system, events that require the government and the profession to take appropriate action.

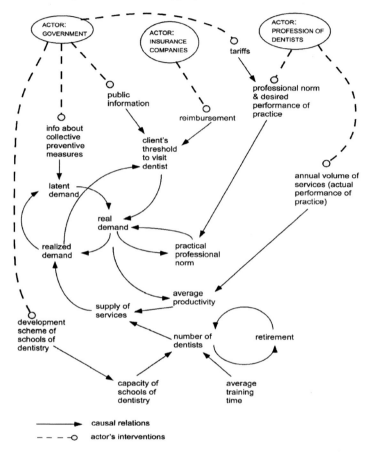

Figure 8.3. Causal network of DENTIST

The government – based on the available annual budget for health care – allocates money for education & training in dentistry, for preventive measures, and together with the insurance companies, takes measures to control expenses of dental care for the individual patient. The government can reduce or enlarge the capacity of schools of dentistry, and it sets the tariff structure for coded treatments.

The dentists/practitioners will determine their desired (average) turnover for a dental practice on an annual basis. Based on the tariffs, they have available the following degrees of freedom for handling their practices:

- The practical professional norm, which guides their treatment decisions in agreement with the patients;
- The number of treatment hours per year the dentists are willing to allocate annually.

Both options provide dentists a good basis for ensuring the desired annual turnover of their practices. To a large extent it is beyond government's control. The game operator may introduce events such as, technological innovations, which influence the quality, and/or the efficiency of treatment.

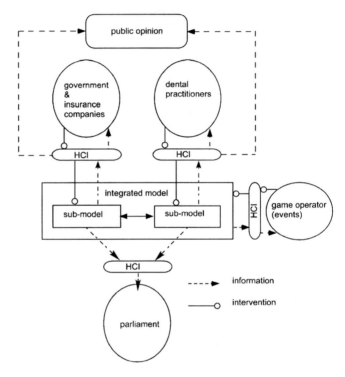

Figure 8.4. Representation of the DENTIST game

A multi-actor simulation such as DENTIST enables us to perform policy exercises. After entering the magic circle, the actors engage in a *policy dialogue*: a conversation about policy issues, causes, impacts and options. The macro- and micro-cycle of the DENTIST game is as follows:
- BRIEFING: The participants are informed about the propose of the game, the game procedures, and they receive their role descriptions;
- MICRO-CYCLE: During each simulation period, the actors complete the following sequence of steps:
  1. Each actor defines its general policy, and the objectives for the forthcoming year;
  2. Strategy formulation – measures to realize the long- and short-term goals are defined;

3. Consultation among the actors about the policies and strategies;
4. The actors specify their strategic measures for the forthcoming period;
5. They implement those measures;
6. Calculating (simulating) the impacts of those measures on the state of the health care system during the current year;
7. Presentation & evaluating the results;
8. Start of the next cycle: Adjustment of goals and policies, etc.

- DEBRIEFING: Assessing the game session according to the framework presented in Chapter 3 (see Figures 3.1 and 3.2). Emphasis is on the implications of the partial observability and control on the system's behavior. During the debriefing it is also possible to monitor the outcomes of various scenarios. Running the games takes on average 4-6 hours, and 6-20 people can participate.

Artifacts such as DENTIST take on board five elements of policy making that, according to Vickers (1972), are commonly ignored:

- Endurance through time: Policies are concerned with conditions and relationships that should be maintained through time;
- Management of conflict: The actors will deal with conflicting and competitive goals and finite resources;
- Value adjustments: Through performing policy negotiations, the actors create and adjust values;
- Modeling historical process: Historical processes emerge from previous actions and events. They are irreversible. Previous actors construct conditions, and operate in unique space-time settings. They are aware of their potential future impact.
- Steering the artificial: Previous actions propagate through the system, arising from earlier policy measures. They impact on the internal dynamics and give rise to outcomes that occur either in place of, or in addition to those that were intended. Thus, actors intervene partly to adjust previous errors of judgment, which are social constructions (artificial).

Multi-actor simulations such as DENTIST support *normative search* (What is it that ought to happen?) and *conflict and bargaining approaches* to social problem solving.

PROSPECTS OF INTERACTIVE SIMULATION

System Dynamics per se, does not limit the scope to simulation mode I, or II, discussed above. In fact, distributed access to SD models has been discussed in the literature (Davidsen, 1994). Software is being released that supports multiple role and/or user games in local area networks (Davidsen & Myrtveit, 1994). It also supports the design, implementation and operation of web-based games (Powersim Metro TM). Whether such options include simultaneous distributed access to one integrated SD-model, similar to the DENTIST framework, is not clear.

The SD approach underscores the dual relationship between structure and behavior – how structure creates behavior and how behavior, endogenously, modifies structure that is, shifts the relative dominance of structural components in the system: shifting loop dominance (Davidsen, 1996). Software packages such as, DYNAMO and STELLA, have traditionally focused on analysis: the derivation of behavior from structure, and not synthesis: the modification of structure to generate desired behavior. Such capability is more in line with the recent trend in software development as a basis for participate model development. It also provides conditions for experimenting with the duality of structure, as pointed out in Chapter 4. An object-oriented approach is one of the standard features that are supported. Moreover, new software will also support on-line modification of structures during a game. The related connectivity offers instrumental conditions for enhancing interactivity between the actors, thus providing a basis for multi-actor simulation, and shaping systems of interactions to self-reproduce social systems (Klabbers, 1996). Through in-flight model expansions, policy and model structure modifications will be facilitated. Although the conditions for participative model development have improved, distributed access to the model-base is still cumbersome. Either SD software does not permit that option, or for administrative reasons, the operating system of the computer configuration that is being used, hampers distributed access. Due to safety, and privacy measures, the operating system may restrict access to one model to one user only. In conclusion, the recent developments of software for SD modeling and simulation have brought the field considerably closer to satisfying the requirements imposed by simulation mode II and especially by mode III. Technical barriers are disappearing. Leveling out organizational and mental barriers is however more difficult.

The three simulation modes call for different capacities and skills. Simulation mode III will be most difficult for the participants. It requires the most expertise and sophistication of both participants and model builders. It not only requires a high level of competence in model building, it furthermore presupposes first hand knowledge about the reference system that is to be modeled. Note, however, that the degree of complexity to be handled, including the strategic actions of the participants, pose also high challenges on facilitators when it comes to interpreting the simulation results, and thus optimizing and securing the learning effects.

Assessments, based on the strictly logical positivist approach of the analytical science (see Chapter 7), have proven to be too limited in scope to bear results. I have argued why the variable approach for assessing the effectiveness of interactive simulation should be avoided. I will underpin my argumentation with the lessons learned from the following PhD studies. Vennix (1990) conducted his PhD study by setting up an experiment to evaluate computer-based learning environments for policymaking. He applied the analytical science method, more particularly the variable approach, focusing on variance theory of causality. The experimental group conducted interactive simulations with an existing model, embedded in a gaming environment. To prepare themselves, before the first session, both the experimental and the control group received a general introductory text on the most important characteristics of the subject matter. Before each session, the learners received more detailed information relevant for that session. The control group of experts received information about the subject matter in written form: the traditional way. The written text reported the results from runs with the simulation model.

The experimental group was put into the interactive learning environment, represented by Table 8.2, simulation mode II, level 2 (one actor), the control group in a learning environment, represented by Table 8.1, simulation mode I, level 1 (zero actor). Knowledge gained by the experimental and control groups was measured in terms of:
- knowledge about the structure of the system;

- knowledge about the dynamic characteristics of the system;
- knowledge about the relationship between structure and system's behavior.

The policy theory, which is the total set of assumptions underlying a policy, was tested via cognitive mapping, representing the network of causal relations.

Two results are interesting to mention. Both groups, due to the written information provided before the sessions, showed a significant increase on two aspects of knowledge: structure and the relationship between structure and behavior. However, no differences were found between the experimental and the control group (Vennix, 1990, p. 202). Also, as for the policy theory, differences between both groups were not significant.

Based on testing the effectiveness of the interactive learning environments (Table 8.2, level 2, compared with Table 8.1, level 1), the interactive mode was not superior to the traditional way of conveying information about experiments with the model.

In a follow-up PhD study, Verburgh (1994) tested effects of participative modeling, distinguishing between domain-specific and strategic (across domain) knowledge. Verburgh used Vennix's research method. The domain-specific knowledge referred to the subject matter, the strategic model to SD concepts such as feedback loops, delays etc. The interactive learning environment used in this approach is similar to Table 8.3, simulation mode III, level 2 (one actor). Also, here the analytical science method was used as a basis for the assessment of results. The results showed no significant differences in the quality of the conceptualization of the system, neither with respect to the domain-specific nor with the strategic knowledge dimension. This applied as well to the individual and the inter-individual dimension (Verburgh, 1994, p. 224). Based on the evidence of Vennix and Verburgh's studies, their evaluation approaches did not bear fruit. New avenues need to be explored, more in line with the design science methodology. We have learned from both studies that a strict positivist assessment approach is too narrow a view on knowledge transfer.

Although for example, Larsen, Morecroft, and Murphy (1991), and Morecroft (1992) have reported on the successfulness of participative policy modeling as a tool for supporting the policy making process, hardly any empirical evidence for this support has been given. I offer a few suggestions for improvement that are in line the frame-of-reference provided in Part II of this book.

- Theoretical notions about social systems should be sorted out adequately. From an epistemological point of view, the distinctions presented in Chapter 4, make a difference in the way steering and control in social systems, are to be understood.
- The architecture of games and simulations (see Chapter 2, Table 2.10), and the design science evaluation methodology (see Chapter 7) should be used as a framework for setting up adequate assessment procedures.
- The learner (actor) should explicitly be put into those interactive simulation environments, taking on board the arguments about the different knowledge claims, discussed in Chapter 3.
- SD models should not be considered truth machines. The related simulation environments are tools to explore different sets of assumptions and values about steering in social systems. These assumptions and values do not refer only to the subsystems of rules and resources of social systems. They should in addition explore assumptions about the motives of the actors and the normative rules and related attitudes that govern them.

These requirements are necessary to study their potential for the self-reproduction and transformation of the existing social system.
- Senge's five disciplines underlying the learning organization should be assessed with respect to their internal consistency. They now implicitly draw on different systems theories and learning metaphors. Consequently, since the constraints of the SD related learning environments are not made explicit, it is difficult to assess the effectiveness of the tools he provided.

The design of interactive simulation to advance the idea of the learning organization could be improved considerably if the notions on social systems theory and learning metaphors expressed in previous chapters, are made the subject of dialogue between SD specialists and decision makers. Complex adaptive systems theory of the kind discussed in Chapter 4, offers new perspectives, showing that classical systems theory with its mechanical approach, is a special case of complexity science. Classical systems theory is in terms of Ashby a more special (i.e., technocratic) treatment of conditionality between parts of 'the organization'. Instead of thinking about the learning metaphors (paradigms) – discussed in Chapter 3 – as two mutually exclusive ways of dealing with knowledge transfer, it could be more fruitful to live with both views on knowledge, and to embrace their valuable perceptions. They complement one another. The acquisition metaphor relates to a state description of knowledge – the result – while the interaction metaphor refers to process description – the road to beat. Both are two sides of one coin.

SD models are empirical models that catch both generic and local knowledge about organization and ways of organizing of companies and institutions. Due to this understanding, model building and interactive simulation are means for setting up conditions for testing consequences of that knowledge, while participating in a learning community. These qualities I see as the fundamental meaning of the usability of *interactive* and *multi-actor simulation*.

NOTES

[i]Forrester, 1961
[ii]Forrester, 1969
[iii]Forrester, 1971
[iv]Meadows, 1972
[v]Gould-Kreutzer Ass., Cambridge MA.
[vi]Meadows, 1984
[vii]Meadows, 1988
[viii]Ventana Systems, Harvard, MA
[ix]Klabbers et al. 1980

MANAGEMENT OF HUMAN CAPITAL

Following the case of dental health care, described the Chapter 8, in this chapter I will illustrate another project at the science/policy interface. It started in the 1980s and continued until the beginning of the 21st century. During its development, the basic ideas, the conceptual framework, and methodological approach did not change drastically. What changed were the clients and their needs, the contexts of use and the intended audiences. These changes impacted on the form and content of knowledge, embedded in the design, the utilization of the subsequent artifacts, and on their media of representation. Gradually also the themes (fashion terms) changed, following the trends in management literature. We started in the 1980s with the keyword *manpower planning*, which was followed during the 1990s by the term *human resource management* (HRM). Then came *strategic HRM*, and currently, we prefer to use the term *human capital*. I will highlight the historic developments of the artifact, covered by the generic term PERFORM (PERsonnel FORMation).

MANPOWER PLANNING OF UNIVERSITIES IN THE NETHERLANDS

The Dutch Ministry of Education & Science, and thirteen Universities in the Netherlands commissioned this project during the 1980s. They were the clients. The goal was to develop a set of tools for manpower planning and policy design. The project team consisted of researchers from the University of Technology Eindhoven, Utrecht University, and the University of Technology Delft. What prompted the need for the project?

The explosive growth of Dutch universities during the 1960s and 1970s, and budget cuts during the 1980s put considerable pressure on the administration of universities. As a rule of thumb, 70% of the university budget is for covering personnel costs. The increasing financial constraints became a difficult challenge for a number of reasons, because budgets cuts directly impact on the available, and future manpower, and as a consequence on research and education. The universities at that time were practically completely financed by the national government. For obvious reasons, the Ministry of Education & Science played an important role in University management. On the other hand, universities, and within their internal organization – the faculties – pursued their independent hiring and firing, and career policies. Therefore, manpower planning and policy formation take place on three interacting managerial levels:

- Ministry;
- University;
- Faculty.

Differences between staffing could not be explained solely by the differences in research and teaching of faculties, since similar faculties at different universities could carry out quite different career policies. In addition to the explosive growth in the previous decades, and budgets cuts in the 1980s, universities anticipated that the staffing, in terms of their age structure, would become increasingly unbalanced in the near future. Providing the tenure system of the scientific staff, their careers would last for several decades, making the staffing little flexible in terms of its composition: capacities to take on board new assignments, distribution over ranks, and age. Manpower decisions made in the 1960s, and 1970s would lag for decades, having a considerable impact on the total budget. Therefore the need was felt to have available adequate planning and policy support tools with a time horizon of two to three decades. The specifications of the design of these tools were as follows (Wessels, 1983):

- *No technicalities for users*: Pending extensive data manipulation, the artifacts should be used by staff members of the administration departments, who had no mathematical training or knowledge about computer programming;
- *Credible and simple tools*, close to the practitioner's locus of control and experience;
- *Decision making based on the user's knowledge and needs*: no built-in algorithms with optimization qualities;
- *Transparent decision-making structure* making visible the effects of decisions made on three managerial levels. This condition was considered important to demonstrate potential interferences between the three levels. The option of feedback on and tuning of policies was needed;
- *Portability* of models and computer programs, combined with the *flexibility* to include new functionality.

Four kinds of tools have been developed:

- Basic models for manpower streams with forecasting or extrapolation options;
- A set of tools for conversational (interactive) planning and policy formation with respect to classes of the manpower system (FORMASY);
- A framework for interactive simulation games with actors on different decision-making levels (PERFORM);
- A set of tools for developing new options within the context of tools 1, 2, and 3.

The modeling framework distinguished categories of personnel. The members of the scientific staff were classified at a certain moment in time in their career, and when time evolves they switch between those classes with a certain probability. We used the following basic features to classify the personnel of faculty, and university.

- Rank, position, or function (full professor, associate professor, etc);
- Grade-age (numbers of years occupying that function);
- Age

Additional features were:

- Participating universities;
- Expertise level;
- Type of expertise;
- Gender;
- Department;

- Employment fraction (full-time/part-time);
- Type of contract (with or without tenure);
- Mobility index;
- In-service time.

The result was a state-space model (Markov model) with transition probabilities connecting in each time period, one class to another. Based on these classifications, the manpower system was loaded with empirical data from faculties, universities, groups of departments within one university, all medical schools in the country, etc. The transition probabilities were partly driven by labor rules that apply to Dutch universities, partly by career policies and decisions within financial constraints, and partly by natural rules, such as, aging. The empirical model mapped the distribution of staff over the classes. Over time, changes in the distribution can be observed with members of staff moving from one category to another. The model frame has been embedded in the computer program FORMASY, allowing conversational use, and interactive simulation. The multi-actor simulation (PERFORM) embedded FORMASY, and was used for developing staffing policies by faculties within a university setting. Faculties had to tune their manpower planning to the university policy, and the financial constraints of the university.

Purpose of PERFORM

PERFORM has been designed to enhance the policy formation process, more particularly to make bureaucratic procedures more efficient, less time consuming, and more transparent to the stakeholders involved. As a consequence, the ultimate goal for designing PERFORM (design-in-the-small) was to enhance the development and implementation of tested personnel policies at Dutch universities (design-in-the-large). Consequently, the project team aimed at improving coherence between the actors (faculties and university board), operating at different organizational levels: department, faculty, and university. Various university board members had expressed that as regards staffing policies they had the feeling of "flying blind", and that it made them feel uneasy about what they were doing. PERFORM has been designed to teach them to cope with the many ambiguities of matching functions, tasks and people in a research and teaching environment, as well as to stimulate them to experiment with new ideas.

Architecture of PERFORM

For the sake of designing a transparent artifact that would demonstrate key issues, we decided to model a hypothetical university consisting of two faculties (a faculty of law, and a faculty of chemistry), and a university board. The following actors were involved:
- University board – supported by
    o The university council, and
    o University planning staff;
- Dean of the Faculty of Law – supported by
    o The Faculty council, and
    o Faculty planning staff, and
- Dean of the Faculty of Chemistry – supported by

o   The Faculty council, and
o   Faculty planning staff.
The architecture of PERFORM is shown in Figure 9.1.

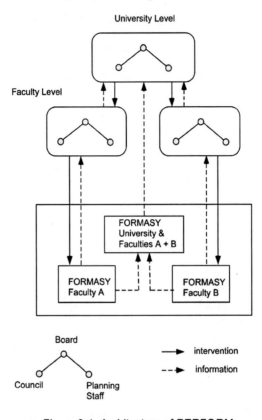

Figure 9.1. Architecture of PERFORM

While developing a policy, and for each game cycle to make a decision, each board developed proposals that were checked for their consequences by the planning staffs. The councils at each level have to approve proposals. Each of the actors, providing their positions, responsibilities, and interests, negotiated workable options. As a rule, the university board allocates the annual budgets to be approved by the University Council. Both faculties operated within those financial constraints defined by the university board. The faculty boards are responsible for the actual manpower planning and implementation. Each actor had only access to its particular task domain, a situation of distributed access. The University board – having common access – could not directly intervene in the personnel formation of both faculties. It has access to all relevant information.

PERFORM's content

For demonstration purposes, PERFORM was loaded with the actual data from two faculties: a faculty of law with a strong tradition in teaching, and a faculty of chemistry with a strong position in research.

As can be expected, the initial personnel formation of both faculties was different in number and composition. The numbers of students were expected to increase for the faculty of law, and to level off for the faculty of chemistry.

The university board was dealing with diminishing financial resources from government, while both faculties were to maintain the quality of research and teaching, and even had to improve their performance. During the game sessions, the participants learned to cope adequately with these tensions. To scale down the variety of options, the game was loaded with three viable scenarios.

Intended audiences and context of use

PERFORM was intended for administrators, planners, and decision-makers of universities, and public officials from the Ministry of Education & Science. It was a stand-alone computer-supported game. Running the game took one day.

Steps of play

PERFORM is a rigid-rule game. During the briefing the participants received manuals and role descriptions. The micro-cycle evolved through the following iterative sequence of steps.

- Initial conditions & preparation of policy. The participants receive the following information:
  - Summary of trends for the previous period of time (5 years time horizon), including costs of salaries and student inflow;
  - Estimates for the forthcoming period of 5 years with numbers of full time equivalents (FTE's) needed, budgets for salaries for the university as a whole, and for each faculty, students inflow expected, maximum number of full professors (chairs);
  - Summary of current personnel composition.
- Evaluation of current situation;
- Framing of policy intentions by the three main actors;
- Tuning and negotiating feasible options between the actors;
- Implementing policies for the next period of time by adjusting the relevant parameters of FORMASY, and returning to step 1.

Important indicators are:
- Distribution of personnel over ranks;
- Distribution of personnel over age, 25-65 years of age;
- Unbalanced distribution of ranks and age over time.

While using PERFORM with members of the university and faculty boards, it turned out that it took too much of their scarce time to take advantage of the opportunity. They were less interested in the technical details of manpower planning, and more keen to understand PERFORM's potential for conveying staffing dilemmas. To address that need, we decided to design a board game that visualized PERFORM in three-dimensional space. Thus, while keeping form and content of PERFORM intact, we adjusted the medium of representation. We used that version to run only one sequence of steps of play. We have used the board game subsequently for training board members, and members of administrative staff.

Within the broader political context of budget cuts, the administrators experienced PERFORM as a zero-sum game. Although in principle that view was not correct, it defined the initial atmosphere of play. Pending the initial framing of the question by the University Board, mutual mistrust and suspicion set the stage for negotiating the allocation of diminishing financial resources. The way the University Board conveyed their role turned out to be crucial. A wrong beginning – due to wrong wording and lack of strategic vision – could easily screw up the whole problem solving process. In that respect, PERFORM was a good indicator of the real tensions within and between universities, and of the horse trading that resulted.

Referring to the distinction between design-in-the-small and design-in-the-large as discussed in Chapter 6, FORMASY, and PERFORM are examples of design-in-the-small. Conditions for using both artifacts as part of a design-in-the-large effort that is, to enhance manpower planning and improve policy development, were not favorable for reasons that I will address at the end of this chapter.

HUMAN RESOURCE MANAGEMENT AND THE BANKING BUSINESS

During the next stage of the project, we shifted attention from academia to the European banking business. During the early 1990s it became clear that due to the increasing impact of information technology solutions on banking, drastic changes in the numbers and capacities of bank employees were to be expected. Especially information technology was expected to have a great influence on the service concepts of banks.

Turmoil in the European business landscape

Since the 1980s we have been witnessing tremendous institutional change in Europe. The emerging European Union and its new member states, are shaping form and content of the EU-Constitution, and as a result changing the relative autonomy of national governments vis-à-vis European government. These changes are offsetting a process of restructuring government and industry both in the manufacturing as well as in the service sectors of the national economies, such as the banking and insurance business. Rajan (1990) mentioned four routes of restructuring business: mergers and acquisitions, internal restructuring, improved efficiency and corporate deaths, routes, which are not mutually exclusive.

Especially, the banking and insurance industry has been facing drastic changes since the start of the European Central Bank (ECB), and the introduction of the Euro. It is simultaneously dealing with:
- Deregulation and decentralization on the national level and increased regulation and centralization on the European level;
- Extension of international networking through Information Technology (IT): the Internet and Intranets;
- Electronic banking, making banks more accessible although not necessarily more customer friendly;

- A search for new markets and customers and offering new and customized services;
- Increased competition as a result of a stronger market-orientation.

In this situation of flux and rapid transformation, managers are challenged to continuously position themselves by asking questions such as:

- What is happening in our socio-economic environment?
- Where do we stand?
- What sorts of business are we really in?
- What are the characteristics of those businesses?
- What are the limits − in terms of values and financial boundaries − to the sorts of activities that we are prepared to undertake?
- Will this business be the same tomorrow?
- What makes our company distinctive?

These questions are difficult to answer as management of large and medium sized companies find themselves in a world more and more characterized by increasing complexity of interaction patterns, processes and issues, due to the many new regulations by the European Commission, and the emerging internal market with its highly diverse economies from nations such as, Germany, France, the UK, the Netherlands, and Poland, Estonia, Hungary, etc. Especially the European banking business has to cope with completely new business conditions. In addition, it has to innovate its service concept because of the rapid advances in Information Technology (IT). During processes of restructuring, the banking and insurance business need to address the following questions:

- How adaptable is the personnel to changes in products, services, technology, and to restructuring the internal organization and workplace?
- Will the employees be able to perform more abstract work using codes and symbols, which are embedded in a continuously evolving IT-infrastructure?
- Will they take more initiative instead of plainly carrying out orders?
- Will the employees be aware of the wider geographical scope of external relations and transactions?
- In general, will management be competent to cope with all these changes?
- Will it be able to make the business more innovative and resilient?

In order to be innovative, more products and services − entering the market − have to be developed during shorter periods of time. As a consequence, managers are being challenged to deal with tensions such as *flexibility versus control, standardization versus customization, interdependence versus autonomy.*

THE BUSINESS ECO-SYSTEM AND HRM

The frame of reference of ecosystems is a metaphor to describe business processes from an evolutionary perspective. I will use it to distinguish two different strategies that are relevant for understanding the position of human resource management (HRM) within the broader scope of general management.

R-strategists

The term "R" represents the reproduction rate of species within the ecosystem. R-strategists exploit resources rapidly, and succeed best by exploring the habitat (*the market*) quickly. They reproduce rapidly to use the resources before other competing species (companies) exploit the habitat, or before it disappears completely. R-strategists disperse in search of other new habitats as the existing one becomes inhospitable (*outsourcing to other economies, when market conditions become too restrictive*).

K-strategists

K-strategists operate in longer-lived habitats, such as for example, an old forest, a traditional rural society, or in terms of De Geus (1997) a living company. Those of the species, with which they interact, are consequently at or near their saturation level K, which represents the carrying capacity of the environment (the current capacity of the economy). It is important for them to honor competitive ability, in particular the capacity to seize and hold a piece of the environment (*market*) and to extract the energy produced by it. A K-strategy enables companies to learn from experience and to store memories. Companies, managed by K-strategists, become more complex and need a longer period to mature. They need to invest more in training and educating their staff, to sustain a viable knowledge community that stores memories. They represent a larger social investment as compared to R-strategists, and gradually become more valuable. They are characterized by a longer period of vulnerability (Gould, 1977).

Sustaining social networks is an example of a K-strategy. For a social system such as a company, which is produced and reproduced by its internal and external stakeholders, it is important to assess in which phase of development it sees itself. Mature industries such as, the banking and insurance business are for various reasons in favor of pursuing a K-strategy. One important reason is that building and sustaining trust with individual and corporate clients takes much time, and requires a continuous effort.

K-strategy & HRM

One may notice an interesting link between these R- and K-strategies, and two major corporate governance paradigms: shareholder, and stakeholder value. Shareholder value focuses on the short-term revenues, by maximizing shareholders value. A favorable assessment by the financial markets requires that concerns fiercely acquire other companies and sell parts of their companies, and that a cunning program is in place to manage the increasing revenues. All these measures should offer the financial analysts something to go by. If in addition the boards of directors of companies – quoted on the stock exchange – possess shares and options of shares, they will feel challenged to reap of the benefits of their efforts in a short period of time. Shareholders expect that the yields per share grow faster than the related value of the company. Companies that emphasize shareholder seem to prefer an R-strategy.

Stakeholder value accepts and endorses the idea that a company is owned by a variety of interested parties (stakeholders): shareholders, management, employees, pension funds, banks, cities, state, etc. It offers a broader perspective and responsibility than the shareholder value. Companies that act according to the stakeholder regime, show similarity with K-strategists. For R-strategists human resources are mainly a cost factor, which should be kept low. When they outsource such resources to cheaper regions, they tend to ignore that the human resources represent current and future production capacity and long-term knowledge potential for innovation. K-strategists acknowledge human resources as key assets of their companies. Accordingly, they are willing to invest more in education, training, and career development than R-strategists. The personnel department of K-strategy companies plays a more vital role in strategic management then in R-strategy companies, which as regards HRM restrict themselves to administrative procedures, control, and operations management.

The following elaboration on human resource management is mainly relevant to K-strategy companies. In the Netherlands the banking and insurance business is very cautious about its personnel policy. Commotion, and unrest among employees about working conditions have a negative impact on the image of trust that is being conveyed. Banking, and insurance are knowledge intensive branches of industry, requiring the daily processing of vast amounts of data and information concerning money and the handling of financial risks. This information flow is the primary resource in banking, information that is in a continuous flux. As a consequence, this business depends increasingly on the quality of smaller numbers of staff. Human resources form the assets that make banks innovative, resilient, and customer oriented. Know what, know how, skills, and work style are the assets of the human resources to keep firms innovative and competitive. Rapid technological developments require in addition a continuous improvement of knowledge and competence to develop and adapt new service concepts. Available knowledge and skills define the quality and flexibility of the human resources. Therefore, management of human resources is a key factor for the banking and insurance business on the road to success.

STRATEGIC POSITION OF HRM

The various strategic factors that influence human resource management are illustrated in Figure 9.2 (Klabbers, 1993-a). Societal changes, institutional reforms in government, and new rules of corporate governance impact in various ways on industry. We have seen radical changes in the internal organization of many multinationals, due to mergers and acquisitions, and internal restructuring. They have offset fundamental transformation processes in business, and new approaches to corporate governance, accountability included. Due to volatile market conditions, management is increasingly involved in a continuous process of strategic positioning.

The resource-based approach the firm offers an interesting perspective on strategic management. The focus of the field is shifting from strategic positioning in a competitive market game to the focus on the firm's unique resources and capabilities. That new strategic game is a resource limited, goal-directed game of invention and communication. Particularly the human resources are considered the main repository of the organization's knowledge to address future challenges.

Strategic management and the resulting organizational change can only be successful if human resources are managed adequately. Rapid technological developments offer both opportunities and risks. Strategic human resources management is becoming the key to success especially in knowledge intensive

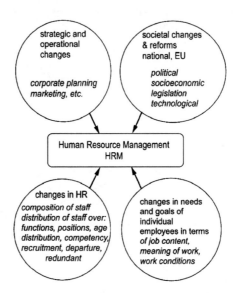

Figure 9.2. Factors influencing human resource management (Klabbers, 1993-a)

sectors of the economy such as banking, and insurance. Strategic HRM defines the short- and long-term demand of human resources, which have to be balanced by internal and external supply of competent staff.

Strategic management measures will impact on the size and structure of the company, on the technological infrastructure and on market conditions. These factors influence the demand for human resources in terms of quantity, quality and timing. Changes in products, services and customers also influence the capabilities and number of employees. In order to be able to assess the internally available human resources, information on age, gender, term of office, function, salary, education, competency, and other qualities of employees are needed. Externally available human resources from the labor market provide the potentially external supply, augmenting the internal supply where and when necessary. Quality and flexibility of the internally available human resources can be maintained and improved by training, education, job rotation, job structuring etc.

Balancing demand and supply of human resources, HR-management is engaged in tuning recruitment, career and departure (redundancy) plans. Such characteristics of human resources management are illustrated in Figure 9.3.

HRM^{SUPPORT} BANKING BUSINESS

The frameworks of Figures 9.2 and 9.3 were used to develop the prototype HRM^{SUPPORT}. The Commission of the European Communities financially supported the project, and the European Association of Cooperative Banks hosted the 1992 Conference on Human Resource Planning in the Banking Sector, during which it was demonstrated. We used a relational database software system to design the artifact, making a distinction between numerical and semantic data. To demonstrate the usability of the approach, after consulting bank directors, we decided to use HRM[SUPPORT] as a *policy exercise* about the merger of two local banks.

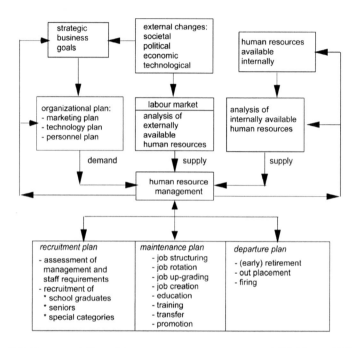

Figure 9.3. Representation of human resource management (Klabbers, 1993-a)

During the 1990s large national banks were planning to drastically re-shape their internal organization by a process of merging local banks.

DESCRIPTION OF THE POLICY EXERCISE: MERGER OF TWO LOCAL BANKS

Due to advances in Information Technology, the bank business is facing ongoing changes. In banking considerable changes were expected and a diversification of services. Automatic tellers, and Internet-banking in general will provide opportunities for limited financial services at small banks and high quality and complex services at regional banks. These types of reorganization were not expected to automatically bring forward a reduction of the total work force. Administrative personnel of small banks such as typists, cashiers and tellers would gradually change over to more qualified jobs. It was expected that new jobs would be created concerning commercial activities, consultancy for individual clients, handling of complicated data files, financial consultancy & engineering, venture capital, etc. Administrative personnel would gradually move to these more

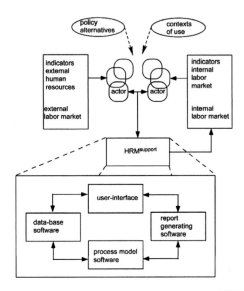

Figure 9.4. Representation of HRM^{SUPPORT}

commercial and controlling jobs. It was not expected to be a smooth process, as in banking staff might not fit well into the new job qualifications. Therefore qualified staff and middle management were to be recruited.

To stay competitive in a European banking market typified by diversification of products and services, we noticed a need for mergers of local banks, and acquisitions at the national level. In cooperative banks this process would percolate through regional and local banks as small local banks would have to redefine their position in local markets in terms of market share, and product- or service diversification. Advancing IT-infrastructure fundamentally affects the primary process in banking, impacting on managerial strategies. The chain of activities that link the banking business with the market increasingly becomes intertwined. Strategic management has to balance flexibility and stability of the internal organization in order to provide continuity in such turbulent circumstances. One of the issues that was expected to arise concerned the optimal size of local banks. Many local banks were considered too small, triggering during 1990s a process of mergers between local banks.

Mergers make high demands upon management and require considerable investments with respect to finances as well as involvement of personnel. Financial authority of the existing local banks has to be re-assigned to the new bank. Mergers will deeply impact on the culture and structure of the local banks involved. As various stakeholders will have different interests, it is obvious that the process will have to be managed very carefully over a prolonged period of time.

At all levels, positions and career perspectives are being questioned not in the least at the level of boards of directors, chief executive officers and managing directors. Jobs will disappear, and new jobs will be created. Job-content and workplace may change, and work conditions and informal work procedures are questioned. Consequently most of the time mergers are viewed more as threats than opportunities.

A scenario for merging banks

Because mergers are delicate processes they have to be managed very carefully. We took the following steps into account. In reality the process of merging takes several years. During the policy exercise presented here, time is compressed into a short period of simulated time allowing the participants to observe some important features of the merger that might take months or years to observe in real life.

Preliminary phase (duration 1-2 years):
- First rapprochement between the potential partners
- Making known intentions to progressing cooperation
- Further investigation for cooperation
- General agreement on prerequisites for merging
- Policy formation by board of directors and managing directors
- Preliminary decision to merge
- Consultation of workers council and unions (compulsory in the Netherlands)
- Laying down of the social plan
- Ratification of merger.

Integration phase (duration 2-5 years)
- Integration top management
- Setting up project management concerning merger of constituent organizations
- Planning of the integration course (board of directors)
- Integration of supporting departments (Personnel Departments, Economic and Administrative Departments)
- Establishment of image of the new organization (mission)
- Organization design:
- Goal setting
- Rules and programs
- Specification of organizational structure
- Personnel formation planning/staffing
- Allocation of employees
- Implementation social plan
- Occupying the new facility.

Post-merger phase
- Training, education
- Evaluation.

Conditions of social policy

In the preliminary statement and in the announcement concerning the plan to merge the following conditions and constraints are established.

1. No forced redundancies under the condition of willingness to accept new functions.
2. Careful attention to be given to the following social aspects:
   - Nature and timing of dissemination of information to employees, worker's council and unions, according to generally established codes of conduct;
   - Decision-making procedures;
   - Early information on the social consequences;
   - Defining measures for easing the consequences;
   - Procedures for mitigating effects on labor conditions.
3. The worker's council should have the opportunity to make recommendations.
4. Informing the unions according to general agreements on mergers and creating opportunities to make recommendations.
5. Preparing and implementing merger and decision-making process according to plan
6. Registration of interests and assessment of abilities and capacities of each employee.

The merger report

The merger report is an important document for all stakeholders involved. Generally it contains the basic information sketched above. In the respective report reasons for the merger are being submitted. As an example the following reasons are mentioned:
   - In the banking business, mergers create opportunities for operating on a larger scale. Due to streamlining the organization, efficiency should be improved.
   - Operating on a larger scale will allow:
       o Service to big clients: industry, government, service sector, wealthy individuals;
       o Hiring and training of professionals to improve competence and quality of service;
       o Utilization of advanced techniques for supporting business administration and consulting individual clients;
       o A more profitable cooperation with headquarters.

Subsequently the initial conditions of the new bank are defined: balance sheet, number of Full Time Equivalents (FTE), average personnel costs, wage costs ratio, training quota, etc. The composition of personnel – staffing – is defined. This *personnel formation plan* is combined with the *personnel plan* describing the human resources internally available and the desired human resources in the (near) future, both quantitatively and qualitatively.

Next the social plan, as discussed above, is defined and the worker's council and/or unions will comment on it. Finally labor conditions and -agreements are stated.

Development of social plan

During the preliminary phase a so-called social plan is being developed. It includes:
1. Schedule of the merging process, including:
   - The nature of participation of the employees, the union and the worker's council;

2. Formation plan (staffing) including:
- Organizational structure; departments, units, functions
3. Personnel plan of the new (merged) bank, covering:
- Human resources available after the merger in full time equivalents (FTEs);
- Primary and secondary labor conditions;
- Re-allocation of functions;
- Training and education as a consequence of re-allocation of functions, and outplacement;
- Salary;
- Career opportunities;
- Employees participation;
- Any additional aspects of social policy.

Summary

This outline of the merging of cooperative banks provided the scenario for the policy exercise on the basis of HRM^{SUPPORT} (Klabbers, 1993-b). During the policy exercise, the task of the participants was to prepare the merger-report and the social plan.

THE POLICY EXERCISE STEP BY STEP

The Policy Exercise in three phases:
- Preparation Phase
- Policy Formation Phase
- Follow-up Phase.

The project team was responsible for the preparation and follow-up phases:
- Preparation involved organizing the exercise;
- Developing and loading HRM^{SUPPORT} with data and information;
- Coordinating the participants contributions to the content of the workshop;
- Preparing the initial scenario.

The follow-up involved the preparation and dissemination of the final report of the policy exercise.

The heart of the Policy Exercise was the Policy Formation Phase. The initial scenario handed out contained relevant information on two banks that had decided to merge. Objectives of the managing directors of the constituent banks were:
- Enactment of the adequate size of the new bank, taking into account its service concept: nature and level of services, market share, and fixing rates for the clients.
- 20 % reduction of total costs.

During the round table discussion the participants develop and interpret one or more strategies concerning human resource management. They use HRM^{SUPPORT} to construct the strategies. Policy Formation proceeds according to the following steps:

Step 1
The facilitator distributes the initial scenario about the intended merger to both Management Teams, consisting of members of the board of directors respectively managing directors of the constituent banks.

Step 2
Both Management Team members discuss the scenario. They take into account among others the service concept of the new bank i.e., nature and level of services, market share, and fixing rates.

Step 3
Each team inspects the available information in HRM^{SUPPORT} concerning their respective bank on three levels of aggregation:
    3.1   Organizational level;
    3.2   Functional level;
    3.3   Employee level.

Step 3.1 Organizational level:
3.1.1. Both Management Teams discuss jointly the current situation, the options available and the initial conditions of the new bank on this level of aggregation.
3.1.2. Both Management Teams prepare their respective strategies and discuss the overall strategy.

Step 3.2. Functional level:
3.2.1. Both Management Teams discuss jointly the current situation, the options available and the initial conditions of the new bank on this level of aggregation.
3.2.2. Both Management Teams prepare their respective strategies and discuss the overall strategy.

Step 3.3. Employee level:
3.3.1. Both Management Teams discuss jointly the current situation, the options available and the initial conditions of the new bank on this level of aggregation.
3.3.2. Both Management Teams prepare their respective strategies and discuss the overall strategy.

Step 4
The audience deliberates on the feasibility of the strategies, on the relevance of the elected indicators. They integrate their perspectives and capture consensus in a revised scenario.

Step 5
The audience discusses the revised scenario (see step 2)

Step 6
The audience inspects broadly the available information in HRM-support in the context of the new scenario.

Step 7
The facilitator leads a joint debriefing of both Management Teams and the audience, asking the participants to consider the underlying framework of HRM-support and to interpret the scenarios produced.

Step 8
The final task of the workshop is to analyze and assess the implications of the scenarios for the social plan and merger report.

During the Conference on Human Resource Planning in the Banking Sector, in Leuven, Belgium in March 1992, we ran the policy exercise with a group of German and Dutch bank managers in front of a large audience of European bank managers and representatives of labor unions of several European countries.

UTILIZATION OF HUMAN CAPITAL

The most recent phase of this long-term project concerned the training of managers of a major Dutch pension fund, one of the major players in the world. At the end of the 1990s it had been transformed from a government agency, in charge of the managing the pensions of civil servants, to an independent company, securing its huge funds, as a major global investment fund, to secure the pensions of a million Dutch people. Pending the volatile global financial market, the company had to transform itself in a few years time from a rigid bureaucracy to a flexible performance based organization, while maintaining its quality of service to the retired civil servants, and securing future commitments for retired people. Linked to this drastic transformation process was a Masters Program, specifically designed to train those managers, who in the near future will become members of top management. Part of the program was the training on strategic HRM to improve the short- and long-term capacity of human capital, and to implement lessons on staffing policies in the various business units. In service companies, the quality of the performance is directly connected to the quality of the human capital – people doing their jobs in a suitable organizational setting. Therefore, the broader aim of PERFORM was to enhance the ongoing transformation process with adequate knowledge about and experience with staffing policies. The tailor-made version of PERFORM (design-in-the-small) became closely linked in the re-design of the company (design-in-the-large).

CONCEPTUAL FRAME

Organized complexity in a company can take many forms such as, hierarchical, divisional, or laterally distributed structures. A fruitful way to structure the internal organization is by means of the composition of personnel performing groups of tasks. One might see it as the fingerprint of available human resources. It represents the company's history as well as potential, resulting from the flux of people entering the company and moving from one position to the next one, or leaving the company. The evolving personnel composition reflects its history, its current capacities, and its future potential. The personnel composition depends on the economic web of relationships between a company and its stakeholders. They shape the institutional context in which a particular company is operating, the wider socio-economic and political business environment, the life style of people, and the business design – infrastructure – and personnel to operate it. These considerations are taken into account when dealing with strategic HRM. When a company is in a process of fundamental change, one of the major foci of attention is the composition of the personnel formation vis-à-vis the internal organization. Shaking up the internal organization implies reshaping the organizational design, its structure, the composition of functions and tasks, and as a consequence the staffing: the allocation of tasks among the staff. When the transition is from a hierarchical, bureaucratic type of organization to a more flexible performance based company, than it is not only the current structure that is at stake, more importantly, it is the company culture that needs attention. People will have to learn to act and interact differently, break old habits, learn new skills and competencies. The transformation process is illustrated in Figure 9.5.

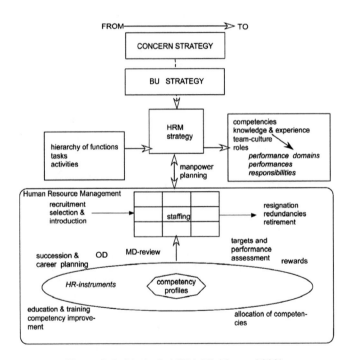

Figure 9.5. Strategic HRM (Klabbers, 2002)

Traditionally, HRM is concerned with the instrumentality of staffing, related to performing short-term administrative tasks, taking into account legal and labor market policies. Its main focus is applying techniques such as recruitment, selection, staffing, remuneration, organizational development, performance assessment, education and training. HRM primarily supports business-as-usual in the capacity derived from financial and production targets. Many impacts of HRM on the standing organization remain intangible, especially those, which relate to business strategy, and knowledge management. In addition, to which extent HRM techniques are based upon a coherent view on competencies, and subsequently linked to the long term dynamics of the personnel formation, career patterns, and innovative potential is difficult to grasp, and often poorly managed, particularly when outsourcing HRM functions. Strategic HRM is not yet well defined. Interrelationships between company strategy, evolving task structure, personnel formation, traditional HRM techniques and competence management, are depicted in Figure 9.5.

The framework of Figure 9.5 captures the notions of organized complexity, modes of coordination and the related value orientations, presented in Chapter 4.

DESIGN CHARACTERISTICS OF THE MANAGEMENT GAME PERFORM

PERFORM-P is part of an in-company Management Development program. Its aim is to enhance the ongoing transformation process from a government agency to a global market player. PERFORM-P integrates HRM with strategic management, dynamics of the labor market, and competency management. One of its major aims is to handle co-evolution of the business units as part of integrated management.

The company is a composition of business units (BU) – internal actors – linked to various external stakeholders. These BUs produce the company as a historically located actor, partly under the conditions of its own choosing. The organization is not conceptualized as simply placing constraints upon the internal actors, but as enabling them to act and to shape the game they play. Both the company and each composite actor within PERFORM-P, shape an adaptive complex system. Each Business Unit acts on local knowledge, and is capable of modifying its internal organization to improve its performance. The performance of the whole company builds upon the co-evolution of its constituting Business Units.

PERFORM-P represents a major company in the service sector of the economy. It consists of five teams: the Board of Directors, Concern Staff, the business unit Concern Information Systems (CIS), and two business units (BU) providing different types of financial services: managing pensions, and handling capital investments. These two BU's operate in two completely different markets. Business Unit A is a global player in the volatile financial markets. Business Unit B operates nationally in a market characterized by ongoing deregulations and increasing competition. Performances of the BU's are closely connected both on a short- and long-term basis, as they mutually provide financial resources to each other for conducting their operations. Performance of the overall concern depends on the co-evolution of both BU's with IT services provided by CIS. CIS implements the business and information policy of the concern vis-à-vis the distinct information policies of both BU's. It operates in a regional market of ICT providers and consultants, implying that it is able to outsource certain short-term capacities to meet ICT targets. Competitors, government, employers' organizations, and unions constitute the economic web of the concern. The structure of PERFORM-P is represented in figure 9.6.

The teams have freedom to act according to rules they agree upon with one another. The emergent properties of their organization result from the way the participants interact and mutually shape meaning and knowledge during the game session.

The game-session evolves through four phases (Figure 9.7). During Phase 1, focus is on an assessment of the internal organization with emphasis on the strengths and weaknesses of the current personnel formation. Phase 2 pays attention to the external organization with special emphasis on changes in the institutional arrangements within the public domain, and their consequences for the concern strategy, particularly their potential impact on personnel policies. Both phases 1 and 2 provide the strategic landscape, and the conditions for selecting feasible projects during phase 3. In this phase, the managers assess and select several innovations – turn key projects – in terms of their strategic advantages, and impacts on HRM. These projects can only be carried out in close collaboration between the two BU's and the Concern Information Systems unit. Precondition for the success of each of these projects is the timely hiring of highly qualified professionals, taking into account the current supply of the labor market, and the competencies needed. If the hiring is only partly successful, than the projects cannot be carried out according to schedule, and performance targets. This will hamper the necessary innovative capacity, and on the long run weaken the innovative potential and competitiveness of the concern.

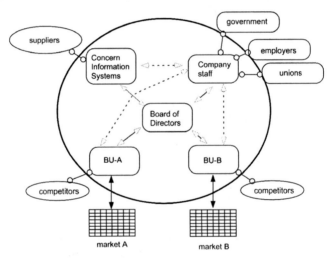

Figure 9.6. Organization of PERFORM-P (Klabbers, 2002)

The core activities during phase 3 are:
- Assessing the potential of the proposed projects for strengthening the concern;
- Developing a personnel plan for each of the proposed projects in terms of the number of staff and the composition of tasks needed: capacities, competencies, and age distribution;
- Designing the competency profiles for key functions as input to the staffing (see Figure 9.5).
- Developing recruitment plans for the projects, taking into account the internal and external labor market.

Competency profiles were framed on the basis of a model that distinguished between *core competencies* such as, entrepreneurship (leadership), business skills, customer service, teamwork, and professional & technical knowledge, and directly related task competencies such as, taking initiative, making well-reasoned decisions, following them through, recognizing problems, coaching, making timely decisions, presenting ideas simply and clearly, listening actively, building consensus, seeking involvement, sustaining working relationships, improving existing processes, adding expertise to others, acting dependably, etc.

This exercise not only required the participants to think carefully about the staffing of the project teams, while being involved in this challenging task, that frame also became self-referential with regard to their own role in the company.

At the end of phase 3, the managers assessed the overall situation, and made final decisions on the feasibility of the innovation projects, and the recruitment plans. During phase 4, they negotiated the concern strategy, with special emphasis on strategic HRM, taking on board the strategic choices made during the previous phases. To ensure an effective implementation strategy, they presented an action plan covering the personnel policies for the whole company and the BU's, and they prepared an information and communication plan. The game session – the macro-, and micro-cycle included, lasted one and a half day.

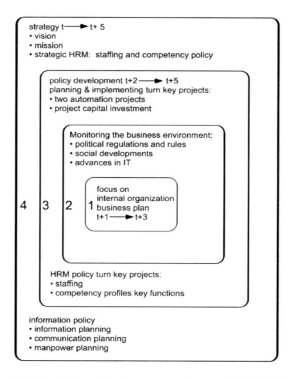

Figure 9.7. Illustration of the four game phases of PERFORM-P

On the basis of these design characteristics, one should realize that every PERFORM-P session is unique in its dynamics, and its self-reproduction of structure, and (lack of) order. It is a self-organizing learning environment. No general explanations, or algorithms can adequately describe the relevant process. A specific causative configuration of actions, interactions, and events would be needed to explain its unique history. Due to the emerging properties of the game, such configuration is not available. The specific organization, structure and process of each session, produces and reproduces order within a theoretically huge sequence space. That order may eventually be understood and explained through knowledge of structural, systemic, and environmental histories and knowledge of the extent of information and the various means of interpretation.

COPING WITH BARRIERS TO CHANGE

In terms of Christopher and Smith (1987), PERFORM-P is not a *closed game*, which means that the managers do not follow the instruction: This is the problem. How will you solve it? It is an *open game*. The managers step into the situation and are asked: How will you deal with it?

The participants are aware that, to gain overall success for the company, co-evolution between the business units is a necessity. This goal is not achieved easily. One of the major barriers is the prevailing company culture, and organizational structure that the participants enact right from the beginning of the game session. The managers are free to choose the way they shape their organization, configuring their company as they see fit. They are invited to experiment with new approaches, and ways of doing things. However, as the real company is in a process of fundamental change, its culture and structure are being transformed. Old habits and routines have to be broken down, which is a time consuming and painstaking process. The ongoing transformation from bureaucratic to performance-based company is illustrated in Table 9.1.

Table 9.1. Direction of transformation process (adapted from Klabbers, 1999)

From	To
Inside: rapid and efficient production	*Outside*: tuning technological potential vis-à-vis markets needs
Old: reduction of complexity	*New*: creative problem solving
Determination: control/steering of operations	*Emergence*: setting the context and conditions for new ideas, processes and systems
Learning by *assimilation*	Learning by *accommodation*
Barriers (blockades) *to change*	*Tolerance and variety*
Narrowly defined responsibility: territory exploitation; short-turn shareholders' return on investment	*Freedom*: tolerance & adaptability; flocking and mobility; knowledge creation; resilience and continuity.

Managers, who had made their career in the "old" company, had difficulty in adapting to the new circumstances and requirements, and in achieving new competencies, needed in the "new" company. They had to change attitudes, local knowledge about work routines, and more importantly their tacit procedural knowledge to understand the ongoing processes and their position in them. They had to re-calibrate their organizational navigation system. In general, they were in a process of transforming the company's culture and communication patterns.

PERFORM-P demonstrated that playing the game is a voluntary attempt to overcome unnecessary obstacles. On the basis of observations made during the sessions, understanding gained during the subsequent debriefings, and written summaries of the gamed processes, I will summarize a few general game patterns.

ATTRACTOR PATTERNS

In Chapter 4, I have discussed the concept of attractor in complex systems, making a distinction between trajectories over time of system's behavior, and structure attractors that capture the tendencies of organizations to maintain contingent forms, configurations, or structures. With respect to PERFORM-P it is worthwhile to notice if and what type of configurations – structure attractors – emerge during the game sessions.

The participating managers have the freedom to choose their preferred form of *organized complexity*. In this interactive learning environment, although free to experiment with new forms of organization, managers tend to start reproducing the organization they are familiar with, even if they express that they are in favor of changing it. Once that structure is in place, they are tempted to produce a new type of organization. However, transitions such as sketched in Table 9.1, take time to settle.

Based on their experience with and knowledge about organizations, managers have mentally available a stock of organizational forms, each with different ways to communicate, each securing their positions and interests in different ways. These ways are viewed as preferences from which they can choose a particular organizational form, which then acts as an *attractor*. Most of the time, this choice is being made implicitly through the way the players interact with each other, a shared form of tacit knowing. In this particular company, during the series of game sessions, two organizational attractors have emerged.

Dependent on their capabilities and preferences, the participants established two different organizational patterns right from the start of the sessions. From the potentially available forms of interaction (depicted in Figure 9.8), they implicitly chose either the distributed one-boss arrangement, or a mixed core-/star-network configuration. Initially, at the beginning of the transformation process pf the concern, the participants started PERFORM-P with the distributed one-boss arrangement, and gradually as time passed, they deliberately started with a core-/star-network configuration. Both initial conditions set the tone for further mutual engagement during the game session.

The distributed one-boss arrangement resembles the past, the core-network/star-network the emerging future of the concern. This was also shown by the way the managers interacted with one another, and in particular how they managed time. Time is a definite constraint in PERFORM-P, and only if all managers share information efficiently, are they able to stay in tune with the needed pacing of the game. In the one-boss arrangement, tasks are performed hierarchically. In the core-/star-network configuration, they perform tasks in parallel activities, implicitly applying the core idea of co-evolution of actors in complex adaptive systems. The main ideas, underlying Table 9.1, helped to understand the different group dynamics of the related sessions.

Distributed One-boss Arrangement

By choosing the hierarchical one-boss arrangement the managers enacted a number of obstacles, which they had to overcome subsequently. As PERFORM-P is a free-form game, these planning and communication obstacles were the managers' own social constructions. They were not included in the rules of the game. I will sketch some obstacles.

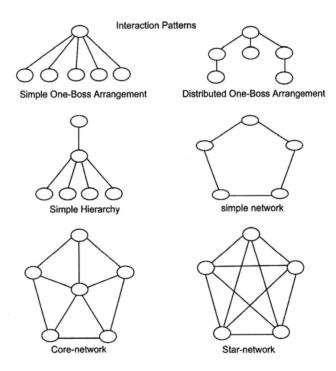

Figure 9.8: PERFORM-P interaction patterns (Klabbers, 2002)

Teams tended to be focused on their internal dynamics, meaning that the gamed company was inner-directed. Emphasis was on making sense of the situation, and especially for the Board of Directors, to gain control over the process. This myopic view on the concern hampered framing suitable conditions for creative and timely problem solving. Sequential and hierarchical communication among teams and emphasis on control of operations formed a barrier to change. Time management became a major obstacle to the point that in one session, the Board of Directors and the Concern Staff lost control, and the BU's managed mutually their affairs without further interference of the Board. Responsibilities were narrowly defined, and existing territories were exploited at the cost of effective co-evolution. The managers emphasized control over content, while loosing track of the process. They were not able to sustain effective mutual relations among the teams. Frustrations about the way things evolved were not canalized among groups, and the managers groused outside the game space, while taking a break to have a cigarette, or drinking coffee. While having a short time-out, they emotionally stayed within the magic circle. In balancing the tension between determination and emergence, their emphasis was on determination.

Several barriers hindered adequate actions. Conformity and secrecy were stressed, nurturing an atmosphere of distrust. Power relationships dominated the scene. Communication was stratified, formal, and centralized. Planning was rigid, and cost driven. Most importantly, the managers suffered from a continuous lack of information and time. This became most manifest during phase 3 – performing the feasibility studies of new and innovative projects – during which the Board lost complete control over the rapidly evolving sequence of events. The situation became chaotic, and the game dynamics were nearing an inflection point, forcing the teams to drastically change course, or to finish in a deadlock. They chose to reshuffle the interaction rules, shifting from a vertical to a more horizontal type of configuration.

The Network Arrangement

Gradually, during the period that the concern's transformation process was getting shape, at the beginning of the game, the managers playing the roles of Board started triggering a collective management structure, resembling the core-network. They stressed the big picture, set the context and conditions for new ideas, and provided general rules to manage the process. By doing so, they arranged a flexible and workable framework for both simultaneous and parallel interactions between teams and members of the teams. They shaped conditions for mutual trust. As a consequence, the gamed company became more outer-directed. The company culture they shaped is characterized by the following keywords: tolerance, variety, adaptability, flocking and mobility between teams, and resilience in managing time.

The resulting setting enabled the teams to level out many barriers. Due to the freedom to move around, the managers were much less inhibited and spontaneously shared ideas, convictions, and objections. Power relations were based on mutual respect, with a keen eye for quality of the emerging organization. The concern structure was flat, and consequently communication patters horizontal, enhancing direct interactions. "Doors were not closed", and the Concern Staff acted as a viable and reliable information resource and go between, much appreciated by everyone. Organized complexity was managed through simultaneous actions within a mutually accepted communication framework. Many processes ran in parallel due to an effective partitioning and coordination of actions. Consequently, time management was effective and efficient. Even during phase 3, handling the rapid sequence of events was done efficiently and effectively. The added value of each team, and each team member in the overall results was high. The spirit was high during the game, and the managers expressed a feeling of accomplishment and satisfaction. The participants expressed that general understanding during the debriefing.

SUMMARY

The terms *manpower planning, human resource management (HRM), people management*, and *human capital management etc.* denote the evolution of socio-economic thinking, and trends in management science about the position of employees in companies. Depending on the way the wind blows, personnel is viewed as a cost or a production factor. If it is viewed as a cost factor, then the management decision to outsource HRM seems straightforward. In that case, applying HRM techniques is a matter of administrative routine. However, it will hamper implementing innovations when they are needed. The three cases of human capital management – covering a period of more than two decades – referred to institutions and companies in the service sector of the economy: universities, baking, and insurance business. In all cases the capacities of the employees is a key "production factor". Universities cannot exist without scientists who are responsible for research and teaching, bank and insurance companies heavily rely on the qualities of its employees to sustain relationships with corporate and individual clients to offer adequate services. In all three cases, drastic socio-economic changes triggered interest in the projects, in the design of policy support systems to enhance the handling of this sensitive issue. Once the artifacts had been designed and tested, the design-in-the-small effort, the next stage of using the games to support the related social problem solving, the design-in-the-large effort, required a receptive political arena. The political arena for manpower planning at universities can best be characterized as mutual distrust among faculties, university boards, and the Ministry of Education and Science. One important indicator for this mistrust was the great reluctance to timely provide the needed information and data to load FORMASY and PERFORM. Both artifacts have demonstrated to be usable. In addition, and more importantly, their initial use for demonstration purposes made their potential also clear.

A similar situation occurred with the banking project. During the 1990s it was foreseen that tens of thousands of European bank employees would become redundant. Representatives of European Unions, present during the demonstration of the prototype HRM^{SUPPORT} at the conference in Leuven, Belgium, showed a keen interest. They were willing to support the further development, on the precondition that they would also have access to the data and information. Bank managers were reluctant to share that information. Those distinct interests put the European Commission in a difficult position. Finally, it decided not to go ahead with financing the next stage of the project.

The conditions for PERFORM-P were more favorable. The transformation process was in full swing. All parties involved had agreed on the political constraints, and the Master Program, of which PERFORM-P was a part, was an in-company training program. In addition, the game was tuned to the ongoing developments. It raised awareness about the strategic position of human capital management through a tailor made learning environment. Moreover, it offered tools that could be used in practice. During the debriefings, participants conveyed that while playing the game, it became difficult for them to distinguish between the gamed reality and daily experiences on the job. Apparently, PERFORM-P triggered the explicit, tacit, local, and encultured knowledge (mental equipment) of the concern to the extent that it generated usable meaning about how to carry on with the transformation process.

From a design viewpoint, on the instrumental level the three projects were very different. Their purposes, context of use and intended audiences were distinct. Yet, the issues have been very similar. On the methodological level, the projects were based upon the same framework. In general, the composition of the personnel formation is made up of the following interrelated classes: numbers, grades, functions, tasks, age, gender, capabilities, etc. The resulting cohort models − state space models − define the way employees move through that system over time. A realistic time horizon for such processes is 5-30 years. Markov models, such as used in FORMASY, require sufficiently large numbers of employees to make reliable statistical estimates of the transition probabilities between states. This precondition could not be met with the banking and insurance company projects. So, we had to adapt the media of representation. For HRM^{SUPPORT} we chose a relational database to model the system's resources. For PERFORM-P, we used paper & pencil matrices as media of representation. Because we applied a robust methodology we were able to smoothly tune our approach to shifting circumstances. If we had continued on the level of instrumental reasoning per se, then we would have had difficulty in understanding the common ground between the projects.

We have learned one major lesson from these projects at the science/policy interface. A precondition for designing effective artifacts is the availability of reliable empirical data and information. Transparency for the client/user is a prerequisite. Yet that transparency is the first casualty when it comes to using gaming artifacts in a highly political arena. The key issue of the design easily shifts from the quality of the artifact and its potential to the question: Who will be allowed to enter the magic circle to play with it, and take advantage of its usability. Working under those conditions makes project teams vulnerable, and running those projects a tricky affair.

POLICY OPTIONS ADDRESSING GLOBAL CLIMATE CHANGE

Developing policy options for dealing with global climate change (GCC), in the context of sustainable development, is a tricky problem. It is complicated not only because of the complex dynamics of the climate system, but also because of the potential societal and political ramifications in the near and distant future. The relevance of reducing greenhouse gas emissions varied among policy makers of different ministries, members of parliament, industry, non-governmental organizations (NGOs) and scientists. Some of these actors considered greenhouse gas emissions by industry and agriculture a potentially serious problem; others were of the opinion that it was still too early to draw any definite conclusions. In order to deal with the apparent gap in perception, the project "Development of policy options for dealing with the greenhouse effect on sustainable development" has been set up to enhance communication between the parties involved and to identify viable policy options. The project was part of the Dutch National Research Program 'Global Air Pollution and Climate Change' (NRP), which ran from 1989-2002.

The development of an international climate policy builds on national policy perspectives. These are dependent on the perceived risks of climate change, socio-economic and cultural characteristics of nations and regions involved, and technical feasibility of policy measures. Scientific and technological research support the policy making process about these issues. The perspectives of the scientific community and the policy makers differ and as a consequence communication is often troublesome. Knowledge construction and utilization under such circumstances can only be effective if all parties involved engage in a continuous dialogue about causes, effects, impacts and responses (Klabbers, et al. 1996). In this chapter I will describe a project carried out in the Netherlands. It had as its major objective the articulation of a variety of perceptions and positions related to climate change. Research questions focused on the risks of and on feasible social, economic, cultural and technological responses to climate change.

Objectives of the project

- To enhance the communication between policy makers, third parties and scientists;
- To identify and explore the range of options to further Dutch climate policy;
- To generate a series of research and policy questions for programming purposes of NRP.

Intended audience

The project involved major actors from government, industry, and NGOs. Eight ministries (Director-Generals, and Directors), members of parliament, political parties, captains of industry, employers' federations, unions, Dutch NGOs, and consumers' associations have been involved. All major Dutch players have actively engaged in the series of dialogue workshops, and through their efforts, they contributed to the overall success of the project.

Multiple realities in issue driven research

Although the greenhouse metaphor has been introduced by the natural sciences, the subsequent linkages of scientific research with policy making implied a broadening of scope. The rationalist approach of the natural sciences was no longer predominant in that debate, as also knowledge from other scientific disciplines such as, the social and behavioral sciences, was needed to deal with social aspects of GCC. Because of the complexity of the problem and the existing scientific uncertainties about GCC, various competing reality definitions about causes, impacts, and responses existed, that were based on the different positions and interests of the major actors involved. Dealing with these multiple views on the issue with the purpose of achieving a coherent approach was the most important challenge of the project. Consequently, the project team had to acknowledge that the scientific method applied in laboratory research was too limited in scope to adequately deal with this tricky issue. We were dealing with what Funtowicz and Ravetz (1993) called, issue-driven research in a context of hard political pressure, high economic interests, values in dispute, high decision stakes and high epistemological and ethical systems uncertainties.

Coherence

During the project there was no integrative framework imposed in advance, because it did not exist, and if it – according to some scientists – did exist, it would have been biased in view of the multiple meanings about GCC. We aimed at developing a coherent framework, taking on board the diversity of ideas about and approaches to GCC. This diversity resulted from the multiple scientific knowledge domains involved, and the various interests of stakeholders is society such as the chemical industry, the transport sector in the economy, agriculture, more particularly the horticulture, the energy supply sector, etc. *Coherence* should allow for many kinds of connectedness between key concepts, encompassing logic but also associations of ideas and intuition, intimations of resemblance, conflicts and tensions, and imaginative leaps. Coherence is open to change and imagination, while true to the many facets of concepts and their interrelations about GCC. During the project coherence was found where the participants of the dialogue workshops could discover and establish relations among various areas of knowledge, understanding and skill, yet where loose ends remained, inviting a reweaving of conceptions to the unknown future of climate change. Participants were invited to figure out how different facts, even those that seemed incongruous, could be connected and made to work in acting and thinking. They needed to frame and continued reframing the (domain specific) facts and significance of facts to which they were attending. They framed as well the policy contexts in which they attended to those facts. Building *trust* between the project team and the participants of the workshops was a precondition for success. We sustained trust by being explicit about the role of the project team. It would act as a facilitator of the policy formation process, and in no way would it present itself as expert with definite ideas about what was correct or wrong, feasible or unrealistic. This was not always easy, because the project team consisted of experts in specific areas of GCC research. Occasionally, members of the project team were tempted to step into an ongoing debate during a workshop. Would that have happened then they would have been no longer in the position to facilitate the process effectively. Therefore, the project team did not act as one of the conversation partners concerning content.

ENHANCING POLICY DEVELOPMENT & IMPROVING THE SCIENCE/POLICY INTERFACE

Dialogue workshops

The project was set up as a series of concatenated dialogue workshops (Klabbers et al. 1994, 1996) (Figure 10.1). The output of one workshop was used as input to the next one in time. The term *dialogue workshop* referred to the framing of interactions between the participants on the basis of specifically designed games, loaded with information gathered from the institutional actors involved.

The first workshop addressed the formulation of key questions that concerned policy makers, business executives, unions etc. They have been used as input for two parallel workshops: one elaborating on those questions that were relevant for the natural sciences, the second one addressing socio-economic and technological questions. The two groups of scientists were asked whether science was capable of addressing the questions, and of producing adequate knowledge about the related questions in the near future. The basic question put forward to the natural scientists was:" Does the greenhouse effect exist, and if so, what are the risks?" The main concern articulated to the social scientists was:" If climate change is in danger of coming out, how can we cope with it from socio-economic, technological and behavioral points of view?" The output of both workshops, combined with the questions generated in the first workshop, became the input for the third workshop – a series of round tables, during which policy- and decision-makers identified and explored a range of feasible options. The discussions focused on the potential impact of the information provided, on the positioning of the participants in the policy debate and on the actions they thought appropriate. From the round tables the project team distilled five rough policy options for further exploration. Finally during the fourth workshop, based on a conceptual framework emerging from these workshops, these five options were reviewed, and assessed. During the first day of the workshop, the dialogue about the scientific issues was stimulated and structured using a frame game, specifically designed to trigger communication between the participants. During the second day, each participant was asked to join a working group tied to one particular option with which he/she felt most comfortable. Each group further developed its option corresponding to the structure of a work document prepared for that meeting. The participants based their contribution to the option-development process on their judgments of climate and socio-economic risks.

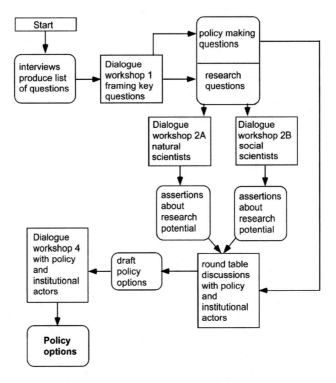

Figure 10.1. Schedule of project (adjusted from Klabbers et al., 1996)

POLICY DEVELOPMENT CYCLE

Climate research for policy-making purposes is a dynamic, iterative processing of meaning. It is a continuous dialogue at the science/policy interface. Policy development includes five basic functions of scientific knowledge construction and utilization (Klabbers, 1982, 1985) (Figure 10.2). (For more details about design-in-the-large and design-in-the-small, see Chapter 6.)

- *Formulation of goals:* problem identification: formulation of the issue;
- *Development of artifacts:* development of explicit procedures and methods for constructing knowledge for surveying the field: design-in-the-small and use of artifacts;
- *Knowledge production:* using the artifact to provide inputs to planning and decision making processes;
- *Science linking:* coupling of research to intended users, leading to changing perceptions through assimilation or accommodation of usable knowledge;
- *Science utilization:* information feedback to actors to adjust goals and interventions.

In Figure 10.2, the development and use of the artifact form a cycle, which is similar to the macro-, and micro-cycle of gaming session, as discussed in Chapter 3. In this climate change policy development project, we have used several artifacts during the four workshops. In fact, we went five times through the "design-in-the-small and use of artifacts" cycle (including two times for workshops 2A and 2B).

The design-in-the-large cycle illustrates a recursive process. Feedback of knowledge into the policy development process happens after a time delay of months to years. In the meanwhile it may happen that the initial question that prompted the project has changed due to changing political circumstances. Were that the case then the facts and their significance would have changed, probably causing available knowledge to be adjusted. Therefore, it is important that the development cycle be tuned to the pacing of policy development, otherwise potentially usable knowledge may become obsolete. Dependent on the policy context, the cognitive domains of the actors involved vary. Moreover they deal with different ideas about usable knowledge.

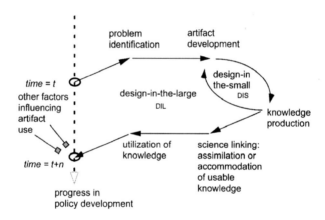

Figure 10.2. Illustration of the policy development cycle

During the round tables the project team confronted the societal actors (policy makers for government, private sector and NGOs) with the results of both scientific workshops. Their response included a cautious exploration of policy options to take into account the scientific understanding of the problem of climate change and sustainable development. At this stage, the discussions were stressed to some extent due to the simultaneous political debate about the second Dutch National Environmental Policy Plan. Fortunately for the project, before dialogue workshop 4 began, the negotiations concerning the governmental Environmental Policy Plan had been settled. This enabled a constructive sharing of strategic visions among the members of each of the groups. As this workshop was problem-driven and action-oriented, emphasis was placed on mutual understanding and a shared will to bring forward viable options.

POLICY OPTIONS

At the start of the fourth dialogue workshop, the project management proposed the following five policy options. These options should not be viewed as mutually exclusive policy alternatives. They rather represented viable courses of action that did not contain specific end-states to be achieved in a distant future. The options were based on a review of the round table discussions:

- No-regrets;
- Least-regrets;
- Acceleration;
- Technological innovation;
- Institutional-cultural change.

No-regrets. Within the no-regrets option it was considered uncertain whether substantial reductions in emissions of greenhouse gases would be necessary. Within this option, priority was given to instruments that serve other (socio-economic and environmental) objectives, simultaneously resulting in a reduction of greenhouse gas emissions. No-regrets instruments will pay off even if climate change will not occur.

Least regrets. Within the least regrets option it was also considered uncertain whether climate change will occur. A trade-off was made between risks linked with the occurrence and non-occurrence of climate change in relation to the policies selected. The policies included all no-regrets instruments supplemented with anticipatory policies aimed at limiting risks resulting from climate change. Emissions are not reduced to the maximum possible, but policies anticipate a very substantial reduction. If reduction proves to be not necessary, part of the effort is lost. If reduction proves necessary, further reductions were expected to be more efficient than they would have been if only a no-regrets policy was implemented.

Acceleration. With this and following options, the context of the proposed policies shifted gradually from climate change to sustainable development. Climate policies are to be developed as part of the general pursuit of sustainability. Acceleration focuses on synergies and positive feedbacks within society. Forces within society that are consistent with sustainable development are reinforced and blockades are removed.

Technological innovation. According to this strategy, technological development is essential for the future. Technological development is the only way to match the demands of an ever-increasing world population with the carrying capacity of the natural environment. This requires a long-term cooperation between government and private enterprise. Government directs technological development by providing opportunities and constraints for the required development and through setting norms and standards.

Institutional-cultural change. Within this option it was assumed that technological solutions would not be sufficient to create a sustainable society. In addition, social, cultural and institutional changes are required to reach such a goal. Furthermore it was assumed that sustainable development could only be achieved through processes of change within society. The role of government is limited to setting proper conditions and providing political support.

Preliminary conclusions

As mentioned above, because of the complexity of the problem and the existing scientific uncertainties, a variety of competing reality definitions existed, which were based on the different perceptions and positions of the major actors involved. This made clear that policy makers' appreciation about what science can do in such an arena is not straightforward and not self-evident. The perceived controversy about climate change among scientists appeared to be a main stumbling block for the public at large and policy makers to decide on the urgency of preventive measures. It was also noted that communication between the science and policy communities should be improved considerably. Scientists should more actively get involved in the public debate. Social and technological scientists should go beyond the stage of writing reports based on analytical studies. In order to disseminate their ideas, they should be encouraged to show by demonstration projects that advocated measures contribute to a solution.

The policy context of each of the five options is different. Therefore, each option should be understood as being supported by a particular coalition of policy makers and third parties. *No-regrets policy* was not considered to be a climate change policy. *Least-regrets, acceleration and technological innovation* were options, specifically aiming at mitigating climate change. *Acceleration and institutional-cultural change* were viewed as mainly sustainable development policies.

The project has produced two types of results. The first result included the policy options mentioned above. The second result was related to the learning processes of all persons involved. It was similar to organizational learning involving many parties. Walking through the subsequent dialogue workshops many participants (about 120 representatives of the institutional actors) were involved. They were very engaged during the policy dialogues. They kept a global perspective on the issue, while searching for Dutch solutions.

The five options could not simply be combined into one overall option through consensus building. This would not have done justice to the complexity of the problem regarding causes, uncertainties, international interdependencies, and the values and norms that are at stake. Instead of striving for unity in points of view it was considered more rewarding to acknowledge the divergence of views and interests of all players, and strive for convergence on actions rather than common goals. The policy options and the basic strategies as produced during the fourth workshop showed a wide range of strategic visions. The plans of actions, however, as proposed by the various groups showed much more commonality than expected. Similarities in the plans of action may have resulted from a lack of creativity or time pressure. It may also reflect a relative consensus on a number of viable actions.

The options were formulated in terms of opportunities and risks. The participants were strongly aware of the notion that the Netherlands should operate on this issue in an international context, dominated by mutual interdependence. Such recognition offered a fruitful basis for an open dialogue among all actors where creativity has a better chance than negotiating in a very polarized setting.

With regard to the steps taken during this project, it was believed that a solid basis has been laid for a continuing fruitful communication between the researchers of the national research program and policy- and institutional actors from all sectors of society. During the project it became very clear that there was an additional field of knowledge on climate change outside the scientific community that had not yet been tapped: risk management. Through the project that knowledge was mobilized and it served as an extra source of inspiration both for policy actors and researchers. Climate risk management clearly called for a new way of communicating between the scientific and policy-making communities.

As said before, the major role of the project team was to provide a fruitful framework for the participants to express their views, to engage in multiple dialogues, during the workshops and round table discussions. The main purpose was to create an open atmosphere enabling and enhancing conversations to challenge their imagination and to avoid deadlocks. The members of the team acted as facilitators. They did not act as experts. The gaming techniques used provided the right conditions for the participants to enjoy their performances. They became highly motivated and put in considerable efforts to generate the results discussed here. At the end the participants considered themselves co-owners of the outcomes.

The results of the project have changed the science/policy interface between the National Research Program on Global Air Pollution and Climate Change (NRP) and the major policy − and institutional actors. The second phase of NRP (1996-2002) has been more explicitly policy-oriented, and the dialogue between science, policy- and institutional actors has become an integral part of the second phase of NRP. The project improved communication and mutual understanding between scientists of different disciplines, potentially increasing the usability of research in this complex interdisciplinary area of climate change. During the science workshops economists, engineers, psychologists, sociologists, philosophers and natural scientists revealed large discrepancies in their view of and approach to the problem, implicitly basing themselves on different paradigms to persuade each other.

Clearly, enhancing communication alone would not bring about convergence in the policy arena. Progressing scientific evidence of climate change, at various levels of aggregation, expressed in terms of socio-economic risks and opportunities was considered necessary. Nevertheless, increased communication should facilitate progress by opening up the minds of single-minded scientists and single-theme policy makers for new crosscutting knowledge domains, and integrating political action to the challenging issue of climate change.

A follow-up activity was proposed to improve the science-policy interface at the national level. This should promote the assimilation, or more importantly accommodation of scientific results by policy actors to help identifying the most relevant research questions. Related to this is the importance of broadening the scope of communication between the science community and policy actors from the private sector, national and local governments and public interest groups. It was recommended to pay attention to issues of climate change and sustainable development that are specifically relevant for special sectors of the economy such as, energy supply, transport, building, etc. In this way, the policy options could be elaborated, deepened, and tuned to the needs and wishes of local and regional government.

GOVERNING RISK & COPING WITH UNCERTAINTIES

The policy options project discussed above, being part of the Dutch National Research Program 'Global Air Pollution and Climate Change' (NRP), is an example of a national effort dealing with a global problem. NRP was related to the ongoing involvement of the United Nations to scientifically underpin climate change policy making.

The United Nations Framework Convention on Climate Change (FCCC) coordinates the *governing relationships* between 161 countries concerning policy making on Global Climate Change (GCC). The terms of the treaty provides the context and conditions for *executive decision making* to implement the agreed measures. In addition, the scientific community continues struggling with major uncertainties and knowledge gaps. I will look at the issue of GCC in more detail from the viewpoint of policy-making, supported by evolving scientific evidence. Governmental policy-making is not only seen as part of the solution, I will argue that is also part of the problem, as it is an additional source of uncertainty in handling GCC.

The debate about uncertainties in GCC is taking place among different parties, running from policy-, and decision-making bodies to multiple scientific disciplines. To take this diversity of viewpoints into account, I will distinguish two levels of judgments: *policy making* in a strict sense, and *executive decision-making* (Vickers 1965). In addition, I have distinguished six relevant scientific domains (Klabbers, et al., 1998). This framework relates to the basic building blocks of social systems: actors, rules and resources (Figure 2.1). Policy-making is a process of appreciation that links two types of judgment: a judgment of facts and a judgment on the significance of these facts for the appreciator (policy actor). Executive decision-making is based on instrumental judgment. It refers to technical issues such as, carrying out policies, and finding the right instruments to implement them. It focuses primarily on maintaining or realizing over time a complex pattern of relationships among decision-makers, based on standards, targets and timetables, and constraints, which previously have been defined through the governing relationships.

Although policy actors, while framing governing relationships, may be confronted with the serious policy problem of global climate change (GCC), this does not imply that they will define the related executive problems. For a variety of reasons, policy actors may refrain from formulating the executive problem. Vickers (1965) pointed out that once a policy actor realizes that there is a policy problem, it is up to him to decide whether it should be put on the political agenda, and if so, what the executive problem will be. Subsequently, it is up to the executive decision-makers to solve it. As the Kyoto protocol is showing, policy-makers themselves, while defining executive problems, constitute important sources of uncertainty for decision making at the executive level. For example, in April 2006, the incoming Canadian government announced that – although it had ratified the Kyoto protocol to reduce greenhouse gas emissions – it is planning to withdraw its support from it. Based on the agreement, it had promised to reduce the emissions over the period 2008-2012 by six percent. Currently, the emissions are 25% above that level. Therefore, the government considers those targets not feasible. The Canadian minister of environmental affairs conveyed being in favor of the US policy. The US government did not ratify the treaty, and is cooperating with Australia, Japan, China, India, and South Korea to invest in technological innovation to curb greenhouse gas emissions. Remarkably that option is one of the options resulting from the policy options project, described earlier. Canadian NGOs disagreed with this policy, expressing that such measures are inadequate. This example shows that when the policy context shifts, related executive problems will shift swiftly and probably dramatically. The Canadian government, while adapting the national GCC roadmap to suit domestic preferences, is increasing uncertainties about global political efforts. Actually, by switching to the US led coalition, it is changing the governing relationships with those nations who have ratified the Kyoto protocol.

Wynne (1992) noticed that the climate change discussions about uncertainty seemed to rely implicitly on the naive notion that inadequate control of environmental risks is due only to inadequate scientific knowledge. He criticized this idea, and added the concept of *indeterminacy* as a category of uncertainty. Indeterminacy refers to the open-endedness (both social and scientific) of the processes of environmental damage caused by human intervention. Indeterminacy introduces the idea that contingent social behavior, including decision and policy makers' behavior, has to be related to the analytical and prescriptive scientific framework. It also acknowledges the fact that many of the intellectual commitments, which constitute knowledge, are not fully determined by empirical observations. The latter implies that scientific knowledge depends not only on its degree of fit with nature, but also on its correspondence with various social constructions of reality. As demonstrated by the policy options project, the richness and reach of knowledge transfer depend on its success in building and negotiating trust and credibility for science. In addition to Wynne's comments on knowledge construction, and discussed in Chapters 6 and 7, it is worthwhile to realize that different scientific disciplines define knowledge differently, and that these differences play an important role in the debate about GCC (Klabbers *et al.* 1996; Klabbers *et al.* 1994). In this regard I have distinguished the *rationalist* and *nominalist* research traditions. Wynne's notion of the social construction of knowledge follows the nominalist tradition being related to as *post-normal science*.

MAPPING KEY UNCERTAINTIES

Considering the long time delays of climate change, and the spatial diversity of its occurrences, we have distinguished a structural (and spatial), and a time component of uncertainty (Klabbers et al., 1998).

Structural and spatial uncertainties of GCC

Table 10.1 depicts a few key uncertainties that relate to the components of social systems: actors, rules, and resources. We have focused on those uncertainties that can be influenced (partly) by human interventions.

Temporal uncertainties

It is important to understand the different time scales for the significant changes that typically occur in the various domains. Considerable GCC uncertainties and risks are usually noticed when processes change rapidly, having significant effects on the state of area involved, and when these changes cannot easily be predicted and/or controlled. Table 10.2 illustrates temporal uncertainties and related time scales.

Table 10.1. Structural uncertainties in GCC (adjusted from Klabbers et al., 1998)

RESOURCES	Uncertainties about resources
1. Geophysical and atmospheric domain	Stability of thermo-hyaline circulation and ice shelves; role of aerosols in climate system; biogenic feedbacks; etc.
2. Ecology domain	Adaptability of ecosystems over time and space; physical harm to biosphere, ecosystems, biotopes; multiple stress; etc
3. Geographic domain	Land use patterns over time; intrinsic unreliability of regional climate projections used in impact studies;
4. Technology domain	Rate and direction of progress in performance, and cost of low carbon emitting technologies; rate of adaptation of these technologies; etc.
5. Socio-economic domain	Geopolitical stability & international trade relations; manufacturing or sale of products and services that cause damage or hazards; vulnerability of sectors of the economy to impacts of climate change; energy supply infrastructure; etc.
6. Population, demographic domain	Demographic developments (mainly in developing countries); consumption patterns; lifestyle changes; risk distribution among individuals, classes, cohorts and populations; etc.
RULES	Uncertainties in executive decision-making
7. Institutional domain	Volatility of political domain and fuzzy transformation of (international) policy problems into national executive decision problems; malfunctioning of institutions; malfunctioning operating procedures; inadequate effectiveness and efficiency measures; disjoint, incremental planning procedures among ministries, leading to suboptimal strategies;
ACTORS	Uncertainties in sustaining governing relationships
8. Political domain	Multiple objectives of risk perception such as equity, fairness, health impairment, safety, control and resilience, requiring participation by interest groups and the affected public; shaping and maintaining inadequate national and international governing relationships for dealing with GCC; etc.

Table 10.2. Temporal uncertainties and time scales (adjusted from Klabbers et al., 1998)

RESOURCES	Uncertainties about resources
Geophysical and atmospheric domain	Natural resources change over a time scale of millions of years. Ocean currents: uncertainties about thermo-haline circulations – time horizon, decades to centuries: if occurring, then climate changes within a time frame of 5-20 years.
Ecology domain	Ecosystems can change within a time horizon ranging from 20 years to centuries.
Geographic domain	Human settlements take decades to transform.
Technology domain	Energy supply, and demand technology typically take 20-50 years from introduction to maximum share. Lifetime of energy infrastructure and buildings is of the order of centuries; interdependencies between technologies also matter for the rates of change (e.g. Houses currently being built are not suitable for electric heat pumps); utilization of technologies and operational decisions: effects can be instantaneous.
Socioeconomic domain	Changes in the capital market and human capital market of the socioeconomic domain show a wide range of time frames, from a maximum of one generation (30 years) to a minimum of 3-5 years.
Population, demographic domain	Composition of population: 30-50 years, lifestyle: 10-20 years.
RULES	Uncertainties in executive decision-making
Institutional domain	Transformation processes of public administration on the basis of changing budget allocations.
ACTORS	Uncertainties in establishing and sustaining governing relationships
Political domain	Elections and government, switching rapidly to new governing relationships: transitions every four years; shifting political agendas; shifting dominance of ministries;

Although policy- and decision-makers prefer to have available uncertainties expressed as probabilities, the nature of many of the uncertainties mentioned in Tables 10.1 and 10.2 does not allow a quantitative approach for an integrated assessment of governing the climate change risks. Nevertheless, quantitative approaches are considered valuable for partial analysis. The question remains how to interpret and communicate those uncertainties.

GOVERNING RISK SOCIETY

Global Climate Change is an example of the risks that nations are facing. GCC is a man-made risk from industrial societies that heavily rely on natural energy resources.   It is expected that mainly the underdeveloped countries are most vulnerable to the impacts of climate change. Nuclear proliferation by states that support terrorism is another example or risk. It results from a mixed blessing of advancing nuclear technology by unreliable national regimes, unreliable in terms of sustaining peaceful governing relations with fellow states. In addition to political and environmental risks, it is worthwhile to pay attention to technological risks with respect to safety and health.

Political, environmental and technological risks expose individuals, groups and populations to hazards such as, lack of economic security, health hazards due to migration of diseases because of climate change, food safety related to risks of hormone treated beef, extreme weather events and threats to safety, exposure to toxic substances, and large-scale accidents resulting from terrorist attacks.   The animal feed sector still cannot fully guarantee the quality of its products due to many unknown, or uncontrollable risk factors at the beginning of the food chain. The trade disputes that result from different domestic regulations in a global market are more than economics. They are about social issues and cultural traditions. The costs of trade quarrels are easy to assess. The benefits are difficult to estimate: the value of safer food is hard to quantify, because they may have long-term and intergenerational effects. The various stakeholders in the dispute convey different perceptions on food safety. Consumer-rights activists and environmental groups may not be susceptible to economic reasoning because they value safety more than immediate costs. To resolve those disputes, scientists are often called to help dealing with the incidence, distribution and control of hazards that many times are higher-order consequences of advances in science and technology.   Accordingly, science plays a double role in the debate about societal risk. Beck (1992) has addressed this issue by pointing out:

> Two constellations can be differentiated in the relationship of scientific practice and the public sphere: *primary* and *reflexive* scientization. At first, science is applied to a 'given' world of nature, people and society. In the reflexive phase, the sciences are confronted with their own products, defects, and secondary problems that is to say; they encounter a *second creation in civilization*. .... and paradoxically enough, in the scientifically partitioned and professionally administered world, the future perspectives and possibility for expansion of science are also linked to the critique of science.   Science becomes more and more necessary, but at the same time, *less and less sufficient* for the socially binding definition of truth (p.155-156).

Complexity & risk

In trying to understand industrial societies two interrelated concepts play a key role: *complexity* and *uncertainty*. Although safety hazards may be highly uncertain, their impact when such events occur may be considerable, implying that the risks are high. Complexity refers to the many components and their interrelationships that are difficult to monitor and to handle in time and space. The concept of complexity is related to *connectivity*: the coupling of parts, subsystems and systems. They influence the way disruptions ramify through the system, and can be handled independently by each component. The term connectivity refers to linkages in the technical infrastructure, while the term *interactivity* refers to linkages among humans, and humans interacting with technological artifacts. Through information and communication technology, as for example the Internet, people are connected. The way they make use of this infrastructure, that is, through the content, meaning and context of their messages, reflects the idea of interactivity. Two types of connectivity play a role:

- *Linear connections*, which follow an expected sequence of activities, in which the segments are well defined and segregated. These connections are transparent. In linear systems, segments are well defined and segregated.
- *Complex connections*, which show unfamiliar, unplanned and unexpected sequences that are neither visible or nor immediately comprehensible although, in retrospect, they may not be incomprehensible.

Complexity is inherent in social systems and in some forms of technology. It arises due to:

- Multiple branching paths of events and processes;
- Multiple feedback loops;
- Jumps from one linear sequence to another;
- Visible interaction because of proximity;
- The 'environment' impinging on multiple components of the system (Perrow, 1984)

Table 10.3. Comparison between loose and tight coupling (adapted from Perrow, 1984)

Loose coupling	Tight coupling
Processing delays possible	Delays in processing not possible
Order of sequences can be changed	Invariant sequences
Alternative methods available	Only one method to achieve goal
Slack in resources possible	Little slack possible in supplies, equipment, personnel
Buffers and redundancies fortuitously available	Buffers and redundancies are designed-in
Substitutions of supplies, equipment, personnel fortuitously available	Substitutions of supplies, equipment, personnel limited and designed-in
Local units adapt to local conditions without requiring changes in system – loose coordination	Whole system adapts to multiple local conditions – tight coordination

Visible interaction in social systems can occur via the Internet, telephone, video-conferencing, TV and radio, etc. So, people may be at very different and distant locations with respect to space, but in each other's vicinity with respect to time. The global information and communication infrastructure gives rise to increasing connectivity and interactivity. Consequently, the world is growing increasingly complex.

Combined with interactivity and connectivity is the *type of coupling* between the parts of relevance. Systems can be loosely or tight coupled. This distinction refers to the internal organization of systems: their horizontal and vertical communication and coordination structure (see Table 10.3). Perrow (1984) characterized tight and loose coupling within organizations as follows. In combining the two dimensions of connections and coupling, Perrow developed a grid of four quadrants. The quadrant with complex connections and tight coupling encompasses the high-risk organizations. Examples are nuclear plants, genetic engineering firms, chemical plants, and space missions.

RISK & RISK PERCEPTION

In general, the term *risk* is connected to the *probability* of an event, and its *impact* when it occurs. If the occurrence of the event can be estimated through a probability distribution, and the impact is known in terms of health and social hazards and financial damage, then stochastic reasoning allows for making rational decisions as part of risk management. In terms of rational executive decision-making, that would be the end of the story. In the political arena – based on sustaining and improving governing relations – that is the beginning of the story of risk society.

Beck (1992) has argued that risk and the perception of risk condition each other. A problem of risk is not an objective fact. Facts and the significance of facts through valuations by people imply that risk problems are social constructs (Hoppe & Peterse, 1993). Risk and the perception of risk are the same. Only from the viewpoint of a narrowly technical rationality, there is a difference. It enforces a division between experts and non-experts in the public debate. That debate is about the dominance of one particular definition of reality, that is, the view of the risk expert. Beck articulated that position as follows.

> The 'irrationality' of 'deviating' public risk 'perception' lies in the fact that, in the eyes of the technological elite, the majority of the public behaves like engineering students in their first semester ... They only need be stuffed full of technical details, and then they will share the experts' viewpoint and assessment of the technical manageability of risks, and thus of their lack of risk. Protests, fears, criticism, or resistance in the public sphere are a pure problem of information ... This perception is wrong. Even in their highly mathematical or technical garb, statements on risks contain statements of the type that is how we want to live – statements, that is, to which the natural and the engineering sciences *alone* can provide answers only by overstepping the bounds of their disciplines (Beck, 1992, p. 58).

I would add to this argumentation, that technical experts not only limit the debate to uncertainty about facts, by excluding the appreciation of the facts from the debate. They moreover reduce the knowledge domain to analytical, functional rationality. By emphasizing first-order productivity, linkages to higher-order consequences are neglected.

Beck said that the origin of the critique of science and technology is the 'irrationality' of the critics. It is the failure of techno-scientific rationality in the face of growing risks, and threats from civilization. This failure is systematically grounded in the institutional approach to science, which is based upon the analytical science methodology. Beck pointed out that these institutions shape an overspecialized division of labor, and a concentration on methodology and theory. The analytical sciences and the related communities of observers request a determined abstinence from practice because of the prerequisites of the scientific method (see Chapters 6 and 7). Beck argued that science is entirely incapable of reacting adequately to civilization risks, since it is prominently involved in the origin and growth of those very risks. Science has become the legitimating patron of a global industrial pollution and contamination of air, water, foodstuffs, as well as the related generalized sickness and deaths of plants, animals and people (Beck, 1992: 59).

So, institutions of science and technology find themselves in a dual position. On the one hand they represent a major force in generating first-order knowledge to increase productivity and the related second-order risks and threats. On the other hand, they are the lenses through which those hazards and dreads are made visible. As risk and the perception of risk condition each other, it is worthwhile to take note about the perception of risk.

Slovic et al. (1981) conducted a large study with ninety hazards and eighteen risk characteristics. The factor analysis brought forward three dimensions of perceived risks. The first factor was labeled *dread risk*. It was associated with:

- Lack of control over the activity;
- Fatal consequences if there were a mishap of some sort;
- High catastrophic potential;
- Reactions to dread;
- Inequitable distribution of risks and benefit (including the transfer of risks to future generations);
- The belief that the risks are increasing, and not easily reducible.

Nuclear power, nerve gas, and crime were high on this factor. Providing current knowledge, I would add this list: global climate change, and terrorism.

The second factor was labeled *unknown risk*, referring to events and processes that are:

- Unknown;
- Unobservable;
- New;
- Delayed in their manifestation.

High on this factor were, DNA research, space exploration, genetically engineered foods, and nuclear power. Also here I would add: global climate change.

The third factor covered *societal and personal exposure to risk*. It referred to the number of people exposed and the rater's personal exposure. Hazards that loaded heavily on this factor were motor vehicle accidents, alcohol beverages, smoking, herbicides and pesticides. If climate change occurs, many people on earth will become exposed to the consequences. Climate change loads heavily on all three factors. It is a health and socio-economic hazard, and no one can hide from it.

The first factor was the best predictor of perceived risk. Solutions to those risks cannot be reduced adequately by technological fixes, based on instrumental knowledge. Of the many hazards those that strike most fear are those which show a lack of control over the activity, have potentially fatal consequences, are of high catastrophic potential, have inequitable distribution of risks and benefits (including the transfer of risks to future generations), have the belief that risks are increasing and not easily reducible, and include an invisible risk, and a threat of loss of sovereignty over assessing the dread. These hazards require the sensory capacities of science in order to make them visible and tractable, long before they may occur. In this respect research on global climate change acts as an early warning system for policy-makers.

ROLES OF SCIENCE IN HANDLING RISKS

Problem framing in the public domain

Handling risks is a form of *social problem solving*, which takes into account people's perception of risks. If that were initially to be ignored, in democratic societies, it will eventually become a political problem. Social problem solving is the outcome of a collective decision making process among stakeholders (actors), advancing future opportunities, while avoiding risks. In this regard the term *problem framing* is more suitable. It is a process in which, interactively, the actors name the elements and attributes to which they will pay attention, and in addition, frame the contexts in which they will address them (Schön, 1983).

In problem framing two heterogeneous elements are linked together: normative elements (norms, values, beliefs, principles, ideals, goals) and situations or conditions: empirical elements (Hoppe and Peterse, 1993; Douglas and Wildavsky 1983). Values, norms, beliefs, and ideas are valuations to objects, products, processes, systems, and relations, attributed by people. Therefore, problems refer to gaps between what is, and what should be. They are social constructs. Problems and situations are shaped by a variety of ideas and frameworks. Moreover, scientists from different disciplines represent different knowledge claims.

In pluralist societies it is common practice to distinguish between consensus and dissension about values (and norms). In addition, the perception of existing and the anticipation of future situations are based on more or less certainty about available knowledge to deal with them. Both viewpoints result in the following framework.

Table 10.4. A typology of policy problems (adapted from Hoppe & Peterse, 1993)

Knowledge Values	Certainty about knowledge	Uncertainty about knowledge
Consensus (competitive goals)	*Manageable knowledge problems*	*(In-)tractable knowledge problems*
Dissension (conflicting goals)	*Tricky ethical problems*	*Tricky governance problems*

On the basis of this scheme, the following can be pointed out.
- Manageable knowledge problems can be solved, because mutual agreement on values and norms, and available knowledge are sufficient conditions to come to a conclusion, and reach a decision.
- With regard to (in-)tractable knowledge problems, there is agreement on ethical standards, but uncertainty with respect to knowledge that should be or become available to reach a decision. If knowledge becomes available through further research, then the problem becomes tractable. Most R&D problems are in principle viewed as more or less tractable knowledge problems.

- Dealing with tricky ethical problems implies that, although knowledge is available, there is no consensus about norms and values. Tricky ethical problems underlie strategic questions about the products, and services. They are related to social and political dilemmas.
- Tricky governance problems relate to issues about which not only available knowledge is uncertain, more importantly, those who will take responsibility, also have to deal with dissension about values and norms. Those problems can only be dealt with ('solved') via people interacting with each other, with the purpose to frame and reframe the issues at stake to find common ground for action.

Dread risk, according to Slovic's definition present nations with tricky governance problems. In terms of Wynne (1992), they are indeterminate, and the actors involved will have to deal with *conflicting certainties*.

As argued above, the scope of the analytical science approach to risk is too limited to adequately deal with dread risk, and tricky ethical, and governance problems. The major and ultimate goal of research on risk is to change current conditions (threats, hazards) to become less threatening. That – by definition – is a design science goal, more particularly the purpose of design-in-the-large. The roles of the design scientists addressing issues of risk are twofold:

- Framing proper conditions for all actors involved to engage in fruitful policy dialogues to 'experiment with viable options' to enhance joint capacities. These are options that refer to design-in-the-small;
- Helping to frame right conditions for social problem solving on the basis of the lessons learned from experimenting with viable options, ensuring transparency of the process, controllability of policy development, and accountability of the policies made. These efforts belong to the design-in-the-large.

Design scientist will only be effective in these two capacities, if they have good knowledge about the subject matter, have great experience in managing social problem solving processes, and are sensitive about the intricate relationships between policy makers and scientists at the policy/science interface.

POLICY OPTIONS PROJECT REVISITED

The Policy Options project as summarized in Figure 10.1, has been an example of participative risk assessment and policy formation about Global Climate Change in the Netherlands. All stakeholders (actors) that mattered have been involved during either one, or more of the subsequent steps of the project. The project scheme was similar to the ideas presented by the USA Presidential/Congressional Commission on Risk Assessment and Risk Management (1997) and depicted in Figure 10.3.

The five policies: *no-regrets, least regrets, acceleration, technological innovation and institutional cultural change* were supported by action and communication plans to be taken on board by the Dutch Ministry of Environmental Affairs, and the other participating ministries. The results were also presented to a special parliamentary committee that prepared a policy document and position paper for the Dutch government.

Through using a gaming approach in the project, we have been able to:

- Take into account equity and justice issues about climate change policies;

- Tap and utilize explicit, local, and tacit knowledge, and mental equipment of the stakeholders, during intensive conversations;
- Represent and communicate indeterminacy, uncertainties and risks among the actors concerned;
- Integrate risk perceptions with approaches to risk from the analytical sciences;
- Enhance stakeholder participation in order to cope with conflicting certainties in the political and institutional domains, and to share risks and uncertainties.

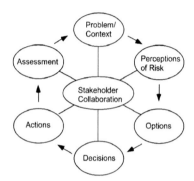

Figure 10.3. Participative risk assessment and management (adapted from USA Presidential Commission Report, 1997)

The gaming approach was fruitful in demonstrating that it can adequately address climate change policy development, dealing with a complex global issue about which major uncertainties exist. Through its transparency, it was supportive in building and maintaining trust among the stakeholders − major institutional actors − who represented distinct positions and interests. All stakeholders had common access to available data and information, and all their views were included in the material to be given serious consideration in due gaming process. During the project we raised awareness about the following issues.

Scientific assessments should focus on uncertainties, including the assumptions underlying models, theories and experiments. Sub-domains of the problem, for which little knowledge is available, should not be ignored. Uncertainties and values need to be made explicit and transparent. Multiple assessments and the use of counter-expertise will enhance the quality of the science policy dialogue. Science should not limit its scope of only paying attention to what seems feasible. This will obscure the political debate addressing dread risks, unknown risks, and societal and personal exposure to risks.

Policy makers should realize that the framing of the issue of GCC and the options to solve it are inseparable. GCC policy is molded by personal and institutional loyalties and interests as well as by cultural preferences. Problem reformulation leads to different options, leading to reframing the issue. Consequently, the GCC debate will never be completed. It is interlinked with risks and opportunities in many sectors of the economy. It is dynamic in nature. Each political commitment triggers action by stakeholders, which rapidly renders the original problem formulation obsolete. The quality and fruitfulness of this dynamic learning process can be improved by enhancing the level of stakeholder participation and by fostering explicit problem framing activities. GCC is unique in scope and scale, and history provides little guidance. Society can only beat that road by walking it. Science can help to build the roadmap, and to provide an educated guess about viable directions. Gaming methodology – applied in the policy options project, and discussed in Part II of this book – is vital to meet that challenge.

LESSONS LEARNED

Lessons on substance

- A shift has occurred in the perception of decision-makers about climate change from a deterministic, cause-effect view on climate change to more thinking in terms of uncertainties, risks and opportunities. A broadly shared view of the participants in the project was that a shift in the policy approach could enhance the effectiveness from a mechanistic top-down governmental approach to a risk- and opportunity-based bottom-up approach. Risk management calls for another mode of communication between the scientific and the policymaking communities than a one-way communication approach, in which science presents facts and policy decides on measures.
- The bureaucratic approach reduces the process of public administration to routine work. The related procedures of "set goals and objectives and go for them", and "organize rationally, efficiently and clearly" have shown to have severe limitations, when it is needed to adapt national environmental policy making to changing economic and political circumstances.
- The policy options: *no-regrets, least regrets, acceleration, technological innovation and institutional cultural change*, are rather rough indications of approaches to the problem. The five options that have been generated cannot simply be combined into one overall option through consensus building. This would not do justice to the complexity of the problem with respect to causes, uncertainties, international relationships, and the values and norms that are at stake. Instead of aiming at unity of points of view and common goals, it was more rewarding to acknowledge the divergence of the views and interests of all players, and to work towards convergence of actions.
- In this project, it was believed that a solid basis has been laid for a continuation of the fruitful communication between the researchers and the policy actors from all sectors of society. During the project it became clear that there is a vast body of knowledge available outside the scientific community that should be tapped. Different but valid perceptions exist about the various aspects (risks) of climate change and climate change policy outside the scientific community. Through the project these have been mobilized and can now serve as an important source of inspiration both for the policy actors and researchers.

Lessons on process

- The people involved used the interviews to express their opinion. In addition, they took the opportunity to blow off steam about politics and the way the issue was handled by the various governmental departments and about the scientific community, which should produce "consistent signals instead of generating ambiguity and controversy".
- In order to build a sufficiently strong basis of trust in the work of the project team, the variety of perceptions and positions on climate change should be honored in the variety of policy options that were taken into account. Only in this way a viable win-win strategy could be explored.
- Researchers, researcher directors, and decision makers were able to work together to develop a comprehensive set of research goals that are responsive to the needs of decision makers.
- Priority setting is a very complex process. With groups as diverse as that assembled, it is difficult for the decision-making and research communities to agree on priority setting. Decision makers often cannot wait for the impacts of curiosity-driven science. Identifying decision makers' needs and researchers' opportunities to react is enhanced by encouraging both to meet face-to-face and interact more frequently.
- It was difficult for different scientific disciplines to agree on priorities. There was a tendency to see only one's own particular research as important and relevant. The process helped the participants understand the perspectives of other disciplines.
- Discussions in the science workshops revealed that economists, engineers, sociologists, psychologists, philosophers and natural scientists showed rather large discrepancies in their view of the issue based on the paradigms used in their approach. Consequently identification of issues via policy makers did not lead to a straightforward scientific assessment of climate change. An integrated assessment based on trans-disciplinary communication should aim at finding the right frame of reference to address climate policy development. Therefore, the scientific assumptions underlying the disciplinary positions should be made explicit in advance.
- Communication among *researchers from various disciplines* is critical, but poorly understood or practiced. Discussions at times produced only a limited mutual understanding of the underlying assumptions that support the scientific assertions and expectations. Whether this provides a necessary and scientific basis for policy action has still to be tested.
- On the other hand communication between researchers and policy makers is critical for global climate change but poorly understood and badly practiced. Discussions produced some mutual understanding of ideas and concerns.
- Many climate change issues require more integrated types of interdisciplinary research and more international means of conducting it than is generally practiced. During the project the different positions of decision makers, who are issue driven, and researchers, who are curiosity-driven, became even more obvious. Future dialogue could prove interesting, as representatives of both communities will have to challenge each other's underlying assumptions for action.

- The project in enhancing the dialogue at the policy/science interface was able to realize continuous improvements in the information exchange (including recommendations) readily useful and available to public officials and private citizens whose decisions affect, or are affected by global climate change. The approach chosen supported a mutual learning process in coping with the complexities and uncertainties of global climate change.

Lessons on project management

- Projects like the one discussed here, should be carried out in direct contact with the decision-making bodies in order to enhance communication and dissemination of results. Participants of dialogue workshops should be able to receive direct feedback of (intermediate) results in order to assimilate the insights gained. That was considered a necessary condition for setting up and maintaining a viable network of involved decision-makers. Also here the gaming approach turned out to be productive.
- The project team, in the role of change agent, constituted proper conditions for fruitful interactions among actors/participants. It managed and nourished among others:
  - A shared need for change;
  - An educational strategy as a means to increase variety and build trust;
  - Emphasis upon experiences and action (learning and doing);
  - A need for collaborative relationships;
  - A social philosophy: personal involvement through circulatory, recursive interactions, leading to co-ownership of process and to stable results;
  - A set of shared purposes;
  - A new cohesive and coherent set of relationships.

GENERAL CONCLUSION

Global Climate Change policy development illustrates key characteristics of a complex adaptive system (see Chapter 4). National, regional, as well as global GCC policy developments can only progress through co-evolution of the major institutional actors involved. In the Dutch Policy Options project, we have demonstrated how such processes evolve over time. In that project – through the concatenated dialogue workshops – we also have demonstrated the fruitful interplay between design-in-the-small and design-in-the-large. At this sensitive science/ policy interface we have dealt with the four kinds of rhetorics, discussed in Chapter 6. This was not an easy task, as some members of the project team – being specialists in one of the many areas of climate change – tended to emphasize rhetorics 1 and 3, while decision makers and practitioners were more keen on rhetorics 2 and 4. The general image about risks and uncertainties, expressed through Tables 10.1 and 10.2, conveys that a meta-disciplinary perspective is needed to cover this wide-ranging issue of climate change adequately. In Part II, I have argued why that perspective is worthwhile.

CHAPTER 11

GENERAL MANAGEMENT GAME: FUNO

In this chapter I will discuss the design and use of the integrated management game FUNO. It is called 'integrated', because it interconnects the various functional management areas such as, production, marketing, finance, purchasing, personnel, etc. Before discussing the design specifications, I will sketch a historic perspective on business organization. The various forms of industrial organization express different management views on running a company, different images of man included. That perspective is needed to understand the broader scope of FUNO in the tradition of industrial management. The participants engage in a process of strategy development, while coping with *organized complexity* that is to a large extent a product of their own making: their social construction of the FUNO company.

AT ISSUE

Since the first Industrial Revolution, we have been witnessing the emergence and proliferation of different organizational configurations such as the *machine bureaucracy*, the *professional bureaucracy*, the *divisional form*, the *simple structure*, the *adhocracy*, the *open systems* form, the *matrix*, and the *project organization*. In addition, we have become familiar with management attitudes expressed in the ideas of the *mechanistic, organic*, and the *learning organization* (Taylor, 1911; Weber, 1947; Burns & Stalker, 1961; Kast & Rosenzweig, 1973; Mintzberg, 1979, Senge, 1990). New forms of organization show an increased fluidity in the external appearances. They are known as *chains, clusters, networks, strategic alliances,* and *virtual organizations* (Clegg & Hardy, 1996; Handy, 1995). Some of these forms are not mutually exclusive. Effective organization depends on developing and maintaining a cohesive and coherent set of relations between company culture, structure, personnel, technology, strategy, and age and size of the company in connection with the conditions of the industry and market in which it is operating (Woodward, 1965; Miller & Friesen, 1984). Within this context *organizational development* (OD) can have several meanings. It could imply large-scale multiple system intervention to further improve organizational effectiveness and efficiency within the boundaries of the existing configuration. It could mean as well, transforming the organization from one form into another. For example, management made the decision to transform the company from a machine bureaucracy into a network organization. To support such a transition, various management techniques such as, Organizational Development (OD), Total Quality Management (TQM), Business Process Re-engineering (BPR), Quality of Working Life, Outsourcing, etc. could be used. Such a transformation will require the re-shaping the existing internal organization, and framing of a new set of relations, of which cultural change is most difficult to manage.

OD is a conceptual approach, a process, and a product. It covers:
- A need for change;
- A set of shared purposes;
- A need for collaborative relationships;
- An educational strategy as a means to increase variety and build trust;
- Emphasis upon experiences and action (learning and doing);
- Use of change agents to help the client system;
- A social philosophy: personal involvement through circulatory, recursive interactions that lead to co-ownership of process and to stable results;
- A new cohesive and coherent set of relationships (adapted among others from Bennis, 1966).

OD is a total organization and primarily a behavioral science approach. Its frame of reference is well established for existing organizations such as firms and institutions, which are in a process of change. Its connotation is the social, and behavioral dimension of management, aimed at changing attitudes, capacities, and skills that is, the cultural and personnel dimensions of organization. Action research – a research method in organization development and education – aims to solve practical problems while expanding scientific knowledge. By blurring the demarcation lines between design and analytical science methods, it is in two minds about its position in science. On the one hand action researchers are participants, and the other hand observers. That dual position brings forward methodological problems of the type discussed in Chapter 7. Action research presents itself as an applied science. If it would position itself explicitly as a design science, then it could operate on two levels: developing meta-artifacts, and applying them while developing action programs with clients (design-in-the-large). Process methodology will enhance understanding why things work, or do not work. Baskerville and Myers (2004) pointed out that unlike research methods of the analytical sciences – observing organizational phenomena but not changing them – action researchers induce organizational change and simultaneously study the process. It is an iterative process that builds upon learning by both researchers and practitioners within the context of the social system involved. Actions research is a clinical method putting the researcher in a helping role with the client, the practitioners. It is a two-stage process: the diagnostic, and the therapeutic stage. Action researchers bring knowledge of action research and general schemas (meta-artifacts), while clients bring situated, practical knowledge. Baskerville and Myers (2004) argued that the four key action research premises are: Peirce's tenet that human concepts are defined by their consequences, James' tenet that truth is embodied in practical outcome, Dewey's logic of controlled inquiry (rational thought linked with action), and Mead's tenet that human action is contextualized socially, and human conceptualization is a social reflection (see *schemas*, Chapter 3).

Structural change such as Total Quality Management, Business Process Re-engineering (BPR), Outsourcing, etc. are techniques related to management science. Although from theoretical perspective OD, TQM, and BPR all aim to improve the effectiveness and efficiency of the standing organization, each of them focuses on a limited set of relations, dependent on their points of views. OD emphasizes the human and cultural dimensions. TQM and BPR pay mainly attention to structure, technology and market. The game FUNO represents a synthesis of these ideas about organization development (OD) and structural change such as, BPR, TQM etc.

Needs for change

If companies are to succeed in the global economy, then every part will need to adapt to shifting circumstances and conditions. Increasing competition is the most important driver for change. Porter (1996) has pointed out that companies must be flexible, in order to be able to respond rapidly to competitive market changes. They should benchmark continuously to achieve best practice, and outsource activities to gain efficiencies without losing innovative potential. In addition, they should nurture a few core competencies in the race to stay ahead of rivals.

Companies dealing with circumstances of fundamental and rapid change, need to be highly adaptable that is, capable to change. This requires both the ability of reflective monitoring of core processes, and the flexibility of continuously tuning the internal organization to external conditions. In pursuing the goal of being the leader of their class, companies have adopted a variety of improvement programs, such as total quality management (TQM), DFM (Design for Manufacturability), lean manufacturing, BPR, bench marking, time-based competition, outsourcing, partnering, and change management. All these management tools aim at improving operational efficiency. Porter (op cit.) stated, that although the resulting operational improvements often have been dramatic, many companies have been frustrated by their inability to sustain short term profitability, as competitors by pursuing similar tactics, catch up sooner or later with the front runner. Apparently a narrowly minded operations approach produces if any, only short term benefits. Do they also lead to viable competitive positions in the long run? Contrary to Porter's use of the term *effectiveness*, he actually was speaking of *efficiency*. Thus, operational efficiency is being improved by performing similar activities better than rivals perform them. Strategic positioning however means performing activities that are different from those of the rivals, or performing similar activities in more effective ways. Thus, measures to improve effectiveness and efficiency refer to different activities. Operational efficiency focuses on better utilizing its existing resources, on continuous business-as-usual improvement. Strategic positioning aims at finding new market positions with more or less virtuosity. Brandenburger & Nalebuff (1995) have summarized wittily the related management attitude and motivation by stating, that successful business strategy is about actively shaping the game you play, not just playing the game you find. Flexibility as coined by Porter is mainly focused on operational flexibility. Strategic positioning under turbulent (chaotic) circumstances requires first and foremost an open-minded workforce with a positive attitude to change, which thrives on trust, honesty and compassion. Where operational efficiency aims at structure and technology, strategic positioning pays attention to culture and vision, and thus on assets such as strategic human resources and knowledge management. This type of flexibility is first of all the product of a negotiated order. The organizational structure of such flexible companies contains units, glued together by logic of trust.

As mentioned above, the emerging new forms of organization show an increased fluidity. Consequently, the internal organization has to mirror that fluidity through breaking down formal compartmentalization into empowered, flat, and flexible organizations. Compared with the functionalist management paradigm, the individual in such an organization is not considered a stable constellation of essential characteristics, or traits, but a socially constituted subject. By maintaining, modifying and transforming inter-organizational relationships, companies can construct their own environments, their own markets, while seeking allies to which they can bond for periods of mutual benefit (Clegg & Hardy, 1996; Daft & Weick, 1984; Fairtlough, 1994). Hamel and Prahalad (1994) argued that these new organizational forms and the related image of man would offer new opportunities for radical innovation, to re-invent the future. The new company will look a lot different from the traditional bureaucracy. Clegg (1990) sketches it as follows. The new company is:

- Decentralized;
- Distributed, with team based leadership and relational network competence;
- Laterally structured to coordinate and control actions across people, knowledge, time and space.

Drivers of and barriers to change

While being involved in processes of change, companies have to adequately deal with and balance the following drivers and barriers of change (Table 11.1) (Van Gundy, 1992; Maslow, 1971).

Individual barriers may be more difficult to level out than the other barriers, as they are much less tangible, and moreover belong to the domain of the individual persons involved. On a time scale of change, the cultural, social/political, and often the individual drivers and barriers of change take many years (5-10 years) to adapt to new circumstances. Structural, technological, procedural, and resources drivers and barriers are more easily to adapt, and they may become balanced in a few years time (1-3 years).

How can large, complex organizations solve the problems of normal functioning that is, efficient operations, reduction of complexity, control, and governance, and still embody the tensions which power innovation? Complex organizations have difficulty with innovation. They have to perform a delicate balancing act between opposing forces and coalitions.

For effective product innovation the following sets of dialogic activities need to be taken into account (Dougherty, 1996, p. 19):

1. Conceptualizing the product to enable the integration of market needs and technological potential (market-technology linking): *balancing the tension between outside and inside;*
2. Organizing the process to accommodate creative problem solving: *balancing the tension between old and new;*
3. Monitoring the process (value chain): *balancing the tension between determination and emergence;* and
4. Developing commitment to the effort of innovation: *balancing the tension between freedom and responsibility.*

These tensions impact on the forces of change in many confusing ways, because actors involved may favor a mixture of these opposing forces. A production manager, for good reasons may be inclined to choose for improving the technological potential (inside), taking on board, advances in technology (new), keeping in control of the existing production process (determination), and staying committed to the available production capacities (responsibility). The marketing manager for good reasons may be in favor of addressing the market needs (outside), opportunities (new), new markets (emergence), and flexibility to act swiftly (freedom).

Table 11.1. Forces of change

Forces of change	Drivers	Barriers
Cultural	Diversity; pluralism; openness; tolerance; shaping the future; freedom of choice; individuality vs. groups;	Conformity; secrecy; groups vs. individuality; sticking to the past;
Social/political	Pluralism; freedom of flocking; flexible reward systems; corporate governance through transparent accountability; distributed, team-based leadership; actively shaping the game you play;	Power relationships; rigid reward systems; corporate governance through old boys networks; playing the game you find;
Individual	Self-confidence; creativity; entrepreneurship; high synergy; courage; trust; spontaneity; expressiveness; relational network competence;	Fear; defense mechanisms; inhibitions; sticking to the past; low synergy (struggling to cope with the polarity between primary and secondary processes);
Structural	Fluidity in the external appearances (chains, clusters, networks, strategic alliances, virtual organizations); laterally structured organizations to coordinate and control actions across people, knowledge, time and space;	Stratification; formalization; centralization; functional specialization;
Technological	Research & Development	Disparate languages of crafts
Procedural	Participative, and interactive planning; performance driven management;	Rigid planning; over-control; cost-driven management;
Available resources	Sufficient competent people; money; equipment; information; time;	Lack of competent people; money; equipment; information, time;

In management practice, during the ongoing negotiations about suitable strategies, coalitions emerge, or are built by actors on opposite sides of the tension scales. Agreeing or disagreeing on explicit and local knowledge may turn out to be easier than on the less tangible tacit understanding and enculturated knowledge, because the actors involved may not be fully aware of the way they convey that silent language. As a consequence, their body language may express a message different from their spoken and written messages.

MANAGING ORGANIZED COMPLEXITY

Problem solving in FUNO means that all participants are shaping a system of interactions to generate an outcome that is beneficial to all parties involved. This system of interactions constitutes forms of organized complexity, in which company policies, economics, technology, and social choice are entangled. The related strategic goal setting can be characterized as follows (Kalff, 1989). Personal and social characteristics, loyalties, and interests mold the strategic problems. Therefore, they are dynamic and lack a definite expression. Each strategic commitment triggers actions, which make the original problem formulation rapidly obsolete. The process of formulation and reformulation of strategy is ongoing. The formulation of what is at stake, and the options to solve it are inseparable. Reformulation leads to different options, leading to reformulation of the issue. Strategic goal setting has no closure. Restructuring the company's socio-economic system sows the seeds for the next round of restructuring. It is interconnected with managing risks and opportunities in areas such as, finance, material resources, human capital, information, government policies, etc. Strategic problems are unique; history provides the actors with little guidance.

In Chapter 1, I have referred to business and behavioral simulations. To compare FUNO with these forms of play, I will present a framework of integrated management, Figure 11.1.

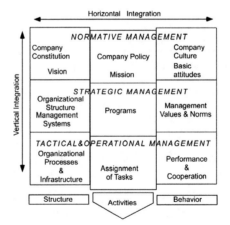

Figure 11.1. Representation of integrated management (adapted from Bleicher, 1991)

Bleicher (1991) developed this framework for integrated management, distinguishing two types of integration: horizontal integration of structure, activities, and behavior, and vertical integration of normative, strategic, and tactical & operational management. Each management level takes responsibility for distinct aspects of the company's structure, activities, and behavior. Eventually, normative management takes care of both forms of integration.

In the management gaming literature, most emphasis is on the tactical & operational, and the strategic levels. In general, the related games are rule-driven. They are used to train the basic skills of managing a company within a well-defined frame. They are similar to the use of flight simulators. I will describe a few well-known games to illustrate my point.

Tactical & operational games

The BEER GAME (1966): an example. The Beer Game is an operational game, during which decisions are made repetitively. It has been developed in the 1960s at the Sloan School of Management of MIT. It represents a production/distribution system, and maps a value chain for producing and shipping commercial goods into a market. Beer is produced and distributed via the marketing director of a brewery to wholesalers, who ship it to retailers, who sell it to their customers. It is a cascade of ordering and shipping of goods. Each player is manager of one of the companies in the chain. The participants team up in groups of four players.

During each time period, the players follow a strict sequence of steps. This allows the game operator to synchronize the activities of the teams. Each individual manager is trying to maximize profits, particularly by reducing the costs. During the game session, players are not allowed to talk, or otherwise communicate with each other. They make individual decisions on the basis of available information.

After the game, each individual player calculates the total costs and analyzes the process that took place in his production/distribution system. The time series data of orders, inventory, and order backlog are put into a diagram. Each production/distribution system calculates the overall costs and connects the diagrams of each company in the chain to learn to understand the dynamics of the total value chain. By comparing, lessons are drawn from each individual manager in the chain and from each of the parallel teams. Finally, comparing the time series of the game with the simulation runs of the SD simulation model deepens lessons learned.

The BEER GAME is a rule-driven board game. The players make tactical and operational management decisions within a tightly bounded cascade structure. Through the game the trainees learn to understand that,

- The game structure influences their individual behavior;
- Individual behavior influences the overall pattern of the chain, causing production/distribution cycles;
- Parallel teams generate similar behavior of boom and bust cycles;
- Players can only change those patterns by changing the structure that is by, changing the rules.
- The players fail to eliminate instabilities that occur within each team, because they did not fully understand how they create the instability in the first place. During the debriefing they will have the opportunity to learn about the instabilities and make suggestions to improve individual and system's behavior. Their suggestions usually are focused on restructuring the flow of information.

The BEER GAME – a tactical & operational management game – is an example of a behavior simulation. Within the existing structure of the organization, focus is on organizational processes, and performance and cooperation are important behavior indicators. Board games are suitable media of representation to show the working of operational management processes, which map the management of social system's resources.

Strategic management games

General management simulations – business simulations – such as, INTOP (1963), INTOPIA (2000), TOPSIM (1994), etc. are computer supported strategic and tactical management games. Behavior equations of the firm, representing micro-economic theories, are included in a black box: the computer. Six to ten management teams operate in the same market(s), manufacturing and selling the same products. They compete against each other under conditions of uncertainty about the market dynamics, which are defined by the micro-economic model. When the players enter the magic circle, they accept those conditions. This makes it difficult for them to understand the rational of the model, and its underlying assumptions. They learn to understand the supply and demand characteristics of those markets while playing. During the game, they are not allowed to challenge the underlying assumptions of the model. After making and implementing their decisions into the computer, the teams receive extensive feedback. The computer produces every cycle many data, requiring a fair amount of data processing to help the players to develop a pattern of the market behavior, and to gather an idea about the relative positions of the companies in it. Decision-making is more complex than in the Beer Game. These general management games are competitive, with distributed access to available information.

The teams are competitive, and usually very eager to get the best results in terms of revenues, market share, and profits. Initially, the functional management roles: production, finance, marketing, etc. although differentiated, may not stress their distinctive features. The team may start working together to figure out the options available. Often, the financial manager takes the lead, to perform the business accounting and do the calculations. The other functional managers respond with filling in the questions put forward by the 'controller'. Gradually, the finance, the production and marketing managers start building a coalition within the team, with the other managers for materials handling, personnel and R&D potentially becoming satellites. It will influence the system of interactions: the internal dynamics of the teams.

Those companies, which manage to build a strong team, usually perform better than the ones that have problems in carrying out a common course for their company. The team leader – CEO – has an important role in coordinating the management team, especially in conflict resolution and ongoing internal negotiations on strategy. As the decisions of each period are presented in numerical form, the participants are very much focused on quantitative data. To be effective, they need to be able to understand their underlying meaning. One of the challenges is to translate consistently the general strategy of the company, formulated at the conceptual level, into yearly numerical decisions for each of the interrelated functional management areas. Emphasis is on business economic data. When they fail to understand this, it will hamper the quality of their decisions, and consequently will influence the performance of their company.

The experience of decision-making under conditions of risk and uncertainty is difficult to handle for players who are not familiar with microeconomics. It makes them feel uneasy. For example, while choosing the selling price of the products and estimating the related production volume, it is not uncommon that the teams initially expect that all goods produced will be sold, independent of the current state of that market. Sometimes it is also difficult for them to understand the meaning of inventory costs, causing teams to buy too many resources for safety purposes. Generally, tuning production to the needs of the market is difficult to grasp for newcomers. Coping with these challenges from the 'driver's seat' to run their companies, is a primary goal of business simulations. They enable for example students in business administration to relate explicit, abstract knowledge about microeconomics, with a tacit understanding of how that knowledge works in (gaming) practice. Business simulations allow little freedom to handle the company structure, and the management system. Making strategic decisions implies utilizing adequate company values and norms to develop a suitable brand image to the market. Main activities include adequate financial and production programs to balance costs/effectiveness. Often, players try to open the black box, to fool the model, and beat the system instead of focusing on their relative position among the teams. Their incentive is less on learning about the mutual impact of various companies, operating in the same market. During the debriefings, these motives should be discussed in terms of lessons learned.

FUNO is a normative and strategic management game, and it should in principle be open to various forms of organization to address forces of change, presented above. FUNO should address issues that industrial companies are facing in contemporary Europe. It questions the company's constitution, requires a re-assessment of the company policy, and it challenges the FUNO management to consider a culture re-shape. FUNO is a tailor-made game for a client with a long and strong track record in management training in the Netherlands. Before discussing its use, I will present details about the game architecture, using the framework Table 5.9 (Chapter 5).

DESIGN SPECIFICATIONS OF FUNO

Who is the client?

The client is a major management-training institute in the Netherlands. Accountable for the design was the then deputy director of the institute. The *problem owner* was the then head of Research & Development, in charge of setting up the new training program "The New Manager".

What is the purpose, and what is the context of use?

The purpose was to design an integrated (general) management game that should be positioned at the beginning of the new management-training program. It should at the start of that program enable the participants to assess their strengths and weaknesses as a manager, and to help them to detect blind spots in self-perception about their way of functioning in a company. Therefore, FUNO is not aimed at training certain skills. It should address potential capacities and learning needs to improve management competency. Those needs are addressed during the following phases of the training program. As the institute had ample experience with business simulations, a precondition for FUNO was that it should not be a computer-supported game. It was made clear by the client – right from the beginning – that such games would give the participants the wrong impression about managing a company. It would give them the wrong idea that, if they were successful in mechanistically managing a company through such a business simulation, they might wrongly view themselves as competent managers in an increasingly volatile economy. The institute expressed that conveying such a message through a standard business simulation, would contradict common experience that management (including leadership) is an ongoing process of structuring the company. The program consists of seven modules, spread over a period of one year. FUNO is part of module two: "strategic management and cooperation". It should enhance the framing of a Personal Development Process profile (PDP), including the core competencies needed as defined by each individual participant. FUNO should run for 2-3 days, for 20-25 participants.

What is the subject matter?

FUNO should address the following issues, which are embedded in goals of the overall training program: integrated management & business administration, strategic and change management, entrepreneurship, leadership, vision, guts, adaptability, strategic understanding, supporting drivers of change, depicted in Table 11.1, and helping the participants in achieving their goals.

Intended audience

FUNO aims at senior managers, board members, and entrepreneurs, motivated to improve their capacities to handle ongoing change and innovation processes. They have 10-20 years of managerial experience, and are between 33 and 48 years of age. FUNO should improve their competency as company leaders. As classes of The New Manager include 20-25 participants, FUNO should provide each of the participants a meaningful role to play.

The profile for participants, and therefore of FUNO is sketched as follows:
- You have experience in various management functions;
- You lead change processes in your organization;
- You are up to a more challenging function;
- You invest in your career, and improving competency is important for you;
- You aim at improving your impact in the organization;
- You want to change the course of events and are aware that the key to success is your behavior, your integrity;
- You are a people manager during change processes;
- You are interested in broadening your scope, beyond the kinds of knowledge taught at traditional business schools. More explicit knowledge does not imply more capacity to know how and when to act.

Subject matter

The management game represents a multi-national company "Furnitura Nova" (FUNO), designing, manufacturing, and selling high quality furniture for homes and offices. The organization chart of FUNO is depicted in Figure 11.2.

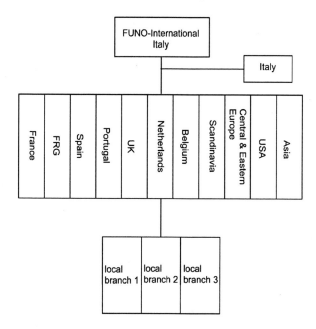

Figure 11.2. Organization chart of FUNO

Its headquarters are located in Northern Italy. It manages companies in various nations and regions of the world. It is a family-owned firm that is: an Italian family is major shareholder. Two brothers are on the Board of Directors in the capacity of Chief Executive Officer (CEO) and Chief Marketing Officer (CMO). Together with other managers, they run the company, overseeing the regional and national companies. For various reasons FUNO needs to set up a new roadmap for the future.   The Dutch national branch with three local branches is assigned the prestigious task of developing a viable strategy in close cooperation with the Italian headquarters, and the three Dutch local branches. That strategic plan will, once accepted, become the benchmark for the other national companies.

Design procedures

Because of the complexity of the subject matter, as designer I played the roles of "composer and conductor", orchestrating the input of project members from the client who had expertise in the various functional management areas such as, finance, marketing, staffing, purchasing, etc.   Once FUNO was ready for use, I trained the trainers (facilitators) for two years. I will elaborate the reasons for such extensive coaching below.

ARCHITECTURE OF FUNO

I will discuss FUNO's architecture, using Table 5.9 as the framework.

CHAPTER 11

ACTORS

Actors – Syntax

Number of players & game places of actors: 25 players (individual actors) divided over 5 teams (aggregated actors), each with special tasks.

Actors – Semantics

Roles. Board of Directors – Italy: CEO FUNO; Marketing Director; Director Design also in charge of Central & Eastern Europe; Director Procurement also in charge of Asia; Director Logistics & Production; Director Finance also in charge of USA.

Headquarters in the Netherlands: General Director; Marketing manager; Logistics (Purchase/Distribution/Transport); Financial manager; Manager Information & Organization; Manager Personnel & Organization.

Branch 1: Commercial manager-showroom; Manager stock keeping; Manager Assembly.

Branch 2: Commercial manager-showroom; Manager stock keeping; Manager Assembly.

Branch 3: Commercial manager-showroom; Manager stock keeping; Manager Assembly.

Workers Council: Chair Personnel & Organization Committee; Chair Strategy & Organization Committee; Secretary Strategy & Policy Committee.

Labor Union representative.

In addition, the facilitators, or a specially invited group of experts, will act as an "Advisory Board" to assess the strategic plan, and subsequently to advice the CEO about its feasibility.

Actors – Pragmatics

Kinds of steering. Autopoietic steering (from the inside). FUNO is a self-organizing learning environment. The actors co-produce the internal organization of FUNO, particularly its culture, communication & coordination structure, and its system of interaction. They shape their specific form of organized complexity.

Kinds of knowing. Learning about the company through interacting with each other, and building a temporary learning community (organizational learning).

RULES

Rules – Syntax

Preparatory rules. The participants receive general information about FUNO several weeks in advance. They are invited to read that material. When the game starts, they are briefed about the game, and receive a general manual with information about Furnitura Nova, its internal organization and the roles. They are informed that FUNO will take place in one large meeting room, and that they are supposed to leave only for a lunch break, and dinner. Coffee etc. will be available within the room. For allocating the teams and roles two options are available. The participants are free to arrange themselves as they see fit. More preferably, during the first week of the course The New Manager, the teaching staff, while learning about the interests and needs of the participants, develops preliminary profiles, and allocates them to the FUNO-roles. They receive their role descriptions, and while reading the material, they start assuming their roles. Subsequently, the first team meeting is arranged to discuss a common view, and to share idea on how to act. That finishes the first meeting during the evening when FUNO starts. The second day FUNO gets shape.

The *start and stop rules* define the beginning and the end of the session on the second day. The facilitator is in charge of upholding the *rules of nature*: start & stop rules, rules for Time-Outs, etc. Only one important rule applies: The Managing Director of the Netherlands will present the strategic plan at the end of the day at a certain moment in time. For the rest of the day, the participants are free to engage in framing the strategy. Once in a while events happen they are free to address or to ignore. For all those reasons, FUNO is a *free-form game* with no rules for engagement. The actors are free to move and interact as they see fit.

Initial game positions. At the beginning of the second day, in the room, all furniture, chairs and tables, are arranged along the walls. The room is in the middle an open space with no initial structure. The actors are free to model the room according to their preferences about FUNO's internal organization.

Steps of play. FUNO unfolds in four phases during which the actors produce intermediate results (Figure 11.3).

The meaning of debriefings I, and II have been described in Chapter 3.

The final game position emerges from the game dynamics and is defined by the relative positions of the teams at the end of the game. These positions are included in the strategic plan.

Rules – Semantics

Relationship between roles. Except for the CEO in Italy, and the General Director in the Netherlands, all other actors are functional managers such as, Finance, Marketing etc. The aggregated actors (team actors) are responsible for the whole company, or for parts: the national and local branches. The actors are free to enact their roles according to their views, knowledge, and beliefs. The actors shape the communication rules − rules for engagement − themselves. Accordingly they construct their particular system of interactions and procedures, within the overall spacing of time as depicted in Figure 11.3. They are free to interpret data and information provided, in ways that suit their purposes. They are also free to interpret their roles and experiment with behavior.

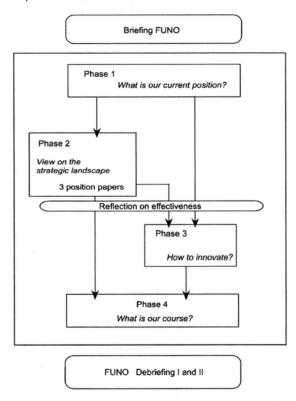

Figure 11.3. Time space of FUNO

The *evaluation of resource allocation and the relative positions* of the actors are not defined up front. They emerge during the game as a result of the ongoing negotiations and decisions. Criteria for evaluating the information are not provided. Judgments about the conditions under which the company is operating are open to debate. They are part of the knowledge, experience, and attitudes of the participants, gained during their career. Their individual and shared *schemas* (see Chapter 3) define how they will judge the evolving situation.

Rules − Pragmatics

Team of facilitators. One or two experienced members of staff facilitate FUNO. In addition, three observers make notes for the debriefing: one observer for the Italian management team, one for the Dutch management team, and one for three local branches. They use observation schemes developed for FUNO.

Assessment functions. As the game format is free-form, the facilitator and an "Advisory Board", which at the end of the day assesses the strategic plan, proposed by the Dutch team, and more particularly by the General Director of the Dutch national branch, represent the assessment function. They comment on the strategic plan and judge it on the basis of its feasibility and company vision. The facilitator continuously monitors the game dynamics, and only intervenes when needed, to help the actors handling conflicts.

RESOURCES

Resources – Syntax

Game space & game positions. The resources of the company define the game space. Resources are material and equipment to manufacture furniture, transport, and sell it, financial resources, personnel, infrastructure (buildings), information, etc. Each actor – dependent on the position in the company – receives information and data that are relevant for managing their task domains. FUNO is not a board game.

Resources – Semantics

The data and information provided, depict the internal organization of the company, its recent history, its recent performance, its position in the various markets, changes in life style of its customers, profiles of competitors, etc. Those data and information are partitioned and distributed among the actors to fit their positions within the company vis-à-vis the market.

Resources – Pragmatics

To run FUNO, a large room with sufficient space for 25 participants, and five game facilitators, are needed together with tables, chairs, flip charts, overhead projectors, PCs and a beamer. As the game runs for three days and two nights, hotel accommodation is needed as well.

THE FUNO PROFILE

FUNO is a so-called free-form game. The participants are provided with a complex management situation, including various bottlenecks. They are asked: "Providing the situation, how do you interpret it, and what will you do?" They are free to name the concepts and their interrelationships to which they will pay attention, both as individual managers and as teams. The participants also frame the management context in which they paid regard to them. Shubik (1983) has pointed out, that this kind of game is not completely known to all players. Playing the game serves as a means, both for shaping rules, and generating a better understanding of those rules.

The participants, during FUNO, have the opportunity to operate from different perspectives. They are invited, even challenged, to become an actor and a referee, and to be pro-active, producing their own goals and resources of motivation. They are freed from a dependence on the game operators, they reason for themselves and thus are made productive in their learning process. The participants are in charge of the flow of events. The game facilitators only provide feedback, when appropriate, which is only on rare occasions. They support the trainees to be reflexive, in evaluating their own progress.

Based on the general information, the participants have all freedom to give shape to FUNO, taking on board their explicit, tacit, local, and enculturated knowledge, gained during their career. Thus, FUNO provides a self-organizing learning environment (Klabbers, 1996).

According to the learning goals of FUNO, each participant is challenged to develop and shape his/her own learning goals. On a meta-level, the main goal of FUNO-company is to interactively construct meaning out of a variety of data and information, which are related to managing the company. They have to develop a core vision, values and purpose, to be able to set out a viable strategy for the future. FUNO triggers mainly conceptual problem solving.

FUNO catches the flavor of the more fuzzy and less structured sort of work of the upper level of management, involved in long term strategic, normative decisions and entrepreneurship based on ideas and beliefs. For that reason it is difficult to play. FUNO is challenging. Compared to the bureaucratic type of work to be done during business simulations (see above), this type of game places more emphasis on conceptual skills, on participating in the teams and on the individual qualities of the participants. The participants are challenged to show their level of expertise and sophistication in handling strategic management issues.

Due to its free-form structure, FUNO gives the actors little grips on events and processes. For people, used to well-defined codes of conduct in regular companies, experiencing the openness of the game may initially bring much confusion, feelings of both anxiety and opportunity. FUNO offers a management world that only gets structure by engaging in the game, and subsequently shaping and understanding the rules. Engaging in FUNO follows the recipe (Carrol, 1865; Weick, 1979): "How can we know what we think until we hear what we say?" "How can we know what we want until we see what we do?" Both recipes imply a notion that participants only learn to understand the meaning of management concepts by playing the game. They will experience differences between their wishes and expectations, between what they say, and what they do. They will experience a gap between explicit knowledge – their *espoused theory* – and the way they handle management questions in practice: their *theory-in-use*. They also will learn to understand that in principle all management knowledge is a combination – a synthesis – of explicit, tacit, and local knowledge, bounded by the particular circumstances of the company, embedded in their enculturated knowledge (mental equipment).

Summarizing, FUNO as a free form game is a self-organizing system and an open-ended self-constructing (interactive) narrative.

EMERGING PATTERNS

The theoretical reflection on complex adaptive systems, presented in Chapter 4, brings forward a need for a coherent description of emergent behavior patterns of FUNO sessions. It may reveal among others how the actors

- deal both with autopoietic and dissipative features of social systems;
- connect both the outside (observer) and inside (participant) perspective;
- link cognition and action in a coherent handling situation;
- convey indeterminacy, uncertainties and risks, and disseminate ideas that support management to handle complexity;
- enhance participation in order to cope with conflicting certainties in the various managerial domains, and to handle indeterminacy.

Describing games is possible at different levels. The views on complex adaptive systems, discussed in Chapter 4, apply to FUNO. In addition, games are characterized according to their architecture (see above), describing FUNO in terms of actors, rules and resources. A third level description takes into account organizational and group dynamics via the evolving system of interactions. At a fourth level FUNO can be described as an interactive narrative that is, a story jointly shaped and shared by the players. All levels interconnect, and together they tell the "full story", both from an inside and outside perspective.

In the context of emerging patterns of organization, I will focus on the system of interactions, which represents the autopoietic forces within social systems.

Building blocks of communication patterns

The basic building block of the system of interactions is the "double interact" (Weick 1979:89). An action by actor A evokes a specific response in actor B. This is an example of an inter-act. B's response evokes a response in actor A. Acts can be accepted, with or without modification, they can be rejected, abandoned or revised. This whole sequence, depicted in Figure 11.4, is called a *double inter-act*. The double inter-act illustrates a communication loop. As a matter of convenience, a straight line in the following figures symbolizes it.

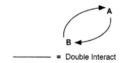

Figure 11.4. Illustration of a double interact

Human relations are based upon evolving double interacts. In social systems numerous actors shape a system of interactions, a collective network that is more or less stable over time. Some actors interact directly with each other. Some interact indirectly via others. The resulting collective structure is an emergent property of such an organization. Communicative acts entail content, context and relationships (meta-communication) (Watzlawick et al., 1967). It is out of the scope of this chapter to discuss in detail characteristics of the interactions, such as the potentially devastating effects of double binds on the functioning of teams.

In FUNO, the teams constitute aggregate actors: wholes with limited autonomy. Their system of interactions is illustrated in Figure 11.5 for five individual actors. Such aggregate actors are reflexive and self-reproduce their internal organization that is, they self-organize their teams.

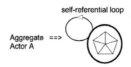

Figure 11.5. Building block of interaction patterns in complex social systems

In the following example, I will describe FUNO, and sketch a typical game session via interaction patterns.

At the start of FUNO it is argued that "Furnitura Nova" is in need of change. The once successful strategy needs revision. Time has come to envision a new company-wide strategy. The current product-market mix is becoming less well tuned to the taste of its consumers, and advances in information technology require a new ICT infrastructure within the company. Moreover, the family owned multi-national needs a cultural reshape to ensure that the major actors are better tuned to each other, and to the market demands.

The initial condition of the game is illustrated in Figure 11.6. First the individual actors internal to aggregate actors A, B, C-1, C-2, and C-3 have to establish their collective structure, which means that each geometric figure actually starts from the vertices. The individual actors build their common web.

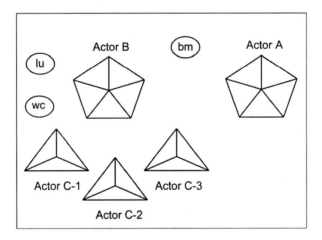

Figure 11.6. Initial condition of FUNO

Five management teams (actors) are responsible for steering FUNO in a viable direction. Actor A represents the board of directors in Italy. Actor B represents the Dutch management board, and actors C-1, C-2, and C-3 represent the three sales branches in the Netherlands. Actor A consists of a CEO and five functional managers. Actor B has a similar structure. In addition, three actors represent the following stakeholders, an advisory board of management (bm) for assessing the strategic plan, the labor union (lu), and the works council (wc).

In FUNO the actors A, B, C-1, C-2, C-3, bm, wc, and lu form the initial subassemblies of the internal organization. During the game, gradually behavior of the individual and aggregated actors becomes increasingly interlocked. Without going into detail, I will sketch a typical way in which the resulting collective structure evolves over time, see Figure 11.7 -a, -b, -c, and -d. Moving through the four phases, the collective structure evolves in a way that it is difficult to comprehend for each individual participant. They are all facing a situation of distributed access to information.

At the start of an FUNO session the participants are challenged to act freely. They have to obey only two main rules: to present their general strategy at a certain moment in time, and to carry out all game related activities in one room. They have all opportunities to shape FUNO according to their personal and collective views and wishes, to shape their company in a way that it fits their imagination and interests.

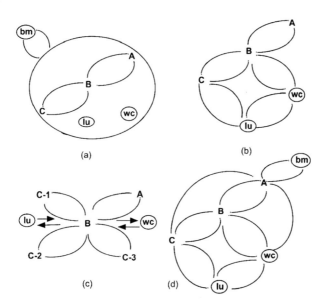

Figure 11.7. Emerging interaction patterns of FUNO

During a session gradually the collective network of FUNO is building up. It resembles usually the reconstruction of a traditional, hierarchical organization with a clear demarcation of power and the Italian CEO definitely in control. Underlying the double-interacts between actors A and B is surprisingly a feeling of mutual mistrust about each other's motives. The initial actions of the CEO and the Dutch Director fuel mutual distrust. This is surprising. All actors are members of the same company, and they are in principle involved in a cooperative game with distributed access to information (Table 2.6, Chapter 2). There is no rule that forbids them from sharing information. So, what in principle should be a cooperative game becomes rapidly a competitive game, probably fueled by the enculturated and tacit understanding of the participants, the mental equipment they bring into the game from their daily experiences. The managers shape rules of competition, and consequently draw boundaries that influence a particular system of interactions.

The emerging company (FUNO) is shaped through *co-evolution between the teams* (company) in combination with its *adaptation to the environment*. Evolution of one aggregated actor (one of the management teams) depends partially on the evolution of the others. In other words, the management teams change in the context – local environment – of the other teams. Co-evolution takes place via the interacting actors that change in terms of internal dynamics during the same time span. This happens within the magic circle of FUNO sessions.

Gradually, the double-interacts are being charged with a competitive attitude. Although the content of the interactions was related to talking business, the meta-communications conveyed that the FUNO managers rejected their mutual relationships. Combined over many sessions, we sense that the actors B and C (C-1, C-2, and C-3) – the Dutch branches of the multinational – tend to build subassemblies, that are most rewarding for them in the local market, while ignoring the overall advantages or disadvantages for the whole company. Actor A is generally considered a threatening outsider. It is interesting to observe that mistrust, for which initially there is no overt reason, is not tested during initial interactions by both actors A and B. It is tacitly accepted as real. As such the CEO and the Dutch Director – both key players in the drama, usually avoid testing their mutual mistrust. They set the stage for an agonistic kind of game. Consequently, mistrust occurs right from the beginning, gradually picking up momentum as the game evolves. The tension between these key actors results in a circular interaction pattern – positive feedback loop – that picks up its own momentum. This circular process with a high negative potential has occasionally caused actor B to start seriously considering the option of a management buy out: breaking loose from the mother company.

Actor B, and especially the Director of the Dutch national branch of FUNO – the key actor in the network – is the linking pin between the local Dutch branches, and the headquarters in Italy. The success of the efforts to construct a viable strategy depends to a large degree on the capacities and abilities of the Dutch Director to set up and maintain good working relations with Actors A and C, and to frame a viable roadmap at the beginning. If that actor fails initially to present a clear vision and approach, then s/he is in for trouble. From Figures 11.7-a, -b, -c, and -d, it can be gathered that the Director is the linking pin in the FUNO network.

The circulatory, recursive interaction patterns, emerging during the game, and depicted by Figure 11.7, represent on a conceptual level the complexities of adaptive social systems. As discussed in Chapter 4, in complex adaptive systems such as FUNO, the actors never possess a perfect model of their environment, which contains other actors that are continuously changing. They acquire information about it only through interacting with them, never having total information about the current state of FUNO. The actors co-evolve while playing. They deal with distributed access to information, and have limited information and knowledge about the various functional management areas. Therefore, they are not capable of holding a large group of potential models of their working environment, including models of the fellow actors. Through increasing synergy, FUNO can far exceed the capacity of single actors. Through decreasing synergy, FUNO may collapse, not being able to produce a feasible strategy.

FUNO IN PRACTICE

In the previous section I have described the evolving system of interactions of FUNO sessions. The schemes of Figure 11.7 show that the Dutch team and particularly its Director is the linking pin, and key to understanding the internal dynamics of the game. In this section, I will sketch characteristics of the content of that system of interactions during game sessions.

FUNO has been operational since 1990, and more than 3000 senior managers have participated in it. Although designed for the course The New Manager, it is also used as a *stand-alone game for in-company training*. In that context of use its purposes are among others:

- *Unfreeze* – legitimizing that companies should allow its members to experiment with innovations and to create a proper atmosphere for learning over prolonged periods of time. It relates to the term *flocking* in organizations, as coined by De Geus (1997). He said that organization should leave space for innovators, "so that they do not feel squelched and their innovations have time to develop" (p. 135).
- *Diagnosis* (test) for participants to clarify for themselves their learning needs. FUNO functions in this regards as a self-referential learning environment (a mirror). During the first debriefing multiple realities emerge. The players become aware of them and they start sharing their experiences. Multiple stories are shared about each particular session. This interactive narrative invites the players to open up, and become receptive for constructive feedback. It is a precondition for the second debriefing that addresses the key schemas in relation to gaps in individual competency. To be effective, a precondition for fruitful debriefings, and specifically debriefing II, is mutual trust. (For more details about the two debriefings, see Chapter 3).
- An *example* for clarifying the existence of *multiple realities* in companies.
- *Catalyst* in team building.

In the following, I will describe some remarkable impressions, gathered over many FUNO sessions.[2]

Gaming and new behavior

Participants who are very much involved in FUNO – as if it were their regular work environment – sometimes make decisions and take actions that come as a great surprise to them. This applies especially to the roles of the FUNO CEO and Director of the Dutch national branch. It happened that during a FUNO session the role of FUNO CEO was assigned to the management development officer of a large construction firm. The Director of the Dutch branch had approached her with the request to make up current deficits. As the Italian Board had other plans, she rejected the request. The Director, having extensive experience as a marketing manager, did not accept this. When discussing the decision of the CEO with his Dutch management team, he devised the trick to earn extra cash money via a "sale & lease back of real estates" construction. The Italian Board reminded the Director that such authority did rest with the headquarters and not with a national branch.

---

[2] I thank Paul Riegen and David Jan van Stolk for sharing their extensive experiences with FUNO since 1990.

Therefore, the Director had overstepped his authority. The tension between both managers rose to the point that, suddenly and within the time span of a few minutes, the Italian CEO fired the Director. The Italian Board appointed a successor, and the game went on. The former Director stayed in the room during the rest of FUNO as an observer.

During the debriefing the CEO mentioned that such a thing had never happened to her in her long career. She expressed being shocked and upset by what had occurred, especially that it had happened "so naturally". She was emotional about what had happened, very surprised by her authentic behavior. The Director involved – a strong manager – who got himself fired, remarked years later that the experience had been traumatic, haunting him for years.

Differences in management culture

An international audience once played FUNO. The then acting CEO – a Frenchman – called a meeting for all Dutch managers without consulting the Dutch Director. The Director was furious about it, because he considered it an undermining of his position and authority. The Director acted in line with the Dutch hierarchical communication tradition. The French FUNO CEO considered his behavior normal – in line with French standards. He explained that his initiative aimed at empowering the Dutch Director. What seems to be honesty and fair play in one culture is considered manipulation and power play in another one.

Mirror

A well-known manager became a member of the management team of one of the local branches. In addition, he assumed the role of member of the Worker's Council. He played that role with fervor, being very keen during the negotiations. During the debriefing he was asked how he could have played that role so well. He responded that he was very familiar with the role of members of the Worker's Council in his capacity of being an employer – the role of his opponents. He knew how Worker's Council members act, and disliked that kind of behavior. It triggered dark corners in his mind. He said that now he had played their role, understanding their position, he had become aware of what harm he did to them. He was frightened by the experience, and in shame. In the future, he would never act again as he had done in the past.

Risks for (dreads to) further cooperation

As FUNO is positioned at the beginning of a yearlong course, building good working relations during the game is important. FUNO is a challenging experience in this regard. Often it is difficult to locate the boundaries of the magic circle, to distinguish between play and reality. It has happened that clashes during the game were experienced as-if in real life. It seems that especially managers keen on power, and disrespect for colleagues are susceptible to such confusion. When it happened, even after clarifying things during the debriefings, occasionally good working relationships were not restored for the rest of the course.

Dutch culture is vulnerable with respect to dealing with situations that require both honesty and ambition, and that stress excellent performance of individuals in teams. FUNO stresses such behavior. Fellow managers discourage their colleagues wanting to excel during the game. The following saying expresses well Dutch common opinion: Just be your normal idiotic self. Participants showing a drive to excel during the game, risking one's neck, are easily finished off. When such events happen during the game, it is very important during the first debriefing to pay extensive attention to this issue. It is a precondition for learning to handle good working relations within performance-based organizations. For multi-nationals with a high degree on cultural diversity, FUNO sessions make such power issues explicit. With respect to personal development, this issue and the related tensions among fellow managers are difficult to handle during the second debriefing when they have not been addressed adequately during the first debriefing. People involved tend to become defensive, not open for constructive feedback.

Trust

As mentioned earlier, FUNO is a cooperative game with distributed access to information. All players assume roles as members of one company. They all are involved in "climbing the same mountain." That is the espoused design theory. The theory in use is that at least with the Dutch managers involved, FUNO becomes easily a competitive game with distributed access to information. Agôn qualities – competition among the teams – become the main drive to play the game. By striking the right note at the beginning of the game, the Italian CEO and the Dutch Director could start building trust. They could keep in mind the following principles for handling trust (Handy, 1995):
- Trust is not blind: only people one knows can be trusted;
- Trust needs boundaries: confidence in someone's competence is within a given context;
- Trust demands learning: a constantly changing network requires flexibility to adapt;
- Trust is tough: those who cannot be trusted must leave;
- Trust needs bonding: people have a need to be acknowledged;
- Trust needs touch: personal contacts are needed;
- Mutual trust requires members to temporarily take the lead.

It is common practice with FUNO that the session starts from a sense of mistrust between the Italian team, and the Dutch national team. The related attitudes are neither included in the roles, nor in the rules of the game. They are embedded in the mental equipment of the participating managers. As a matter of fact, both teams are Dutch managers. Feelings of mistrust become the basis of action. They are nurtured as a self-fulfilling prophecy. Managing misunderstanding becomes the 'daily routine.' Paraphrasing, and exaggerating Handy, I notice the following from FUNO sessions.
- Mistrust is myopic: even people one knows cannot be trusted;
- Mistrust exceeds boundaries: questions about someone's competence surpass a given context;

- Mistrust prohibits learning: in a constantly changing network it hampers flexibility to adapt, it avoids trust to be tested;
- Mistrust spoils relationships;
- Mistrust hampers bonding;
- Mistrust disregards touch: personal contacts are avoided;
- Mutual mistrust hampers members taking the lead. They wait and see.

FUNO sessions tend to internally alternate between these attitudes of trust and mistrust. When asked during the debriefing whether there were initially any reasons for suspicion, the answer was "no". When asked subsequently, whether the persons involved did check whether mistrust was realistic, the answer usually keeps floating in the air, as if this is the first time that the question has been raised. Maybe among Dutch managers a tacit understanding about mutual mistrust is part of their management culture.

Management competency

During the final stage of the game, the Director of the Dutch national branch presents the strategy that should improve the performance of FUNO. That plan is both assessed by the Italian Board, and an Advisory Committee to the Italian CEO. Moreover, it should demonstrate the competency of the Dutch management team. Although FUNO has not been designed for assessing explicit knowledge about finance, marketing, staffing, etc., the quality of the Director's report gives a good indication about the related capabilities of the managers. The strategy report and the preceding negotiation process provide the participants with a good understanding about their strengths and weaknesses, and the resulting learning needs to fill in the gaps in their competency.

The FUNO managers tend to start focusing on solutions without asking first: What is going on? What is causing these problems? They seem to tacitly assume that, everyone shares the same perception on the situation. They do not test these assumptions. If some managers have the guts to raise these questions, due to the hectic situation at the beginning, they are sidelined quickly and easily.

Task perception of the Italian Board

The Italian board (of Dutch managers) is constitutive in shaping an adequate consultation structure. Instead of being alert about staging fruitful conditions for framing a viable strategy, the Italian Board usually is inner-directed, lacking leadership in arranging good working conditions for the Dutch team. It does not seem to be aware of the organizational climate in which it is operating. It is startled when the Dutch national branch approaches the Board with some tricky questions. Only then does it become aware of its outer-directed tasks and responsibilities. While mentally not being well prepared for the task, the Italian Board is inclined to demonstrate authoritarian, highhanded, behavior, by burdening the Dutch national branch with questions that it should already have addressed and answered itself. Maybe that social setting is the trigger for mistrust, described above. The facilitators and observers often remark that if this is an indication of the Dutch business climate, then it is a bad omen.

It occurs that the Italian Board is not in the mood to appreciate the Dutch efforts. Instead of supporting its Director and Dutch management team, and promoting social cohesion, it tries to find 'creative' ways to undermine the position of the Dutch managing Director. Double-crossing and subtle forms of demoralizing the Dutch team happen conveying the message that the Director is no longer considered an asset to FUNO. An interim manager could do that job as well. The Italian Board always has the option of selling the Dutch branch. If against all these odds, at the end of the day, the Dutch Director succeeds, s/he is showered with compliments.

Often the task perception of the Italian Board is disappointing. It focuses on middle management questions that it actually should have delegated to the Dutch national branch, and even local branches. It then shows that it has no sense of top management questions and company governance. Tasks and opportunities of top management seem to be unknown territory.

Task perception of the Dutch National branch

The Dutch headquarters are always in a sandwich between the Italian Board and the local branches. That linking pin position is not enviable. Nevertheless, the Dutch team and the Director enjoy the challenge. Considering that key position, the most stressing question at the beginning is: Where and how to start? The chance of becoming overloaded with questions from above and below in the hierarchy is real. If that happens the Dutch national team runs the risk of being torn apart by centripetal forces. Instead of conveying its vulnerability, also the Dutch team tends to adopt an authoritarian communication mode. Instead of opting for the support of the local branches, it destroys the chances for support and cooperation. If that happens, then the local branches are inclined to seek direct contact with the Italian Board, bypassing the Dutch national board. It will diminish the added value of the Dutch headquarters. This brings forward the following dilemma for the Dutch headquarters. Will it initially keep the doors closed for the local branches, until it has framed a clear strategy and roadmap, or should it first start building relationships, letting the local branches know that 'content' comes later. Should it first try to solve the problem internally – similar to the approach of the Italian Board – or should it apply the maxim: Why don't we talk, and while doing so, become aware of what we think? It seems that all managers are inclined to look first for instrumental problem solving, and only afterwards start asking questions about strategic positions. That management mode does not provide fruitful conditions for adequate leadership to address uncertainties and insecurities among the staff.

Task perception of the Dutch local branches

The teaching staff of The New Manager (FUNO observers included) in general considers the roles of the local branches in FUNO less important than the roles of the Italian Board and the Dutch national management team. This attitude turns up during the allocation of roles at the briefing. The sequence is, first the Italian Board, then the Dutch national branch, and finally the local branches. The most outspoken managers opt for the CEO and Dutch director's roles, etc. The least outspoken participants finally become managers of the local branches. That general teaching staff attitude is not very motivating for the local branch managers. From general management viewpoint, that conception about the minor role of the local branches is wrong. They play the key role in implementing the strategic plan, as the local branches have to carry out the ideas. During the ongoing negotiations they test the feasibility of ideas. They feel the heat and chill of the market, and therefore are more sensitive for the consequences of a wrong strategy than the general managers.

During FUNO, the local branches often turn out have a great impact on the game dynamics, and the outcomes at the end of the day. Much depends on the initial conditions the teaching staff frames during the briefing, while distributing the role descriptions and manuals. When it tacitly conveys the message that the local branches belong together, then there is a great chance indeed that they will join forces. If role allocation and distribution of manuals happen separately for each individual branch, then the local branches may be inclined to go their own way. The separate branches may suffer from their minor influence, as it allows the Dutch headquarters – in its authoritarian mode – to play 'divide and conquer'. Also here it is curious that the cooperative game is twisted to become a competitive game. Only shrewd local managers can capitalize on their chances.

SUMMARIZING REMARKS

Many anecdotes have been told about FUNO game sessions. For many managers it has become a common and worthwhile experience, often told with amusement. For some the experience is painful, even traumatic beyond the boundaries of the magic circle of FUNO. The way these experiences and lessons learned are being handled to a large extent depends on the quality of the two debriefings. When the debriefings are facilitated on the basis of mutual trust – in a safe learning environment – then painful experiences are integrated constructively in the response repertoire of the managers, improving their capacities in handling complex innovation & change processes in organizations.

The general image about the business climate and managerial competency that emerges from 16 years of experience shows that FUNO touches upon sensitive issues addressed above that need continuing attention through education and training.

Providing the complexity of the game, and the intricacies of the evolving system of interactions, facilitating and debriefing FUNO is not a straightforward and simple task for reasons expressed in the previous section. It took two years to train the trainers to adequately handle FUNO.

Several times I have remarked that in principle FUNO is a cooperative game with distributed access. So far FUNO has turned out in practice to become a competitive game with distributed access. It may demonstrate Dutch business relations and the Dutch business climate – the mental equipment – that the managers bring in when they start playing. Competition seems to be a stronger drive than cooperation.

In terms of the classification of games by Caillois (2001) (see Chapter 2), FUNO turns out to be a regulated competition (agôn), a dramatic spectacle before an audience (mimicry), and a game of chance, due to events that happen (alea). The agôn element refers to rules that the players enforce on each other (ludus). The combination of agôn and alea demonstrates a free act of will, stemming from the satisfaction felt in overcoming arbitrarily conceived and voluntarily accepted obstacles. Referring to the mimicry element, and the internal rules through the improvising managers – a feature of paida – FUNO may simulate behavior in terms of make believe. Would this have been the case, then we might talk about a temporarily split personality, a split between the real person and the person playing the role of FUNO manager. Even following dramatic events sketched above, during the debriefings, the participants discussed their authentic behavior, and did not refer to make belief. So, although they played their roles, simulating the FUNO managers, they enacted their real personality. FUNO conveys their basic habits and reflexes.

In Chapter 4, I have addressed the term complex adaptive system, and distinguished "the system", and "this organization." I have referred to complementary antagonistic forces. They demonstrate the more fundamental of forces of organization and disorganization. Learning in FUNO is to disorganize and increase variety. To organize is to forget and reduce variety. FUNO sessions are often chaotic, and through this chaos new order emerges. This implies that through organizational learning, the parts, their interrelationships, the whole, and emergences will change. These forces are at work during the game, and it is intriguing to watch. Participants mutually shape their emergent organization, experience dialogic forces that are of their own making, and learn to handle organized complexity. The debriefings give the participants ample opportunity to mutually reflect on the evolving system of interactions (Figure 11.7) and its impact on the company as a global unit, as well as on their experiences and feelings. By acting and reflecting, they learn to handle this complex adaptive system. By displaying simultaneously various kinds of cooperative and competitive behavior, they steer FUNO in surprising directions, in ways, which are beyond the control of one single actor.

The emerging organization during a FUNO session results from the interaction patterns shaped by the participants themselves. They constitute that complex whole, and can blame no one else for it when things go wrong. By being aware of their co-ownership, the demarcation line between game and reality blurs. The boundary of the magic circle becomes semi-permeable. During the debriefing they learn through their shared experience to understand the meaning of the term organization, relations between the whole and the parts, unity-multiplicity and emergences. They also realize that organized complexity is a co-production.

While playing, the FUNO managers co-construct their view on the company. During the debriefings, they interactively shape the narrative, their combined FUNO history, by pulling together the multiple pieces of gamed reality.

More recently, we have used the FUNO approach to design a web-based game: Model United Nations Online (MUNO) (Matthys & Klabbers, 2004). It concerned a policy exercise using Web-based gaming. By adapting the FUNO frame to the Internet infrastructure, we used the Web as the medium of representation.

CHAPTER 12

EPILOGUE

INTRODUCTION

In the former chapters, I have discussed principles of gaming and simulation. Providing the high diversity of gaming approaches, a meta-disciplinary perspective is needed to bring coherence to the field. I have also argued why gaming interconnects the design with the analytical sciences. Part III addresses several large-scale case studies, in which gaming played a crucial role. Playing games involves drama, sometimes a comedy, more often with a streak of tragedy. I have sketched in Chapter 11 some of the drama unfolding in FUNO sessions. Playing and more importantly, facilitating numerous games over many years for a great variety of audiences, I have learned that they trigger authentic behavior that exceeds the bounded area of the magic circle. In game sessions, some players consistently show a tendency to cheat, to double-cross, and to agree on A and secretly do B. However, most players are honest, show courage, and occasionally show their vulnerability. I have noticed a whole spectrum of human behavior during game play. After immersing in a game, and demonstrating their mimical capabilities, players express their personality and basic character, most of the time being unaware of the way they embody their presence in the game, and the silent language they convey. While facilitating tailor-made games for dedicated audiences in well-defined contexts of use, players have often approached me, telling me that they could no longer distinguish between what was play and what real. So, gaming has helped to set the stage for players to enact real life situations. In addition, the debriefings have set fruitful conditions for reflecting on those multi-layered experiences, to help the players to become more aware of the intricacies of social systems, and their roles of players in shaping drama. The debriefings are con-ducive to co-constructing interactive-narratives.

In this epilogue, I will wrap up some key issues, underlying gamed drama in relation to moral behavior, and start with summarizing a theory of knowledge that addresses ethical questions about gaming.

PLAY & ONTOLOGY

In this section, I will address key questions about gaming in relation to ontology. The basic ideas of Levinas will help in offering a suitable frame-of-reference. Levinas (1984) has reflected on key qualities of people meeting each other face-to-face. He paid attention to related ontological and epistemological questions (*ontology*: study of essence of things, properties of existence; *epistemology*: theory of knowledge, justification for knowledge claims). The following text wraps up Levinas' main thoughts.

Authentic ontology coincides with the factuality of our temporal existence. Our knowledge of being in general presupposes an actual situation for the knowing mind. *Contingency* and *factuality* are not facts, which are offered to us as faculties that help us to comprehend. They are abilities that facilitate our knowledge and understanding. They are the *acts* by which we comprehend. They enhance the transitivity of comprehending facts and their meaning. Levinas said that, in order to comprehend a tool, it is not sufficient to see it. We must use it.

To comprehend our place in the world we should not define it, for that would put us in the position of observer, an outsider, who first wants to grasp and clarify, and subsequently by virtue of that knowledge wants to be in control. We should relate to reality affectively, for that makes us participants. To comprehend what it means to be, we must exist. In Western philosophical tradition, thinking is similar to observing, with the sciences in the role of communities of observers.

Levinas' views imply a break with this tradition. He stressed that thinking is acting, embarking for the dramatic events to happen, events that are part of our being in the world. By acting in a certain way we have done many things that we did not intend to do. Every act has unintended consequences for the good and for the bad. Our awareness of reality does not coincide with our living in the world. If, as a result of this split, clumsiness of an act turns out to be counterproductive and counterintuitive then we are in the midst of a tragedy. Most of the time we are. In other words, our awareness and control of reality – through that awareness – do not exhaust our relation with it. We are both fully present in it, and also part of it.

Heidegger (1927) has argued that comprehending an object means relating to it, seeing it as a special case of being. Objects are perceived (observed) against the wider horizon of our existence. Comprehension means relating to the particular through our knowledge of the universal. For example, relating to this spoon of sugar that is, glucose or fructose ($C_6H_{12}O_6$) as examples of monosaccharide, means relating to it as a subclass of polysaccharides, which is a subclass of carbohydrates, which is a subclass of organic matter. We take possession of a thing through the idea of that thing. We deny its individuality by considering it as an element of calculation and as a particular case of an idea. The way in which the perceptual world shows its universality, via relationships with all other elements of the image/representation, is through its *form* of this reality. This form of knowledge is outside the relationship with the acting subject. It hides the perceptual world. We submit the perceptual reality by capturing it in a category (see also Hacking, 1999, and 2002 on classification, Chapter 5). The concrete thing is caught in a system of relationships. By classifying it, we conquer it.

According to Levinas, this ontological view on objects does not apply to the fellow human beings ('the other'; 'autrui'). Our relation to the other person does not only require learning to know him or her, it moreover requires sympathy and affection, beyond cool observation as if that other person were an object. A person does not come close to us from the wider horizon of a universal concept or idea. That person – as a being – asserts him- or her-self, and acts accordingly, in the same way as I do. It is impossible to reach the other person without (verbally and non-verbally) communicating with him/her. Thinking and expressing oneself with regard to the other person are inseparable. This implies that it is not possible to transfer an idea as if it is poured into the mind of the other person (as a mental container). It must be borne from the knower him-/herself. Expressing oneself does not mean articulating what I share with the other right from the beginning of the meeting. Prior to any participation in a shared meaning, expressing oneself means: establishing a bond via a relationship that cannot be reduced to comprehension as an act of knowledge about an object. Levinas argued that our relation to other human being is beyond ontology. A relationship with another person cannot be reduced to an image of the other. It coincides with invoking the other, an act, which is not preceded by the act of comprehending such as with comprehending an object. Does this mean that such an act precedes thinking?

In the relationship between human beings, the object of such an encounter is both given and associated with us. What is named a being is at the same time spoken to. We communicate with the other being when we give him/her a name. Contrary to comprehending an object, tool, or chemical substance by enlightening it against the horizon of being, meeting another person does not imply that we become their owner. Considering things to be no more than things results from our way of relating to them. As entities they borrow their meaning from the whole to which they belong, from our way of classifying them. I comprehend the group, class, or category from the perspective of their being-in-general. They place themselves at my disposal in the form of my comprehension, and as a result of that act, become my mental property. An entity does not have a meaning in itself. It derives its meaning only from being a silhouette against its enlightened horizon. That horizon is shaped by a human act. The human face is granted a meaning in a way, which is different from making sense of an object. It signifies a relationship with this being, based on a moral awareness (consciousness). A human being only commits him/herself in a relationship, which according to Levinas does not contain power. Does Levinas mean that meeting another person for the first time precedes power relations, and that we are − or should be − of good nature in such a relationship?

In his introduction to Levinas, Peperzak (1984) expressed that Levinas' radical criticism of ontology concerns the most important and thoroughgoing event: the experience of the other human being. In ontology it had not been addressed before. The question concerns: what do I experience and see when another person stands in front of me? The universe is the playground of my thinking: the beings (objects, entities) are parts and linkages that help me to reconstruct the big picture. However, when someone stands up in front of me, it is a decisive moment, which reveals something completely new to me. I am not able to classify that person similarly to the way I classify objects that I use as my property, for work and pleasure. That person cannot be viewed as a phenomenon amongst all other phenomena against the background of an encompassing horizon. The other person is not an event in a larger whole. The other presents him- or herself. S/he watches me, and even before one word has been exchanged, her face speaks to me. Therefore, the other is not a phenomenon of which I should reveal its essence. S/he does not wear a veil, but reveals him- or herself directly. Her countenance, her eyes are absolutely open: naked. Then I know: her eyes (not her will, or tyrannical mood) dictate to invite her to enter my house and world as a foreigner who becomes my guest. Then I have a conscience: not I but s/he commands.

This raises a key question: When individuals meet for the first time, does it mean that they invoke one another, through an act of relating purely based on affection? If that is the case, then our limbic system may be the trigger for emotionally relating to one another, prior to any act of thinking and classifying.

Depending on these fundamental views on human relations, it makes quite a difference to play a game where everybody is present in the same room, meeting face-to-face, or where every participant communicates indirectly through cyber-space. In terms of meeting people, fundamentally distinct human qualities are at stake in these different contexts of use.

When people meet in a public space, often they are persons acting in a certain capacity, playing a certain role, and being an actor. They are not as naked as Levinas seems to imply. To which extent does such meeting (role-play) influence the direct and silent body language, or is it the other way around? Does body language stage the meaning of the meeting? Initial encounters during a game session may play a vital and maybe crucial role for the rest of the game. Maybe that 'chemistry' influences the underlying – hidden – motives, of which the players are not aware. Levinas pointed out that in situations of human beings, meeting each other, thinking is acting. Prior to any participation in sharing meaning with the other person, expressing oneself means first establishing a bond via a relationship that cannot be reduced to comprehension similarly to an act of knowing about an object. The other speaks to me too. That signifies a moral awareness in any game, in life. Those qualities of the human condition precede and condition the playing of games.

THE MAGIC CIRCLE AND WHERE TO DRAW THE LINE

Huizinga (1955, p. 58), referring to the competitive basis of cultural life (agôn) in archaic society, mentioned a custom, practiced by certain Indian tribes in British Columbia. It is known as the *potlatch*. The potlatch is a great feast, during which one group, with much pomp and ceremony, makes gifts on a large scale to the other group with the specific purpose of showing off its superiority. The only return expected lies in the obligation of the receiving group to reciprocate the feast within a certain period and if possible to surpass it. Everything can be an occasion for arranging a potlatch: a marriage, a death, etc. Potlatch percolates the communal life of the tribes: their rituals, law, and art. The main thing is the distribution of goods. By taking part in the feast, the other clan accepts tacitly the obligation to give a potlatch on a still grander scale. Should it fail to do so, it wastes its honor and rights. In the potlatch one group is trying to prove its superiority by offering lavish gifts, and moreover and more strikingly, by the complete destruction of one's possessions to show that one can do without them. Potlatch is a peculiar example of agôn – a form of contest and competition. It is connected to winning, to being superior, and hinges on glory, group-honor, prestige, and last but not least, on revenge (Huizinga, 1955, p. 59). Potlatch related customs have been traced in Greek, Roman, Old Germanic, Ancient Chinese, and pagan Arabian of pre-Islamic culture. Huizinga – referring to Maunier (1924) – told the following story from an Egyptian newspaper:

> Two gypsies had a quarrel. In order to settle it they solemnly called the whole tribe together and then proceeded each one to kill his own sheep, after which they burned all the bank notes they possessed. Finally the man, who saw that he was going to lose, immediately sold his six asses, so as to become victor after all by the proceeds. When he came home to fetch the asses his wife opposed the sale, whereupon he stabbed her.

This sad story illustrates that the term *playful gaming* should not always be connotated with joyful gaming. It raises questions about where to draw the line between inside and outside the magic circle, about cause-effect sequences of events and actions, and about start- and stop-rules, exceeding the territory of the circle. The wife, opposing her husband, was she in or out of the magic circle, and if out, was it her personal decision? Apparently, she was out of it, present as participating observer, and in addition, a close relative, objecting to the consequences of the rules. Was she just trying to convince her husband to violate the rules, or did she intend to play another game? Did she try to convince her husband to cheat the rules, pretending at least to protect them, or was she simply not a good sport? The story does not recall whether the matter was taken to court, and whether the Egyptian judge accepted the potlatch rules as an acceptable and reasonable motive for killing the wife? If that would be common law in Egypt, the story does not recall either, whether the whole potlatch ceremony was set up as a pretense of the gypsy to kill his wife, and get away with it.

This disastrous story is not about a spontaneous outburst of passion. It resulted from acting out a formalized custom. Huizinga (op cit.) argued that the underlying principle of the potlatch is the pure and simple agonistic 'instinct', a violent expression of the human need to fight. In the original Dutch version of the book Huizinga (1985), referred to other Potlatch examples: Cleopatra outdoing Mark Anthony by dissolving her pearl in vinegar, and Dutch student rituals of the ceremonial smashing of glassware. Potlatch is a serious, fateful, sometimes bloody and fatal, and sacred play, raising the individual or group to a higher power.

Competition, and the resulting merit, is at the root of sacred rites such as, potlatch. Huizinga stated that from childhood onwards to the highest achievements of civilization one of the strongest incentives to perfection, both individual and social, is the desire to be praised and honored for one's excellence. In praising another, each praises oneself. We want to be honored for our virtues (Huizinga, 1955, p. 63). Longing, yearning, and craving are deeply felt human motives for action.

In Chapter 1 I have referred to outdoor gaming and to David Berreby (2005) who described some interesting outdoor programs to underpin his ideas about the emerging science of "tribal" psychology. I have wrapped up the intriguing experiment by Muzafer Sherif, a social psychologist, and the emergence of "tribal" behavior of two groups of youngsters, first becoming "artificially at war" with one another, and later – after changing the resources of their combined habitat – becoming partners. Sherif ensured that the experiment remained playful, no harm done to the kids. Berreby told another story. In 1963, Lufty N Diab, psychology professor at the American University in Beirut tried to repeat Sherif's experiment. He chose a group of eight Christian and 10 Muslims. Given the historic tensions between communities in Lebanon, it was not surprising that fighting broke out between the two teams of campers, the Blue Ghosts and the Red Genies. After three Genies threatened a Ghost with knifes, Diab decided to break up the camp before it could reach the reconciliation stage, as previously staged in Sherif's experiment. Striking about this camp was that the fighting did not occur along religious lines. The Blue Ghosts consisted of five Muslims and four Christians, and so did the Red Genies. The three Genies with the knives were all Christians, but so was their Blue Ghost victim. Fourteen of the boys had come from fiercely religious schools. During the camp – taking part in that magic circle – they could easily have chosen to see themselves as Christians versus Muslims. When confronted with the option between their religious "us" and "them", they chose Ghost versus Genie instead. The magic circle had apparently drawn a new demarcation line between 'tribes'.

To further illustrate his point about tribal psychology, Berreby gave another example, this time not from a social psychological experiment. One of the people convicted of war crimes during the Rwanda genocide was a Hutu nun, Sister Gertruda, who had called in a militia to massacre Tutsi refugees. She did not turn over her fellow nuns who were Tutsis. Berreby used the following phrasing to support his thesis about tribal psychology. "Had she been more of a Christian, and less of a Hutu militant, she would have not called in the murderers. Had she been less of a Christian, she would have let the Tutsi nuns perish too. The important point is that all three choices – her own hideous compromise, or a more religious decision, or a more ethnically based one – were plausible" (Berreby, 2005, p. 10). To explain this kind of behavior, Berreby argued that we are not slaves of our identities, and neither slaves of our instincts. We should understand such human behavior as rooted in its context. Berreby phrased this moral behavior in the neutral language of psychological theory, stripped of its ethical value and moral choice.

Preliminary conclusion: It seems relatively easy to trigger aggression and destruction in temporary social settings such as the potlatch, and field games. How does it come to be so easy? Why do people cross the line of moral behavior so easily? What is at stake? Or should I rephrase that question by asking: Is morality of behavior ingrained in (confined by) the wider meaning of the rules of the game, however local they might look like from an outsider's position? Are we talking about moral behavior in a context that not only allows it, and more importantly, justifies it? Does it mean that civilization is just a thin layer of veneer, covering our animal aggressive instincts?

In "Our inner ape" (De Waal, 2005) argued that answering those questions is not so straightforward as it seems. He said that we have long attributed man's violent, aggressive, competitive nature to his animal ancestry. But what if we are just as given to cooperation, empathy, and morality by virtue of our genes? He described primate social behavior of two closest cousins from the ape family – the famously aggressive chimpanzee and the lesser-known egalitarian, erotic, matriarchal bonobo – linking them to the most provocative aspects of human nature – power, sex, violence, kindness, and morality. He positioned man in relation to our cousins: crueler than the chimpanzee, and more empathic than the bonobo, who is capable of saving a sick bird. He observed that in a clear hierarchy fewer conflicts occur, because everyone knows what to do, and what not to do. Culture transfer is built into our biological substructure (basis), similar as with chimpanzees, bonobos, and other primates. Our added advantage is language, which allows us to give explicit instructions. The resulting symbolic structure influences in its turn biological relationships. De Waal mentioned that this language capacity also covers many aspects of human communication, more specifically the hidden messages from body language. He said in an interview (NRC, January 28, 2006) that people cannot lie to a deaf student of his, and that they do not understand this. She told de Waal that she only watches their hand gestures and facial expressions. So, explicit (spoken) language may as well distract from other important signals. Non-verbal communication is important to understand power relationships, and we are very sensitive to them. De Waal pointed out that people unconsciously tend to tune the lower pitches of their voices (below 500 hertz) to each other. The one who adjusts that deeper pitch most in relation to the other has a lower status in the hierarchy. These are characteristics man has in common with those apes. Moral behavior of man is not a veneer. It is an old quality in evolutionary terms. De Waal referred to cognitive science experiments – scanning brain activities when subjects are solving tricky moral problems. It has turned out that those activities occur in parts of the brain that are old from an evolutionary perspective: the limbic system connected to emotions. De Waal concluded that social-emotional, we are similar to our hairy cousins. We take moral decisions very quickly, instinctively, and only afterwards we start rationalizing them through language. Young male chimpanzees are very keen on power relations, and when they notice that their male caretakers are sensitive to such relations too, they start provoking and ragging them. The caretakers always lose. Therefore, most caretakers are female. They are more patient. De Waal made a distinction between power and influence. He observed that female chimps might not be dominant, however they might exercise considerable influence. From his observations, he noticed that men are more capable of handling conflict than women. Women are more capable of preventing conflict from happening. According to de Waal, men are better at bringing about peace; women are better at sustaining it. From this perspective, the stories about the gypsies, and Sherif and Diab's field games – mentioned above – do not allow a simple and straightforward causal link between man's violent, aggressive, competitive nature with his animal ancestry. Something else should help complete the picture about moral behavior.

Above, I have said that we want to be honored for our virtues (Huizinga, 1955, p. 63). Longing, yearning, and craving are deeply felt human motives for action. Competition (agôn) is an important drive to achieve what we are longing for. Others may have what we long for, which makes us envious. Girard (1976) has referred to this human capacity, calling it *mimetic desire*. He illustrated his theory by two examples. When giving plenty of toys of strictly the same kind to a group of children, the kids start to dispute and fight each other for the same object, while ignoring plenty of other toys left. In another example, he described a common experience of the neglected wife, who once again becomes attractive to her husband when another man courts her. Girard stressed that mimetic desire has neither subject nor object. It is always the imitation of the desire of another person. That person becomes a *model* to be imitated or copied. The simultaneous convergence of desires of people defines the object of desire. It starts rivalries and models become obstacles in fulfilling desires. We desire what others desire because we imitate their desires. The potlatch story, as well as Sherif and Diab's descriptions exemplify mimetic desires. The nature of the desire is never for the object itself. It is what the other desires. Girard has analyzed masterpieces from writers such as, Shakespeare, Dostoyevsky, Camus, Hugo, Dante, Cervantes, Proust, Freud, etc. for revealing various mechanisms of human desire. In general, such desire is not a linear sequence of actions. Desire is triangular: subject – model – object, implying a third presence: an object, a subject, and a third person toward whom the envy is directed (Girard, 1965). He argued that envy might be reduced to mere irritation when our desires are accidentally thwarted. However, true envy is infinitely more profound and complex. It always contains an element of fascination with the 'insolent' rival. This mimetic desire is the immediate interference of the desire of the imitator with the imitated desire. In other words, the desire of the one imitates (copies) the desire of the other, and shows what is desirable when desiring. It is a dynamic pattern that makes rivalry out of imitation in a continuously reinforcing imitation. It is a circular logic of positive feedback. Mimetic desire is coded and mediated (unknowingly) by the model. An external observer may notice the incompatible, conflicting process of on the one hand the merging of imitation, and on the other hand the differentiation – distinction – in desire. The protagonists – the rivals – being soaked up in their mimetic dance, do not perceive the characteristics of their actions and motives by virtually stepping out of their magic circle, which leads to such circular memitism. The model or rival may be real as in Shakespeare's "Julius Caesar", symbolic, as in Camus' "The Stranger", or transcendental as in Cervantes' Don Quixote.

I consider this mimetic quality a typical human characteristic, requiring a cognitive complexity not yet observed among primates. Visual objects in their environment immediately trigger the desire of chimpanzees and bonobos: no mimicry. Combining de Waal and Girard's views, moral behavior is ingrained in our evolution is similar ways as in chimpanzees and bonobos. Therefore, that is not the distinctive quality when it comes to understanding the roots of the most provocative aspects of human nature – power, violence, kindness, and morality. Mimetic desire comes closer. The triangular dynamics it sets in motion very well can explain the potlatch story, the outdoor game experiences, and great stories told by famous writers. Moreover, the tri-angular dynamics of rivals shape a magic circle with emerging properties that have a definite meaning for the actors involved, which is different from the perspective of external observers. They may notice a destructive action pattern, a peculiar kind of violence, eloquently described by Shakespeare et al. It is a game, but usually not a nice game that unfolds when *mimetic desire* is at stake. I guess that as regards FUNO (Chapter 11) – in principle a cooperative game, developing consistently in a competitive zero-sum game – rivalries are linked to the mediated desire: control over the Dutch branch as a crown jewel of the company.

The *mimetic desire* elaborated by Girard, enlightens an interesting and often destructive combination of *agôn*, and *mimicry* (Callois, 2001, see Chapter two). In all cases in which *agôn* plays a role, the competing players rely upon their own resources, wanting to triumph and prove supremacy. That is their basic drive and ambition. In the potlatch example, the competition is regulated, institutionalized (*ludus*). Providing Girard's ample descriptions of mimetic desire in literature, the triangular rivalry is to a minor extent influenced by institutionalized rules. That desire drives the protagonists – blindly – into a contest – confined by the peculiar quality of *paida*: agitated players, engaged in a dark and destructive dance. *Agôn,* involving the struggle of the will against (external) obstacles, is the opposite of *alea*, which assumes a player, submitting to a supposed omen, or verdict of destiny. It presupposes a fatalistic attitude full of superstition, magic, and miracles. Lotteries are good examples. Characters driven by agôn qualities are distinct from characters floating by alea incentives. Gamblers, playing games of the alea type, may envy people who are successful in playing competitive games (agôn). They are more inclined to *alea* – games of chance – to have success in life than entering the magic circle of competition. Cultures may also be characterized by such opposing qualities in similar ways.

Caillois (2001) paid attention to the interdependence of games and culture, to the reciprocal relationship between a society and the games it likes to play. He illustrated this among others with the Argentine card game of TRUCO, related to poker and manilla. It is essential for each player to let the partner know the cards in hand, without the opponents learning about them. The single cards, and combinations are symbolized via various facial expressions, each corresponding to different individual cards and sets of cards. The signals are part of the rules of the game. They must be meaningful to be effective for the partner, and incomprehensible for the opponents. Skill is required to communicate with the partner, and to deceive the opponent. Such game qualities, so prevalent as a characteristic of this almost national pastime, "may excite, sustain, or reflect habits of mind that help give ordinary life, and possibly public affairs too, their basic character – the recourse to ingenious allusions, a sharpened sense of solidarity among colleagues, a tendency toward deception, half in jest and half serious, admitted and welcomed as such for purposes of revenge, and finally a fluency in which it is difficult to find the key word, so that a corresponding aptitude must be acquired" (Caillois, op cit., p. 84). In terms of cause and effect relations, it may be that TRUCO has impacted on the Argentine culture. It may also be the other way around. Argentine culture, favoring ingenious allusions, has embraced TRUCO, because it reinforces existing habits and values. It also may be the case that Argentine culture and TRUCO form a positive feedback loop, reinforcing one another. The question is whether this connection between TRUCO and Argentine culture, observed and hypothesized by Caillois in the 1950s, still exists in contemporary Argentine, or whether another game has become a national pastime? Moreover, it could as well be the case that TRUCO was a good escape from oppressing, upsetting government.

Based on these examples, we could state that groups, tribes, sects, and even nations co-construct magic circles, shaping social systems – (mini-) societies – with their particular rules of play. They play a mix of cooperative and competitive games with or without distributed access (Table 2.6). The rules of those games, and their tacit understanding become integrated in structural conditioning, and subsequently become drivers of social interaction (Table 4.2). If this view on social systems is correct, then the different hierarchical scales of the systems – from individuals to groups, to nations – embody different time scales for the magic circle. The time scale of a group playing a card game is small as compared to the time scale of sects, tribes, and nations. The boundary line – the interface – between the game space, and its environment is more or less semi-permeable, dependent on who are in charge of boundary control.

FINAL REMARKS

This brings me to a final remark. Above, I have referred to social and tribal psychology, to ethology, and mimetic desire, and great literature. In previous chapters, I have elaborated social systems theory, as a meta-disciplinary frame-of-reference for the study of gaming. The main reason for discussing advances in the social and biological sciences was to address moral behavior and ethics, very much ingrained in the practice of gaming. I have connected 'our inner ape' (De Waal, 2005), with mimetic desire (Girard, 1976), to shed more light on rivalry, aggression and the potential of mutual destruction among protagonists in competitive games (agôn), as illustrated in the Huizinga's potlatch story (Huizinga, 1955), and Berreby's (2005) references to experiences with field games. These considerations should be interpreted in terms of Levinas' basic view on people meeting face-to-face. With respect to the ethics of gaming, I will take on board the distinction between good and bad. These notions relate to what Amos Oz (2005) in his acceptance speech of the Goethe Prize, has called the tree of knowledge of good from evil. He referred to two universal characters: god and the devil, and remarked that the devil is an egotist, only helping others to serve his own ends. His main thesis was that since the book of Job we knew that God and Satan played on the same chessboard, man being their game-piece, and that the intellectual innovation, called social sciences has blurred that distinction. The knowledge of good and evil used to be clear and distinct categories. Although it is hard to define good, evil has its unmistakable odor. Every child knows what pain is. When we deliberately inflict pain on another, we know that we are doing evil. Subsequently, Oz made an important point. Oz stated that the social sciences have blurred the clear distinction between good and evil that humanity has made since the beginning, "since the Garden of Eden". Social sciences entering Western culture in the 19th century have brushed evil aside, denying its very existence. Oz said:

> For the new, self-confident, exquisitely rational, optimistic, thoroughly scientific practitioners of psychology, sociology, anthropology, and economics – evil was not an issue. Come to think of it, neither was Good. To this very day, social scientists simply do not talk about good and evil. To them, all human motives and actions derive from circumstances, which are often beyond personal control. ... We are controlled by our social background. For about 100 years now, they have been telling us that we are motivated exclusively by economic self-interests, that we are no more then marionettes of our subconscious. In other words, the modern social sciences were the first major attempt to kick good and evil off the human stage.

He continued listing those causes which are to blame: society, painful childhood, the political, colonialism, imperialism, Zionism, globalization, etc. Systems are evil. In the ancient sense of the word, as presented in Book of Job, and by Macbeth, Yago, or Faust, individual men and women cannot be 'bad'. Oz viewed these opinions ethical kitsch. "The ultimate evil in the world is not war itself, but aggression". We have a spectrum of choices whether to inflict pain or not to inflict it, to look it in the face or to turn a blind eye to it. That spectrum confronts each one of us several times a day.

Playing games triggers a whole spectrum of choices, and from an ethical viewpoint, the game designer and facilitator should always build into them the following ground rules, or meta-rules: The players should not be brought in a position that they harm each other. If the situation becomes harmful, the game should be stopped immediately. If for unforeseen reasons harm is done, the facilitator should make everybody aware of it, restore conditions for proper conduct, and during the debriefings pay extensive attention to causes, and impacts, in order to mutually achieve a constructive assessment. Lessons learned from such serious events should become common knowledge and tacit understanding among the participants to prevent that in the future something similar will happen again.

The added value of reflecting on game experiences is the lessons learned about our basic motives and drives in their contexts of use, and the choices actors make pending their foreseen and unforeseen consequences. Eventually the facilitator should make clear that the rules of the game do not prescribe that the players act, as if they were robots. The individual and the aggregate actors always take responsibility for making choices for the good or the bad. Gaming offers great opportunities to bring to the fore the linkages between explicit, local, tacit and encultured knowledge, and the related value judgments. They emerge through persons (actors) meeting one another face-to-face, and interacting with one another. In terms of Levinas, the resulting relationships among the players in the magic circle are above all, ethical.

BIBLIOGRAPHY

CHAPTER 1

Andlinger, G. R. (1958). Business games B play one. *Harvard Business Review, 26*(3), 115-125.

Arai, K. (2003). Contributions of JASAGA to simulation and gaming. *ISAGA/JASAG Symposium II on the 34th Annual Conference of International Simulation and Gaming Association (ISAGA).* Kazusa Akademia Park, Japan.

Aumann, R. J. (1959). Acceptable points in general cooperative n-person games. In A. W. Tucker & R. D. Luce (Eds.), *Contributions to the theory of games,* Volume IV (Annals of Mathematics Studies, 40) Princeton: Princeton University Press.

Barth, F. (2002). An anthropology of knowledge. *Current Anthropology, 43*(1), 1-18.

Bernard, J. (1954). The theory of games of strategy as a modern sociology of conflict. *American Journal of Sociology, 59,* 411-424.

Berreby, D. (2005-a). Us and them (and me and you): The emerging science of "tribal" psychology. *Update: The New York Academy of Sciences Magazine,* Nov/Dec, 10-13.

Berreby, D. (2005-b). *Us and them: Understanding your tribal mind.* New York: Little, Brown and Company.

Caillois, R. (2001) (first ed. 1958). *Man, play and games.* Chicago: University of Illinois Press.

Eigen, M., & Winkler, R. (1975). *Das Spiel. Naturgesetze steuern den Zufall.* München: Piper & Co.

Eberle, T. (2004). Effects of experiencing outdoor challenges – Canyoning. In W. C. Kriz, & T. Eberle (Eds.), *Bridging the Gap: Transforming knowledge into action through gaming and simulation.* Munich: SAGSAGA.

Gamson, W. (1961). A theory of coalition formation. *American Sociological Review, 26,* 373-382.

Gamson, W. (1968). *SIMSOC: Simulated society* (3rd ed.). New York: The Free Press.

Grunfeld, F. V., Vié, L., Williams, G., & Bell, R. C. (1994). *Your move: Board- and table games from all over the world.* Kosmos: Utrecht (in Dutch).

Huizinga, J. (1955). *Homo Ludens: A study of the play element in culture.* Boston: The Beacon Press.

Huizinga, J. (1985) (8th ed). *Homo Ludens: A study of the play element of culture.* Groningen: Wolters-Noordhoff (in Dutch).

Kato, F., & Arai, Y. (2003). *The past, present, and future of JASAG.* Contributions of JASAGA to simulation and gaming. *ISAGA/JASAG Symposium I on the 34th Annual Conference of International Simulation and Gaming Association (ISAGA).* Kazusa Akademia Park, Japan.

Klabbers, J. H. G. (1996). Problem framing through gaming: Learning to manage complexity, uncertainty and value adjustment. *Journal Simulation & Gaming, 27*(1), 74-92.

Klabbers, J. H. G. (2004). On cross-fertilization: A tale for two JASAG gaming communities. *Studies in Simulation & Gaming, 14*(1), 28-37.

BIBLIOGRAPHY

Luce, D., & Raiffa, H. (1957). *Games and decisions: Introduction and critical survey.* New York: John Wiley & Sons.
Makedon, A. (1984). Playful gaming. *Simulation & Games, 15*(1), 25-64.
Miles, R. H., & Randolp, W. A. (1985). *The organization game.* London: Scott, Foresman.
Maturana, H. R., & Varela, F. J. (1980). *Autopoiesis and cognition.* London: Reidel.
Nash, J. F. (1950-a). Equilibrium points in n-person games, *Proceedings of the National Academy of Sciences of the United States of America, 36,* 48-49.
Nash, J. F. (1950-b). The bargaining problem. *Econometrica, 18,* 155-162.
Nash, J. F. (1951). Non-cooperative games. *Annals of Mathematics, 54,* 286-295.
Nash, J. F. (1953). Two person cooperative games. *Econometrica, 21,* 128-140.
Popper, K. R. (1963). *Conjectures and refutations: The growth of scientific knowledge.* New York: Routledge and Kegan Paul.
Priest, S. (1986). *Outdoor leadership preparation in five nations.* Unpublished Doctoral Dissertation. University of Oregon, Eugene, OR, USA.
Schelling, T. C. (1960). *The strategy of conflict.* Cambridge, MA: Harvard University Press.
Shubik, M. (1983). Gaming: A state-of-the-art survey. In I. Ståhl (Ed.), *Operational gaming.* Oxford: Pergamon.
Stadsklev, R. (1974). *Handbook of simulation gaming in social education.* Institute of Higher Education Research and Services. The University of Alabama.
Thorelli, H. B. (2001). Ecology of international business simulation games. <u>Journal</u> *Simulation & Gaming, 32*(4), 492-507.
Von Neumann, J., & Morgenstern, O. (1944). *Theory of Games and Economic Behavior.* Princeton: Princeton University Press.
Walker, P. (1995). http://william-king.www.drexel.edu/top/class/histf.html.
Wittgenstein, L. (1968). *Philosophical investigations* (translated by G. E. M. Anscombe). (3rd ed.) New York: Macmillan.

CLUG (1966). Riverside, NJ: The Free Press.
INTERNATION SIMULATION (1966). Chicago, IL: Science Research Ass.
INTERNATIONAL OPERATIONS SIMULATION, (1963). INTOP: PLAYER'S MANUAL. Thorelli, H. B., Graves, R. L., & Howells, L. T. New York: The Free Press.
INTERNATIONAL OPERATIONS SIMULATION, (1995). INTOPIA/ MARK 2000: EXECUTIVE GUIDE. Thorelli, H. B., Graves, R. L., & Lopez, J.C. Englewood Cliffs, NJ: Prentice Hall.
METROPOLIS (1964). New York: Gamed Simulations, Inc.
METRO-APEX (1964). Los Angeles: COMEX
METRO (1965). Ann Arbor: Multilogue.
STARPOWER (1969). Del Mar, Cal: Simile II.

CHAPTER 2

Aarseth, E. J. 1997). *Cybertext: Perspectives on ergodic literature.* London: The John Hopkins University press.
Abt, C. C. (1968). Games for learning. In S. S. Boocock, & E. O. Schild (Eds.), *Simulation games in learning.* Beverly Hills: Sage.
Brown, R. G., & Nilsson, J. W. (1962). *Introduction to linear systems analysis.* London: Wiley.

Caillois, R. (2001) (first ed. 1958). *Man, play and games*. Chicago: University of Illinois Press.

Christpoher, E. M., & Smith L. E. (1987). *Leadership training through gaming*. London: Kogan Page.

Ellington, H., Addinall, E., & Percival, F. (1982). *A handbook of game design*. London: Kogan Page.

Empson, W. (1955). *Seven types of ambiguity*. New York: Meridian Books.

Giddens, A. (1993). *New rules of sociological method*. Cambridge: Polity Press.

Heylighen, F. (1990). A new transdisciplinary paradigm for the study of complex systems? In F. Heylighen, E. Rosseel, & F. Demeyere, F. (Eds.), *Self-steering and cognition in complex systems: Towards a new cybernetics*. London: Gordon and Breach.

Huizinga, J. (1955). *Homo Ludens: A study of the play element in culture*. Boston: The Beacon Press.

Huizinga, J. (1985) (8th ed). *Homo Ludens: A study of the play element of culture*. Groningen: Wolters-Noordhoff (in Dutch).

Klabbers, J. H. G. (1996). Problem framing through gaming: Learning to manage complexity, uncertainty and value adjustment. *Simulation & Gaming, 27*(1), 74-92.

Klabbers, J. H. G. (2003). Gaming & Simulation: Principles of a science of design. *Simulation & Gaming, 34*(4), 569-591.

Klabbers, J. H. G., (2006). A framework for artifact assessment & theory testing. *Simulation & Gaming, 37*(2), 155-173.

Klabbers, J. H. G., & van der Waals, B. (1989). From rigid-rule to free-form games: observations on the role of rules. In J. Klabbers, W. Scheper, C. Takkenberg, & D. Crookall (Eds.), *Simulation-gaming: On the improvement of competence in dealing with complexity, uncertainty and value conflicts*. Oxford: Pergamon.

Marshev V, & Popov, A, (1983). Element of a theory of gaming. In I. Ståhl (Ed.), *Operational gaming*. Oxford: Pergamon Press.

Maturana, H. R., & Varela, F. J. (1980). *Autopoiesis and cognition: The realization of the living*. Dordrecht: Reidel.

Moore, O., & Anderson, A. (1975). Some principles for the design of clarifying educational environments. In C. S. Greenblat, & R. D. Duke (Eds.) (1982). *Principles and practices of gaming-simulation*. Newbury Park: Sage.

Morgan, G. (1986). *Images of organization*. London: Sage.

Mouzelis, N. P. (1991). *Back to sociological theory: The construction of social orders*. London: St. Martin's Press.

NRC-Newspaper, 14.09.2002.

Ornstein, D. S. (1989). Ergodic theory, randomness, and "chaos". *Science, 243*, 182-187.

Rollings, A., & Adams, E. (2003). *On Game Design*. Boston, MA: New Riders.

Shubik, M. (1983). Gaming: A state-of-the-art survey. In I. Ståhl (Ed.), *Operational gaming*. Oxford: Pergamon

Sutton-Smith, B. (2001). *The ambiguity of play*. Boston, MA: Harvard University Press.

Weber, M. (1947). *The theory of social and economic organisation*. London: Oxford University Press.

Weick, K. E. (1979). *The social psychology of organizing*. London: Addison Wesley.

BIBLIOGRAPHY

BAFA-BAFA (1973). Simile II, Del Mar, California.
BEER GAME (1966). Cambridge, Mass: MIT Sloan School of Management.
CLUG (1966) Riverside: Free Press.
DENTIST (see chapter 8)
FUNO (see chapter 10)
HEXAGON (1976). Ann Arbor: Multilogue.
PERFORM (see chapter 9)
SIMSOC (Gamson, W. A. 1978). SIMSOC, Simulated Society. New York: Free
    Press.

CHAPTER 3

Anderson, J. R., Reder, L. M., & Simon, H. A. (1996). Situated learning and
    education. *Educational Researcher, 25*(1), 5-11.
Anderson, R. C., & Pearson, P. D. (1984). A schema-theoretic view of basic
    processes in reading comprehension. In P. D. Pearson (Ed.), *Handbook of
    reading research*, Vol. 1. New York: Longman.
Bandura, A. (1996). *Self-efficacy: The exercise of control*. New York, Freeman.
Barth, F. (2002). An anthropology of knowledge. *Current Anthropology, 43*(1), 1-18.
Bereiter, C. (1997). Situated cognition and how to overcome it. In D. Kirshner, & J.
    A. Whitson (Eds.), *Situated cognition: Social, semiotic and psychological
    perspectives*. Mahwah, NJ: Erlbaum.
Booth, W. C. (1987). The idea of a University as seen by a rhetorician. The 1987
    Ryerson Lecture. The University of Chicago.
Brown, J. S., Collins, A., & Duguid, P. (1989). Situated cognition and the culture
    of learning. *Educational Researcher, 18*(1), 32-42.
Chi-Yue Chiu's, (2002). Comments on Barth's paper. *Current Anthropology, 43*(1),
    11-12.
Cole, M. (1996). *Cultural psychology: A once and future discipline*. Cambridge, MA:
    Belknap Press of Harvard University Press.
Dennett, D. C. (2003). The self as a responding − and responsible − artifact. In J.
    DeDoux, J. Debiec, & H. Moss (Eds.), *The self: From soul to brain*. Annals of
    the New York Academy of Sciences, Vol. 1001. New York, NY.
Dewey, J. (1981). Experience and nature. In J. A. Boydston (Ed.), *John Dewey:
    The later works, 1925 -1953, 16*. Carbondale: Southern University Press.
Dewey, J. (1989). Appendix 1. In J. A. Boydston (Ed.), *John Dewey: The later
    works, 1925-1953, 16*. Carbondale: Southern University Press.
Diggins, J. P. (1994). *The promise of pragmatism*. Chicago: University of Chicago
    Press.
Duke, R. D. (1974). *Gaming: The future's language*. London: SAGE.
Fodor, J. A. (1998). *Concepts. Where cognitive science went wrong*. Oxford:
    Clarendon Press.
García-Carbonell, A., Rising, B., Montero, B. & Watts, F. (2001). Simulation/
    gaming and the acquisition of communicative competence in another
    language. *Simulation & Gaming, 32*(4), 481-491.
Gill, J. H. (2000). *The tacit mode: Michael Polanyi's postmodern philosophy*.
    Albany: State University of New York.
Goleman, D. (1995). *Emotional ontelligence: Why it can matter more than IQ*. New
    York: Bantam Books.

Greeno, J. G. (1997). On claims that answer the wrong question. *Educational Researcher*, 26(1), 5-17.

Hacking, I. (1999). *The social construction of what?* London: Harvard University Press.

Holland, D., & Cole, M. (1995). Between discourse and schema: Reformulating a cultural-historical approach to culture and mind. *Anthropology and Education Quarterly*, 26(4), 475-490.

Hoopes, D. S., & Pusch, M. D. (1979). Definition of terms. In M.D. Pusch (Ed.), *Multicultural education*. Boston: Intercultural Press.

Huizinga, J. (1985) (8th ed). *Homo Ludens: A study of the play element of culture.* Groningen: Wolters-Noordhoff. (in Dutch)

Johnson, M. (1987). *The body in the mind: The bodily basis of meaning, imagination, and reason.* Chicago: University of Chicago Press.

Kant, I. (1929). *Critique of pure reason* (N. K. Smitth, Trans.). New York: Cambridge University press.

Klabbers, J. H. G. (1996). Problem framing through gaming: Learning to manage complexity, uncertainty and value adjustment. *Simulation & Gaming*, 27(1), 74-92.

Klabbers, J. H. G. (2003). Interactive learning what? In F. Percival, H. Godfrey, Ph. Layborn, & S. Murray (Eds.), *The international gaming yearbook, Volume 11: Interactive learning through gaming and simulation.* Edinburgh: SAGSET.

Kolb. D. A., & Fry, R. (1975). Toward an applied theory of experiential learning. In C. Cooper (Ed.), *Theories of group process,* London: John Wiley.

Kriz, W. C. (2003). Creating effective interactive learning environments and learning organizations through gaming simulation design. *Simulation & Gaming*, 34(4), 495-511.

Krogh, von, G., & Roos, J. (Eds.) (1996). *Managing knowledge.* London: Sage.

Le Goff, J. (1977). *Pour un autre Moyen Age.* Paris: Gallimard.

Lewis, M. (2003). The emergence of consciousness and its role in human development. In J. DeDoux, J. Debiec, & H. Moss (Eds.), *The self: From soul to brain.* Annals of the New York Academy of Sciences, Vol. 1001. New York, NY.

Marconi, D. (1998). *Lexical competence.* Cambridge, MA: MIT Press.

Mayer, J., Salovey, P., Caruso, D. R., & Sitarenios, G. (2001). Emotional intelligence as a standard intelligence. *Emotion*, 1, 232-242.

McClelland, D. C. (1985). *Human motivation.* New York: Scott Foresman.

McVee, M. B., Dunsmore, K., & Gavalek, J. R. (2005). Schema theory revisited. *Review of Educational Research*, 75(4), 531-566.

Moore, O. & Anderson, A. (1975). Some principles for the design of clarifying educational environments. In C. S. Greenblat, & R. D. Duke (Eds.), *Principles and practices of gaming-simulation.* Newbury Park: Sage.

Moss, H. (2003). Implicit selves: A review of the conference. In J. DeDoux, J. Debiec, & H. Moss (Eds.), *The self: From soul to brain.* Annals of the New York Academy of Sciences, Vol. 1001. New York, NY.

Piaget, J. (1952). *The origins of intelligence in children* (Margaret Cook, Trans.). New York: International Universities Press.

Polanyi, M. (1964). *Personal knowledge.* New York: Harper and Row.

Polanyi, M. (1966). *The tacit Dimension.* Garden City, N.Y: Doubldeday.

Prawat, R. S. (1998). Current self-regulation views of learning and motivation viewed through a Deweyan lens: The problems with dualism. *American Educational Research Journal, 35*(2), 199-224.

Prawat, R. S. (1989). Promoting access to knowledge, strategy, and disposition in students: A research synthesis. *Review of Educational Research, 59*(1), 1-41.

Premack, D., & Woodruff, G. (1978). Does the chimpanzee have a theory of mind? *Behavioural and Brain Sciences, 4,* 515-526.

Rein, M. (1976). *Social science and public policy.* New York: Penguin Education.

Rogoff, B. (1990). *Apprenticeship in thinking: Cognitive development in social context.* Oxford: Oxford University Press.

Romme, A. G. L., & Putzel, R. (2003). Designing management education: Practice what you teach. *Simulation & Gaming, 34*(4), 512-530.

Rumelhart, D. E. (1984). Schemata and the cognitive system. In R. S. Wyer, & T. K. Scrull (Eds.), *Handbook of social cognition.* Hills, NJ: Lawrence Erlbaum.

Ruohomäki, V. (2003). Simulation gaming for organization development. *Simulation & Gaming, 34*(4), 531-549.

Schön, D. (1983). *The reflective practitioner.* New York: Basic Books.

Schön, D. (1987). *Educating the reflective practitioner.* San Francisco: Jossey-Bass.

Sfard, A. (1998). On two metaphors for learning and the dangers of choosing just one. *Educational Researcher, 27*(2), 4-13.

Sternberg, R. J. (1998). Abilities are forms of developing expertise. *Educational Researcher, 27*(3), 11-20.

Sternberg, R. J., Wagner, R. K., Williams, W. M., & Horvath, J. (1995). Testing common sense. *American Psychologist, 50,* 912-927.

Sternberg, R. J. (1985). *Beyond IQ: A triarchic theory of human intelligence.* New York: Cambridge University Press.

Sutton-Smith, B. (2001). *The ambiguity of play.* Boston: Harvard University Press.

Vygotsky, L. S. (1978). *Mind in society.* Cambridge: Harvard University Press.

Vygotsky, L. S. (1986). *Thought and language.* Cambridge: MIT Press.

Weick. K. E. (1979). *The social psychology of organizing.* London: Addison-Wesley.

Wenger, E. (2002). *Communities of practice: Learning, meaning, and identity.* Cambridge, UK: Cambridge University Press.

Wittgenstein, L. (1961). *Notebooks, 1914-1916.* New York: Harper.

THE WORK FLOW GAME (1998). Finnish Institute of Public Management, Helsinki University of Technology, Laboratory of Work Psychology and Leadership.

CHAPTER 4

Abbot, M. M., & Van Ness, H. C. (1972). *Theory and problems of thermodynamics.* New York: McGraw Hill.

Allport, F. H. (1962). A structuronomic conception of behaviour: Individual and collective. *Journal of Abnormal and Social Psychology, 64,* 3-30.

Alvarez de Lorenza, J. M. (2000). Closure, open systems, and the modeling imperative. In J. L. R. Chandler, & G. Van de Vijver (Eds.), *Closure: Emergent organizations and their dynamics.* New York: Annals of the New York Academy of Sciences, Vol. 901, 91-99.

Archer, M. (1995). *Realist social theory: The morphogenetic approach.* Cambridge, UK: Cambridge University Press.

Atmanspacher, H. (1997). Cartesian cut, Heisenberg, cut, and the concept of complexity. *World Futures, 49*, 321-343.

Ashby, W. R. (1968). Principles of the self-organizing system. In: W. Buckley (Ed.), *Modern systems research for the behavioral scientist.* Chicago: Aldine.

Bergstein, T. (1972). *Quantum physics and ordinary language.* New York: Humanities Press.

Bonabeau, E., Dorigo, M., & Theraulaz, G. (2000). Inspiration for optimization from social insect behaviour. *Nature, 406*, 39-42.

Boxer, Ph. J. and Cohen, B. (2000). Doing time: The emergence of irreversibility. In J.R. Chandler, & G. Van De Vijver (Eds.), *Closure: Emergent organizations and their dynamics.* New York, Annals of the New York Academy of Sciences, Vol. 901.

Burns, T., & Stalker, T. G. M. (1961). *The management of innovation.* London: Tavistock.

Casti, J. (1994). *Complexification. Explaining a paradoxical world through the science of surprise.* London: Abacus.

Clegg, S. R., & Hardy, C. (1996). Introduction: Organisations, organisation and organizing. In S. R. Clegg, C. Hardy, & W. R. Nord. *Handbook of organisation studies.* London: Sage.

Cohen, J., & Stewart, I. (1995). *The collapse of chaos. Discovering simplicity in a complex world.* New York: Penguin.

Dewey, J. (1960). *The quest for certainty.* New York: Capricorn.

Dougherty, D. (1996). Organization for innovation. In S. R. Clegg, C. Hardy, & W. R. Nord. *Handbook of organisation studies.* London: Sage.

Gharajedaghi, J. (1999). *Systems thinking: Managing chaos and complexity.* Oxford: Butterworth-Heinemann.

Giddens, A. (1993). *New rules of sociological method.* Cambridge: Polity Press.

Goguen, J. A., & Varela, F. J. (1979). Systems and distinctions: duality and complementarity. *International Journal of General Systems, 5*(1), 31-43.

Hacking, I. (1999). *The social construction of what?* Cambridge, MA: Harvard University Press.

Handy, C. (1995). Trust in the virtual organisation. *Harvard Business Review, 73*(3), 40-50.

Havel, I. M. (1996). Scale dimensions in nature. *International Journal of General Systems, 24*(3), 295-324.

Joslyn. C. (2000). Levels of control and closure in complex semiotic systems. In J. L. R. Chandler, & G. Van de Vijver, G. (Eds.), *Closure: Emergent organizations and their dynamics.* New York: Annals of the New York Academy of Sciences, Vol. 901.

Jørgensen, S. E. (1999). A tentative Fourth Law of Thermodynamics, applied to description of ecosystem development. In C. Rossi, S. Bastianoni, A. Donati, & N. Marchettini (Eds.), *Tempos in science and nature: structures, relations, and complexity.* Annals of the New York Academy of Sciences, Vol. 879.

Kampis, G. (1991). *Self-modifying systems.* Oxford: Pergamon.

Kast, E., & Rosenzweig, J. E. (1973). *Contingency views of organisation and management.* Chicago: Science Research Associates.

Katz, M. J. (1986). *Templets and the explanation of complex patterns.* Cambridge, UK: Cambridge University Press.

Kaufmann, S. A. (1993). *The origins of order. Self-organization and selection in evolution.* Oxford, UK: Oxford University Press.

Klabbers, J. H. G. (1986). Improvement of (self-)steering through support systems. In F. Geyer, & J. van der Zouwen (Eds.), *Sociocybernetic paradoxes*. London: Sage.

Klabbers, J. H. G. (1996). Problem framing through gaming: Learning to manage complexity, uncertainty and value adjustment. *Simulation & Gaming, 27*(1), 74-92.

Klabbers, J. H. G. (2000). Learning to handle complexity in social systems. In I. P. McCarthy, & T. Rakotobe-Joel (Eds.), *Proceedings of the International Conference on Complexity and Complex Systems in Industry*. University of Warwick.

Klabbers, J. H. G. (2001). Complexity & game theory: A new foundation for experimental, empirical and experiential social systems research. In E. Musci (Ed.), *On the edge of the millennium: A new foundation for gaming simulation*. Bari: Edizioni B.A. Graphis.

Klabbers, J. H. G. (2002). Enhancing corporate change: The case of strategic human resource management. In: G. Frizelle, & H. Richards (Eds.), *Tackling industrial complexity: The ideas that make a difference*. Proceedings of the 2002 Conference of the Manufacturing Complexity Network, University of Cambridge.

Kuhn, T. S. (1962). *The structure of scientific revolution*. Chicago: University of Chicago Press.

Küppers, B. (1995). Understanding complexity. In N. Russell, N. Murphy, & A. R. Peacock (Eds.), *Chaos and complexity. Scientific perspectives on divine action*. Berkeley, CA: The Center for Theology and the Natural Sciences.

Maturana, H. R., & Varela, F. J. (1980). *Autopoiesis and cognition: The realization of the living*. Dordrecht: Reidel.

Mintzberg, H. (1979). *The structuring of organisations*. Englewood Cliffs, NJ: Prentice Hall.

Morin, E. (1999). Organization and complexity. In C. Rossi, S. Bastianoni, A. Donati, & N. Marchettini (Eds.), *Tempos in science and nature: Structures, relations, and complexity*. Annals of the New York Academy of Sciences, Vol. 879.

Mutch, A. (2002). Actors and networks or agents and structures: Towards a realist view of Information systems. *Organization, 9*(3), 477-496.

Parsons, T., & Shils, E.A. (Eds.) (1951). *Toward a general theory of action*. New York: Harper & Row.

Pascal, B. (1897). *Les pensées*. Paris: L. Brunschvicg.

Piaget, J. (1980). The psychogenesis of knowledge and its epistemological significance. In M. Piatelli-Palmarini (Ed.), *Language and learning*. Cambridge: Harvard University Press.

Rosen, R. (1991). *Life itself*. New York: Columbia University Press.

Sallach, D. L. (2000). Classical social processes: Attractor and computational models. *Journal of Mathematical Sociology, 24*(4), 245-272.

Schrodt, P. A. (1988). PWORLD: A precedent-based global simulation. *Social Science Computer Review, 6*, 27-42.

Senge, P. M. (1990). *The fifth discipline*. London: Double Currency.

Simon, H. A. (1969). *The sciences of the artificial*. Cambridge, MA: MIT Press.

Stewart, P. (2001). Complexity theories, social theory, and the question of social complexity. *Philosophy of the Social Sciences, 31*(3), 323-360.

Taylor, F. W. (1911). *Principles of scientific management*. New York: Harper & Row.

Thévenot, L. (2001). Organized complexity: Conventions of coordination and the composition of economic arrangements. *European Journal of Social Theory*, 4(4), 405-425.

Van der Werf, E. C. D. (2004). AI techniques for the game of Go. Ph.D. thesis. Maastricht, NL: Maastricht University Press.

Von Foerster, H. (1973). On constructing a reality. In F. Preiser, (Ed.), *Environmental Design Research*. Dowden, Hutchinson & Ross, Stroudberg.

Von Foerster, H. (Ed.) (1981). *Observing systems*. Seaside, CA: Intersystems.

Von Foerster, H. (1984). Principles of self-organization in a socio-managerial context. In H. Ulrich, & G. J. B. Probst (Eds.), *Self-organization and management of social systems*. Berlin: Springer.

Von Glasersfeld, E. (1991). *Radical constructivism in mathematics education*. Dordrecht: Kluwer.

Weber, M. (1947). *The theory of social and economic organisation*. London: Oxford University Press.

Weick. K. E. (1979). *The social psychology of organizing*. London: Addison-Wesley.

Weick, K. E., & Westley, F. (1996). Organizational learning: Affirming an Oxymoron. In S. R. Clegg, C. Hardy, & W. R. Nord (Eds.), *Handbook of organization studies*. London: Sage.

Wenger, E. (2002). *Communities of practice: learning, meaning, and identity*. Cambridge, UK: Cambridge University Press.

CHAPTER 5

Abrahamsson, P., Salo, O., Ronkainen, J., & Warsta, J. (2002). *Agile software development methods: Review and analysis*. VTT publication 478. Oulu: Julkaisija.

Baldwin, C. Y., & Clark, K. B. (1997). Managing in an age of modularity. *Harvard Business Review*, 75(5), 84-93.

Beck, K. (2000). *Extreme programming explained*. Boston: Addison Wesley.

Bekey, G. E. (1971). Mathematical models in large systems. *IEEE Systems Man and Cybernetics Group. Annual Symposium Record*, California.

Boehm, B. (1988). A spiral model of software development and enhancement. *IEEE Computer*, 21(5), 61-72.

Cockburn, A. (2002). *Agile software development*. Boston: Addison Wesley.

Churchman, C. W. (1970). The client and the model. In R. M. Stogdill (Ed.), *The process of model building in the behavioural sciences*. Ohio State University Press.

Cunningham, W. (1995). *Episodes: A pattern language of competitive development*. http://c2.com/ppr/episodes.html

Evans, P. B., & Wurster, T. S. (1997). Strategy and the new economics of information. *Harvard Business Review*, 75(5), 70-84.

Hacking, I. (1999). *The social construction of what?* Cambridge: Harvard University Press.

Hacking, I. (2002). Inaugural lecture: Chair of Philosophy and History of Scientific Concepts at the Collège de France 16 January 2001. *Economy and Society*, 31(1), 1-14.

Hanken, A. F. G., & Reuver, H. A. (1973). *Introduction to systems theory*. Leiden: Stenfert Kroese (in Dutch).

Jacobson, I., Booch, G., & Rumbaugh. (1999). *The unified software development process*. Longman: Addison Wesley.

Katz, D., & Kahn, R. L. (1966). *The social psychology of organizations*. New York: John Wiley.

Klabbers, J. H. G. (1974). Human computer decision-making: Notes concerning the interactive mode. In M. Mesarovic, & E. Pestel (Eds.), *Proceedings of the Symposium Multilevel Model of World Development System*. IIASA: Laxenburg, Austria.

Klabbers, J. H. G. (2000). Learning as acquisition and learning as interaction. *Simulation & Gaming, 31*(3), 380-406.

Morgan, G. (1986). *Images of organization*. London: Sage.

Randers, J. (1972). *Model validity versus the utility of a model*. Lecture at the System Dynamics Summer Institute, Hannover, Germany.

Rollings, A., & Morris, D. (2004). *Game architecture and design*. Boston: New Riders.

Schön, D. A. (1983). *The reflective practitioner*. New York: Basic books.

Schwaber, K., & Beedle, M. (2002). *Agile software development with Scrum*. Upper Saddle River, NJ: Prentice Hall.

Von Bertalanffy, L. (1968). *General system theory*. New York: George Braziller.

Von Foerster, H. (1984). Principles of self-organization in a socio-managerial context. In H. Ulrich, & G. J. B. Probst (Eds.), *Self-organization and management of social systems*. Berlin: Springer.

Wenger, E. (2002). *Communities of practice: Learning, meaning, and identity*. Cambridge, UK: Cambridge University Press.

CHAPTER 6

Apple, M. W. (Ed.) (1995). *Review of research in education*, Volume 21. Washington, DC: American Educational Research Association.

Apple, M. W. (1999). What counts as legitimate knowledge? The social production and use of reviews. *Review of Educational Research, 69*(4), 343-346.

Beck, U. (1992). *The risk society*. London: Sage.

Blasi, L., & Alfonso, B. (2006). Increasing the transfer of simulation technology from R&D into school settings: An approach to evaluation from overarching vision to individual artifact in education. *Simulation & Gaming, 37*(2), 245-267.

Bonabeau, E., Dorigo, M., & Theraulaz, G. (2000). Inspiration for optimization from social insect behaviour. *Nature, 406*, 39-41.

Bonabeau, E., & Meyer, C. (2001). Swarm intelligence: A whole new way to think about business. *Harvard Business Review, 79*(2), 106-116.

Booth, W. C. (1987). The idea of a *Uni*versity as seen by a rhetorician. The 1987 Ryerson Lecture. The University of Chicago.

Bourdieu, P. (1993). *The field of cultural production*. Cambridge: Polity Press.

Brown, J. S., Collins, A., & Duguid, P. (1989). Situated cognition and the culture of learning. *Educational Researcher, 18*(1), 32-41.

Campbell, D. T. (1969). Ethnocentrism of disciplines and the fish-scale model of omniscience. In M. Sherif, & C. W. Sherif (Eds.), *Interdisciplinary relationships in the social sciences*. Chicago: Aldine.

Casti, J. L. (2000). Bizsim – The world of business – in a box. In I. A. McCarthy & Th. Rakotobe-Joel (Eds.), *Complexity and complex systems in industry.* University of Warwick.

Cecchini, A., & Rizzi, P. (2001). Is urban gaming useful? *Simulation & Gaming, 32*(4), 507-521.

Committee on Facilitating Interdisciplinary Research, Committee on Science, Engineering, and Public Policy (2005). Washington, DC: The National Academic Press.

Foucault. M. (1979). *Discipline and punish: The birth of the prison* (A. Sheridan, Trans.). New York: Random House.

Foucault, M. (1972). *The archeology of knowledge & the discourse on language* (A.M. Sheridan Smith, Trans.). New York: Pantheon.

Funtowicz, S. O., & Ravetz, J. R. (1993). Science for the post-normal age. *Futures*: September, 739-755.

García-Carbonell, A., Rising, B., Montero, B., & Watts, F. (2001). Simulation/ gaming and the acquisition of communicative competence in another language. *Simulation & Gaming, 32*(4), 481-491.

Hacking, I. (1999). *The social construction of what?* Cambridge: Harvard University Press.

Hacking, I. (2002). Inaugural lecture: Chair of Philosophy and History of Scientific Concepts at the Collège de France 16 January 2001. *Economy and Society, 31*(1), 1-14

Huizinga, J. (1985) (8th ed). *Homo Ludens: A study of the play element of culture.* Groningen: Wolters-Noordhoff (in Dutch).

Hoppe, R., & Peterse, A. (1993). *Handling Frozen Fire: Political culture and risk management.* Oxford: Westview Press.

Klabbers, J. (1996-b). Problem framing through gaming: Learning to manage complexity, uncertainty and value adjustment.*Simulation & Gaming,* 27(1), 74-92.

Klabbers, J. H. G. (2003). Gaming & simulation: Principles of a science of design. *Simulation & Gaming, 34*(4), 569-591.

Klabbers, J. H. G. (2004). Enhancing policy development through actor-based simulation. In R. Shiratori, K. Arai, & K. Fumitoshi (Eds.), *Gaming, simulation and society: Research scope and perspective.* Springer-Verlag: Tokyo.

Klabbers, J. H. G. (2006). A framework for artifact assessment & theory testing. *Simulation & Gaming, 37*(2), 155-173. DOI: 10.1177/1046878106287943.

Klabbers, J., van der Sluijs, J., & Ybema, R. (1998). Handling uncertainties in global climate change. Special issue of the *Journal of Environmental Sciences, 13*(5), 286-296.

Klabbers, J., Swart, R. Janssen, R., Vellinga, P., & van Ulden, A. (1996-a). Climate science and climate policy: Improving the science/policy interface. *Mitigation and Adaptation for Global Change* 1, 73-92.

Klabbers, J. H. G., Swart, R. J., van Ulden, A., & Vellinga, P. (1995). Climate Policy: managing organised complexity through gaming. In D. Crookall, & K. Arai (Eds.), *Simulation and gaming across disciplines and cultures.* London: SAGE.

Kuhn, T. S. (1962). *The structure of scientific revolution.* Chicago: University of Chicago Press.

March, S. T., & Smith, G. F. (1995). Design and natural science research on information technology. *Decision Support Systems, 15,* 251-266.

Meadows, D. L. (2001). Tools for understanding the limits to growth: Comparing a simulation and a game. *Simulation & Gaming, 32*(4), 522-536.

Noy, A., Raban, D. R., & Ravid, G. (2006). Testing social theories in computer-mediated-communication through gaming and simulation. *Simulation & Gaming, 37*(2), 174-194.

Polanyi, M .(1964). *Personal knowledge.* New York: Harper and Row.

Popkewitz, T. S. (1991). *A political sociology of educational reform: Power/ knowledge in teaching, teacher education and research.* New York: Teachers College Press.

Popper, K. R. (1963). *Conjectures and refutations: The growth of scientific knowledge.* New York: Harper.

Schön, D. (1983). *The reflective practitioner.* New York: Basic Books.

Schön, D. (1987). *Educating the reflective practitioner.* San Fransisco: Jossey-Bass.

Simon, H. A. (1969). *The sciences of the artificial.* Cambridge, MA: MIT Press.

Starkey, B. A., & Blake, E. L. (2001). Simulation in international relations education. *Simulation & Gaming, 32*(4), 537-551.

Thorelli, H. B. (2001). Ecology of international business simulation games. *Simulation & Gaming, 32*(4), 492-506.

Von Gigch, J. (2002). Comparing the epistemologies of scientific disciplines in two distinct domains: Modern physics versus social sciences. *Systems Research and Behavioral Science, 19*(6), 551-562.

Von Krogh. G., & Roos, J. (1996). *Managing knowledge.* London: Sage.

Wenger, E. (2002). *Communities of practice: Learning, meaning, and identity.* Cambridge, UK: Cambridge University Press.

Wenzler, I., Kleinlugtenbelt, W.J., & Mayer, I. (2005). Deregulation of utility industries and roles of simulation. *Simulation & Gaming, 36*(1), 30-44.

Wynne, B. (1992). Uncertainty and environmental learning. *Global Environmental Change, 2,*111-127.

CHAPTER 7

Bateson, G. (1972). *Steps to an ecology of mind.* New York: Ballantine.

Blasi, L., & Alfonso, B. (2006). Increasing the transfer of simulation technology from R&D into school settings: An approach to evaluation from overarching vision to individual artifact in education. *Simulation & Gaming, 37*(2), 245-267.

Boulding, K. E. (1956). *The image.* Ann Arbor: The University of Michigan Press.

Boulding, K. E. (1968). General systems theory – The skeleton of science. In W. Buckley (Ed.), *Modern systems research for the behavioural scientist.* Chicago: Aldine.

Campbell, D. T., & Stanley, J. (1963). Experimental and quasi-experimental designs for research. In N. L. Gage (Ed.), *Handbook of research on teaching.* Chicago, IL: Rand McNally.

Chatterji, M. (2005). Evidence on "What works": An argument for Extended-Term-Mixed-Method (ETMM) evaluation designs. *Educational Researcher, 34*(5), 14-24.

Compton, A. H. (1935). *The freedom of man* (3rd ed.), cited in Popper, K.R. (1979). *Objective knowledge: An evolutionary approach.* Oxford: The Clarendon Press, p. 207.

Cook, T. D., & Campbell, D. T. (1979). *Quasi-experimentation: Design and analysis issues for field settings.* Chicago, Ill: Rand McNally.

Dugdale, J., Pallamin, N., & Pavard, B. (2006). An assessment of a mixed reality environment: Toward an ethnomethodological approach. *Simulation & Gaming, 37*(2), 226-244.

Eddington, A. (1958). *The nature of the physical world.* Ann Arbor: University of Michigan Press.

Frege, G. (1892). Ueber Sinn und Bedeutung. *Z. Phil. und phil. Kritik, 100,* 25-50.

Gill, J. H. (2000). *The Tacit Mode: Michael Polanyi's Postmodern Philosophy.* Albany: State University of New York.

Goguen, J. A., & Varela, F. J. (1979). Systems and distinctions: Duality and complementarity. *International Journal of General Systems, 5*(1), 31-43.

Graham, C. H. (1964). Visual perception. In S. S. Stevens (Ed.), *Handbook of experimental psychology.* New York: Wiley.

Hacking, I. (2002). Inaugural lecture: Chair of Philosophy and History of Scientific Concepts at the Collège de France 16 January 2001. *Economy and Society, 31*(1), 1-14

Hacking, I. (1999). *The social construction of what?* Cambridge: Harvard University Press.

Hume, D. (1739). *A treatise of human nature* (Edited by L. A. Selby-Bigge). Oxford: Clarendon (1967).

Joslyn. C. (2000). Levels of control and closure in complex semiotic systems. In J. L. R. Chandler, & G. Van de Vijver (Eds.), *Closure: Emergent organizations and their dynamics.* New York: Annals of the New York Academy of Sciences, Vol. 901.

Klabbers, J. H.G. (1996). Problem framing through gaming: Learning to manage complexity, uncertainty and value adjustment. *Simulation & Gaming, 27*(1), 74-92.

Klabbers, J. H. G. (2001). The emerging field of simulation & gaming: Meanings of a retrospect. *Simulation & Gaming, 32*(4), 471-480.

Kriz, W. C., & Hense, J. U. (2006). Theory-oriented evaluation for the design of and research in gaming and simulation. *Simulation & Gaming, 37*(2), 268-283.

Kuhn, T. S. (1962). *The structure of scientific revolution.* Chicago: University of Chicago Press.

Mallon, B., & Webb, B. (2006). Applying a phenomenological approach to games analysis: A case study. *Simulation & Gaming, 37*(2), 209-225.

Maturana, H. R., & Varela, F. J. (1980). *Autopoiesis and cognition.* London: Reidel.

Maxwell, J. A. (2004). Causal explanation, qualitative research, and scientific inquiry in education. *Educational Researcher, 33*(2), 3-11.

Mohr, L.B. (1982). *Explaining organizational behavior.* San Francisco: Jossey-Bass.

Noy, A., Raban, D. R. & Ravid, G. (2006). Testing social theories in computer-mediated-communication through gaming and simulation. *Simulation & Gaming, 37* (2), 174-194.

Polanyi, M. (1964). *Personal knowledge.* New York: Harper and Row.

Popper, K. R. (1979). *Objective knowledge: An evolutionary approach.* Oxford: The Clarendon Press.

Prigogine, I., & Stengers, I. (1984). *Order out of chaos.* New York: Bantam books.

Rossi, P. H., Freeman, H. E., & Lipsey, M. W. (1999). *Evaluation: A systematic approach* (6th ed.). Thousand Oaks: Sage Publications.

Rouchier, J., & Robin, S. (2006). Information perception and price dynamics in a continuous double auction. *Simulation & Gaming, 37*(2), 295-208..

Shadish, W. R., Cook, T. D., & Campbell, D. T. (2002). *Experimental and quasi-experimental designs for generalized causal inference.* Boston, MA: Houghton Mifflin Co.

Spector, P. E. (1981). *Research designs.* Berverly Hills, CA: SAGE.

Tarnas, R. (1991). *The passion of the western mind.* New York: Ballantine Books.

Toffler, A. (1984). Science and change. In I. Prigogine, & I. Stengers, *Order out of chaos.* New York: Bantam books.

Von Foerster, H. (1984). Principles of self-organization in a socio-managerial context. In H. Ulrich, & G. J. B. Probst, (Eds.), *Self-organization and manage-ment of social systems.* Berlin: Springer-Verlag.

CHAPTER 8

Ashby, W. R. (1968). Principles of the self-organizing system. In W. Buckley (Ed.), *Modern systems research for the behavioural scientist.* Chicago: Aldine.

Barlas, Y. (1996). Formal aspect of model validity and validation in system dynamics. *System Dynamics Review, 12*(3), 183-210.

Barlas, Y., & Carpenter, S. (1990). Philosophical roots of model validation: Two paradigms. *System Dynamics Review, 6*(2), 148-166.

Checkland, P., & Scholes, J. (1990). *Soft systems methodology in action.* New York: Wiley

Churchman, C. W. (1970). The client and the model. In R.M. Stogdill (Ed.), *The process of model building in the behavioural sciences.* Ohio State University Press.

Davidsen, P. I. (1994). Perspectives on teaching System Dynamics. Coupling structure and behaviour, annotating simulations, and supporting Just in Time Open Learning (JITOL), *Proceedings of the 1994 International System Dynamics Conference,* Microworlds.

Davidsen, P. I. (1996). Educational Features of the System Dynamics Approach to Modelling and Simulation. *Journal of Structured Learning, 12*(4), 269 - 290.

Davidsen, P. I., & Myrtveit, M. (1994). Der Rütli Management Simulator − A new concept in system dynamics based management flight simulators, *Proceedings of the 1994 International System Dynamics Conference,* Education.

Forrester, J. W. (1961). *Industrial dynamics.* Cambridge: MIT Press.

Forrester, J. W. (1969). *Urban dynamics.* Cambridge: MIT Press.

Forrester, J. W. (1968). *Principles of systems.* Cambridge: Wright Allen Press.

Forrester, J. W. (1971). *World dynamics.* Cambridge: Wright Allen Press.

Klabbers, J. H. G. (2000). Learning as acquisition and learning as interaction. Special issue on System Dynamics & Interactive Learning Environments, *Simulation & Gaming, 31*(3), 380-406.

Klabbers, J. H. G. (1996). Problem framing through gaming: Learning to manage complexity, uncertainty and value adjustment. *Simulation & Gaming, 27*(1), 74-92.

Klabbers, J. H. G., van der Hijden, P., Hoefnagels, K., & Truin, G. J. (1980). Development of an interactive simulation/game: a case study of DENTIST. *Simulation & Games, 11*(1), 59-86.

Larsen, E. R., Morecroft, J. D. W., & Murphy, J. (1991). *Helping management teams to model: A project in the consumer electronics industry.* System Dynamics Conference, Utrecht.

Meadows, D. L., Behrens III, W. W., Meadows, D. H., Naill, R. F., Randers, J., & Zahn, E. K. O. (1974). *Dynamics of growth in a finite world.* Waltham, MA: Pegasus Communications.

Morecroft, J. W. D. (1992). Executive knowledge, models and learning. *European Journal of Operations Research, 59,* 9-27.

Senge, P. M. (1990). *The fifth discipline: The art and practice of the learning organization.* New York: Doubleday.

Senge, P. M. (1994). *The fifth discipline fieldbook.* New York: Doubleday.

Sterman, J. D. (2000). *Business dynamics: Systems thinking and modeling for a complex world.* New York: McGraw-Hill.

Vennix, J. A. M. (1990). *Mental models and computer models: Design and evaluation of a computer-based learning environment for policy-making.* Dissertation, Radboud University (the Netherlands).

Verburgh, L. (1994). *Participative policy modelling.* Dissertation, Radboud University (the Netherlands).

Vickers, G. (1972). Commonly ignored elements in policy-making. *Policy Sciences, 3.*

Weick, K. E., & Westley, F. (1996). Organizational learning: Affirming an Oxymoron. In S. R. Clegg & W. R. Nord, *Handbook of organization studies.* London: Sage.

FISH BANKS, Meadows D. (1988). IPSSR Hood House, UNH, Durham NH 03824, US.

STRATAGEM. Meadows D. (1984). IPSSR Hood House, UNH, Durham NH 03824, US.

CHAPTER 9

Christopher, E. M., & Smith, L. E. (1987). *Leadership training through gaming.* London: Kogan Page.

De Geus, A. (1997). *The living company.* Boston: Harvard Business School Press.

Gould, S. J. (1977). *Ontogeny and phylogeny.* Cambridge: Harvard University Press.

Klabbers, J. H. G. (1999). Gaming in professional education & management considerations for the design of a new class of management gaming/ simulations. In Y. M. Porkhovnik, & M. M. Novik (Eds.), *Simulation and gaming in professional education and management.* St. Petersburg: Evropeyskiy Dom.

Klabbers, J. H. G. (2002). Enhancing corporate change: The case of strategic human resource management. In G. Frizelle, & H. Richards (Eds.), *Tackling industrial complexity: The ideas that make a difference,* Proceedings of the 2002 Conference of the Manufacturing Complexity Network, University of Cambridge, UK.

Klabbers, J. H. G., & Sweere, P. (1993-a). HRM[Support]: A policy support system for human resource management. In B. J. van Tol (Ed.), *Human resource planning in the banking sector* (pp. 47-60). CERA: Leuven, Belgium.

Klabbers, J. H. G., & Sweere, P. (1993-b). The policy exercise. In B. J. van Tol (Ed.), *Human resource planning in the banking sector* (pp. 63-78). CERA: Leuven, Belgium.

Rajan, A. (1990). *A zero sum game*. London: The Industrial Society.

Wessels, J. (1983). Manpower planning for universities in the Netherlands. In J. H. G. Klabbers, J. A. E. E. van Nunen, P. G. M. de Rooy, & J. Wessels, *Some aspects of manpower planning within the Dutch Universities*. Project Manpower Planning within the Dutch Universities, ppp-report 8. University of Technology Eindhoven, the Netherlands.

CHAPTER 10

Beck, U. (1992). *The risk society*. London: Sage.

Douglas, M., & Wildavski, A. (1983). *Risk and culture*. Berkeley: University of California Press.

Hoppe, R., & Peterse, A. (1993). *Handling frozen fire: Political culture and risk management*. Oxford: Westview Press.

Klabbers, J. H. G. (1982). Futures research and public policy making: A context of use for Systems Theory and Gaming. In D. B. P. Kallen, G. Kosse, H. C. Wagenaar, J. J. J. Kloprogge, & M. Vorbeck (Eds.), *Social science research and public policy making*. Windsor: The NFER-Nelson Publishing.

Klabbers, J. H. G. (1985). Instruments for planning and policy formation: Some methodological considerations. *Simulation & Games, 16*(2), 135-160.

Klabbers, J., Van der Sluijs J., & Ybema, J. (1998). Handling uncertainties in global climate change. *Journal of Environmental Sciences, 13*(5), 286-296.

Klabbers, J., Swart, R., Janssen, R., Vellinga, P., & van Ulden, A. (1996). Climate science and climate policy: Improving the science/policy interface. *Journal Mitigation and Adaptation for Global Change, 1*, 73-93.

Klabbers, J., Vellinga, P., Swart, R., van Ulden, A., & Janssen, R. (Eds.) (1994). *Policy options addressing the greenhouse effect*. Bilthoven: NRP Programme bureau-RIVM, the Netherlands.

Perrow, C. (1984). *Normal accidents*. New York: Basic Books.

Presidential/Congressional Commission on Risk Assessment and Risk Management (1997). *Framework for environmental health risk management*. Washington DC.

Schön, D. A. (1983). *The reflective practitioner*. New York: Basic books.

Slovic, P., Fischhoff, B., & Lichtenstein, S. (1981). Perceived risk: Psychological factors and social implications. *Proc. of the Royal Society of London, A376*, 17-34.

Vickers, G. (1965). *The art of judgement: A study of policy making*. London: Chapman & Hall.

Wynne, B. (1992). Uncertainty and environmental learning. *Global Environmental Change 2*, 111-127.

CHAPTER 11

Baskerville, R., & Myers, M. D. (2004). Special issue on action research in information systems: Making IS research relevant to practice-foreword. *MIS Quarterly, 28*(3), 329-335.

Bennis, W. G. (1966). *Changing organisations*. London: McGraw-Hill.

Bleicher, K. (1991). *Das Konzept integriertes Management*. Frankfurt: Campus Verlag.

Brandenburger, A. M., & Nalebuff, B. J. (1995). The right game: use game theory to shape strategy. *Harvard Business Review, 73*(4), 57-71.

Burns, T., & Stalker, T. G. M. (1961). *The management of innovation*. London: Tavistock.

Caillois, R. (2001) (first ed. 1958). *Man, play and games*. Chicago: University of Illinois Press.

Carrol, L. (1865). *Alice in Wonderland*. London: MacMillan.

Clegg, S. R. (1990). *Modern organisations; organisation studies in the postmodern world*. London: Sage.

Clegg, S. R. & Hardy, C. (1996). Introduction: Organisations, organisation and organizing. In S. R. Clegg, C. Hardy, & W. R. Nord, *Handbook of organisation studies*. London: Sage.

Daft, D. L., & Weick, K. E. (1984). Towards a model of organisations as interpretation systems. *Academy of Management Review, 9*(2), 284-295.

De Geus, A. (1997). *The living company*. Boston: Harvard Business School Press.

Dougherty, D. (1996) Organization for innovation. In S. R. Clegg, C. Hardy, & W. R. Nord, *Handbook of organisation studies*. London: Sage.

Fairtlough, G. (1994). *Creative compartments: A design for future organisations*. London: Adamantine Press.

Hamel, G., & Prahalad, C. K. (1994). *Competing for the future*. Boston: Harvard Business School.

Handy, C. (1995). Trust in the virtual organisation. *Harvard Business Review, 73*(3), 40-50.

Kalff, D. J. A. (1989). Strategic decision making and simulation in Shell. In J. H. G. Klabbers, W. J. Scheper, C. A. Takkenberg, & D. Crookall (Eds.), *Simulation-gaming: On the improvement of competence in dealing with complexity, uncertainty and value conflicts*. Pergamon, Oxford.

Kast, E., & Rosenzweig, J. E. (1973). *Contingency views of organisation and management*. Chicago: Science Research Associates.

Klabbers, J. H. G. (1996). Problem framing through gaming: Learning to manage complexity, uncertainty and value adjustment. *Simulation & Gaming, 27*(1), 74-92.

Maslow, A. H. (1971). *The farther reaches of human nature*. New York: Pinguin Books.

Matthys, K., & Klabbers, J. H. G. (2004). Model United Nations Online (MUNO): A study of a policy exercise using Internet gaming. In W. C. Kriz, & Th. Eberle (Eds.), *Bridging the gap: Transforming knowledge into action through gaming and simulation*. Munich: SAGSAGA.

Miller, D., & Friesen, P. H. (1984). *Organisations: A quantum view*. Englewood Cliffs, NJ: Prentice Hall.

Mintzberg, H. (1979). *The structuring of organisations*. Englewood Cliffs, NJ: Prentice Hall.

Porter, M. E. (1996). What is strategy? *Harvard Business Review, 74*(6), 61-78.

Senge, P. M. (1990). *The fifth discipline*. London: Double Currency.

Shubik, M. (1983). Gaming: A state-of-the-art survey. In I. Ståhl (Ed.), *Operational gaming.* Oxford: Pergamon.

Taylor, F. W. (1911). *Principles of scientific management*. New York: Harper & Row.

VanGundy, A. B. (1992). *Idea power*. New York: AMACOM.

BIBLIOGRAPHY

Watzlawick, P., Beavin, J. H., & Jackson, D. D. (1967). *Pragmatics of human communication.* New York: W.W. Norton.
Weber, M. (1947). *The theory of social and economic organisation.* London: Oxford University Press.
Weick, K. E. (1979). *The social psychology of organizing.* London: Addison-Wesley.
Woodward, J. (1965). *Industrial organisation: Theory and practice.* London: Oxford University Press.

BEER GAME (1966). Cambridge, Mass: MIT Sloan School of Management.
TOPSIM, 1994, Högsdal, B., UNICON Management Systeme. Meersburg, BRD.
INTERNATIONAL OPERATIONS SIMULATION, (1963). INTOP: PLAYER'S MANUAL. Thorelli, H. B., Graves, R. L., & Howells, L. T. New York: The Free Press.
INTERNATIONAL OPERATIONS SIMULATION, (1995). INTOPIA/ MARK 2000: EXECUTIVE GUIDE. Thorelli, H. B., Graves, R. L., & Lopez, J.C. Englewood Cliffs, NJ: Prentice Hall.

CHAPTER 12

Berreby, D. (2005). Us and them (and me and you): The emerging science of "tribal" psychology. *Update: The New York Academy of Sciences Magazine,* Nov/Dec, 10-13.
Caillois, R. (2001) (first ed. 1958). *Man, play and games.* Chicago: University of Illinois Press.
De Waal, F. (2005). *Our inner ape.* London: Granta.
Girard, R. (1976). *Critique dans un souterrain.* Lausanne: L'Age d'Homme.
Girard, R. (1965). *Deceit, desire & the novel.* Baltimore: The Johns Hopkins University Press.
Hacking, I. (1999). *The social construction of what?* Cambridge: Harvard University Press.
Heidegger, M. (1927). *Sein und Zeit* (Being and time). Tübingen: Max Niemeyer Verlag (English translation (1962), New York: Harper & Row).
Huizinga, J. (1955). *Homo Ludens: A study of the play element in culture.* Boston: The Beacon Press.
Huizinga, J. (1985) (8th ed). *Homo Ludens: A study of the play element of culture.* Groningen: Wolters-Noordhoff (in Dutch)
Levinas, E. (1984). *The human face.* Baarn: AMBO (in Dutch).
Maunier, R. (1924). Les échanges rituals en Afrique du Nord, *L'année sociologique N.S., II*(5), 81.
Oz, A. (2005). Goethe Prize Speech. Aggression ist die Mutter aller Kriege (Aggression is the mother of all wars). *Frankfurter Allgemeine Zeitung,* August 29, 2005, 33.
Peperzak, A. (1984). Introduction to Levinas, *The human face.* Baarn: AMBO (in Dutch).

SUBJECT INDEX

325

Printed in the United States
137411LV00002B/10/P